BETWEEN LAW AND POLITICS

BETWEEN LAW & POLITICS

The Solicitor General and the Structuring of
Race, Gender, and Reproductive Rights Litigation

RICHARD L. PACELLE, JR.

Texas A&M University Press
College Station

Library of Congress Cataloging-in-Publication Data

Pacelle, Richard L., 1954–
  Between law and politics : the Solicitor General and the structuring of race, gender, and reproductive rights litigation / Richard L. Pacelle, Jr.— 1st ed.
     p. cm. — (The presidency and leadership; no. 14)
Includes bibliographical references and index.
  ISBN 1-58544-234-8 (cloth : alk. paper)
  1. United States. Solicitor General. 2. Political questions and judicial power—United States. 3. Civil rights—United States. 4. Race discrimination—Law and legislation—United States. 5. Sex discrimination—Law and legislation—United States. 6. Birth control—Law and legislation—United States. 7. Law and politics. I. Title. II. Series.
  KF8790 .P33 2003
  342.73'0873—dc21
                                          2002013746

To Fenton
For Everything and More

Contents

Contents

Figures

Tables

Tables

Acknowledgments

WHEN I STARTED THIS PROJECT, I had a great idea: I would make myself a character in the book, maybe an attorney in the Civil Rights Division or in the Office of the Solicitor General. I would construct conversations that never occurred and create memos that did not exist and use them to investigate the role of the solicitor general. In the end, I settled for a basic academic study.

I have many people to thank for their assistance over the last three years. I received a Research Board Grant from the University of Missouri–St. Louis to give me a year to conduct much of the interviewing, gather the data, and begin the writing. The Department of Political Science provided me with assistance from the development through the gestation of the project. As always, I need to thank Jan Frantzen, Lana Vierdag, and Sandra Beins for their help and just for making the department a nicer place. I was fortunate enough to have excellent research assistants during the gestation of this research. Professor Barry Pyle, Yan Huang, Yvette Dulaney, Marc Hendershot, and Andrea Pyatt all did a great deal to facilitate the completion of this project. I owe a particularly enormous debt to Maureen Gilbride Mears who was my research assistant during my leave and through the early stages of the project.

I am deeply indebted to all the people from the solicitor general's office, the Justice Department, and the Civil Rights Division, past and present, who took their valuable time to talk with me and answer my questions. In particular, I want to thank Professor Drew Days, the first person I interviewed. He was kind enough to allow me to invoke his name when I called others. Judge Charles Fried met with me after hearing oral arguments. Judge Kenneth Starr was gracious enough to take time out from other pressing matters you may have read about to talk to me. Professor Walter Dellinger welcomed me into his home on a Sunday morning to discuss the office with me. Solicitor General Seth Waxman talked to me less than forty-eight hours after he was sworn in.

I want to thank all the people who were gracious enough to talk to me in person. I also spoke to a number of individuals over the phone. I especially want to thank those who were willing to answer the questions of a disembodied voice they did not know. In the Appendix, I have listed the names of all of those who kindly endured my odd questions and gave some of their time to inform, enlighten me, and, on more than one occasion, correct my misperceptions. One theme came through virtually in all the interviews: a great respect and affection for the office. In his book, *The Tenth Justice,* Lincoln Caplan relates a story about Frank Murphy that reflects the respect held for the solicitor general. Upon ascending the Court, Murphy asked if any previous justice had held as many important offices as he had. He was told that William Howard Taft had been solicitor general, a Court of Appeals judge, president of the Philippines Commission, secretary of war, president, as well as chief justice. The dejected Murphy responded: "He was Solicitor General, too?"

I owe special thanks to a former student, Jon Jennings. If I had a former student who was an assistant coach for the Boston Celtics and one who was a presidential aide, it would be a real question of which of them was more successful. In Jon's case, he has done both. He helped get me access to people in the Justice Department and a tour of the White House. I was in Washington doing my first set of interviews when the Monica Lewinsky scandal broke and there were odds on whether President Clinton or Vice President Gore would give the State of the Union address.

I want to thank those people who housed me as I visited various cities to do my interviewing. My brother, Wayne, and Kirsten Rosenberg put me up during my visits to Washington, D.C. My stepson, Craig Martin, then a graduate student at Harvard, and Kathleen Christian hosted my trips to Boston. Craig let me use his car to travel to Yale. I thought it better that I did not tell him where I was going. My friends, Barbara and Jim Halporn, were kind enough to allow me to stay when I interviewed people at Harvard Law School. Of course, my parents had to put me up (and put up with me) when I was in New Haven. My aunt, Harriet Kral, was nice enough to let me stay with her as well. My former colleagues, Professors Michele Hoyman and Mike MacKuen, hosted me when I gave a talk at the University of North Carolina. Michele was instrumental in obtaining the interview with Professor Dellinger. On our many pilgrimages to Yankee Stadium, my best friend, Ed Mongillo, an expert on the Kennedy administration and Justice Department, discussed civil rights and the 1961–65 period. As the commercial says: "priceless."

A number of the experts on the solicitor general's office, Professors Stephen Puro, Jeffrey Segal, Rebecca Salokar, Kevin McGuire, and Chris Zorn shared manuscripts, information, the names of contacts, and data with me. I want to thank Professors MaryAnne Borrelli and Janet Martin, a graduate school colleague of mine. Janet called to ask me to contribute a chapter to an edited volume that she and MaryAnne were constructing and asked me to recommend someone to write a chapter on the solicitor general. I suggested names. None of them were available, so I got the job by default. When MaryAnne and Janet had to tell me that I needed to cut quite a bit from the draft of my chapter, they cushioned the news by suggesting that I take my research and try to turn it into a book manuscript and recommended the project to Texas A&M University Press. I want to thank the series editor, Professor Jim Pfiffner, for his assistance. I also want to thank Karol Lorenz for her careful editing of the manuscript. She saved me from a number of errors. I also want to thank Craig Crawford of the Department of Justice for the picture that graces the cover.

Professors Roy Flemming and Steve Puro read portions or all of the manuscript and provided me with important feedback. I want to apologize to Professor Flemming's graduate seminar, which read the original manuscript (which was 40 percent longer than this version). I understand a number of the members of that seminar quit graduate school. Professor Larry Baum, my long-term advisor, also read portions of the manuscript and offered his cogent analysis. Larry also updated and gave me his famous Baum Adjusted Scores. He is an excellent scholar and an even nicer person. It was a stroke of brilliance on my part to study under his direction. Professors Mike MacKuen and Jim Stimson were kind enough to share updated data with me.

I want to thank Professor Austin Sarat and Dr. Louis Fisher, who reviewed the manuscript. They offered a number of excellent suggestions that have improved the book immeasurably. You would think that having all this help would allow me to share any blame. Unfortunately, I bear the responsibility for all remaining errors of commission and omission.

I want to thank my parents, Patricia and Richard, Sr., for all of their constant love, support, guidance, and encouragement. They have been waiting patiently for the book. I hope it was worth the wait. They now know more than any of their friends about the solicitor general. That may explain why they do not get invited to parties anymore.

I dedicate this book to my wonderful wife, Fenton Martin. I cannot possibly list all the things she has done to help me on this book and in general. Her love and support have been unwavering. And if that wasn't enough, and don't you think it ought to be, she has served as an invaluable research source for my constant questions. Together we have authored about twenty books. Honesty compels me to report they have almost all been hers. I have always thought of her as "my award-winning wife" and the Office of Women's Affairs at Indiana University proved me right when it made her the initial recipient of a new award for someone who furthers the research and teaching mission of the university. I might be prejudiced, but I think it was truly an inspired choice.

BETWEEN LAW AND POLITICS

Part I

THE SOLICITOR GENERAL AND AMERICAN POLITICS

I N THE FEDERAL JUDICIARY ACT OF 1870, Congress created the Office of the Solicitor General (OSG) "to represent the interests of the United States"[1] and assist the attorney general. The statute required that the solicitor general be "learned in the law." Even justices of the Supreme Court are not required to meet that standard.[2] Charles Fahy, a former solicitor general, noted that upon creation of the office, the requirement that the attorney general be "learned in the law" was eliminated.[3]

The solicitor general was given some of the authority that had formerly belonged to the attorney general. Control of litigation was not centralized under the attorney general; many agencies had their own solicitors. The creation of the solicitor general was an attempt to establish centralization and coordination. The solicitor general has become, in fact, what the attorney general is in name.[4]

The solicitor general, a presidential appointee, plays a critical role in translating the policies of the government, the president, and the executive branch into litigation. The solicitor general decides which of the cases the government lost in the district courts and the courts of appeals should be appealed. The office also assumes full control over government cases appealed to the Supreme Court. Though these are formidable powers and give the solicitor general a major voice in the construction of judicial policy, the influence of the office extends even further. The solicitor general often enters cases in which the government is not a party through an *amicus curiae* brief.[5] This permits the solicitor general to influence the structure of doctrine and advocate a position even though the government is not involved in the particular case.[6] Over time, the office has earned a high degree of credibility with the justices. One manifestation of that credibility is that the Court will, on a number of occasions, ask for the views of the solicitor general. In these instances, the Court formally invites the solicitor general to express its views on the case before it.

The OSG is a small, elite law firm that has been populated by some of the greatest legal minds and attracts the best staff attorneys.[7] The office gets a great deal of respect from the legal community, the attorney general, and the Supreme Court.[8] Studies demonstrate that the reputation of the solicitor general plays an important role in the Court's decision making.[9] The OSG has hundreds of cases it could appeal to the Supreme Court, but the office carefully screens petitions to bring only the best cases.[10] The Court, in turn, grants a higher percentage of the solicitor general's petitions and the government is more successful on the merits than any other litigant (winning more than two-thirds of its cases).[11]

More significantly, the Court often adopts, sometimes verbatim, the arguments the solicitor general propounds in its briefs and oral arguments. Given the demonstrated excellence of its attorneys, knowledge of the proclivities of the justices, and the number of potential cases, the OSG has an unmatched ability and opportunity to litigate strategically.[12] In theory, this gives the president the potential to exert significant influence over the development of legal policy. But there lies the rub: the success of the solicitor general is partially a function of the fact that the office is free to ignore the president. Because the OSG must defend legislation, the office also needs to consider the position of Congress. How the solicitor general balances the need to attend to political duties and legal responsibilities is the subject of this analysis.

This study focuses on the work of the OSG in three issue areas: civil rights, gender discrimination, and reproductive rights. These issues have been prominent in presidential, congressional, and judicial policies. Many have argued that race has been a realigning issue and abortion has had that kind of potential.[13] The three issues have produced periods of policy convergence and periods of competition between the branches.[14] The issues provide a range of policy activity: race issues started as constitutional and became largely statutory, gender issues are predominantly statutory, and reproductive rights are constitutional.[15] Though these issues have different foundations, they are related to one another structurally or by analogy. Gender and racial equality are cut from the same constitutional cloth: the Fourteenth Amendment. Gender and reproductive rights, although housed under different constitutional principles, are both central to concerns of women.

The issues provide a context for evaluating the work of the solicitor general under special conditions and for studying the balancing of constituencies. Dealing with these issues poses a number of constraints for the solicitor general. Because these issues have divided the political parties, changes in party control of the presidency created different priorities. Because they are visible issues, such changes affect the agenda of the solicitor general's office. At times, the Court strongly supported reproductive rights and racial and gender equality. At other times, the Court sought to overturn or limit such rights. While the major precedents in these areas, *Brown v. Board of Education, Reed v. Reed,* and *Roe v. Wade,* have not been overturned, two have been weakened substantially.

RESEARCH DESIGN

This analysis examines the role the solicitor general has played in structuring civil rights, gender equality, and reproductive rights policy in the Supreme Court. I focus on the competing demands placed on the solicitor general in these areas and the consequences of attempts to satisfy those demands. All issues present constraints, but they are magnified in controversial areas.

I use a triangular approach for studying the role of the solicitor general. I use aggregate analysis to examine macro-level trends in support and success for civil rights and gender rights by the solicitor general. To understand the context under which the solicitor general operates and the dynamics of decision making, I conducted thirty-four interviews about a range of topics with past solicitors general, principal deputy solicitors general, career deputies, and assistants in the OSG, as well as with a number of assistant attorneys general for civil rights, chiefs of the Appellate Section of the Civil Rights Division (CRD), a ranking member of the Employment Section of the Division, and a former attorney general (see Appendix). I questioned the solicitors general, deputies, and assistants about the dynamics of the office, the contours of the three issues, and individual cases. I questioned members of the division about policy priorities, their relationship with the OSG, and individual cases.

Finally, I examined the briefs and decisions in all Supreme Court cases in the three issue areas over the past half-century: 225 civil rights cases, ninety-three gender rights cases, and thirty reproductive rights cases.[16] Of that universe of cases, the solicitor general participated in 178 civil rights, fifty-eight gender rights, and nine reproductive rights cases. I coded the briefs and decisions on a number of variables and in those cases in which the government was involved, I analyzed the briefs to determine the position that the solicitor general adopted in the case and the office's success on the merits.

I coded briefs and decisions that favored reproductive rights and ended programs that discriminated as pro-women's rights. I used similar coding for decisions that ended discrimination against racial minorities. Support for affirmative action on race or gender grounds was coded liberal. I coded support for benign programs that were based on stereotypes as opposed to gender equality.[17]

I use aggregate numbers to determine trends and variation across presidential administration and type of participation. I also use spatial models to compare the positions adopted by the solicitor general under different sets of conditions and compare the position of the office to the desired policy stances of Congress and the president.[18] In subsequent chapters, I examine the most important cases.

This analysis focuses on two aspects of the solicitor general's work in race and gender equality and reproductive rights: how the office handles competing constraints and how that balancing act is resolved. The first question is the relative influence of the various factors that influence the solicitor general and how they have changed over time. The roles assumed by the solicitor general in race, gender, and reproductive rights cases are a function of the evolution of those issues, the convergence between the agenda of the administration and that of the solicitor general's office, and the predilections of the Court tempered by the influence of Congress. Second, is the "so what" question: given the competing demands, how did the solicitor general structure race, gender, and reproductive rights doctrine? What influence did different solicitors general have in helping the Court formulate doctrine?

Before I turn to those questions in Parts II and III, I establish the strategic, institutional, and policy context within which the solicitor general operates in Chapters 1 and 2. In evaluating the influence of the president, Congress, and the Court, it is important to remember that there are institutional dynamics that every solicitor general faces and relations in political time, the period of the individual solicitor general's tenure.

CHAPTER I

Between Law and Politics

The Role of the Solicitor General

WE OFTEN CONCEPTUALIZE law and politics as if they comprised different ends of a continuum. Law is conceived of as neutral and above politics. The legal realm is typically distinguished from policy making, and courts are supposedly neutral arbiters. In theory, the differences distinguish "reason and learning from will and power."[1] At the same time, distinctions between the legal and political represent a false dichotomy. As Oliver Wendell Holmes remarked, "Every important principle which is developed by litigation is, in fact and at bottom, the result of more or less definitely understood views of public policy."[2] And yet, members of the Justice Department speak freely of distinctions between law and politics even if they cannot define the concepts precisely. Perhaps no one embodies the tensions that divide law and politics better than the solicitor general of the United States. It is not difficult to find the source of those tensions.

The solicitor general is subject to politics by virtue of the appointment process. The solicitor general is nominated by the president and answerable to the attorney general and the president. In many respects, the nomination of a solicitor general parallels that of a Supreme Court justice. The criteria are similar: both are well respected, have legal experience, and often share the legal philosophy of the administration. There is often an "agenda" issue that dominates the administration's concerns as a litmus test that might affect the choice of a justice and a solicitor general.[3]

Choosing justices and judges, on one hand, and the attorney general and solicitor general, on the other, are means by which the president can affect judicial policies. A carefully chosen solicitor general can provide an important resource for the administration and further its litigation priorities. The Justice Department sets priorities for legal matters and the OSG formulates the administration's agenda in the federal courts. If the president is unhappy with the direction that the solicitor general or attorney general is taking, he can replace them. Most presidential appointees are constrained by the arena in which they act. For the solicitor general that arena is the Supreme Court[4] and its trappings, precedent and doctrinal development, provide the legal context for the solicitor general.

Politics and law are at the intersection of the solicitor general's responsibilities. The frequency of participation in front of the Supreme Court makes the solicitor general an important ally of the justices, who rely on the office's expertise to control their docket and help structure doctrinal development. But the mode of selection and the duties of the solicitor general generate the tensions that define the office. As a presidential appointee, the solicitor general might be expected to "carry water" for the administration. Complicating matters is the fact that part of the work of the president and the executive branch involves neutral law enforcement and is supposed to be above politics. At the same time, a large portion of the work of the judiciary, particularly the Supreme Court, is policy-oriented and profoundly political, further blurring distinctions between the legal and political realms.

There is another element to the hypothetical dichotomy between law and politics. The solicitor general operates in a dynamic political environment, but is charged with imposing stability upon the law and legal positions. The solicitor general must pursue a changing executive agenda, but also assist the Court in imposing doctrinal equilibrium. The solicitor general is also expected to formulate consistent positions on various issues, regardless of the president. Kenneth Starr, solicitor general under President George H. W. Bush, considered this consequential: "We need to respect continuity and stability in the law. As someone who had the privilege of serving as a judge, I appreciate that stability and predictability in the law are very important. I tried to make sure that I took those enduring values of predictability and stability in the law into account to guide us."[5]

The office is entrenched in tradition that carries over to the formal morning coat that the solicitor general wears when arguing cases. Tradition helps the solicitor general maintain support from the Court and some autonomy from the political forces. From the earliest periods, the attorney general did not try to control the solicitor general. This established an ethos of independence for the office.[6] Empirically, this translates to the fact that 95 percent of the solicitor general's decisions are made without outside consultation.[7] Regardless of political persuasion, the solicitor general has to protect the office, a responsibility that is particularly cumbersome in controversial areas of litigation.

Although the OSG is relatively invisible, it has become "an immensely important reservoir of governmental power."[8] The role of the solicitor general has grown in proportion to the power of the Supreme Court. Because the solicitor general operates in a context that is structured by the Court, its agenda will bear more than a passing resemblance to the agenda of the Court.

The office is an important link to the Court for the president and the agencies. Members of the office see themselves as critical legal advisors, but minimize their role in policy making. Deputy Solicitor General Lawrence Wallace sounded the theme: "Litigation is not a policy making position; you need to make changes at the administrative level. We were not appointed to make policy." Seth Waxman, solicitor general under President Bill Clinton, argued, "I do not critique policy decisions of a group or agency; I accept the substantive policy judgments of the president and program administrators." But as Philip Heymann, who served as an assistant in the office, noted, "The Solicitor General normally claims that the office does not make policy. But that hides all the differences in the world." According to Walter Dellinger, acting solicitor general under Clinton, "There is a dangerous attitude in the Solicitor General's Office that there is no politics. The attorneys in the Office often pretend that they can be above politics. The Office is above politics, in a sense, but it had its own political position. In some ways, it is a political position with political judgments." Andrew Frey, a former deputy, makes the crucial distinction, "The work involves policy making, but not political considerations." If the solicitor general does not "make policy" in the narrow sense of the word, the office's decisions have clear policy implications.[9]

This is a study of the manner in which the solicitor general balances law and politics. We tend to assume that most actors are unconstrained and that they act on their sincere preferences. In reality, most actors have to act in a more sophisticated fashion. Most actors cannot achieve their sincere preferences and need to act strategically to achieve their most preferred goals given the constraints they face. The differences between sincere and strategic preferences are reflected in the tensions between politics and law. Pursuing the administration's sincere goals puts the solicitor general on the political end of the spectrum. Solicitors general act strategically when they anticipate the actions of others and, in doing so, move toward the legal end of the spectrum.

I start with the notion that the solicitor general is a strategic actor, balancing politics and law, the need to serve the president and the Court, and trying to adhere to existing precedent, while moving policy in a desired direction. While the solicitor general must be learned in the law, he is asked to litigate legal questions and political issues. Drew Days summed up the dilemma:

> Despite the unique confluence of factors which in a sense demand the Solicitor General to strive toward the ideal, the path is not easy. For all the impressive powers of the Solicitor General and the special role that he plays in the management of federal litigation, in fact the job is filled with difficult conflicts with respect to issues such as who is one's client, how does one separate policy and law, what are long-range as opposed to short-range interests of the United States, and where does one draw the line between the demands of one's duty as an advocate for the Executive Branch and one's responsibilities as an officer of the Court. The ideal and the reality are sometimes in painful tension.[10]

The solicitor general is a strategic actor, who must make decisions and achieve institutional and personal goals in a dynamic environment. Implicit in the notion of litigating strategically is that the repeat player is reacting to the Court and existing precedent.[11] The solicitor general has a more complicated calculus that includes the president, the Justice Department, Congress, the relevant agency, as well as precedent and the Court.

THE SOLICITOR GENERAL AS A STRATEGIC ACTOR

Solicitors general understand that their ability to achieve their goals is dependent on other actors. These actors, the president, the attorney general, the agency, Congress, and the Court, have the ability to influence the office's decisions. The president, Congress, Court, and the head of the CRD (the agency for civil rights and gender issues), have different time frames, serve different constituencies, and face different institutional contexts. In arriving at the decision whether to proceed with a case, file an *amicus* brief, which side to support, and how to frame the ultimate argument, the solicitor general must synthesize these different perspectives.

Solicitors general act strategically when they consider the preferences of other actors. According to Days, "As Solicitor General, I get up every morning prepared for a day of complex calculations and calibrations required to establish the nature and scope of the legal representation expected of me." Within such a system of interdependent powers and responsibilities, the solicitor general must consider the preferences and possible actions of other actors. Days claimed that "my responsibilities imposed additional constraints upon the nature and intensity of my advocacy that I had not experienced in private practice."[12] Thus, it is important to understand the context in which solicitors general operate in order to understand their decisions to pursue some cases, file *amici* briefs, and the positions they adopt.

This study utilizes a neoinstitutional perspective to examine the work of the solicitor general. According to John Aldrich, "The 'fundamental equation' of the new institutionalism is that political outcomes are the result of the interplay of actors as they seek to realize their goals, of the institutional settings in which they act and which they may help to shape, and of the historical context in which their decisions are set."[13] Neoinstitutionalism bridges the gap between traditional legal analysis, attitudinally based theories, and institutional analysis.

According to Lee Epstein and Jack Knight, there are three components of the strategic model: goals, strategic interaction, and institutions. Solicitors general seek to attain their goals through strategic interaction with other actors who seek to advance their preferences. Institutions, the context in which the solicitor general operates, structure strategic behavior. Institutions are defined as sets of formal and informal rules that define interactions in particular ways.[14] Although institutional rules and structures are often viewed as constraints on individual behavior, the apparent restrictions may also provide an array of opportunities for political actors. Some institutional arrangements facilitate the solicitor general's goals, while others constrain his ability to achieve those goals. Thus, outcomes are the result of individual, goal-oriented behavior as determined within the constraints and opportunities afforded by the institutions in which the actors function.[15] I adopt this perspective to try to understand how different institutional contexts—combinations of legal, social, and political norms—condition the behavior of the solicitor general.

The solicitor general's activities may be constrained or enhanced by legislation, precedent, and judicial doctrine. Despite the fact that the solicitor general is appointed by the president, the office must cultivate a long-standing relationship with the Court. Thus, to push the president's agenda too aggressively runs the risk of alienating the Court. The solicitor general is a respected advisor and gatekeeper for the Court. Indeed, the solicitor general is often referred to as the "tenth justice of the

Supreme Court." A number of solicitors general have remarked that the office's relationship with and duties to the Court are more important than winning individual cases.[16] Solicitors general also have some responsibility to Congress in that they may be obligated to defend legislation that conflicts with the administration's position. The need to serve two or more masters imposes constraints on the solicitor general. I will discuss the solicitor general's relations with these institutional actors in Chapter 2. Now, I turn to the goals and norms that influence the solicitor general and the office's different roles.

Goals of the Solicitor General

The political science literature sometimes treats actors as single-minded seekers of one overriding goal. Members of Congress want to get reelected,[17] bureaucrats want to enhance their budgets,[18] Supreme Court justices want to further their values and attitudes.[19] In his study of judicial decision making, Lawrence Baum suggests a more elaborate structure of goals.[20] I assume that solicitors general attempt to pursue a variety of personal and institutional goals and fulfill a number of roles in furtherance of their duties. It is not unreasonable to assume that institutional goals are more dominant in noncontroversial issue areas.

As Figure 1-1 shows, at the top of the hierarchy of personal goals, the solicitor general wants to retain the position. Remaining in office permits the solicitor general to achieve one of the dominant substantive personal goals: advancing the president's agenda. Other personal goals involve the solicitor general's place in history and future employment.

FIGURE 1-1

HIERARCHY OF GOALS FOR THE SOLICITOR GENERAL

Personal	**Institutional**
• Maintain Position as Solicitor General	• Maintain Office Independence
• Advance President's Agenda	• Help Supreme Court Impose Doctrinal Stability
• Preserve Future Employment Opportunities	• Protect Supreme Court
• Secure Place in History	• Maintain Relations with Agency
• Maintain Level of Success in Supreme Court★	

★Combination of Personal and Institutional Goals

In controversial areas, the solicitor general would be more likely to care about personal goals.

The institutional goals speak more to the legal end of the politics-law dichotomy and to the need to act strategically. At the peak of the hierarchy of institutional goals is the solicitor general's desire to protect the independence of the office from the political forces. Subordinate institutional goals that help the solicitor general achieve that central goal are protecting the Supreme Court, helping the Court impose doctrinal stability, and maintaining strong working relations with the agencies. One goal that straddles the personal/institutional divide is maintaining a high level of success in the Supreme Court. Personally and institutionally, the ability to achieve these goals will be affected by the roles solicitors general fulfill and the opportunities and constraints they encounter.

Institutions: Norms and Rules

The institutional context includes the norms, rules, and conventions that structure the solicitor general's behavior. For the solicitor general, three norms dominate: precedent, coherent doctrinal development, and deference. The Court is the arena in which the solicitor general operates and it is an environment in which precedent is an important concept. While it is not inviolate, the solicitor general needs to consider existing precedent when deciding whether to file a brief or prepare an argument. As part of its judicial role, the Court needs to impose consistency on doctrine. The solicitor general is expected to help the justices in the development of doctrine. Finally, under the *Chevron* doctrine, the solicitor general and the Court are expected to defer to the position of the relevant agency.[21] This may mean that the solicitor general has to argue a position that he/she opposes.

Precedent. The major institutional norm that influences the OSG is precedent. The solicitor general is constrained by existing precedent. A solicitor general with a personal or a presidential agenda needs to assess the willingness of the Court to gut or overturn established precedent. Even if the Court is philosophically opposed to existing precedent, justices are loathe to overturn it outright. Precedents like *Miranda v. Arizona, Mapp v. Ohio,* and *Roe v. Wade* have been under attack for years, yet the Court stopped short of abandoning them completely.

A direct precedent, one that is on point, structures the behavior of the solicitor general. As Eric Schnapper noted, "When precedent is really clear, it is difficult or impossible to frame an argument for the result the solicitor general or administration might prefer as a matter of policy."[22]

There are opportunities as well. If precedent favors the position the solicitor general wished to take, then the office may be able to transplant it to related areas. If precedent is hostile to the administration's designs, in the short term, the solicitor general can attempt to chip away at it, distinguishing other cases from it. The long-term strategy would be to have the precedent overturned or limited.

Precedent may deter a solicitor general from making a certain argument. According to Waxman, the question the office needs to ask is "In light of Supreme Court precedents and tests, can the particular program be defended in Court?" As Rex Lee, Reagan's first solicitor general, noted, an argument in an area of settled law would "destroy the special status that I enjoyed by virtue of my office . . . I would acquire a new status, equally special. The Court would have written me off as someone not to be taken seriously."[23]

Policy Evolution and Doctrinal Development. Issue evolution can provide opportunities or pose constraints for the solicitor general. Policy is dynamic and path dependent: once the Court stakes out a path, the direction of doctrine and precedent are constrained. The evolution of doctrine refers to the process by which the accretion of legal questions and decisions yield policy. The interpretations of Constitutional and statutory provisions and the definition of rights and liberties result from the resolution of individual cases.

The judicial behavior literature lends credence to the processes by which issues evolve and become more complex over time.[24] The literature suggests that different fact situations have a significant impact on the decisions of individual justices and the Court. The behavior of justices and litigants is expected to vary as a function of different conditions.[25] Issue evolution structures the behavior of the solicitor general.

The construction of doctrine is a dynamic, diachronic process. New issues emerge from landmark decisions, the shock of the punctuated equilibrium model. Once new issues reach the Court, they lay claim to future agenda space. The initial landmark, no matter how sweeping, cannot address all contingencies in that issue area. Consequently, justices need to construct doctrine in a coherent fashion and screen petitions for cases that will help them fill gaps. The Court builds doctrine in layers, settling basic questions before moving to more difficult concerns. Litigants need to structure litigation, build on past efforts, and flesh out emerging doctrine. The tone of the Court's decisions encourages litigants to bring additional cases in that issue area.[26] Confusion in doctrine creates uncertainty for lower courts and generates subsequent cases aimed at resolving unsettled questions. The solicitor general is in the best position to assist the Court in continuing to construct doctrine. The need to construct doctrine can constrain the solicitor general.

In most areas of law, policy evolution proceeds through defined stages.[27] Judicial policy moves from general to specific and from simple to complex: cases tend to get more difficult over time.[28] The landmark establishes general principles that can be extended to related issues. Thus, *Brown v. Board of Education* involved school desegregation, but created an environment for cases in employment, housing, and voting rights. A major decision gives litigants the opportunity to push the policy envelope. Similarly, if the Court retrenches in a specific area, it encourages supporters of that decision to press for further retreats.

There are constraints that arise as policy moves from simple to complex. Litigants supportive of earlier decisions attempt to induce the Court to expand previous decisions. Having settled the core questions, it is uncertain how much further the Court is willing to go. Court support should decline as cases get more difficult. Solicitors general must litigate in this environment, pressing an issue to achieve policy goals and doctrinal equilibrium.

In the initial stage, when the Court defines the emerging issue, the solicitor general is unlikely to get involved unless the government is a party or the Court requests the office's opinion.[29] The office seldom files voluntary *amici* briefs in new areas. As Robert Bork said, "Often the solicitor general does not get involved in path breaking cases. The solicitor general lets the issue percolate in the lower courts at the outset and gets involved later."[30] If the government is a party, then legislation or agency policy is involved, constraining the solicitor general's position. While the solicitor general could have the opportunity to write on a blank slate, the office normally eschews that chance until the issue has developed. The solicitor general will join the fray as soon as the Court has shaped the contours of the issue and it moves to the later stages of development.

Substantively, these are first-generation questions, the core concern of the policy area. There is an expectation that individual justices will attempt to establish doctrinal equilibrium in the area. As members of the Court of last resort, justices have an institutional obligation to decide cases in a consistent manner so as to guide lower courts as part of the judicial role.[31] Part of the role of the OSG is to assist the Court in this process.

This initial stage is marked by the cases immediately preceding and following the landmark. Cases preceding the landmark begin to define the boundaries of the central issue and constrain the range of long-term deviation. The landmark decision defines that question and the cases immediately following define its scope.

At some point, the Court should resolve first-generation questions in a manner that will guide lower courts allowing the issue to progress. This next phase is marked by the increased difficulty of the cases. This later stage is the solicitor general's typical forum.[32] If the goals are political, the solicitor general may be seeking to expand existing policy or have those policies limited. The solicitor general may be constrained by existing precedents and the need to adhere to them. Often, the solicitor general will help the Court as it seeks to impose doctrinal equilibrium, fulfilling legal goals. Typically, the solicitor general is not involved in pushing the envelope too quickly or trying to relitigate previously decided issues. The solicitor general may urge the Court to continue its policies or not to venture forth until doctrinal gaps have been filled.

Given stable membership, the Court should impose consistency on doctrine. This consistency, however, is seldom established because of membership changes or the introduction of additional issues that arise from separate dimensions. Changes in the composition of the Court can have profound effects on issue evolution. In particular, such changes can reverse the trend of policy development. The impact of membership changes underlines the role of the president in selecting justices.

A Court that is antagonistic to precedent can begin to reverse or limit decisions. Normally, the membership change required to achieve policy devolution is extensive. In practical terms, one party would have to hold the presidency through the departures of a number of justices and replace members appointed by the other party. Ronald Reagan and George Bush continued the work Richard Nixon began in reshaping the ideological and philosophical direction of the Court.

The power of the Court's institutional role is such that even in the face of wholesale ideological changes, few precedents are directly overturned. Analysts predicted that the Court would overturn *Roe*. Proponents of reproductive rights had been leaving the Court for a decade and were replaced by justices who had supposedly passed litmus tests on the issue. Yet, a majority could not be constructed to overturn *Roe*.

In most areas, policy eventually evolves in a variety of directions, taking on layers of complexity. The issue may be attached to other issues by litigants or justices interested in pursuing policy goals. For instance, during the gestation of civil rights litigation, freedom of association cases arose involving members of the National Association for the Advancement of Colored People (like *NAACP v. Button*). Some southern states attempted to expose membership in the NAACP, raising First Amendment issues in an equal protection context.

At this stage, the solicitor general typically tries to help the justices by trying to confine the issue to a single dimension. Often, the Court uses the government's briefs and arguments to locate the multifaceted questions in a single issue space. At times, the Court may invite the solicitor general to help determine which of the issues should dominate.[33]

Civil rights evolved in this manner. The Court dealt with a variety of miscellaneous cases until *Brown* defined the issue. Policy then evolved in two patterns. First, it evolved from simple to complex, creating a variety of increasingly difficult desegregation cases and from general to specific, spreading out to employment, voting, and housing. The solicitor general was partially responsible for cultivating the general doctrine and spreading it to individual areas.

Gender discrimination was defined in the context of race doctrine. At the outset, this constrained the development of the issue. The solicitor general, reacting to the Court, tried to fashion a context for gender and had considerable difficulties. Reproductive rights doctrine emerged without the assistance of the solicitor general.

Deference to Agency Policies. While other norms reflect the relationship between the solicitor general and the Court, deference is a function of the relationship between the office and various executive agencies. The solicitor general argues the cases before the Supreme Court, but the office has to defer to policy goals that have been established by the agency. Legal and policy positions are developed before the case reaches the OSG. As Deputy Solicitor General Edwin Kneedler noted, "the attorney-client relationship is defined to a large degree; the *Chevron* doctrine affords the agency wide latitude."[34] I will examine this relationship more closely in Chapter 2.

Part of the variation in the solicitor general's behavior is a function of whether this is a new or existing issue. Existing policy carries issue definitions that structure its development, established agency positions, and legal precedents. A new issue does not have that baggage and can become a battleground over attempts to impose a definition. In addition, there is the relative controversy of the issue. Noncontroversial issues may be invisible to those outside that policy community. For such issues, the legal realm will often dominate. The decisions made by the solicitor general do not typically attract a great deal of attention. But in controversial issues, the scope of conflict is expanded and the political realm becomes dominant. The decisions of the solicitor general in areas like civil rights and reproductive rights are guaranteed to engender pressures from a variety of sources.

ROLES OF THE SOLICITOR GENERAL IN LITIGATION

The institutional context and the norms and rules attendant to it structure the conditions under which the solicitor general operates. The solicitor general is asked to play a number of roles that are dependent in part on the form of participation. The tensions in balancing law and politics and the demands of the actors in the solicitor general's environment are reflected in the different forms of participation. The solicitor general can decide whether to seek a writ of certiorari in cases the government lost in the lower court. The solicitor general may come to the Court as a respondent to defend a lower court victory. Even when the government is not a party, the solicitor general can enter the case with an *amicus curiae* brief when the government is interested in the results. Finally, the Court may ask the solicitor general to participate in a case, seeking advice on how to proceed.

These different forms of participation carry different responsibilities, opportunities, and constraints for the solicitor general. Figure 1-2 shows that the roles that the solicitor general plays vary as a function of these responsibilities. In cases in which the government is a party, the solicitor general most closely resembles the "tenth justice." In cases in which the government is invited to file an *amicus* brief, the solicitor general plays a role closer to the "fifth clerk" of the justices. When solicitors general file *amici* briefs, they play a role akin to the attorney general, an agent of the executive branch.[35]

FIGURE 1-2

PARTICIPATION AND ROLES OF THE SOLICITOR GENERAL

	Type of Involvement	Discretion	Primary Constituency	Role
PARTY	Constitutional	Great	President/Congress	Tenth Justice
	Statutory	Limited	Congress/Agency	
AMICUS	Programmatic	Limited	Agency	Attorney General
	Agenda	Great	President	
INVITED	Federal Interest	Limited	Agency	Fifth Clerk
	No Clear Interest	Limited	Supreme Court	

Solicitor General as Party

The government is involved in thousands of cases a year in the lower courts, giving the solicitor general a myriad of opportunities to seek appellate review. Federal agencies that lose in the lower court and see their power circumscribed may be anxious to go forward in hopes of having the decision reversed. In most of these cases, the solicitor general's client is the agency. The solicitor general serves as a gatekeeper and has to manage the caseload. The solicitor general is constrained by the policy position of the agency and the intent of Congress, but the sheer volume of litigation provides the office with the opportunity to select cases strategically with an eye toward success on the merits. In effect, the solicitor general serves as a judge or mediator, particularly when a case pits two agencies or departments against each other. This makes the solicitor general a critical actor in the policy decisions of executive branch.[36] Most of these cases involve interpretation of statutory provisions, so the solicitor general must pay attention to the intent of the legislating Congress and the will of the sitting Congress.[37]

The relationship between the agency and the solicitor general is important in making the decision whether to file a petition for certiorari. There is bound to be conflict between an agency with parochial views and a solicitor general who is concerned with the broader perspective of the executive branch. The agency is interested in pursuing its policy goals; the solicitor general, on the other hand, has law enforcement and legal goals to pursue. The agency feels it is in the best position to determine its policies and priorities. The solicitor general needs to coordinate the work of many agencies and bring cases that are important and can be won.[38]

As a petitioner, the solicitor general comes closest to representing the so-called "tenth justice" or ally of the Court. As gatekeepers, the solicitor general takes cases the office believes the Court will find worthy. According to former Deputy Kenneth Geller, "Case screening is the most important role of the solicitor general. It involves a great deal of concern over tactics, strategies, and law in deciding which cases to take." In Geller's view, the office's job is to guard the door to the Supreme Court and "we think that we can do a better job of picking most important ones (cases) than the Court can."[39] As a petitioner, the solicitor general helps shape the decision through its briefs and oral arguments. There are opportunities mixed with constraints, as the solicitor general searches for the best cases. The office is composed of professional advocates who are "dedicated to the rational development of law and reinforce their loyalty to the Court by advancing the best arguments in the government's briefs."[40] The solicitor general needs to help the Court impose stability on doctrine.

While there are constraints posed by the agency and Congress, there are opportunities for the solicitor general. For instance, the solicitor general enjoys substantial discretion as a petitioner. As the ultimate repeat player, the solicitor general can play the odds and refuse to bring certain cases. The solicitor general may get specific orders or more subtle forms of interference from the attorney general or the president to take cases the office would otherwise refuse to pursue. In addition, the political agenda of the administration may "encourage" the solicitor general to advance arguments that oppose existing precedents. Certainly in the great majority of cases, the issues fall outside the interests of the president, giving the solicitor general a great deal of "functional independence."[41] According to Days, "a tradition of independence, both within the Department of Justice and Executive Branch as a whole, has developed with respect to the Solicitor General's role. Although the Solicitor General is appointed by the President and works for the Attorney General, it is rare for his decisions to be overruled by either of his superiors. Consequently, for most purposes, the Solicitor General has the last word with respect to whether and on what grounds the United States will seek review in the Supreme Court and determines what cases from the federal trial courts the Government will seek to appeal."[42]

The need to litigate strategically takes on particular significance when the solicitor general needs to respond to litigants who are appealing cases the government won in the lower courts. In these cases, the solicitor general starts in a passive role, unable to choose which cases will go forward. Knowing that justices normally take cases to reverse them is a hint that the lower court decision may be in jeopardy. These cases can threaten the solicitor general's attempts to construct a coherent litigation strategy and may interfere with the government's legal policy. The solicitor general can, and often will, oppose the appellants' brief, asking the Court to refuse to accept the case. The government's vulnerability is limited because the Court can only accept a small fraction of the petitions on its docket. While the solicitor general is constrained in these cases, occasionally the solicitor general will welcome the opportunity to participate because some cases provide useful vehicles for furthering the office's goals.

Because the solicitor general understands that the government is less likely to prevail on the merits when it is a respondent, the office adopts a defensive posture in such cases. The OSG would seek to have the Court refuse the case and, failing that, try to limit the effects of an adverse precedent. In essence, the solicitor general is engaged in damage control in these cases. In the end, the office is remarkably successful, winning over half of its cases as respondent, a success rate unmatched by any other litigant.[43]

Solicitor General as *Amicus Curiae*

Rex Lee divided *amici* cases into two categories. The first category protects the enforcement powers of the government; the second furthers the particular administration's views. The first category involves direct federal law enforcement interests, such as Title VII and voting, in cases in which the federal government was not a party, but a decision would have a significant impact on its interests.[44] All administrations file these types of cases to fulfill the Justice Department's enforcement powers and help the agency. These cases come with constraints and fulfill legal obligations rather than political goals. The solicitor general appears to play the role of the attorney general as neutral law enforcement officer in such cases.

The other cases have less to do with enforcement authority, but are part of the current administration's policy agenda. Voluntary *amici* briefs provide the best opportunity to further executive designs. The division between law and politics is clearest in these cases. As Mark Levy, a former assistant solicitor general, noted, "There is unfettered discretion to participate in such cases. The views of the current Administration get heavy weight and there is generally no countervailing positive law by Congress."[45] Some, advocating the legal view, argue that the solicitor general should never file *amici* in these cases. They believe that pursuit of the president's agenda is not a legitimate objective for the solicitor general. Others argue the political view that the solicitor general should file in almost every case because he is the only person who can speak for the president in the Court. If the solicitor general abdicates, the president's views will not be heard on these important issues.[46] The solicitor general typically hews to a middle path and does not abuse the privilege by filing too many *amici* briefs.

When the office enters a case with an *amicus* brief in this second category, the solicitor general is the least constrained. Because the government is not a party, the cases carry minimal risk because the decisions will not directly affect it. The *amici* better reflect political selectivity than the strategic selectivity that marks the office's work as petitioner.[47] In these so-called "agenda cases," the solicitor general most closely resembles the attorney general as policy advocate for the administration.

In race, gender, and reproductive rights, these cases typically involve state laws. By entering the case, the solicitor general has the chance to argue for uniformity in the law or offer the office's position on a similar federal law that might be challenged later. Most importantly, an *amicus* brief provides the solicitor general with the opportunity to expand or narrow the issue in the case. The solicitor general can enter these cases in hopes of expanding a favorable decision or limiting a negative one.

Responding to Invitations

In the third category of cases, the Court "calls for the views of the solicitor general" (CVSG). The invitation to participate via an *amicus* brief occurs almost exclusively at the petition stage, when the Court is asking the solicitor general whether certiorari should be granted. If the petition is granted, then the office normally files a brief on the merits. The "invitation" to participate is not really a request, but is treated as an order.[48]

When the Court "invites" the solicitor general to enter a case, the office's flexibility is circumscribed. In these cases, the solicitor general is often acting not as an agent of the executive branch but as a legal advisor to the Supreme Court. In inviting the solicitor general's participation, justices normally expect the office to provide a less partisan review of the law and a survey of existing precedent. This resembles the original intention of the *amicus curiae* brief, which was designed to be a recitation of legal positions by a disinterested "expert witness."[49]

Some argue that the reason that it adopts a more neutral position in the invited cases is because the office has no real interest in the case or as Lawrence Wallace put it "we do not have a dog in the fight."[50] This was echoed by Walter Dellinger: "My guess would be that briefs filed in the invited cases give the appearance of greater disinterest and impartiality because the Solicitor General chooses not to file an *amicus* brief voluntarily. . . . The case is not very controversial until some members of the Court thought that the challengers had a better case than the lower court did. The case is lower on the radar screen until the Supreme Court thinks the issue needs ventilation." Or it may be because the issue is very contentious according to Dellinger: "Different branches of government have conflicting views and the Solicitor General declined to get involved to avoid controversy. This can occur when there are very strong views, but they differ from one agency to another. . . . The Solicitor General takes neither position and may draft a brief reflecting the different views of the agencies."[51]

In this capacity the solicitor general is less the "tenth justice" and more the "fifth clerk." According to Days, "The Court is explicitly asking for help. The Court wants a theory for locating the case in terms of the thousands of other cases it needs to address." Thus, the solicitor general serves more as an officer of the Court than as an advocate. The Court is more likely to invite the solicitor general to participate under certain circumstances. The Court will invite the solicitor general when it perceives that a federal interest is involved. The office may be asked to file when there is a new issue without established precedent. The solicitor general is asked to provide a broader context or perspective for the Court to use in approaching the new issue.[52] Invitations are also likely when there is a change in the development of an issue. As issues evolve, they take on a greater complexity and often get attached to other issues. When this occurs, the Court may ask the solicitor general to help formulate the proper doctrinal stream and find a niche for the new fact situation.

While the CVSG can limit the type of arguments the office can make, it provides opportunities as well. First, the invitation extends the government's influence into another area. More broadly, the solicitor general generates a reservoir of good will with the Court that can be borrowed against when the solicitor general has a case the office considers important. Kenneth Starr felt that the invitation to file a brief gives the government a great advantage: "I viewed the CVSG as the Court seeking guidance, but affording the US the courtesy of being heard without putting the US in the position of being in the case *sua sponte*. If the US were doing that with regularity, the government would be charged with being an officious intermeddler." According to Starr:

> The CVSG has a two fold purpose. First, it serves to guide the Court or assist the Court as to whether the case is important enough to merit review. Second, it serves to offer the position of the US on the merits of the issue. With respect to the former—assisting the Court—it is a welcome opportunity for the US as so much litigation affects the government, but we're not involved. It is a courtesy to the government. With respect to the latter—the position of the US—there we followed the professional responsibility of assimilating the views of different parts of the Justice Department and the agencies and putting forth the best argument.[53]

Members of the office estimate that about 50 percent of the petitions in invited cases are granted. If the petition is granted, then the solicitor general typically files an *amicus* brief on the merits. As Wallace said, "if we tell them to take the case and they do, we have an interest. If we ask them to deny the petition and they take it, we look like we are sulking if we do not file on the merits."[54]

Implications. The different forms of participation present a dilemma for the OSG, particularly in periods of divided government. The solicitor general might wish to act on his own preferences or those of the president, but is constrained. If Congress, the president, and the Court have different priorities, the solicitor general could be in a delicate position. In the same term in the same issue area, the solicitor general may be invited to provide a legal argument, may be obligated to defend Congressional policies, and may be filing an *amicus* brief to further the president's agenda. If the office has to argue for a broad interpretation of a statute and then turn around and argue for a narrow constitutional interpretation to fulfill the president's agenda, the potential for doctrinal confusion exists.

In some instances, the goals and roles may conflict. A solicitor general who gives primary attention to legal goals may not fully exercise his prerogatives in the discretionary *amici* cases. More likely and more recently, solicitors general who want to emphasize political goals may use invitations from the Court or law enforcement types of case as vehicles to push the administration's policy designs. The chances for judicial rebuke may be greater in these circumstances.

Part of the answer of which master the solicitor general serves is a function of issue area or policy. Many issues have little salience. Indeed, different administrations would argue similar cases the same way. Richard Seamon, a former assistant in the office, argued that "in 80 to 90 percent of the cases handled, the dispositions did not change that much. Probably 40 to 60 percent were criminal cases. We were still trying to keep the bad guys in jail."[55]

In less ideologically charged issues, the solicitor general's priority may be to help the Court stabilize the law. Thus, legal concerns overcome political ones. These cases permit the solicitor general to be above the fray and earn credibility that could be borrowed against when political cases arose. In controversial cases, the president may have a great deal of interest. Judge William Bryson, a former deputy solicitor general, argued that "98 percent of the cases are not affected by the Administration, but the other 2 percent are white hot and people from the Administration hover over you quite closely, providing support or interference, depending on your view."[56]

CONCLUSION

Balancing law and politics is a difficult task under ideal conditions. That task is further complicated when issues are visible and at the center of national debate. The range of alternatives for the solicitor general may be wider, but the pressures are more intense. The solicitor general must act strategically to adapt to the environment and shape positions. The dynamic nature of the exogenous factors stands in contrast to the stability that the office seeks to impose on policy.

The success of the solicitor general raises a number of questions. Is the solicitor general so persuasive that the office's arguments are adopted because of their excellence? Or does the expertise of the office lie in its ability to predict what the justices will consider acceptable and tailor arguments in that direction? As the consummate repeat player, the solicitor general will bring the types of cases the office believes it can win. The ultimate answer is probably some combination of the two factors. The question can be posed in another fashion: Is the office's success due to strategic decision making on the part of the solicitor general, the experience and expertise of the solicitor general's office, or a function of the deference that the Court shows for the executive branch?[57]

The need to attend to different masters and try to impose consistency on the law can have a dramatic effect on the legacy the solicitor general bequeaths to a successor and policy development. The goals of the solicitor general reflect those constraints. The policy and legal goals of the solicitor general can create a series of conflicts. The attempt to achieve the administration's policy goals may be constrained by the need to achieve legal goals. If these goals are complementary, there are opportunities. To achieve those goals, the solicitor general must pay attention to strategic interaction with the actors in the office's environment. The different types of participation provide different constraints and emphasize different institutional relationships between various actors and the solicitor general. In the next chapter, I turn to a closer examination of the relationship between the solicitor general and the other actors in the office's environment.

CHAPTER 2

The Solicitor General as a Strategic Actor

THE 1937 TERM ESTABLISHED the context for the modern Supreme Court and solicitor general. The Court had upheld challenges to the constitutionality of portions of the New Deal, thrusting itself into a showdown with President Franklin Roosevelt. When the Court eventually capitulated, it averted a constitutional crisis. This forced the Court to redefine its institutional role. In his famous Footnote Four in the *United States v. Carolene Products* decision, Justice Stone argued that the Court should adopt a double standard, exercising restraint in economic matters, but advocating a "preferred position" for individual liberties and civil rights.[1]

Brown v. Board of Education was the most important step in bringing Footnote Four to fruition. *Brown* expanded the use of equity and created a precedent for broad legal remedies.[2] The Court's expansive view of the Constitution and renewed judicial activism encouraged the use of the judiciary by a variety of groups.[3] Increased activism in civil rights and individual liberties meant that the Court was opening its doors to new issues and would have to establish doctrinal equilibrium in those areas. Once the policy window was opened, the Court would rely on the solicitor general for assistance in conceptualizing cases and imposing consistency on doctrine, fulfilling its role as "tenth justice" and "fifth clerk." In addition, the creation of statutory authority through various civil rights and voting rights acts made the government a party to many cases. This allowed the solicitor general to adopt the role of "attorney general as law enforcement officer." The salience of these issues encouraged presidents to use their solicitors general to pursue their agendas and to utilize them in the role of "attorney general as policy maker."

STRATEGIC INTERACTION

The individual solicitor general's ability to achieve his or her goals depends on what the president wants to achieve and how willing he is to use the solicitor general, the goals of the agency, the relationship with and the composition of the Supreme Court, the willingness of Congress to intervene, and constraints imposed and opportunities provided by precedent and doctrinal evolution in individual issue areas. The norms of precedent and doctrinal development implore the solicitor general to help impose stability on the law. The institutional context, which refers to the solicitor general's strategic interaction with other actors, may do the opposite.

The solicitor general tries to achieve a number of personal and individual goals in a dynamic environment that requires strategic interaction. As a strategic actor, the solicitor general has to play a number of different roles. As Drew Days argued "life for the Solicitor General is never simple. Through all of these twists and turns, it is important for the Solicitor General to keep in mind his responsibility to be a forceful and effective advocate for the government while ensuring that he maintains a reputation for 'absolute candor and fair dealing' in the Supreme Court and lower federal courts." The bottom line of this balancing act, according to former Deputy Frey, is that "there is normally a moderating effect on the policies of other parts of the government."[4]

The President

Robert Scigliano argues that the judicial and executive branches were designed by the framers as "an informal and limited alliance against Congress."[5] Presidents facing a Congress controlled by the other party (or an antagonistic wing of their party) may have their programmatic options limited. They can govern by veto or try to use the courts to supplement their agenda. The power to appoint justices and the solicitor general gives the president the opportunity to exert influence.

The solicitor general is a political appointee, but because of the need to operate in the legal sphere, the office is not expected to be politically oriented. Indeed, the solicitor general owns a significant degree of independence within the Justice Department. The need to be "above politics," yet intricately involved in setting litigation priorities places the solicitor general in a peculiar position, balancing different roles and facing a number of constraints.[6] Symbolic of the tensions is the fact that the solicitor general has offices in both the Supreme Court and the Department of Justice.[7]

Solicitors general have to balance law and politics, yet the two clearly intersect. The question for the solicitor general, particularly for controversial issues, is how to maintain independence. Should the solicitor general try to insulate the office from the political forces? Walter Dellinger said no:

> It is important to have independence, but retain the channels to the elected branches. There has to be a policy of engagement with the political forces. Some Solicitors General try to maintain independence by not letting the President and Attorney General in on their deliberations and strategies. I explained things to them early and often, especially on troublesome cases. I would brief them at the beginning of the term and highlight the key cases. I shared the views that opponents of mine held and offered my positions. This gave them procedural cover for those controversial cases.[8]

Presidents attempt to select solicitors general who share their policy views and judicial philosophies. But competing constraints virtually ensure that the solicitor general cannot strictly follow the president's bidding. The president needs to select a solicitor general that the administration can trust to be independent. According to Rebecca Salokar: "The Attorney General has neither the time or resources to supervise every decision of the solicitor general."[9] Because the solicitor general is a repeat player interested in getting favorable decisions that will penetrate through the judicial system, the office must be pragmatic enough to advance cases that have a chance of winning.

Days expressed the dilemma, "The President appoints the Solicitor General and the President, not the Solicitor General, appears in the Constitution. Consequently, the President has the last say, from a constitutional standpoint, as to what the administration's position before the Supreme Court will be. And there have been a few occasions in recent years where Presidents have exercised that constitutional authority by giving explicit instructions to their Solicitors General to advance certain arguments before the Supreme Court and lower federal courts." But he added, "From a pragmatic standpoint, Presidents have concluded that their direct interference in the Solicitor General's decision-making process in a particular case may damage the administration's credibility, especially in the Supreme Court, with respect to its entire litigation program." Most solicitors general believe it is proper to contribute to the administration's agenda, but a wholesale departure from the special status that the solicitor general enjoys would impair that status and the ability to serve the president's objectives would suffer. According to Lawrence Wallace, "The Administration needs an effective voice in the Supreme Court. If the Solicitor General does not provide that, it hurts the Administration."[10]

While the president cannot micromanage the solicitor general, the administration's views get an airing. According to Days, "Given the way that the decision-making process works, by the time a case has reached the point of possible appellate court or Supreme Court review, the policy concerns of the President have usually been fully presented to the Solicitor General by his appointees in the affected departments and agencies."[11]

Each president is motivated by a desire to achieve certain policy goals and write his pages in history. The president may try to use the attorney general and solicitor general to advance his agenda. This can be particularly important when there is divided government and the president does not have the political muscle to move his program through Congress. Race and abortion were agenda issues. Given the constitutional basis of the issues, the Court was the primary arena to contest battles. In reproductive rights and early civil rights cases, the solicitor general was an important resource because most of the activity involved state laws and could be addressed through an *amicus* brief.

In the statutory realm, the interpretation that the solicitor general offers in briefs and arguments can expand or contract legislative intent, giving the president another means of advancing his agenda. In fact, a narrow interpretation can give the president a second chance to "veto" legislation when there is divided government.[12]

The different time clocks of the president and his advisors, on the one hand, and the lawyers in the divisions and the solicitor general's office, on the other, give each different priorities. Those clocks divide the political from the legal. For the president, the long-term relationship between the Court and the solicitor general may be a luxury that can be temporarily sacrificed. Wallace, who served through a number of administrations, was aware of the tensions: "The President's supporters are on a different time clock; they don't like to hear about obstacles. They often go after the messenger."[13]

The institutional context that solicitors general faced changed dramatically over the last half-century. Franklin Roosevelt ushered in a new regime for presidential power.[14] The solicitor general was affected by these changes, but in significant ways, the work of the office helped shape that context in civil rights, gender discrimination, and reproductive rights. Changes in the Department of Justice and the CRD ushered in a new regime for the office.

The Attorney General and the Department of Justice

According to Wallace, "The Department of Justice is the original public interest law firm."[15] Because the OSG is housed in the department, there is an additional chance for executive influence. As the head of the department, the attorney general has responsibilities that are distinctly legal in character: he or she is the chief law enforcement officer of the United States, legal advisor to the president, and an officer of the court. But the attorney general is often a close political ally of the president, part of what has been referred to as "the inner Cabinet."[16] The solicitor general is supposed to be "above politics." Victor Navasky posed the question: ". . . what happens when the Solicitor's idea of his obligation to the court conflicts with the Attorney General's idea of his obligation to carry out Presidential policy?" The attorney general is more likely to focus on short-range political results, while the solicitor general is more concerned with long-range constitutional law implications.[17] According to Dellinger: "There are politics in the Office, but I would trust the solicitor general in the long run. On the whole, the views of the Office are less likely to be tainted by politics. The Department of Justice, in general, is a good place to do legal analysis."[18]

While the attorney general is legally and organizationally the solicitor general's boss, in practice the office enjoys a measure of "independence." But according to Lincoln Caplan, "The solicitors general have treated 'independence' as a paradox. They recognize that they serve at the pleasure of the President and often put the word in quotation marks. Yet they have considered it a fundamental requirement of the Solicitor." The solicitor general regularly meets with the attorney general and priorities are discussed. As Salokar notes: "As a member of the Department of Justice, the solicitor general is subject to the tension between law and politics that permeates the Department itself." In theory, the attorney general makes policy decisions. "But the Attorney General and the President should trust the judgment of the Solicitor General not only in determining questions of law but also in distinguishing between questions of law and policy."[19]

The attorney general is typically less qualified to make legal judgments than the solicitor general. Indeed, only a few attorneys general could be considered qualified to be solicitors general. Attorneys general are typically chosen for their policy-making and management skills. The solicitor general is better positioned to balance agency concerns and place restraints on the administration.[20]

The functions and tensions provide Nancy Baker with the end points of a continuum: the attorney general as neutral at one end and advocate at the other. The advocate is policy-oriented and promotes the president's agenda. The neutral lies at the other pole, he or she is the eminent professional—legalistic and nonpolitical. The advocate is often a presidential advisor on a whole range of domestic and foreign policy issues and infuses the department with a policy orientation that may filter into the OSG. The neutral, on the other hand, reinforces the objectivity that is a hallmark of the OSG. The neutral would be less likely to interfere with the solicitor general. The closer the attorney general is to the advocate end of the continuum, the more pressure he or she would be expected to exert on the solicitor general.[21]

The activism of presidents was reflected in the behavior of their Justice Departments. Even before passage of the Civil Rights Act of 1957, attorneys general had moved beyond the narrow range of options outlined under the law. The primary vehicle was the *amicus* in cases brought by private plaintiffs. The government could participate in private suits and strengthen cases by bringing federal legal resources to bear. Thus the attorney general and solicitor general could coordinate civil rights policy, exercise leadership, and become active in policy development. The breadth of participation made the attorney general a virtual co-plaintiff. The use of the *amicus* permitted the solicitor general to play the roles of "Attorney General as policy maker" and "law enforcement officer."

The Justice Department gained a new arsenal of statutory weapons under the Civil Rights Act of 1964 and Voting Rights Act of 1965. Previous acts had not provided extensive authority for the Justice Department to enforce desegregation and voting rights or included provisions for private accommodations. The solicitor general could "assume the role of creative tactician under a constitutional provision which like the due process and voting rights clauses denotes a developmental principle rather than a settled norm of conduct."[22]

Executive Agencies and Departments

The OSG sits atop dozens of departments, divisions, and agencies in a manner that is similar to the way that the Supreme Court sits at the apex of the judicial system. In this fashion, according to William Brigham, "The Solicitor General is a Junior Supreme Court sitting in judgment on the policies of the various agencies and departments of the government."[23] But the agency poses an institutional constraint because the office needs to defer to its policy position.

The head of the agency is a political appointee, who may attempt to influence the solicitor general. One of the underlying questions will be how political the agencies act in pursuing their charges. The divisions make recommendations as to which cases the solicitor general should appeal to the Supreme Court. As a gatekeeper, the division can influence the priorities of the solicitor general.

The agency is pulled by political and legal forces. The agency normally tries to establish and maintain a consistent position. If the president can affect the agencies through political appointments and issue priorities, he can exert indirect influence on the solicitor general's litigation priorities. That is an onerous task, however, because while the president can choose a handful of political appointees, the vast majority of agency lawyers remain in office despite changes in administration.[24]

Careerists in the appellate sections and legal staff in the agencies provide an institutional memory. Their long-term perspective insulates them from the winds of political change. Careerists are more likely to adopt a piecemeal approach to the construction of legal arguments. They will try to stay the course in their issue area.

Cabinet departments and executive agencies have trial and appellate sections. The trial section takes cases of first impression to the federal district courts. If the government wins, the losing party may decide to appeal. This will activate the appellate section of the agency. If the government loses, the appellate section needs the consent of the OSG to appeal. This gives the office important influence over cases percolating in the lower courts. But it also vests a great deal of control in the trial and appellate sections. Days who served as the head of the CRD before becoming solicitor general, noted ". . . agency lawyers generally will have more intricate knowledge of each case and have more expertise concerning their own programs, regulatory structure, and applicable legal precedent." The litigating sections are tied to the policy-making agencies, so legal and policy positions are developed before the solicitor general gets involved. Frey noted: "Policy is made elsewhere. Our job is to support it if it is defensible."[25]

David Flynn, chief of the appellate section of the CRD, notes that "the role of the Chief of the Appellate Section is intertwined with the functions of the Solicitor General." According to Carter Phillips, who served as an assistant solicitor general, the office "identifies for the agencies issues and questions that might be coming up and starts to formulate a theory." There is a complicated dynamic between the appellate section and the solicitor general. As Deputy Solicitor General Edwin Kneedler noted, "The attorney-client relationship is defined to a large degree; the *Chevron* doctrine affords the agency wide latitude."[26]

According to Flynn, the chief of the appellate section "makes a recommendation as to seeking review or filing an *amicus;* the initial draft of the brief is modified by the solicitor general's office and filed in the Supreme Court." As Wallace notes: "Program responsibility belongs to the agency. We try to keep the broad perspective and intervene sporadically with the agency. We help the agencies with adjustments: what will fly in the Court. We consult with them and help them think through the issues. We need to hear their concerns, problems, and why they take a position." Sometimes that requires close attention according to Kneedler: "The office must make sure the agency made a sound decision before going forward. The agency/division may paper over a problem. We need to look beneath the surface sometimes." There are tensions that define the law/policy duality. As Kenneth Starr noted, "We have to balance the agency's views with the need to provide a consistent legal position in the case."[27]

The process of review can have a number of indirect effects. According to Days: "Through the Solicitor General, the Executive can, for specific legal issues, control policies central to many independent agencies. In fact, even the unexercised threat of such control might alter an agency's litigating strategy; in such cases, in a dynamic similar to a presidential veto, an agency may be forced to reassess or compromise its independent policies to accommodate the Solicitor General's views."[28] By serving as a gatekeeper, the office keeps weak cases off the Court's docket and saves federal agencies from a tendency to overreach.

There is another possible dimension to this dynamic. If the administration can influence the solicitor general, then it has the potential of spreading its influence very broadly. If the OSG is used to monitor all agencies and expand or contract their individual policies, the president has the opportunity to move his agenda. It is more efficient than trying to affect each of the agencies individually.

The relationship between the agency and the solicitor general defies easy characterization. Organizationally, the solicitor general is superior to the agency. But the agency sets the policy priorities. There are tensions inherent in the relationship. Kneedler notes that "the office is often seen as arrogant by the agency. The agency does not appreciate our program."[29] The agency thinks that its particular cases are important. The solicitor general may take a broader view and decide not to pursue the cases. If the agency is upset with the office, the head may try to convince the president or attorney general to intervene and veto the solicitor general's decision.

In theory, this relationship seems to divide law from policy. The agency makes policy decisions; neutral law decisions are left to the solicitor general. Once again, this is too simplistic. The agency's political decisions are infused with legal ramifications and must be couched in legal arguments. The solicitor general's decision to permit the agency to take the case to the next level or to deny permission has clear policy implications. Ability to control the solicitor general can extend the influence of the political forces. Levy claimed that "policy decisions become intertwined with legal positions; they tend to converge over time as the case proceeds."[30]

Though basic policy positions are established by the agency, the solicitor general may need to shape the contours of individual cases. Wallace noted: "People think that we are referees over fully developed positions. Under the stimulus of litigation, we have to think through many issues that someone has not considered before." Levy added that "the Solicitor General has a supervisory role over lower court litigation and helps to shape litigation in the lower courts. The institutional view gets formed at this stage. It is important for the Solicitor General to get involved at this stage."[31]

In a sense, the OSG resembles the Office of Management and Budget (OMB). OMB is a clearinghouse for the budget requests of executive agencies. The solicitor general controls access to the next court level, a decidedly finite resource, much as OMB controls access to the treasury. In the vast majority of the cases (90 percent), the solicitor general refused to honor the agency's request to file in the Supreme Court.[32] Eric Schnapper compares this function of the solicitor general to the senior partner at a private law firm.[33] The solicitor general exercises final authority over strategic and tactical judgments about how to proceed in a given case.

The CRD was the agency with the primary responsibility for civil rights, gender, and reproductive rights issues. Policy is set by the assistant attorney general who heads the division. The modern era of federal involvement can be traced to 1939 when Attorney General Frank Murphy established a Civil Rights Section in the Criminal Division of the Justice Department. *Brown* was the landmark that forced the department to take fuller responsibility and led to creation of the CRD.[34] The division has important enforcement powers, particularly in voting rights. Other agencies such as the Equal Employment Opportunity Commission (EEOC) also have authority to pursue violations based on race or gender.[35] Unlike some divisions, Congress and president care deeply about its policies.

The Office of the Solicitor General

The solicitor general presides over an elite law firm. Beneath the solicitor general, there is a principal deputy, a political appointee, who does not need Senate confirmation. The position, sometimes referred to as the political deputy, was created in 1983 to handle civil rights. On the same organizational level are three to four "career" deputy solicitors general.[36] One deals exclusively with criminal matters, the others deal with various civil matters. Beneath the deputies organizationally are 17–20 staff attorneys, who are generalists (except for the assistant who deals with tax cases). According to Phillips, "The office has great success in getting A-plus lawyers who work hard without an ax to grind."[37]

One means for the executive to influence the Court is to initiate changes through the solicitor general's office. The president selects the solicitor general and political deputy,[38] who set the office's legal priorities. The president and Justice Department will establish policy and legal goals, which the solicitor general will attempt to further. The solicitor general and principal deputy may set their own priorities, but the office has an institutional memory. Many attorneys remain through changes in administration and can affect the ability of the political appointees to further the president's designs.

The long tenure draws careerists closer to the Supreme Court and its concern for long-term doctrinal development. Wallace argued: "Incrementalists accomplish more. They can change the nature of legal debate. Careerists take the long view. The Administration takes the short view, as it must. Our view follows Court procedures: a case-by-case incremental approach. From my experience under seven different presidents, presidents are more apt to get in trouble due to the overzealousness of supporters, rather than the career official's attempts to be more cautious." As Phillips noted: "It is hard to walk into the office and not be respectful of the relationship with the Supreme Court. It is ingrained in the line people and the deputies providing an institutional component."[39]

The process of setting litigation strategies and implementing them in individual cases is based on alternate degrees of specialization. The appellate section is composed of specialists in individual issue areas. When the case moves into the solicitor general's office, it is assigned to staff attorneys, who are generalists. The case then moves to the individual deputy, who is a specialist. The ultimate decision lies with the solicitor general, "the consummate generalist." According to Seth Waxman, this layering has great utility: "It is useful to have a stratum of generalists above the litigating units. It is highly functional to have divisions with a deputy assigned to each one. This allows someone to focus on the development of law in those areas—how briefs are written and arguments crafted." Waxman claims the process

> is the most perfectly devised system for legal analysis given the diversity of views, quality of people, and the imperative to make a decision. It makes for thrilling discussions and decisions. Ten to twenty people thinking about an issue. All are charged with representing the people of the United States. Each asking what is the right thing to do, but each has a different institutional view. Each one has read everyone's analysis and thought about it. They wrestle with jurisdictional issues in the context of real world problems with real time deadlines.[40]

The history and traditions of the office present a formidable dilemma for a solicitor general who wants to push the president's agenda. On the other hand, they provide cover for the solicitor general who wants to treat the law as primary, respect the relationship with the Court, and keep a distance from the administration's goals. The job of screening cases, monitoring litigation across trial and appellate sections, and preparing briefs mandates that the solicitor general rely on the careerists. Maintaining the highest professional standards means that the new solicitor general cannot get too closely tied to the policy views of the administration. As former deputy Geller noted: "It is important to make certain that the solicitor general focuses on the connection to the Court. . . . The careerists must remind the solicitor general of institutional concerns. It is an effort to help the Administration. A bad case can diminish the Court's view of the office. The Administration might get a short-term victory, but at a loss of long-term capital." Days argues that "the Solicitor General is invited by tradition, as well as statute and regulation, to step out from the role of partisan advocate to assist in the orderly development of the law and to insist that justice be done even where the immediate interests of the federal government may not appear to benefit."[41]

According to Donald Ayer, principal deputy for Charles Fried, "The pervasive view of the Solicitor General's office is that there is a body of law that is there and if we work hard enough, we can discover the neutral principles. This is the ideal quest of the Solicitor General's Office if it is not always entirely realistic. It is a noble idea that is worth pursuing, and it becomes ingrained in those who work in the office. They work in a neutral way, stating the principles of law up front." John Roberts, principal deputy for Starr, echoed this notion: "The solicitor general and the careerists share a desire to protect the office."[42]

The solicitor general can also be constrained by the work of his predecessors. In the short term, politics and law may collide when a new solicitor general has to continue cases already in the judicial pipeline. When a change in party brings a new solicitor general to office, there may be a temptation to reverse the government's position in controversial cases. This is a step that is not taken lightly. As James Turner noted, "Changing sides in a case is unusual. It is newsworthy because it is 'man bites dog.'"[43] There are bound to be some changes, but they should be done with great care.[44] A reversal of position raises red flags for the Court. As Geller said, "It has to be a very important case to pay the price before the Court."[45] Interestingly, and symbolic of the division between law and politics, solicitors general are less troubled by the need to change sides than the careerists.[46]

In the longer term, the previous solicitor general provides opportunities and constraints for his successor. A new president may be interested in changing the direction of policy initiatives. This is a difficult task that requires changing an agency's priorities. Years of following and arguing a position in the courts establish a precedent. The solicitor general may be asked to encourage the Court to reverse or limit past decisions. Thus, the dynamics of politics can interfere with the need to impose stability. A new administration can try to chip away at existing doctrine, but it risks alienating the Court if the justices are not so disposed. On the other hand, an entrenched policy position can provide cover for those seeking to stay the course.

If a party takes control of the White House after a long absence, there may be pent up demand for initiating change. The solicitor general may be asked to assume a role in that process. But the new solicitor general is likely to be arguing cases in front of a Court packed by the other party and antagonistic to his designs.

More specifically, the work of an immediate predecessor can constrain the options available to the new solicitor general. If the past solicitor general has embarked on a new area of law, the new solicitor general may be obligated to help the Court with the development of doctrine, even if it conflicts with the views of the administration. In most areas, the new administration would simply follow the script laid down by its predecessors. For controversial issues, however, the chances of policy reversal are considerably higher when a new party takes over the Justice Department.

There is evidence that the OSG has changed in remarkable ways.

When Nixon wrestled the presidency from the Democrats in 1968, he did not change his predecessor's solicitor general. Had Bill Clinton done the same thing, Kenneth Starr would have been his solicitor general. Refusing to change the solicitor general despite a change of party suggests a degree of nonpartisanship that is considered an ideal of the office. A little more than a decade later, the office was charged with being politicized and advancing a controversial agenda.

Changes in the nature of the solicitor general's role have occurred and civil rights and abortion have been more than partially responsible. Some analysts argue that the type of individual chosen as solicitor general has changed. The qualifications of solicitors general have not changed, but recent presidents have made choices that are more ideologically oriented than their predecessors. In addition, recent presidents have chosen solicitors general who do not have the reputations that Archibald Cox, Erwin Griswold, and Robert Bork had.[47] According to Paul Bender, principal deputy under Drew Days: "There was a difference in the background of the Solicitor General. Griswold, Cox, and Thurgood Marshall had independent stature with the President. Days did not have that independent stature."[48] This could have consequences for a solicitor general who tries to stand up to political operatives seeking to advance the president's agenda.

Philip Heymann, who served in the OSG, claimed that there have been significant changes in the way solicitors general have done their jobs: "There was a great reliance on the Hart and Sacks article that argues that there is a determinant legal answer for every legal question. The Solicitor General could tell the president that the office could not take a certain position because it is the law. There has been a movement away from that today. Solicitors General are advocates for a position. It is in this difference that everything lies. This is a matter of how extensive is the area of law versus that of policy."[49]

There has been a widely held perception that solicitors general since the Reagan administration were not as free from political interference. Ideological solicitors general have been chosen before, like Cox and Bork,[50] but they frequently moderated their stances and argued positions that seemed to belie their political views. Recent solicitors general have been less likely to let the trappings of the position moderate their views on sensitive issues. Although there are a number of explanations for these apparent changes, many argue that this is further evidence of the politicization of the office.

There have also been structural changes that are directly tethered to civil rights and abortion. Advisors in the Justice Department argued that the solicitor general needed a political ally, the principal deputy, as an intermediary between the solicitor general and the staff attorneys. This enhanced the political dimensions of already controversial issues. In the past, these issues might be mediated by career experts, who had some insulation from the vagaries of the political winds.

Critics feared that the creation of the principal deputy would inject a unhealthy dose of politics into the office. According to Geller, "The solicitor general and the attorney general recognize that he/she must be a person of the highest legal ability. In retrospect, it has worked out very well; it has been much ado about nothing."[51] Bryson agreed that it has been positive:

> They have been first rate lawyers, certainly not political hacks. They were not moles for the White House. The people selected did not come in with an air of suspicion around them. They had a credibility in speaking with and for the White House, yet they were interested in upholding the highest standards of the Solicitor General's Office. The Principal Deputy served as the person to handle the highly sensitive cases. This was great for the Career Deputies. We did not have to deal with those cases or worry about the political concerns of the White House. It freed us to go about our work. The careerists were shielded from the political winds.[52]

Much of the credit for this has been attributed to Paul Bator, the first principal deputy. He created a precedent by following the same degree of care that has always been a hallmark of the OSG. According to Ayer, who held the position, "The principal deputy argues the difficult, highly charged political issues. But he/she is not a political fix it man. The role of the principal deputy is not to carry political water on controversial issues. It is important that he or she pursue the ideals of the office, which include disinterested logical reasoning."[53]

Claims of politicization at the top of the OSG (the creation of the principal deputy position and the ideologies of recent solicitors general) have been supplemented by claims that politics has infused the selection of assistants. Starr and Days were each accused of using ideology as a criterion for selection. Bender argued that "there was a politicization of hiring in the office that began with Ken Starr. He hired in an ideological way at the assistant level . . . Starr's political hiring changed the office." He defended Days's selections: "Drew was accused of political hiring. We hired people from the Legal Defense Fund and the ACLU; the office had never had lawyers from those organizations. Drew's hiring decisions were not political in nature."[54]

Richard Seamon, an assistant under Starr and Days, said, "There was not an overt or conscious ideological slant to the hiring. Days was interested not so much in getting new people who were on the left as he was in getting people with different backgrounds to get more breadth." Rather a form of natural selection evolved. Seamon added: "A lot of hiring was influenced by contacts, over the transom applications." The solicitor general fields recommendations from contacts in academia or elsewhere. As solicitors general get more ideological, it is likely that their contacts will recommend young attorneys who share an ideological affinity and thus give the impression of political hiring. There is some self-selection involved according to Dellinger: "The best applicants, enthusiasts who are sympathetic to the Administration's view, tend to apply."[55]

The OSG has always been subject to politics, but the degree of political influence seems to have grown. If the principal deputy has not fulfilled the prophesies of opponents, it has been a symbol of the desire of political forces to influence the office. It is clear that the OSG has been the subject of greater attention in the last two decades. According to Deputy Kneedler, "We felt under siege and heavily scrutinized, but to some extent we had it coming. There was an arrogance in the office. We felt that we knew the right answers to legal questions. There was a loss of innocence that came as a result. We had been very isolated as an institution. We are not as isolated now. . . . The office was knocked down a peg or two and that is probably good in the long run."[56]

The Supreme Court

Every solicitor general must pay attention to the long-term relationship with the Supreme Court, but the individual solicitor general also must pay attention to the predilections and jurisprudence of the sitting Court. The solicitor general typically inherits a strong relationship from his predecessor and must bequeath that to his successor. More specifically, the solicitor general also pays attention to the composition of the Court. The office may need to tailor its desired positions to those of a majority of the Court. The solicitor general should have opportunities when the Court is favorable, but faces constraints when the Court is ideologically opposed to the president's positions.

The OSG shares a symbiotic relationship with the Supreme Court. This impairs the ability of the president to influence the solicitor general. The lifetime tenure of the justices and the career track of many attorneys in the office provide each with some insulation from politics. The solicitor general screens cases carefully, keeping many off the Court's crowded docket. Wade McCree, President Jimmy Carter's solicitor general, argued that "it is the duty of the Solicitor General to serve as a first-line gatekeeper for the Supreme Court and to say 'no' to many government officials who present plausible claims of legal errors in the lower courts." The solicitor general also "focuses and directs the development of law," helping the justices impose stability on doctrine. Solicitors general appear before the Court more than any other litigant, thus they are familiar with the predilections of individual justices and the Court.

The office and the Court have developed "a tradition of mutual trust and respect."[57] As Starr noted, "There is a unique relationship between the two branches that is valued and treasured and is a factor that counsels care, caution, and effective lawyering." The result, as James Cooper argues, is that "the long-term advantages of cooperation tend to outweigh strategies of short-term gain." Thus the solicitor general "is likely to have an incentive structure which is less sensitive to politics and more sensitive to the Court." Indeed, Caplan argues: "The ties between the Solicitor General and the Supreme Court confound the textbook notions of checks and balances."[58] The Court and the solicitor general have checks on each other. If the Court is unhappy with the office's screening of cases or the quality of its briefs, it can reject a higher percentage of its cert petitions or give the solicitor general a higher percentage of losses on the merits. Given the volume of potential government litigation, the OSG could flood the Court if it was not satisfied with the justices' treatment of its cases.

This unique relationship provides some special advantages for the OSG. Starr noted: "There is an institutional sense that the relationship between the Office and the Court is an important and enduring one. You are afforded certain courtesies by the Court."[59] The solicitor general is one of the few litigants allowed to submit an *amicus* brief without permission of the parties in the case. The office is also permitted to make use of an extraordinary procedure known as lodging. This permits the office to add supporting materials that are not in the trial record, but will shed light on the government's position. Each of these procedures, along with the sheer number of cases, gives the solicitor general an advantage over other litigants. As David Kendall argues: "In the Supreme Court, the solicitor general's office is the home team."

While the solicitor general gets benefits that are denied other litigants, it has responsibilities that others do not. As Caplan writes, "The Solicitor General plays by different rules because he represents the United States. If the solicitor general's office owes a special duty to the Court, and the Justices hold the solicitor general's lawyers to a higher standard of craft, why shouldn't the Court give those lawyers some extra scope." Waxman viewed it from the opposite perspective:"There is a special relationship between the solicitor general and the Supreme Court; what is special is the additional responsibility, rather than the perks."[60]

This influence is particularly evident when the justices turn to the solicitor general for assistance on legal issues and invite the office to state the government's position. The notion of an "invitation" is a misnomer. In reality, as Levy said, it is tantamount to an order from the queen.[61] This "call for the views of the Solicitor General" (CVSG) is considered the highest compliment that the Court can bestow on the office.[62]

The solicitor general's primary responsibilities are to screen petitions carefully and carry forward briefs of the highest quality. Another important function of the solicitor general is informational. Oral arguments and written briefs are good places for justices to get information. But the Court is bombarded by information. Litigants may fabricate or exaggerate circuit conflicts or misrepresent the impact of a precedent.[63] The solicitor general seeks to provide the justices with accurate and balanced information and assure that the briefs maintain a high level of professionalism. The solicitor general frames positions that strike the appropriate balance between justice and advocacy and identifies the interests and policies of the agency. These activities can make the Court's job much easier. Timothy Johnson found that a third of questions that justices asked at oral arguments came from *amici* briefs.[64] Because the solicitor general files the most *amici* briefs, the office's influence is profound.

There are a number of pragmatic considerations that compel the solicitor general to adhere to a stringent level of candor in dealing with the Court. As the ultimate repeat player, the solicitor general participates in more than half of the cases on the Court's plenary docket. As a result, the quality of the solicitor general's work has an enormous impact on the Court. If the office is not reliable, then the Court cannot utilize its work as a cue. In addition, all of the office's appearances are on behalf of one client, so the presentation in one case can affect the government in other cases. The frequency with which solicitor general handles cases means the office develops a reputation that will affect the credibility of its analysis and arguments.[65] Cooper claims, "As a consequence of this repeated reevaluation, the Solicitor General can serve as a sort of legal brand name, offering some assurance of quality."[66]

While many briefs have problems that force justices and their clerks to do additional research, the solicitor general's briefs and arguments can save the justices time by presenting a thorough and balanced discussion of the facts and legal issues. As one justice's clerk put it: "We jokingly referred to the solicitor general's petition as the answer sheet." Clerks and justices pay close attention to the briefs: "The solicitor general also knows all the catchwords, and they just know how to write a brief."[67]

This assists the justices in understanding the nature of the issues and available alternatives and in framing legal questions. Few clerks have mastered the issues before the Court. Indeed, many are only five years out of college. The solicitor general's office has more resources and experience than the clerks. In particular, the deputies who specialize in particular issues frequently bring more expertise and knowledge to that area than most justices. Though it is a small office, it can draw on expertise from thousands of attorneys in the executive branch. In addition, the office is not constrained by many of the restrictions regarding *ex parte* communications and can marshal research that would be difficult or impossible for the Court to gather.

If the OSG does not give a full and objective presentation, it complicates the work of the justices and its relationship with the Court. Clearly, this can create a tension between the solicitor general's responsibility to inform the Court and its desire to persuade the justices to reach a certain result. According to Robert Bork, "The Solicitor General . . . bears a special relationship to the Court. He owes it complete intellectual candor even when that impairs his effectiveness as an advocate."[68]

Rex Lee summed up the most visible manifestation of the relationship between the office and the Court: "There is a widely held, and I believe substantially accurate, impression that the Solicitor General's office provides the Court from one administration to another—and largely without regard to either the political party or the personality of the particular Solicitor General—with advocacy which is more objective, more dispassionate, more competent, and more respectful of the Court as an institution than it gets from any other lawyer or group of lawyers."[69]

While the office must pay attention to the Court as an institution, the solicitor general must also pay attention to the current configuration of the justices. The office must provide quality briefs and careful screening, regardless of the identity of the president or the nine justices. The scope of those briefs, decisions regarding which losses to appeal, and which cases to join as *amicus* depend to some degree on the composition of the Court. The solicitor general's agenda must be practical. The OSG cannot push cases or arguments that are out of line with the ideological tenor of the Court.

It is the task of the solicitor general to determine whether justices will adhere to precedent or might be willing to depart from it. In deciding whether to file a certiorari petition and which arguments to offer, the solicitor general, as a strategic repeat player, needs to determine how justices will react. As Starr argued, "It is a mistake to view the Court as static. It too has a dynamic with jurisprudential evolution and development. The Solicitor General should be attentive to that dynamic."[70]

The solicitor general must anticipate the type of information and analysis the Court will find useful in deciding cases and continuing doctrinal construction. In trying to determine the concerns of the justices, the solicitor general may need to put aside the administration's designs. If the president wants to use the solicitor general as a policy activist, he must be certain that the Court will accept such behavior. Otherwise, the president stands to lose a significant portion of the influence he has with the Court and the solicitor general would lose effectiveness as a legal representative of the administration.[71] As Wallace said: [The office] "engages in a meaningful dialogue with the Court about the public interest in light of the programmatic interest of the government and the jurisprudence of the Court."[72]

Congress

Congress is a complex institution that presents opportunities and poses constraints for the solicitor general. Congress can provide support for the solicitor general and the administration by passing legislation that makes litigation easier or less necessary. On the other hand, Congress can retaliate if it does not like a Supreme Court decision.

Once the Senate confirms the solicitor general, Congressional influence is lessened. Congress has to pass the office's budget each year, giving it the opportunity to send a message.[73] On rare occasions, Congress can convene oversight hearings to examine the operation of the solicitor general's office. In 1995, the Senate Judiciary Committee used oversight hearings to critique Days's handling of some controversial cases.[74]

The solicitor general has responsibilities to Congress. The interpretation of Congressional intent and language normally involves the solicitor general.[75] As Robert Katzmann notes, "A court that pronounces what Congress meant in such areas as civil rights, voting rights, and gender discrimination will almost certainly be the object of heightened attention."[76] Congress cares about these issues; there is certain to be interest group pressure regardless of the Court's decisions. Presidents Reagan, Bush, and Clinton faced long periods of an intense, often hostile "partisan legislative arena" making the litigation strategy important. It also meant that any success in the judicial arena would be subject to Congressional review.[77]

In statutory and constitutional interpretation, it is the handiwork of Congress that is reviewed by the Court. The solicitor general needs to have a sense of a potential Congressional reaction. As Charles Fried, solicitor general under Reagan, noted: "Congress affected my calculations somewhat. What is the point of an aggressive stance if Congress is going to flip it right away? Sometimes, we went ahead anyway, especially if the lower courts had done the wrong thing. It is Congress' prerogative to review the interpretation."[78]

The question is most dramatic when the constitutionality of an act is at stake. The Justice Department is required to notify Congress if it decides not to defend legislation that has been challenged. If the solicitor general refuses to defend the act, Congress can utilize its own counsel. In such a case, "the executive branch necessarily forfeits its natural monopoly on the function of litigating in the name of the United States." A refusal to defend a statute appears to negate the supremacy of Congress as the lawmaking body. It also calls into question the constitutional mandate that the executive "take care that the laws be faithfully executed." In general, the solicitor general defends the constitutionality of laws, "unless no professionally respectable argument can be made in defense of the statute."[79] Thus, the solicitor general serves as the lawyer for the government, rather than the executive branch.

There are important reasons for the solicitor general to support Congress. According to Days,

> [T]he Solicitor General's traditional willingness to champion the acts of Congress fosters comity between the Executive and Legislative Branches in two important ways. First, by making it unnecessary for Congress to become involved in litigation except in unusual cases, the Solicitor General's policy of defending the acts of Congress ensures that the government speaks with one voice in the Supreme Court while at the same time reinforcing the Executive Branch's status as the litigating arm of the government. Second, the policy prevents the president from using litigation as a form of post-enactment veto of legislation that the current administration dislikes.[80]

Conflicts regarding statutory interpretation are less dramatic, but may raise questions regarding the appropriate role for the solicitor general. When issues of statutory interpretation arise, it is the solicitor general who must address them and provide a viable meaning for the Court to consider. There are more than a few occasions when the solicitor general must defend statutory language the president finds objectionable. The question is what happens when the interests of the president and Congress collide?[81] In most circumstances, in disputes over statutory interpretation, the solicitor general normally takes Congress' side. If the president has opposed legislation, but it passed perhaps even over his veto, the solicitor general must respect Congressional prerogatives.[82] But as Fried noted, "Given the ability of the president to veto harmful legislation, we knew we could proceed with a case even if Congress might balk."[83]

Congress has authority to clarify its intentions through subsequent legislation. Occasionally, the justices "invite" Congress to overturn the Court's statutory interpretations, though few of those invitations occur in civil rights cases.[84] Many issues of statutory interpretation arise in the context of judicial review of independent agency action. In such instances, the original interpretation of the statute has been rendered by an administrative agency. In response, the solicitor general has three choices: adopt a position that reflects the administration's view, advance the interpretation of the agency, or search for the intent of Congress, independent of the position of the agency or president. Ultimately, the office must attempt to speak with one voice for the government. The solicitor general serves as a judge when there is conflict, bringing parties and agencies together to develop a unitary position.[85]

The interpretation of statutory provisions requires the solicitor general and the Court to infer the intent of Congress. The process is complicated by the fact that the solicitor general and the Court must react not only to the Congress that passed the statute, but to the sitting Congress that could retaliate for a decision it finds objectionable.[86] As a consequence, Congress poses a shifting constraint. When the solicitor general argues a case involving a statute, the office needs to consider what Congress meant when it passed the law and how the sitting Congress might interpret the provisions in question.

In the end, even in cases involving statutory construction, the Court is the primary concern for the solicitor general. As Robert Long, a former assistant, noted: "It has been my practical experience that you have to persuade the Court. We needed to consider what have the past Court decisions on statutory interpretation held. We follow some rules of statutory interpretation, but we also pay close attention to how the Court has interpreted the statutes." Former Principal Deputy Roberts concurred: "There was no real concern with Congress on interpretation; there are rules for the interpretation of statutes. But Congress can fix the statute if the members are unhappy."[87]

The solicitor general has greater latitude in constitutional issues.

Congress has little realistic chance of mustering the extraordinary majorities necessary to overturn constitutional decisions. Congress can institute blocking legislation to limit the impact of such decisions or check the
Court in other ways. In statutory interpretation, the solicitor general
faces greater constraints. Congress can pass overriding legislation by a
simple majority. But if there is divided government, the president can
veto such legislation. Unpopular decisions bring Congressional threats
to the Court. The solicitor general might not be a target, but the office
could be an accessory to the process that puts the Court into Congressional crosshairs. The solicitor general is normally interested in protecting the Court.

The impact and role of Congress changed dramatically since the Legislative Reorganization Act. In 1946–63, Congress was largely an obstacle to meaningful civil rights legislation. It was a divisive issue that
could wreck the Democratic Party. Almost half of the Democrats were
from southern and border states, forcing the leadership to "submerge"
civil rights initiatives.[88]

In the following decade, Congress became an important ally of the
Court. During the Reagan and Bush administrations, Congress was
considered the leader in protecting civil rights, overturning a number of
Court decisions.[89] During the Clinton administration, Republican control of Congress and reforms expanded legislative ability to counteract
the president and removed some of the safety net for civil rights.[90]

Since 1952, seventeen of twenty-four elections have yielded divided
government.[91] A president who cannot steer his agenda through a hostile Congress may opt for a judicial strategy. The shifts in the role that
Congress played and the increase in divided government have had important implications for the solicitor general.

SUMMARY

There is no question as to the importance of the solicitor general or the
potential of the office. H. W. Perry claims that "he is surely the most important person in the country, except for the justices themselves, in determining which cases are heard in the Supreme Court."[92] Days argued
that:

> for most purposes, the Solicitor General has the last word
> with respect to whether, and on what grounds, the United
> States will seek review in the Supreme Court and he deter-
> mines what cases from the federal trial courts the govern-

ment will seek to reverse on appeal. In this process, the Solicitor General is not a 'hired gun.' To be sure, he is not a
policy-maker in the sense that other presidential appointees
at the cabinet and the sub-cabinet levels are. But in the
course of acting as a *legal* policy-maker regarding government litigation, the Solicitor General not only advises his
colleagues as to means to achieve certain ends in light of the
wisdom that is often gained from court challenges to federal
policies.[93]

The solicitor general's position subjects the office to a number of
pressures that are particularly prevalent in controversial areas. There are,
according to Lee, "Temptations . . . to consume the Solicitor General's
capital in the interest of particular cases." Those temptations come in
three forms. First, given the success at the certiorari stage, there is pressure to file more briefs. The agency always wonders how filing one additional brief would affect the office's credibility. Lee maintained that this
would increase the justices' workload; they would be forced to do the
screening rather than the executive branch. Wade McCree argued that
"we do not petition the Supreme Court to review adverse decisions unless the case satisfies the stricter standards of exceptional importance applied by the Supreme Court itself. . . . The selfish reason for the Solicitor General's self-restraint in petitioning for certiorari is to give the
Court confidence in Government petitions."[94]

The second temptation involves use of voluntary *amici* briefs. Nearly
every case the Supreme Court accepts is important and the solicitor general would have an interest in most. In every case, according to Lee, the
Court would be better off if it had the views of the solicitor general. But
if the office did that, it would lose credibility. As Lee argued, "It is almost
as if I had a certain number of chips to play." Since many changes involve
judge-made law, Lee maintained that the president's views should be presented: "It is part of the duty of the solicitor general to file *amici* in the
so-called agenda cases and in those cases, the Court does give the solicitor general a little more leeway. There is a realization by the justices that
the solicitor general does carry some of the Administration's policies to
the Court. But all solicitors general feel it would be a mistake to file in
too many."[95]

Finally, there is temptation to use the Court as a forum for airing controversial views. Such arguments could be used to lend symbolic support
to external groups. Should solicitors general offer arguments they know
the Court will reject? Though the Court is certain to disagree, the

solicitor general could start a dialogue that might lead justices to reconsider their positions.[96] The solicitor general could arm its supporters on the Court for the future. Most solicitors general are reluctant to try this tack. There is a good practical reason: the Court's decision would probably be a strongly worded opinion that would create an adverse precedent.

According to Starr, the solicitor general is not always constrained: "If we felt that a particular position on an issue was erroneous, we would state that, even if the Court might disagree. . . . The example I like to summon up involves the solicitors general under Franklin Roosevelt who tirelessly suggested to the Court, with almost no success, that the Court's jurisprudential thrust was wrong. They continued to push that position. That did not mean that FDR and the Justice Department should shy away from the fact that three or four justices take umbrage with the arguments." Fried echoed the sentiments: "The Solicitor General has a professional obligation to maintain the reputation for accuracy and soundness of argument. But you still try to argue your position."[97]

The solicitor general might use cases to speak to external audiences. Lee argued that the OSG cannot do that: "The audience for the briefs and arguments consists of nine people and nine people only." According to Wallace, "The Court does not want political cases in which it is the venue for venting the issue. Our credibility diminishes when we appear to be talking to someone else through the Court." Lee argued that the solicitor general is "not the pamphleteer general nor the neighborhood essayist."[98]

Cooper noted, "Though the Solicitor General may increasingly become the President's mouthpiece, it is the Court that provides him with a stage and an audience, and it is the Court that will control his influence and indirectly his behavior." Kirsten Norman-Major summarized the inherent tensions: "The ultimate role of the Solicitor General will be determined by the relationship between the President and the Court and the Solicitor General's willingness—or determination—to respect the rule of law."[99]

Part of that is a function of the parallel missions of the Court and the office. As one former member of the office noted, "It is the only spot, besides a judgeship, where your job is to figure out what *you* think is the right answer for the law and then to present your argument to the highest court in the land."[100]

Perhaps no one understood the tensions better than Lee, who presided over what critics called a politicized office:

> What lawyer would not value a relationship in which the
> court before which he appears with frequency asks him

'what should we do about this case in which you are not involved?' I think that it is not only proper for the Solicitor
General to use the adversarial advantages that result from
that kind of relationship, it would be a breach of obligation
to the President who appointed him to fail to do so. But it
must be done with discretion, with discrimination, and with
sensitivity, lest the reservoir of credibility which is the source
of this special advantage be diminished, with adverse consequences not only to the government's ability to win cases,
but also to be an important institution of government
itself.[101]

The resulting relationship with the Court has been jealously guarded
by the careerists. It also affects political appointees. All solicitors general
and their principal deputies have balanced the need to serve the president with the obligation to bequeath an amiable relationship to their successors. Presidents and attorneys general have generally respected the
relationship between the Court and the solicitor general and tempered
their requests. It is left to Lee to have the last word: "There has been built
up, . . . a reservoir of credibility on which the incumbent Solicitor General may draw to his immediate adversarial advantage. But if he draws too
deeply, too greedily, or too indiscriminantly, then he jeopardizes not
only that advantage in that particular case, but also an important institution of government. The preservation of both—and striking just the
right balance between their sometimes competing demands—lies at the
heart of the Solicitor General's stewardship."[102]

Part II

THE SOLICITOR GENERAL AND RACE LITIGATION

THE ISSUE OF RACE has been a constant underlying factor in American politics. Key compromises in establishing the Constitution and formulating the structure of government were based on race and slavery. The Civil War was fought over questions of slavery expansion. In the wake of the war, three constitutional amendments, the Thirteenth, Fourteenth, and Fifteenth, were passed to redefine race relations.

Soon after the passage of these amendments, the Supreme Court emasculated the provisions that might have provided equal protection under the law. Into the twentieth century, racial issues were often treated with federal neglect and state hostility. The New Deal seemed to offer some hope of revisiting civil rights issues. The attempt to achieve economic justice included some symbolic and practical measures to correct discrimination. At the same time, race was the fault line under the New Deal political order. Issues of race threatened the New Deal coalition and the Democratic Party.[1] With active Congressional opposition, civil rights progress had to be initiated in the executive or judicial branches. This provided the opportunity to activate the Justice Department and the solicitor general.

Any momentum was stalled by the advent of World War II, but the nation's military needs mandated that the draft include African Americans. Once in the army, black soldiers were placed in segregated barracks. Protests and a successful march on Washington goaded President Roosevelt into issuing "a pathbreaking executive order" creating the Fair Employment Practice Committee (FEPC). The FEPC was hardly the solution to racial discrimination. It suffered from institutional constraints and increasing Congressional opposition.[2] But it created a positive precedent for governmental intervention on behalf of civil rights.

Harry Truman would recreate the FEPC to continue the Roosevelt legacy. Truman was willing to go further and ultimately advanced the cause of civil rights. The Truman plan for civil rights was multifaceted and included a more aggressive stance by the Department of Justice, which eventually brought the issue into the OSG. The success of the solicitor general is dependent on the willingness of the Supreme Court to accept the office's briefs and arguments. In Footnote Four of the *Carolene Products* decision, the justices appeared to articulate an institutional preference for the advancement of civil rights and civil liberties. The Truman administration presided over the beginning of significant changes in the activities and responsibilities of the solicitor general. Some changes in the nature of the solicitor general's role have occurred as a result of civil rights. Many of those changes are the subject of the next three chapters.

Race was an issue that divided the parties and had the constant attention of the other branches, imposing a number of constraints on the solicitor general. Civil rights differed from other issues on a number of dimensions. Perhaps most significantly, the judiciary played a more central role in defining the issue than in most other areas.[3] Congressional assistance came later and structured subsequent waves of litigation while transplanting the issue from the constitutional to the statutory plane. In the area of civil rights, there have been three regimes for solicitors general. One was initiated during the Truman administration. It was marked by a more aggressive use of *amici* briefs and more activism by the solicitor general. The solicitor general has never been completely free from politics, but this regime interjected more political concerns into the office. The second regime was a result of the passage of the Civil Rights Act of 1964. The Civil Rights Act permitted the government, through the Justice Department and the OSG, to become a party to civil rights cases. This allowed the solicitor general to plan litigation in a more strategic fashion. The final regime appeared to evolve in the Reagan administration and was marked by increased external pressure on the office. Changes in the institutional context and the types of solicitors general were responsible. This occurred as the remedies for civil rights, like affirmative action, were beginning to broaden in scope.

The charge has been leveled that Reagan's solicitors general Rex Lee and Charles Fried attempted to pursue a conservative policy agenda through the federal courts when the administration's policies were blocked in Congress.[4] The attempt to use the Court to further a political agenda threatened the relationship between the OSG and the Court. This is particularly relevant because some of the "agenda cases" directly involved issues that were central to racial equality, most notably attempts to limit affirmative action.

In subsequent chapters, I investigate the activity of the solicitor general under different circumstances. To set the context for the substantive analysis, I begin this section with some aggregate analysis of the solicitor general's support levels for civil rights and success on the merits.

While the solicitor general has played an important role in this litigation, leadership initially belonged to the Legal Defense Fund (LDF) of the NAACP. The LDF orchestrated the strategies that led to *Brown*. The solicitor general became a critical ally and provided important symbolic support. After the Civil Rights Act and the Voting Rights Act of 1965, the Justice Department had greater power to initiate activity and exercise policy leadership.

Support and Success: The Solicitor General and Race, 1945–2000

In the aggregate, there were significant differences between the political parties in the office's support of civil rights. As Table II-1 shows, Democratic solicitors general supported civil rights at a considerably higher rate than their Republican counterparts. In fact, Democratic solicitors general only filed one brief against a civil rights claimant. Table II-2 shows that solicitors general who served under Democratic presidents won almost 80 percent of the cases they entered compared to 65 percent for Republican appointees. While these results are not surprising, subsequent analysis suggests that the reasons for these trends are complicated.

Civil rights has moved through three phases. These phases coincided with the three regimes previously alluded to. The initial phase, which lasted until the Civil Rights Act of 1964, was dominated by litigation. There was almost no Congressional assistance for the courts or civil rights during this period. Congress and the president joined the battle in the administrative stage, creating the "federal triangle." Executive leadership and Congressional response created the Civil Rights Act and Voting Rights Act of 1965 and gave the Court needed support. The third

---

Table II-1
Support for Civil Rights Claimants by Political Party in Cases Involving the Solicitor General

	Political Party of President		
Civil Rights Position	*Democratic*	*Republican*	*Total*
Favor Civil Rights Claimants	79	66	145
Oppose Civil Rights Claimants	1	32	33
Total	80	98	178

Table II-2
Success of the Solicitor General by Political Party in Civil Rights Cases

	Political Party of President		
Success on the Merits	*Democratic*	*Republican*	*Total*
Win	63	64	127
Loss	17	34	51
Total	80	98	178

phase, beginning during the Reagan administration, has been marked by an attempt to redefine issues. The Clinton administration attempted to reestablish some protection, but it was often contesting issues on redefined grounds.[5] Figure II-1 represents the dispersion of civil rights issues and the key decisions across the last half-century.

As Table II-3 shows, during the litigation phase, 1945–63, solicitors general supported civil rights in each of the twenty-five cases the OSG was involved with. Table II-4 shows that the OSG was successful in all twenty-five cases. Support for civil rights and success on the merits declined in subsequent phases. In the administrative phase (1964–80), the Court became a secondary actor, interpreting statutes, rather than breaking new legal ground. During this phase, solicitors general still overwhelmingly supported civil rights claimants (86 percent) and were still successful (70 percent), but the unanimity of the previous phase broke down. During the redefinition phase (1981–present), support for civil rights claimants declined to 67 percent. Success on the merits declined to 62 percent.

The different phases were reflected in the type of participation, shown in Table II-5. Through the litigation phase, the government was only a party to four cases, a function of the dearth of legislation. The solicitor general's reluctance to get involved during this phase can be seen in the fact that the solicitor general had to be "invited" to participate in many of the cases. The solicitor general filed eleven voluntary *amici* briefs in this phase. Most of these were "agenda cases."

The growth of Congressional interest, reflected in the Civil Rights Act and Voting Rights Act, had an impact on the type of participation. In the administrative phase, the solicitor general was involved in thirty-one cases as a party. The solicitor general entered fifty-three cases as *amici,* but a number of those were not agenda cases. There are three types of *amici* briefs: invited, discretionary agenda, and those involving agency or statutory power. The third category resemble direct party cases more than the agenda briefs and grew as a result of the Civil Rights Act of 1964, Voting Rights Act of 1965, and the work of the EEOC. The number of invitations declined, a function of the fact that the government was increasingly active in cases at earlier stages, mitigating the need for the Court to force the solicitor general's hand.

In the redefinition phase, as civil rights increasingly became statutory, the solicitor general was heavily involved in cases in which the government was a party. There was also a reliance on *amici,* particularly agenda cases. But a significant number of the *amici* briefs were cases in which an agency or a governmental interest was involved, again resembling the

Figure II-1
The Evolution of Issues and Important Decisions across Presidential Administrations

	Truman	Eisenhower	Kennedy	Johnson	Nixon	Ford	Carter	Reagan	Bush	Clinton
Graduate School Cases		Brown	Goss	Green Southern Resistance	Swann Milliken	Pasadena	Columbus Dayton	Seattle Crawford	Dowell Freeman	

School Desegregation

	Truman	Eisenhower	Kennedy	Johnson	Nixon	Ford	Carter	Reagan	Bush	Clinton
Shelley Henderson	Shelley Henderson	DC v. Thompson	Burton	Heart of Atlanta Alfred Mayer	Sullivan Tillman	Runyon		Patterson		

Public/Private

	Truman	Eisenhower	Kennedy	Johnson	Nixon	Ford	Carter	Reagan	Bush	Clinton
					Griggs Washington v. Davis	Albemarle Paper	Bakke Weber Fullilove	Stotts Wygant Ward's Cove	Metro Broadcasting	Adarand

Employment/Affirmative Action

	Truman	Eisenhower	Kennedy	Johnson	Nixon	Ford	Carter	Reagan	Bush	Clinton
				South Carolina v. Katzenbach			Connor Briscoe Mobile	Thornburgh McCain	Chisholm Clark Presley	Shaw DeGrandy Miller Bush

Voting Rights

61

party cases more than the agenda cases. There was a modest rise in the number of invited cases, which can be attributed to minority district voting disputes.

Each of these phases was dominated by the influence of the first president's solicitor general. The Truman, Johnson, and Reagan solicitors general set the context for their successors, providing opportunities and constraints. This preliminary analysis provides a partial answer to the re-

TABLE II-3

SUPPORT FOR CIVIL RIGHTS BY THE SOLICITOR GENERAL
ACROSS DIFFERENT PHASES

	Civil Rights Position		
Phase of Civil Rights	*Support*	*Opposition*	*Total*
Litigation Phase 1948–63	25	0	25
Administrative Phase 1964–80	76	12	88
Redefinition Phase 1981–2000	44	21	65
Total	145	33	178

TABLE II-4

SOLICITOR GENERAL SUCCESS ON THE MERITS IN CIVIL RIGHTS CASES
ACROSS DIFFERENT PHASES

	Success on the Merits		
Phase of Civil Rights	*Win*	*Loss*	*Total*
Litigation Phase 1948–63	25	0	25
Administrative Phase 1964–80	62	26	88
Redefinition Phase 1981–2000	40	25	65
Total	127	51	178

TABLE II-5

SOLICITOR GENERAL PARTICIPATION IN CIVIL RIGHTS CASES
ACROSS DIFFERENT PHASES

	Type of Participation			
Phase of Civil Rights	*Party*	*Invited*	*Amicus*	*Total*
Litigation Phase	4	10	11	25
Administrative Phase	31	4	53	88
Redefinition Phase	28	7	30	65
Total	63	21	94	178

search questions: how does the solicitor general balance the factors that face the office, and how did it affect policy development? To get a broader perspective, the work of solicitors general beginning with the Truman administration is examined. I examine the political and policy context that each solicitor general faced and discuss the office's role in major civil rights cases through the Clinton administration.

CHAPTER 3

The Solicitor General in the Litigation Phase

1945–63

D URING THE LITIGATION PHASE, there appeared to be no variance in the position or the levels of success in civil rights. Solicitors general supported civil rights and were successful on the merits in each case. Beneath the surface, however, there were some significant differences between administrations. In this chapter, I examine the dynamics set in motion by the Truman administration, how this constrained subsequent solicitors general, and the strategies that allowed the office to balance the forces in its environment and assist the Supreme Court in constructing the emerging doctrine.

The New Deal ushered in new institutional roles for the president and Congress[1] and created the conditions for Footnote Four, a new judicial paradigm.[2] The growth of the central government and executive branch provided a more active role for the solicitor general. The solicitor general assumed a significant role in trying to protect the New Deal, by arguing that the law should be destabilized.[3] This stands in contrast to the normal role of the solicitor general which is to help the Court impose stability on the law. Given negative precedents, solicitors general would have to do the same in civil rights.

From the post-Reconstruction period to 1964, few presidents showed interest and Congress was a graveyard for meaningful civil rights policy. As a result, after 1938 litigation was the primary vehicle for the protection of minority rights. The issue was almost exclusively constitutional because few viable statutes existed. Though there were constitutional provisions that could be used, the Court had been loathe to use them.

Litigation is a piecemeal process and it takes a long period of time to construct doctrinal foundations that can translate to coherent policy. In addition, courts must rely on the good offices of the other branches to implement their decisions. These constraints limit the prospects for social change.[4] But even symbolic victories serve important purposes. Courts may be useful as triggering mechanisms to provide momentum for a nascent social movement or to remove lingering obstacles. A few significant legal victories can create an environment for legislative or executive victories.[5]

If litigation is the only recourse, the solicitor general becomes a critical actor. Solicitors general can link the resources and support of the executive branch to groups using the judiciary. They can help sequence litigation and provide a key to the courthouse door. Assisting a group in its litigation efforts would appear to obligate the executive branch to assist in implementation and policy construction. On the other hand, the failure to join the judicial battle exposes groups to the vagaries of the litigation process.

Under normal circumstances, the solicitor general does not typically get involved in an area until the Supreme Court defines the issue and establishes boundaries. At that juncture, the solicitor general enters the picture to help the justices impose doctrinal equilibrium. Prior to the Truman administration, the work of the solicitor general was even more limited.

An external policy entrepreneur, the NAACP, was responsible for placing civil rights on the agenda. There was almost no precedent for aggressive third-party activity by the government. There was little statutory authority to "force" the solicitor general into court to defend or interpret statutes. The solicitor general had to wait for an invitation from the Court to join the fray. Thus, the dominant role for the solicitor general in civil rights as World War II ended was that of fifth clerk, a role that often carried constraints.

In addition to institutional constraints, there were environmental limitations. Existing statutory remedies had been emasculated by the Supreme Court in the wake of Reconstruction. In the area of civil rights, hostile precedents had interpreted the Fourteenth Amendment out of existence. Because Congress and presidents had ignored civil rights, litigation seemed to be the only outlet. But despite the imperative of Footnote Four, the Court did not seem anxious to confront the issue.

THE ROAD TO TOPEKA: HARRY TRUMAN

The goals of the Truman solicitors general were never really developed. Members of the office took advantage of flux to exert leadership. In doing so, they cast their lot with the Legal Defense Fund of the NAACP.

The need for strategic interaction was limited by the fact that Congress was not a factor and the CRD had not yet been formed. Institutional rules and norms did not augur well for an advancement of civil rights. Existing doctrine was hostile and the Court had not yet fully adopted the preferred position doctrine. Institutionally and doctrinally, there was little reason to expect the solicitor general to be aggressive in civil rights. First, the Democratic Party was leery of the race issue. Second, there was little legislation to allow the solicitor general to be proactive. Third, solicitors general did not often use *amici* to enter as a third party. During the Truman administration, the OSG would alter its institutional role and the dynamics of civil rights litigation. In the end, this would provide constraints and opportunities for subsequent solicitors general.

Executive. Civil rights arose as a political issue when large numbers of black voters in northern urban areas supported Franklin Roosevelt. Harry Truman inherited the unresolved racial questions without the good will that blacks felt toward FDR. Eventually, Truman made civil rights a front page issue, largely because he calculated that it would serve his political agenda. As a result, Truman altered presidential politics and the role of the solicitor general for the next generation.[6]

The rise of civil rights consciousness posed a threat to the Democratic coalition. FDR sidestepped the issue to avoid offending Southerners. Hubert Humphrey had forced Truman's hand with a rousing speech at the 1948 Democratic Convention. Southern delegates left the convention and southern Democrats left the party, seemingly dooming Truman's re-election bid. In the end, according to David McCullough, Humphrey did more to re-elect Truman than anyone else.[7]

Richard Kluger argues that Truman put his political reputation on the line for African Americans like no president since Abraham Lincoln. Truman was willing to use the bully pulpit to support civil rights. Attorneys General Tom Clark, J. Howard McGrath (who was solicitor general under Clark), and James McGranery were willing to do Truman's bidding.[8] The civil rights activity of the Justice Department effectively began with the creation of the Civil Rights Section. Under Clark, the section was aggressive in prosecuting federal violations and trying to persuade state and local officials in the South to monitor and prosecute state violations. Truman used executive orders to integrate the military and create and fund the Civil Rights Commission.[9] The vague language of old civil rights statutes, which had been fallow for decades, limited and undermined enforcement.

Congress. Congress, most notably the Senate, was a barrier to the extension of civil rights. Southern power in Congress was enough to block initiatives that might emerge from the White House. Prior to the Truman administration, six bills to investigate lynchings and end poll taxes died by filibuster.[10] Congress was unwilling to re-enforce Reconstruction era legislation that had been gutted by the Court in the late nineteenth century. But if Congress was unlikely to do anything positive, its ability to modify or reverse a pro–civil rights Court decisions was limited. If Congress could muster support to overturn a decision, Truman could veto the legislation. Most early race cases involved state laws and were based on constitutional grounds, limiting Congressional review.

Supreme Court. On the eve of Truman's ascension to the presidency, the Court was not a likely vehicle for the expansion of civil rights. The Roosevelt Court was in the process of changing its institutional role and in a state of flux. Roosevelt was constantly shifting people on and off the Court. This took a toll on the dynamics of the Court and attempts to establish doctrinal equilibrium.[11] During his tenure as president, Truman certainly did nothing to enhance those possibilities. His appointments are generally regarded as a rather sorry lot.[12] It was a Court adrift with little leadership and facing new, unprecedented issues. The Truman Court was characterized as following a philosophy of judicial restraint, which suggests an unwillingness to rewrite precedents and construct new law.[13] According to the Baum measure of policy change, the 1949–52 Court was considered the most conservative until the 1990s.[14]

Issue Evolution. The Fourteenth Amendment seemed to provide the constitutional basis for equal protection, but the Court had emasculated the privileges and immunities and due process clauses. *Plessy v. Ferguson* (1896) stood as a formidable barrier to equal protection. The Reconstruction Congress had passed a battery of acts to support the new amendments. The Court interpreted them narrowly, limiting Congressional authority.[15] Still, some of the groundwork toward *Brown v. Board of Education* had begun. In the first case of its kind, *Missouri ex rel Gaines v. Canada* (1938), the Court ruled that Missouri could not force an African-American student to attend law school in another state and had to create a separate, but equal law school or admit Lloyd Gaines to the all-white school. More broadly, in *Smith v. Allwright* (1944), the Court ruled that the white primary was state action and thus unconstitutional. Litigants seldom attacked *Plessy,* thus, these narrow decisions had limited application. As Truman took office, the existing patterns of civil rights policy were not favorable, but signs of progress were on the horizon.

Because the Court had decided few civil rights cases, there were no clear precedents and doctrine was unstable. The solicitor general could rely on symbolic Court support, but strategically pushing for an expansion of rights would not have been prudent. Such a barren doctrinal landscape is not ordinarily one the solicitor general wishes to enter.

The policy environment was not shaped by the government in legislation or litigation. Rather, it was the NAACP that was the proactive force behind the emergence of civil rights policy. The government was limited by the fact that most cases involved state law. To get involved, the solicitor general would have to enter the case as an *amicus curiae,* which meant that the government could not structure the sequence of litigation. The problem was that there was little precedent for the use of the *amicus* brief in such a proactive manner. An outside group was pushing civil rights in the face of hostile precedents. The government would be forced to live with the decisions and precedents in those cases.

The Truman Solicitors General

Figure 3-1 shows a spatial representation of the factors that influenced the solicitor general. Truman's support, filtered through the Justice Department, played an important role in the solicitor general's involvement in early civil rights cases. The potential negative impact of Congress was limited by the fact that most cases involved state activities rather than federal legislation. The Court did not have a majority that was willing to support civil rights unequivocally. Precedent was an impediment, but the solicitor general worked on its periphery, refusing to challenge *Plessy* directly, but beginning the process of undermining it.

The OSG led the Court as well as reacting to it. The office was partially responsible for moving the Court to reconsider *Plessy.* Solicitor

---

FIGURE 3-1
ENVIRONMENTAL CONSTRAINTS ON THE SOLICITOR GENERAL:
TRUMAN ADMINISTRATION

SG`

	SGp	SGw	SGc	
Liberal				Conservative
	President	Supreme Court	Congress	Precedent

SGp: Position Solicitor General would adopt if doing the president's bidding
SGw: Position Solicitor General would adopt if winning was the sole goal
SGc: Position Solicitor General would adopt to avoid Congressional response
SG`: Actual position the Solicitor General adopted

General Philip Perlman participated in five civil rights cases: one as a party and four as a voluntary *amici*.[16] But even in the case in which the government was a party, the solicitor general treated the brief like an *amicus*. Perlman was consistent and successful, supporting civil rights and prevailing in each of the cases. The impact of the role of the solicitor general during this period is largely underestimated. Most victories were small, but they established favorable precedents, started the momentum to *Brown,* and maybe most importantly, put the government into civil rights. This structured future litigation efforts and constrained the Eisenhower administration's attempts to avoid these cases.

The first major contribution of the OSG came in the restrictive covenant cases. The work occurred behind the scenes and was more proactive than the office's normal course of action. *Shelley v. Kraemer* (1948) began without the NAACP. Philip Elman of the OSG encouraged the NAACP, American Civil Liberties Union, American Jewish Congress, and other groups to ask the Justice Department to file an *amicus* brief.[17] The government had never done so in a civil rights case in which only private citizens were the litigants. Clark and Perlman were hesitant to get involved, but the African-American vote was important and Truman had been aggressively talking about civil rights.[18]

After the Civil Rights Commission issued a vigorous denunciation of racism and advocated the Justice Department's involvement in the battle against restrictive covenants, Clark and Perlman filed a brief in *Shelley* and *Hurd v. Hodge* (1948).[19] Elman urged the attorney general and solicitor general to get involved and enlisted statements from other government agencies, including the secretary of state, who said that restrictive covenants were an embarrassment in the conduct of foreign relations.[20]

In Court, Perlman argued that restrictive covenants violated public policy and had the practical effect of undermining the government in domestic policies and foreign affairs. He argued that enforcing the covenants constituted state action, which could be attacked under the Fourteenth Amendment.[21] The Court agreed, creating momentum for civil rights groups and favorable precedents. Filing the brief created a precedent for government involvement in civil rights.

In *Henderson v. United States* (1950), the solicitor general and the Justice Department opposed the position of Congress and the Interstate Commerce Commission (ICC) in a case involving segregation in railroad dining cars.[22] Perlman and Elman rejected the pretense that the United States could, in good conscience, defend the "separate but equal" doctrine. In effect, the solicitor general's brief was like an *amicus*. The solicitor general advocated a strong ideological position that had a visible social science component, a portend of the *Brown* brief.

Representative Sam Hobbs of the Judiciary Committee filed an *amicus* brief for seven members opposing the solicitor general. Their brief accused the office of politicization and attempting to usurp legislative prerogatives. They argued that Congress rejected fourteen measures that would have ended segregation. The brief ended with an unveiled threat to slash the office's budget.[23]

Undaunted, Attorney General McGrath argued, for the first time, that *Plessy* was wrong and the Court should overrule it.[24] McGrath conceded that no activity of Congress or the Court could eradicate prejudice, but behavior was shaped in part by the rules of conduct prescribed by law as interpreted by the Court. Thus, the Court's decision could strengthen the barriers established through prejudice or undermine the obstacles and bring them into disrepute. Litigants occasionally offer arguments that have little chance of immediate success to arm their allies or introduce new alternatives for the justices to consider. The justices refused the invitation to overturn *Plessy,* issuing a narrow decision that the railroad's policy was illegal. Given that *Plessy* was a transportation case, this would have been a good opportunity to repudiate that precedent. In the end, the *Henderson* decision was a disappointment to civil rights groups.[25] But the solicitor general had made inroads and continued the momentum toward significant change.

Perlman filed *amici* in two graduate/professional school cases, *Sweatt v. Painter* (1950) and *McLaurin v. Oklahoma Board of Regents* (1950), asking the Court to overturn *Plessy*.[26] Although the students were granted relief, the Court again refused to attack *Plessy* directly. Still, officials from the executive branch were again on record as requesting the reversal of *Plessy.* Ultimately, Perlman was unwilling to launch a full, frontal attack on *Plessy.* He believed that segregation had no place in graduate and professional schools, but refused to support integration in grade schools.

The quantum leap to *Brown* occurred after the 1952 election and only after Perlman's resignation. After scandal forced Attorney General McGrath to resign, McGranery was chosen to be the new attorney general and clashed with Perlman immediately.[27] When Perlman resigned, members of the OSG stepped into the vacuum. Robert Stern and Elman went to McGranery and told him that the Justice Department had supported overturning *Plessy* but that the past solicitor general would not forcefully argue that position before the Court. McGranery gave Stern, the acting solicitor general, his blessing.[28] Still Stern and Elman, acting strategically, doubted the time was right for a direct challenge to *Plessy.* They felt that the Court was not ready to consider wholesale desegregation of southern schools.[29]

The Justice Department, on its own initiative and with Truman's support, entered five cases involving segregation in schools as *amici.* These cases occurred during Truman's lame duck period.[30] Elman's brief was considered more effective than the other briefs. If the Court was willing to reconsider *Plessy,* then the government had arguments designed to eradicate it. The brief argued that "separate but equal" symbolized "a badge of inferiority." Elman provided an escape hatch for the justices if they were reluctant to attack *Plessy* directly. His brief conceded that the Court did not have to overrule *Plessy* because black schools were clearly inferior to white schools.

Elman relied heavily on the Court's recent opinions. He knew part of the Court's reluctance was tied to the need to attach a remedy to the decision. Elman was certain the Vinson Court would never support an immediate, broad remedy. If the Court was to outlaw segregation, Elman claimed that it did not have to be done overnight. He argued that implementation should be carried out by the district courts. The NAACP was not happy with the gradualist approach. The Court refused Attorney General McGranery's request for time to argue the government's position because it did not want "any political speeches." Thus, Elman's brief was the sole vehicle for the government's position. Unfortunately for the OSG, the Court delayed consideration of *Brown,* meaning control over the case would fall to the Eisenhower administration.

Conclusion. Prior to the Truman administration, the solicitor general operated under imposing constraints in civil rights. The government was seldom a party and use of the *amicus curiae* was limited. The Justice Department enacted institutional changes that ushered in a new period for the solicitor general. The OSG adopted the role of attorney general as policy maker, using the *amicus* as a tool for extending the government's influence. The *amicus* provides the solicitor general with the most discretion and imposes the fewest conditions. This change in the rules provided the opportunity for the solicitor general to be proactive and overcome some of the constraints on the office. The solicitor general was aggressive in the one case involving the government as a party, opting to challenge the ICC.

What caused the change and created an environment that would structure the work of subsequent administrations? While the Court had taken steps toward protecting civil rights, there was little to suggest the broad expansion that was in the offing. The administration elevated politics over law in civil rights. The office had not been active in civil rights, vigorous use of third party *amici* had been unprecedented, and while the Court had made a few pro–civil rights decisions, none suggested that a majority was ready to reverse *Plessy*. The solicitor general figured out a way to blunt the impact of the policy environment: argue on narrow grounds to avoid a direct confrontation with *Plessy*. The office had to adopt a political perspective because the legal perspective would have doomed its efforts. If the solicitor general was acting strategically, the office would have kept a distance and allowed the Court to construct a theoretical context and then proceed to help fill in the emerging doctrine. Instead, the OSG cast its lot with the president's policies and the NAACP, rather than judicial doctrine. What made this more implausible is that the motivation for these choices was the careerists in the office, rather than the political forces.

To answer the questions posed at the outset: Did the Truman solicitors general act strategically? And, how did the office structure civil rights litigation? The careerists took advantage of the replacement of the attorney general and solicitor general to establish an aggressive stance. For most solicitors general, the legal component constrains attempts to maximize the administration's position. In a sense, the Truman solicitors general were freed from many of the normal constraints.

As the institutional memory of the OSG, career members are in a position to exert influence over transient political appointees. Normally that entails elevating legal priorities over political ones or using the former to temper the latter. The Truman administration represented a departure. The goals of the careerists were consistent with Truman's position. The president and attorney general set a moral tone and Congress was effectively disenfranchised because these were constitutional issues. The norms and rules constrained a solicitor general who wanted to participate in the expansion of civil rights. Part of the work of the OSG during this period was designed to remove the obstacles and create norms that would provide future opportunities. New precedents, executive support, and the emergence of a new judicial philosophy contributed to changing the office's business.

The work of the solicitor general transformed civil rights and played a dramatic role in structuring litigation. The brief constructed by Elman gave the Court the ammunition to attack *Plessy* directly and provided a blueprint for implementation.[31] The Justice Department launched an initiative against Jim Crow, filing *amici* opposing restrictive covenants and supporting desegregation in higher education.

There were a number of firsts during Truman's term: Perlman defined a positive role for the government and the OSG urged the Court to abandon *Plessy,* expanded the use of *amici* briefs, and lent legitimacy to the NAACP. The solicitor general was present when the evolutionary cycle accelerated with *Brown.* The NAACP and solicitor general were instrumental in changing the direction of issue evolution by beginning to remove doctrinal impediments. The arguments were beginning to push the Court in the direction of civil rights. The most significant contribution was creating a precedent for activity that subsequent administrations were all but forced to follow during the litigation phase.

In the end, the record of the Truman solicitors general was better than the environment might have predicted. It was also very different than expected. The OSG, along with the NAACP, set the framework for the evolution of doctrine, rather than reacting to a context set by the Court. With Congress opposed to civil rights initiatives, the Court limited in support of equal protection and little doctrine, there were formidable obstacles. Only the president, whatever his motives, was willing to exert significant effort in favor of civil rights. Expanding the use of the *amicus* brief was a response to the obstacles.

DWIGHT EISENHOWER: CONFLICTING SIGNALS

If there was no landmark decision, the OSG helped provide critical foundation building work. The Truman administration was prepared to enter *Brown v. Board of Education,* but a delay in consideration of the case brought a new party to the White House. Would the new solicitor general continue its predecessor's policies? Changes in the institutional environment did not seem conducive to an expansion of litigation efforts. The goals of the Eisenhower solicitors general were more tempered than those of their predecessors. The Court would emerge as a major actor and force the solicitor general's hand. The rules and norms also favored the expansion of civil rights. The OSG under Truman had constrained the freedom of its successors, particularly in the *Brown* case.

Executive. Dwight Eisenhower is widely portrayed as being ambivalent about civil rights. He was reluctant to use the bully pulpit even after *Brown.* Indeed, Eisenhower took a passive role, seeing himself as a mediator and defender of the law rather than an advocate or partisan. He did not support use of federal power to combat discrimination. He publicly expressed reservations about the prospects of legislation changing "the hearts and minds of men."[32] His ambivalence allowed opponents to water down the Civil Rights Act of 1957.[33] His most important symbolic action, committing troops to Little Rock, was done grudgingly. There was a window for executive leadership and a chance to further desegregation, but Eisenhower balked and the opportunity passed.[34]

Some have claimed Eisenhower was a "hidden hand" president, who worked behind the scenes. They argue that his policies were designed strategically to push compliance with the law, mollify the South, and make political gains.[35] Eisenhower insisted that leadership on civil rights issues occur at the cabinet level. This was fortunate, because the Justice Department was forceful in expanding the scope of civil rights. Attorney General Herbert Brownell submitted a bill that marked the turning point in the administration's policy toward the issue.[36] Brownell wanted to separate the Civil Rights Section from the Criminal Division and expand its power. The CRD was created by the Civil Rights Act of 1957. The attorney general wanted to include a provision that would allow the government to intervene as a party in desegregation cases, but it was defeated. Brownell also worked hard to ensure the appointment of enlightened judges in the South to carry out desegregation.[37]

After *Brown,* the Justice Department got more involved in civil rights. Brownell used powers and procedures that had not been invoked since Reconstruction. The primary goal was not to create a litany of new rights but to find legal means of enforcing the rights that were increasingly flowing from the Court's decisions.[38] The central focus of the Justice Department in passing the Civil Rights Act of 1957 was to ensure voting rights. Brownell's successor, William Rogers, was less aggressive in supporting civil rights. Kluger points out that the administration began only ten voting rights cases in the three years after the 1957 Act was passed.[39]

Congress. Prior to the 1950s, the Congressional record on civil rights was one of "continual deadlock and failure."[40] According to Carmines and Stimson, "Its collective foot dragging in the 1950s had a clear interpretation to racial activists, presidents, courts, and the public."[41] The Eisenhower period was marked by tension between the Court and Congress over civil rights and internal security issues. Still, the Civil Rights Act of 1957 was the first action of its kind passed by Congress in almost a century. Hostility from Southern Democrats had to be overcome to get the measure passed. Senator Lyndon Johnson was influential in getting the bill enacted, but at a cost. Southern Senators agreed to accept a watered-down version of the bill in exchange for a tacit agreement not to filibuster, a promise broken by Strom Thurmond.[42]

Howard Smith of the Rules Committee and Senator James Eastland of Judiciary used their positions to cripple later civil rights bills. Smith refused to convene hearings on the Civil Rights Bill of 1959, delaying its consideration for a year. To pass civil rights legislation, the leadership had to "use extraordinary measures to circumvent Eastland."[43] The Civil Rights Act of 1960 was minor and largely symbolic.[44] After *Brown,* Congress had become significantly more liberal,[45] but far from a positive force for civil rights.

Supreme Court. Truman supported civil rights, but his judicial appointments did not reflect that support. Eisenhower was the reverse: his support was tepid, but his appointments to the Court were responsible for a revolution in civil liberties and civil rights. It is alleged that Eisenhower claimed that as president he made two mistakes and they were both on the Supreme Court.[46] Earl Warren exercised the leadership that civil rights policy needed to emerge and flourish. The addition of William Brennan pushed the Court further to the left. According to Baum's adjusted scores, the Court got significantly more liberal during Eisenhower's tenure.[47]

Issue Evolution. Civil rights policy was still in the nascent stages of development. Advances during the Truman administration were tentative and limited. Civil rights claimants often won individual cases, but the decisions, most notably those involving graduate and law students, broke little precedential ground. There were concerns that the momentum established under Truman would be slowed or reversed if Eisenhower did not support further expansions. Still, the solicitor general was on record as supporting an extension of doctrine. While the existing state of policy evolution was not a harbinger of immediate success, *Brown* would change that by providing the landmark that introduced disequilibria to civil rights policy. Eisenhower's tenure represented a transition as the Court started to define the issue. The solicitor general would play a central role in that process.

The Eisenhower Solicitor General

Despite conflicting signals from the environment, the solicitor general supported the extension of civil rights. Figure 3-2 shows the spatial relationship between the different factors. Eisenhower was ambivalent, but his Justice Department exerted a positive influence. Congress offered symbolic support, but most cases were outside its reach. The major influence came from a Court ready to dismantle segregation.

Despite the change in party control, the OSG had carryover in personnel, most notably Stern and Elman, who were instrumental in developing the Truman administration's civil rights position. They provided continuity and helped guide the Eisenhower solicitors general to an increasingly broader view of civil rights.[48] The rising tide of *amicus* activity that had begun during the Truman administration was diminished somewhat by the Eisenhower administration's change to an emphasis on legislation rather than litigation.[49]

Solicitors General Simon Soboloff and J. Lee Rankin, who argued all of the civil rights cases except the second *Brown* case, followed the lead established by their predecessors.[50] The OSG participated in eight cases: two as a party, two as voluntary *amicus,* and four at the request of the Court. While the office was successful in each case, there were differences in the approach to the cases based on the form of participation. In the direct cases, supporting the constitutionality of the Civil Rights Act of 1957, the Solicitor General argued for Congressional intent and the power of the Justice Department. In the voluntary *amici* cases, the OSG was more circumspect and conservative. In the invited cases, the OSG was "forced" to adopt a broader view by the work of the previous administration. The solicitors general exercised their prerogatives by refusing to enter a number of civil rights cases.

Rankin submitted an *amicus curiae* brief and argued in *Gomillion v. Lightfoot* (1960), a case involving voting rights and an area of particular concern for the Justice Department. Redistricting had created an oddly shaped district to disenfranchise black voters. Existing precedent seemed to block judicial resolution. The brief concentrated on removing the political question obstacle to allow the Court to consider the case.[51] The solicitor general acted as the attorney general as policy maker in this instance.

The most important briefs were the two *Brown v. Board of Education*

FIGURE 3-2

ENVIRONMENTAL CONSTRAINTS ON THE SOLICITOR GENERAL:
EISENHOWER ADMINISTRATION

SG`

SGw   SGc   SGp

Liberal————————————————————————————Conservative

Precedent Supreme   Congress   President
Court

SGp: Position Solicitor General would adopt if doing the president's bidding
SGw: Position Solicitor General would adopt if winning was the sole goal
SGc: Position Solicitor General would adopt to avoid Congressional response
SG`: Actual position the Solicitor General adopted

cases. The Court invited the solicitor general to participate to ensure that a decision would have support from the administration. The request was delayed until the Court was certain the brief would support desegregation.[52] Brownell polled aides in the Justice Department. The general attitude was a desire to avoid filing a brief. But Stern and Elman told the group that "the Court's invitation to appear at the reargument was tantamount to a command."[53]

Stern and Elman warned against refusing to take a definitive position on *Plessy* because the justices would raise it during oral argument and the Truman administration had argued that it should be overturned. Eisenhower sent a memo to Brownell inquiring about the propriety of the attorney general giving his opinion regarding the constitutionality of segregation. Brownell informed the president it was his duty as an officer of the Court to be prepared to give an opinion. Brownell was sensitive to possible charges that the Justice Department had changed position or was making inconsistent claims, so he did not repudiate any of the arguments in the Truman administration's brief.[54] In effect, the position of the Truman solicitor general tied the hands of the Eisenhower administration.

Brownell pulled the brief out of the OSG and assigned it to Assistant Attorney General Rankin (who would become solicitor general in 1956). The president did what he could publicly to distance himself from the brief, although he took part behind the scenes.[55] The brief reflected the equivocal position of the administration and the differences between political appointees in the Justice Department and holdovers in the OSG.[56] Elman, a former clerk for Justice Frankfurter, had frequent conversations with his mentor concerning the most convincing arguments for the government to advance in the brief.[57] The brief did not directly ask the Court to overturn *Plessy* or argue that segregation was wrong. Rankin and Elman agreed that this supplemental brief to the Justice Department's 1952 brief should confine itself to answering the questions posed by the Court. The brief aligned the government with the NAACP, much to the chagrin of the South, which expected a more balanced treatment.[58]

Eisenhower asked to see the brief and suggested some changes. Caplan argues that it was unprecedented for the solicitor general to clear a brief with the president.[59] Rankin had balked previously when Eisenhower tried to get him to change the brief.[60] The divisions were reflected in oral arguments as justices asked repeatedly for clarifications regarding the government's position. Rankin urged the Court to proceed slowly and turn implementation over to the federal courts. But he did argue that school segregation could be attacked under the Fourteenth Amendment. Ultimately, the Court unanimously agreed that segregation had no place in public education.[61]

The government's brief in *Brown v. Board of Education* II (1955) offered the Court a blueprint for implementing *Brown* I. Solicitor General Sobeloff's position, which reflected the president's desire for a slow moving process, departed from the remedy offered by the NAACP. Sobeloff argued for a gradual process with an emphasis on local solutions rather than a nationally directed remedy with an imposed timetable. The Court adopted the government's position using the phrase "with all deliberate speed."[62]

The solicitor general helped to structure the direction of school desegregation policy, but there were problems that were reflected in the administration's approach. Robert Fredrick Burk argued "*Brown* meant that the full moral weight of the Constitution as interpreted by the Supreme Court was now on the side of the advocates of integration." But the decision increased the pressure on the administration and subsequent presidents. Arguments to delay implementation or to be less aggressive in backing the Court for political or philosophical reasons would bring choruses of criticism.[63]

Conclusion. Eisenhower solicitors general largely played the role of attorney general as law enforcement officer. They tried to protect the statutory power the Justice Department had obtained through the Civil Rights Act. The Justice Department wanted to play the role of fifth clerk in *Brown,* but careerists in the OSG argued that the Court wanted the tenth justice or a policy statement. The tentative steps were a function of divisions in the institutional environment. The Court was increasingly active, but the president was not aggressive. Congress was becoming a factor, but in a less direct manner. As long as the issues were constitutional, the retaliatory impact of Congress could be minimized. But the desire for legislative, rather than judicial, solutions, placed self-imposed restraints on the executive branch.

The policy environment was less than propitious, but important symbolic victories had emboldened the NAACP and encouraged the members of the OSG to press for advances and to consider attacking *Plessy.* Once *Brown* was decided, the policy environment changed from a constraint to an opportunity, but the office failed to exploit it to the fullest.

In each of the nine cases, the Eisenhower solicitors general supported civil rights and were on the winning side. The position of the administration was structured by its predecessor. But the Eisenhower solicitors general were less proactive. More in keeping with the traditional position of the OSG, Sobeloff and Rankin were reactive to the Court.

The goals of the Eisenhower solicitors general were moderate, but still supportive of civil rights. They exercised restraint by avoiding a number of cases and arguing for more limited advances. Despite presidential ambivalence, the rest of the factors in the solicitor general's environment supported the extension of civil rights. Congress passed the Civil Rights Act of 1957, giving additional authority to the Justice Department and creating the CRD. The Court was willing to push the frontiers and tailoring doctrine to that end. The rules and norms were much more favorable, but that was a double-edged sword. They would provide opportunities for careerists who wanted to expand civil rights, but force the hand of the Eisenhower administration.

While the Truman solicitors general pushed their power to the broadest extent, the Eisenhower solicitors general did not fully utilize the support they had. The latter were caught between two extremes: the potential of the Court and the restraint sought by the president. Clearly, the solicitor general adopted strategic preferences and strode the middle path, arguing for civil rights claimants, but adopting more moderate positions than the NAACP. Perhaps, most importantly, the solicitor general did not abandon civil rights despite the change of administration.

The Eisenhower administration wrestled with the legal/political dichotomy for two terms. In this instance, the influence of the legal and political realms was transposed. Normally, the political forces demand sudden change and a break from the stasis that often governs doctrinal development. In this instance, the political forces had hoped to adopt a passive role and move slowly. But they were trapped by the *Brown* precedent and forced by the mix of cases to move quickly. The impetus for more aggressive behavior came from the careerists in the OSG, who normally serve as a brake on change.

The administration opted for the legal perspective over the political. In a sense, the solicitor general tried to return to its traditional role, but it was difficult to put the genie back in the bottle. In *Brown,* the solicitor general took the most forceful step belying the fact that it was invited to participate. The normal expectation is that the solicitor general will temper its view in such cases. The solicitor general went beyond Eisenhower's desires as a consequence of the previous position taken by the office under Truman. But the government's position was less aggressive than the primary policy entrepreneur, the NAACP, desired.

The strategic activity slowed the evolution of civil rights. If *Brown* was an open policy window, the solicitors general did not appear to take full advantage. There were some advances that forecast future developments. Rankin did commit the government to a position in the public-private cases and showed a willingness to enter the reapportionment thicket.[64] Both issues would become ripe during the Kennedy administration.

The solicitors general played a critical role in structuring doctrine. Elman's recipe for *Brown,* all deliberate speed and federal district court supervision, was accepted by the Supreme Court as the controlling principles and was evidence of the office's impact. It also established the context for the Kennedy solicitors general.

JOHN KENNEDY: RELUCTANT TO PUSH WITH A SMALL MAJORITY

The Court's decision to cast its lot with the solicitor general rather than the NAACP was a sign that could be read two ways. Proponents could point to the fact that the Court overturned *Plessy* and try to use *Brown* across a variety of issues. This created rising expectations among civil rights groups. On the other hand, the phrase "all deliberate speed" supported those who wished to move incrementally or thought that was practical. Civil rights groups expected much more from the Kennedy administration.

Certainly, there was every reason to suspect that the goals of Kennedy's solicitor general would be more favorable to civil rights. The institutional environment posed a series of constraints, but provided some opportunities. The Department of Justice and the CRD became more aggressive. Kennedy initially resisted civil rights leadership to avoid antagonizing power brokers in Congress. Later, he submitted a civil rights bill, which limited the solicitor general's options. The solicitor general did not want to preempt potential legislation by pushing broad arguments. The Court seemed to be a favorable forum. Precedents increasingly supported civil rights, but were still in an early stage.

Executive. While civil rights was a cornerstone of his campaign, John Kennedy defended his reluctance to push the issue as a function of his narrow electoral victory. Kennedy was initially unwilling to draw on the moral credit of his office or expend his finite political capital to advance civil rights. He faced constraints in that southern Democrats chaired key committees and had enough votes in the Senate to filibuster.[65] Paul Light argues that Kennedy "could not 'afford' a major civil rights bill."[66] In civil rights, Kennedy was more an evolutionist than a revolutionist.[67]

Kennedy was pressured on all sides: Southerners in Congress fought even the most modest proposals while civil rights proponents, emboldened by judicial success, urged further advances.[68] When Kennedy took office, civil rights proponents strongly advocated the use of executive orders, something the candidate had promised, to supplement the litigation strategy. Use of executive- and judicial-based strategies seemed to be the most promising avenues in the face of congressional deadlock.[69] According to John Doar of the CRD, "The litigation strategy was the only approach which had a chance."[70] But Kennedy did little to effectuate his campaign promises. He abandoned legislation that would have bogged down, did not push executive orders that would have alienated the South, and concentrated on litigation efforts specifically aimed at winning the black vote. Kennedy publicly supported *Brown* and worked behind the scenes to speed desegregation, while appointing African Americans to a number of positions.[71] But some of Kennedy's actions, most notably his appointments to the federal bench in the South, retarded civil rights.[72]

Events in the South in June, 1963, represented a critical turning point, convincing the president that a cautious approach was not working. According to Richard Reeves, Kennedy moved back and forth between meetings on two "war fronts": Saigon and Birmingham.[73] As a result, he gathered key aides and staffers from the Justice Department to come up with a bold new plan to attack school segregation, discrimination in public accommodations, and threats to voting rights.[74] Though his sweeping proposals were blocked in Congress, the debate of 1963 structured the context for consideration of the Civil Rights Act of 1964.[75]

The Justice Department was headed by Robert Kennedy, the embodiment of the advocate attorney general.[76] He wanted to exert more influence in civil rights, but had no formal program. He hoped to achieve integration without disturbing the social equilibrium. His initial activities were responsive and reactive, marked by crisis management and the goal of avoiding violence. He wanted to get limited court orders to mollify leaders of the civil rights movement.[77]

Robert Kennedy wanted to rein in the OSG, but he was intimidated by Solicitor General Archibald Cox. According to Philip Heymann, a member of the office during the early 1960s, "Archie Cox had a very special position in the Administration. If he said this was the way, that was it. Robert Kennedy was very deferential."[78]

The solicitor general's environment began to change in one notable way: the CRD had expanded resources and authority. While its efforts had been dominated by voting, the division was increasingly moving into other areas as the Court paved the way. The division became an advocate for a broader conceptualization of civil rights and wanted Cox to move more quickly and decisively. Kennedy increasingly adopted that perspective, but was reluctant to do anything that might cost the office credibility before the Court.[79]

Cox saw his job as to protect the Court as much as to convince it. This raised questions regarding what should happen when the solicitor general's obligation to the Court conflicts with the attorney general's obligation to the president. The civil rights community believed that the president's policy should prevail. According to Burke Marshall, head of the CRD, "There were no differences in policy views, the differences involved the conception of the role of the Supreme Court, the Solicitor General, and the role of law in the Harvard sense."[80] Cox adopted the judicial restraint of Justice Frankfurter and felt that it was not the solicitor general's job to litigate morality or push the Court too far.

Activists in the Justice Department thought that Cox's definition was too narrow. They argued that the law was in flux and evolving quickly, so the office should decide not on the basis of legal theory but should follow division policy. The evolution of the solicitor general's position was incremental. Cox wanted to make certain that his position would not contradict the Justice Department's policy. But at the same time, Cox felt the Court would only support narrow, piecemeal evolution. He felt that the Court might reject broader requests. He also argued that it would be tougher to get changes effected if they were done through litigation, rather than legislation.[81]

Congress. John Kennedy subordinated his civil rights program so that he could get southern support for the rest of his agenda. Civil rights demonstrations began to galvanize public opinion and move the president and Congress into action. Kennedy responded with the most sweeping legislation since Reconstruction. While observers felt that Congress would gut the bill, in fact the proposed legislation was strengthened before it was blocked.[82] During the administration, Congress was not a strong, positive force for civil rights. Ideologically, Congress was relatively liberal,[83] but key committees and the ability to filibuster, "a powerful and often decisive weapon" in civil rights,[84] could frustrate the aggregate liberal support.

The uneasy balance of a Congress more willing to accept civil rights, yet hamstrung procedurally, left a vacuum that allowed the division to pursue an aggressive tack. Filibusters and committee procedures could bottle up legislative measures, but lack of numbers and a presidential veto would limit the ability of Congress to retaliate if the Justice Department was too aggressive.

Supreme Court. Kennedy replaced Charles Whittaker and Frankfurter with Byron White and Arthur Goldberg. Not only did this make the Court more liberal, it removed Frankfurter, the most forceful advocate for judicial restraint. The changes made the Court the most liberal to that time according to the Baum adjusted measure (72.8).[85] The Court was certainly becoming an appropriate venue for proponents to advance claims and speed the evolution of civil rights policy.

Issue Evolution. As Kennedy took office, civil rights policy was still in its early stages, but it had a powerful precedent in *Brown* and an open policy window. The Court had also decided *Gomillion* to protect voting rights. As part of the post-*Brown* strategy, the Court was letting federal district courts handle the first round of desegregation.[86] The obstructionist tactics of the South were only now working their way to the Supreme Court.

There were mixed signals for the Justice Department and the solicitor general. *Brown* was the type of sweeping landmark that affected related and unrelated issues and the Court's willingness to require desegregation suggested the possibility that the justices would cast the net of equal protection even further. On the other hand, the Court had not made significant moves into employment discrimination, segregated facilities, or other forms of discrimination. The Eisenhower administration was unwilling to push the Court or take advantage of the policy window. The Kennedy administration would also demonstrate uncertainty as civil rights moved to the next stage of development.

The Kennedy Solicitor General

Figure 3-3 suggests an environment that was conducive to expanding civil rights. The Court was receptive and precedents were increasingly favorable. The president supported civil rights, but with a gradualist's ap-

---

FIGURE 3-3

ENVIRONMENTAL CONSTRAINTS ON THE SOLICITOR GENERAL:
KENNEDY ADMINISTRATION

SG`

	SGw	SGp	SGc	
Liberal——————————————————————————Conservative
	Precedent	Supreme Court	President	Congress

SGp: Position Solicitor General would adopt if doing the president's bidding
SGw: Position Solicitor General would adopt if winning was the sole goal
SGc: Position Solicitor General would adopt to avoid Congressional response
SG`: Actual position the Solicitor General adopted

proach. Congress was unable to do much of a positive or negative nature. The spatial configuration suggests that Archibald Cox might have been able to advance an aggressive stance. While Cox supported civil rights, he often adopted a more moderate position and argued cases on narrow grounds.

According to Burke Marshall, "The Court had a lot of confidence in Cox, more so than most Solicitors General."[87] Civil rights and reapportionment were agenda cases for Cox. He was involved in twelve civil rights cases during the Kennedy administration. Cox participated in one case in which the government was a party, six as a voluntary *amicus curiae,* and was invited to participate in five cases. In each of the cases, Cox supported civil rights and the government was on the winning side. Cox's positions were a "logical progression of the Warren Court's development of law."[88] But the solicitor general did not break much new doctrinal ground. Cox felt that the OSG had an obligation not to advocate positions that would cause problems for the justices.[89] Indeed, with few exceptions, the cases were relatively unimportant and served to fill existing gaps and pave the way for the important cases to come.

The aggregate numbers shroud the influence of the office in structuring doctrine. The most important civil rights case during Kennedy's truncated term was *Burton v. Wilmington Parking Authority* (1961), initially filed by Solicitor General Rankin. The OSG urged Cox to pick *Burton* as his first case for symbolic reasons. The brief, constructed by Rankin, was a relatively narrow discussion of state action and provided Cox with his first success.[90]

Because cases involving segregation in public and private facilities were relatively new and without clear precedent, the Court asked the solicitor general to state the government's position. Cox typically opted for a narrow interpretation in these cases, trying to avoid the constitutional issues.[91] Cox believed that the division on the Court justified his narrow interpretation. In general, "when he might have been expected to call for radical changes in the law, Archibald Cox believed that for the good of the Court and the solicitor general's office, he should advocate restraint."[92]

In the five cases,[93] the solicitor general stated that he would reserve judgment on the broader grounds of state action. The Court, over the dissents of four justices, asked the solicitor general to express the government's view on the constitutional issue. The dissenters objected that the Court should not request an additional brief when the government had declined to take a position on the issue. In response, Cox still took a different tack than the NAACP wanted. The solicitor general continued to follow the "standard unaggressive position—that the cases could be decided on narrow grounds,"[94] which contributed to the Court's willingness to avoid constitutional grounds.[95]

The administration was afraid that a broad precedent would thwart its legislative initiatives, most notably an attempt to pass a bill based on the Commerce Clause. A favorable decision based on the Fourteenth Amendment would defuse momentum for legislation and be harder to implement. Cox urged Congress to act and expand the doctrine of state action.[96] Cox was unable to get the Court to delay consideration of the cases until the legislation passed. As a result, he argued that the state was responsible for discrimination if long-standing custom is supported by state law.[97] Cox argued that southern states had encouraged and supported mandatory segregation and discrimination, constituting state action even though there was no specific legislation involved.[98]

The narrow position of the solicitor general was understandable in cases in which the office was invited to submit a brief. A truer test of the OSG can be found when it files a voluntary *amicus* brief. But here, too, Cox took the cautious approach: narrowing the issues in the cases. In *Garner v. Louisiana,* the solicitor general filed a voluntary *amicus* brief on behalf of sit-in demonstrators. But the *amicus* argued it was unnecessary to reach the constitutional questions. Cox believed that he could best assist the Court by focusing on specific issues without involving broader and largely uncharted questions about state action.[99]

Cox claimed that the sit-in cases constituted his only real disagreement with the attorney general. The legal principle of the sit-in cases, state action theory, was the major substantive division. Cox wanted to proceed with narrow grounds, seeking to reverse the convictions of individuals, but avoiding the broader grounds he felt the Court might reject.[100] He advocated a case-by-case approach, while Robert Kennedy wanted a sweeping declaration that could clear the way for broad action.[101] Nicholas Katzenbach said that these were the most difficult issues for the solicitor general: "They involved straight ordinary trespass law. Archie was reluctant to take the cases. It was not easy to persuade Cox. Once he began to find state action in old state laws, he got excited about it."[102]

The policy environment, reflected in the strategic machinations in the executive branch and pending legislation in Congress, affected the divided responses of the justices, seven of whom filed opinions in the five concurrent cases. There was little disagreement about the result; the Court found the discrimination illegal. Disagreement centered on the basis for the decision, whether the Constitution afforded protection.

The result was that the Court left no clear precedent, hoping that Congress would step into the breach.[103]

As the central actor in civil rights, the NAACP was an integral part of the solicitor general's environment. The organization was pursuing its own strategies and, in a sense, constraining the solicitor general's activities.[104] Attorney General Kennedy supported the broad extensions the NAACP was seeking in its litigation efforts. Cox, however, felt that the NAACP was attempting to push the Court too far, too fast. Cox did not think he could get five votes for broad state action.[105]

Cox's major impact came from reapportionment, cases that had enormous consequences for civil rights. Groups challenging malapportionment approached Solicitor General Rankin during the Eisenhower Administration and he supported filing an *amicus* brief.[106] Robert Kennedy wanted to get involved, but Cox felt that precedent was clearly antithetical. The disparities between districts in Tennessee were so extreme that Cox felt compelled to get involved. He urged the justices to remove the political questions barrier, but doubted that he would win. According to Burke Marshall: "The reapportionment cases came through my office. The development of positions required decisions about the basic role of the Supreme Court in constitutional adjudication, the role of the Attorney General and the Department of Justice in constitutional development before the Court."[107]

Cox felt part of his duty was to protect the Court and he worried that an expansive decision would affect the legitimacy of the institution. He sought victory on the narrowest grounds possible.[108] According to Robert Dixon: "His briefs and participation in oral argument as *amicus curiae* tended to shape the Court's perception of the issues and indeed to dominate the litigation at certain stages."[109] During oral arguments, Cox was pressed by Frankfurter who adopted his traditional restraintist position. Cox conceded that "there are wrongs which can only be righted by the people or their legislatures." But judicial inaction in the face of severe wrongs might have worse consequences. Cox argued that a positive decision would remove an impediment and lead to reapportionment. By contrast, a negative decision would stifle reform and remove the incentive to correct malapportionment.[110] Cox argued for general principles of representative equality, but wanted to avoid a hard and fast remedy, preferring to retain flexibility to meet the needs of individual states.[111]

Chief Justice Warren, who presided over *Brown, Mapp,* and *Miranda,* considered *Baker v. Carr* the most important decision of his tenure.[112] Redistricting would give urban areas significantly more power in the legislatures.[113] Cox, however, was "tormented over his role in the victory."[114] The decision set off a firestorm that threatened the Court, as Cox had feared. Bills were introduced in Congress to delay implementation and limit the Court's jurisdiction. A constitutional amendment to overturn the decision was proposed.

Baker opened the door to troubling questions regarding the appropriate scope of a remedy.[115] Attorney General Kennedy wanted to push strict equality, "one person, one vote," but Cox resisted. He had no misgivings about *Baker,* but there was a great deal of difference between showing a constitutional violation and recommending a remedy like "one person, one vote." Cox said, "I was never able to swallow arguing 'one person, one vote' for the state legislature under any and all circumstances."[116] In the end, Cox offered a more narrow approach, but the Court adopted the "one man, one vote" standard in *Reynolds v. Sims.*[117]

Conclusion. Cox let legal and institutional goals dominate policy goals as he hewed to a moderate agenda. He did this despite pressures in his strategic environment that supported expansion. Norms and rules did not pose serious constraints for civil rights advocacy. But the environment was more complicated and provided reasons to proceed slowly. First, Cox felt that the Court was still divided and broad arguments would not attract a majority. Second, important legislation was pending and Cox worried that expansive decisions might kill its momentum.

Despite their differences, the office under Kennedy more closely resembled its counterpart under Eisenhower. Although Kennedy may have been more sympathetic to civil rights, he displayed his predecessor's reluctance to throw his weight behind the issue. That reluctance may have been a decisive factor in the solicitor general's tempered and measured responses. Congress continued to fulfill an indirect role. While it was unlikely to muster any opposition to Court decisions, the administration wanted it to be a positive force. At the same time, the CRD was urging a more sweeping approach. The Justice Department did not want to use litigation to preempt a more inclusive legislative solution. The impact of the Court was less certain. On the one hand, the Court had been rewriting doctrine and showed no signs of slowing down. On the other hand, Cox felt that seeking broad extensions of precedents might fracture the majority. The narrow arguments often won by narrow margins, suggesting that his strategy was wise.[118] But he may have been too risk averse. Given their respect for Cox, the justices may have been willing to go further. It is possible that the minority had attracted all the votes it could and the five justice majority could not be splintered.

In general, Cox's influence under Kennedy seemed to be marginal. The solicitor general did help buttress the foundation of civil rights law.

The contribution was more in sheer numbers of favorable precedents than in monumental additions to doctrine. Cox followed the pragmatic lead of the president. The Justice Department wanted Cox to go further, but lacked the legitimacy to challenge the respected solicitor general. Congress figured into the calculations, not because of what it had done but what it might do. Cox was constrained by issue evolution. The public-private issues involved difficult questions and were confounded by the strategy of waiting for Congress to act.

As solicitor general, Cox certainly acted on strategic preferences that included a conscious avoidance of preempting or defusing the momentum to a legislative solution. President Kennedy supported civil rights in principle, but did little to push any initiatives. Preference outliers in the Senate had the power to block legislation. This made the litigation strategy more important. Cox supported civil rights in each brief he filed, but often appeared reluctant to press for broad precedents despite the fact that the Supreme Court seemed willing to push the envelope.

In terms of structuring litigation, Cox's efforts generally represented a holding pattern. Cox tentatively broke some new ground in the private/public cases. His most important contribution was in an area that had important implications for civil rights: reapportionment.

Cox argued cases narrowly and did not seek frequent involvement as *amici*. In elevating the legal over the political, Cox viewed the Court as his primary constituency. Cox acted as tenth justice and tried to avoid leading the judiciary into precarious decisions that might threaten its institutional legitimacy. Under different circumstances in the Johnson administration, he moved along the continuum toward the political end.

The policy environment was more favorable, but the potential of *Brown* was greater than its practical impact. As a precedent, *Brown* held the promise of spreading out across the civil rights domain. If segregation was unconstitutional in education, why not in employment, housing, restaurants, and other accommodations? Would the solicitor general lend the prestige of the office and the force of the government to efforts to spread *Brown* far and wide? Cox resisted the impulse. He felt that Congress was better suited to accomplish that.

CONCLUSION: THE SOLICITOR GENERAL IN THE LITIGATION PHASE

The NAACP helped push open the doors of the Supreme Court and eventually the OSG joined the battle. Solicitors general in the Truman administration acted more directly on their preferences than any of their immediate successors. In addition, they made major procedural and doctrinal changes in the government's treatment of civil rights. Solicitor General Perlman committed the government to civil rights by opposing restrictive covenants. Although unwilling to challenge *Plessy* directly, the office was establishing the basis to do so. These activities established the context for the next two presidents and their solicitors general.

Truman played a major political role by publicly supporting civil rights and providing a context for the OSG to do the same. Eisenhower and Kennedy, for political reasons of their own, urged their solicitors general to move slowly and follow precedent, mixing legal and political concerns. The office initially sought to destabilize law by asking the Court to overrule *Plessy*.[119] The Court and the solicitor general spent the early litigation phase working toward *Brown* and the decade after it filling in the gaps. The Court adopted the office's language and recommended remedies in *Brown*.

Certainly the highwater mark of the litigation phase was *Brown,* but a number of advances defined the period. The Court was essentially the only institution involved in civil rights during most of this phase. The work of the Truman administration and its successors was important in reducing existing constraints, eliminating some negative precedents, and getting the president and Congress involved in supporting civil rights, providing allies for the Court.

Civil rights issues were expanding from education to other areas. The solicitor general's role was critical because litigation was the sole means of advancing the issue. The NAACP was still the primary force, but the solicitor general added legitimacy and support at a critical juncture. This committed the solicitor general to help doctrinal development. It also created a precedent for an incremental approach to civil rights.

The solicitor general is normally a reactive agent. The office typically waits for the Court to define the context and then it becomes active in helping the Court establish doctrinal equilibrium. A vacuum at the top of the OSG during the Truman administration gave career attorneys the opportunity to establish a new set of policies that increasingly moved the solicitor general to the epicenter of civil rights litigation. The "careerists" became an institutional memory urging the next administration to stay the course. They became policy entrepreneurs who shaped the government's policies for the next generation. The OSG had to be proactive because few cases permitted the government to enter as a party.

Procedurally and substantively, the Justice Department under Truman changed the role of the solicitor general and the nature of civil rights. Solicitors general made active use of *amici* to enter cases and inject the government into the issue. Institutionally, this began to move the solicitor general from the roles of tenth justice and fifth clerk to attorney general as policy maker and enhanced the impact a president could exert over the office.

The Justice Department established a precedent for joining the civil rights issue as a proponent of equal protection. This would constrain subsequent administrations. The Justice Department also created or expanded the arsenal of weapons that the Civil Rights Section (later the Division) and the solicitor general could bring to bear. This would affect the office's treatment of civil rights as well as spilling over to other issues.

Elman developed a coalition of departments and agencies to support his decision to file an *amicus* in *Shelley* and create a precedent for the aggressive use of *amici*. Substantively, staff attorneys filed an official position on behalf of the government. They alternated between calls for narrow decisions that would not upset current precedent and arguments that *Plessy* should be overturned. They committed the government to the issue and, in effect, forced the next president to put the resources and moral authority of the government behind civil rights.

Public policy is often path dependent. The process had been started by the Truman administration, and subsequent presidents were compelled to continue to pursue litigation and support civil rights even though they were reluctant to move too quickly. Clearly, decision making was broadly strategic. The Eisenhower and Kennedy solicitors general may not have pushed the Court as far as they could, but they paired the strategic decisions of avoiding an overreliance on litigation and a desire not to preempt legislative possibilities.

CHAPTER 4

The Solicitor General in the Administrative Phase

1964–80

THE SOLICITOR GENERAL had become an important actor in the civil rights movement and a resource for the executive and judicial branches. But there were limits on the ability of the executive branch and the solicitor general to help the NAACP pursue a constitutional revolution. *Brown* had provided a potent symbol, but its practical effects had been limited. To have civil rights reach the next level of development and penetrate the national consciousness, the Court needed an active president and Congress to provide tangible resources to enforce civil rights.

The administrative phase, which began with the passage of real civil rights acts, ushered in Congress as a real factor in the solicitor general's environment. For decades, Congress was, in a sense, nonexistent. Nothing significant could emerge from Congress because committees and a third of the Senate could block potential legislation. On the other hand, Congress could do little to thwart the Supreme Court. The votes were not available to reverse Court decisions and the president's veto could be brought to bear if they were.

Assistance for the Court came in the form of the Civil Rights Act of 1964 and the Voting Rights Act of 1965. The two acts provided significant authority for the Justice Department and Congress. They changed the nature of the solicitor general's work. Rather than being a passive agent who had to wait for cases to be brought to the Court and to enter them as *amicus,* which meant a lack of control, the Justice Department could sequence litigation. The Civil Rights Act and Voting Rights Act gave the government the statutory authority to join litigation as a party. The passage of these acts also removed a symbolic impediment: Cox had been reluctant to advance broad arguments to avoid preempting these pending statutes.

The unanimity of the legislative phase was broken in the administrative phase. Table 4-1 shows the levels of support and success for the administrations during the administrative phase. Nixon solicitors general opposed civil rights for the first time. In addition for the first time, the government lost civil rights cases. Not only did the government lose cases in which it opposed civil rights, but it lost cases in which it supported the civil rights claimant. This chapter examines the factors that dominated the concerns of solicitors general during this period and how they influenced the development of doctrine.

The administrative phase provided the conditions for effective judicial policy making. Just as the Truman solicitors general shaped the agenda for the next two administrations, passage of the Civil Rights Act and Voting Rights Act constrained the activities of presidents who followed Lyndon Johnson. The legislative provisions were not the last word on civil rights, rather they became a baseline that solicitors general tried to expand through the courts.

TABLE 4-1

SOLICITOR GENERAL'S SUPPORT FOR CIVIL RIGHTS AND SUCCESS
BY TYPE OF PARTICIPATION DURING THE ADMINISTRATIVE PHASE

Support for Civil Rights
Type of Participation

President	Party Pro	Party Con	Invited Pro	Invited Con	*Amicus* Pro	*Amicus* Con	Total Pro	Total Con
Johnson	8	0	1	0	10	0	19	0
Nixon	5	1	1	0	16	5	22	6
Ford	5	3	0	1	4	2	9	6
Carter	9	0	1	0	16	0	26	0

Success on the Merits
Type of Participation

President	Party Won	Party Lost	Invited Won	Invited Lost	*Amicus* Won	*Amicus* Lost	Total Won	Total Lost
Johnson	8	0	1	0	10	0	19	0
Nixon	5	1	1	0	13	8	19	9
Ford	1	7	1	0	4	2	6	9
Carter	7	2	1	0	10	6	18	8

LYNDON JOHNSON AND THE CIVIL RIGHTS REVOLUTION

There was little reason to expect any significant change in the solicitor general's approach to civil rights in the wake of Lyndon Johnson's ascension to the White House. There were no changes in the CRD, Robert Kennedy was still attorney general, and Archibald Cox continued as solicitor general.

The goals of the solicitor general are tempered by strategic interaction and norms and rules. Cox exercised restraint in deference to the Court and precedent and to avoid preempting a legislation solution. The typical norms of the office, though modified by the Truman administration, elevated legal concerns over political. With the passage of the Civil Rights Act, the environment changed dramatically. The president was aggressive in his support for civil rights. Congress had created an arsenal of new authority and the Court was willing to expand that authority. This made the government a party, freeing the solicitor general from some of its traditional restraint.

Executive. As a southerner, Lyndon Johnson was perhaps in the best position to push for the extension of civil rights, the domestic issue that "marked" his administration.[1] The assassination of John Kennedy provided Johnson with the window of opportunity that opened even further with the landslide of 1964. Johnson urged immediate action as a testimony to the late president. With the help of Senator Everett Dirksen, a coalition of northern Democrats and Republicans broke an eighty-two–day filibuster to create the "greatest liberal achievement of the decade."[2] While he could have "treaded softly on racial issues after 1964," Johnson was not content, feeling that momentum could be transferred to other legislation. Breaking southern opposition in the Senate created a window for the passage of a battery of legislation.[3]

For all its benefits, the Civil Rights Act did not eliminate voting problems. Litigation, the primary existing remedy, was a slow process. There were three available alternatives: a Constitutional amendment, legislation taking federal control of voting, or legislation to empower a federal agency to monitor voting. With a large majority and weakened conservative coalition, the administration decided to pursue the third alternative despite concerns about its constitutionality. Similar legislation had been struck down after Reconstruction.

The political forces were in the proper alignment for further action. Johnson and Congress were anxious to act and the Court showed "every indication that the boldest initiatives of the Great Society were constitutionally acceptable." Despite that, the OSG was worried that a bill constructed in haste and built on shaky precedential grounds would be vulnerable to challenge. The proposed bill would grant significant authority to the attorney general to determine if violations occurred and to dispatch federal authorities to enfranchise voters.[4]

The Justice Department exercised its enhanced powers to back the president's initiatives. Attorneys General Ramsey Clark and Katzenbach were closer to the advocate end of the spectrum.[5] The department was aggressive in pursuing and extending civil rights and voting rights. The CRD continued to grow in prominence, in no small part, because of the salience of the issue in the wake of the Court's aggressiveness. In addition, it had the benefit of the expanded authority of the Civil Rights Act of 1964 and Voting Rights Act of 1965.[6] The division was increasingly becoming a clientele agency, viewed by civil rights groups as an advocate for their desired policies.

The Voting Rights Act gave the attorney general the power to suspend literacy tests, appoint election examiners, bring suits, require preclearance for changes in election law, and disallow problematic changes.[7] Section 5 shifted the burden of proof to state governments that had a history of discrimination. These "covered jurisdictions" had to preclear changes in voting procedures with the attorney general or the federal district court in Washington, D.C. Section 2 prohibited discrimination in voting in states not covered by section 5 and applied to discriminatory procedures instituted before 1965.[8] The Voting Rights Act had the potential to restructure the social and political fabric of the South and change national politics.[9]

The success of the Johnson administration paved the way for a multifaceted War on Poverty, an economic complement to civil rights legislation. Johnson hoped to speed desegregation and sustain civil rights gains through the courts and new legislation.[10] But Congress was less receptive, making the courts and the solicitor general important actors. The escalation of the War in Vietnam took a toll on domestic issues. The Great Society, which was rife with implications for civil rights, bogged down. Johnson failed to inspire the public as he had with the Civil Rights Act and Voting Rights Act.[11]

Congress. With better organization in Congress, strong presidential leadership, and favorable public opinion, the powerful Civil Rights Act of 1964 became reality. To pass the bill, the leadership strategically tried forum shopping, sending the bill to the Senate Commerce Committee, rather than Judiciary, headed by James Eastland of Mississippi. In the House, the Judiciary Committee got the bill to avoid the Foreign and Interstate Commerce Committee, headed by Representative Oren Harris of Arkansas.[12] The bill included provisions for race and gender equality and created the EEOC.[13] The liberalism scores for Congress prior to the midterm election of 1966 were the highest in the 1950–85 period.[14] Support in Congress was important because the Civil Rights Act and Voting Rights Act were the subjects of a number of challenges regarding first their constitutionality and later statutory interpretation. Having strong Congressional support reinforced the solicitor general and the Court in these challenges.

Supreme Court. Johnson's replacement of Arthur Goldberg with Abe Fortas did not do much to alter the ideological composition of the Court. According to the Baum adjusted scores there was a slight decline in support for civil liberties, which was probably a function of issue evolution. But the choice of Ramsey Clark to head the Justice Department induced significant change. The father of the new attorney general resigned from the Court allowing Johnson to nominate Solicitor General Thurgood Marshall. Now Marshall could protect the precedents he spent his adult life with the NAACP and OSG constructing. The end of the Johnson term coincided with the highest adjusted support scores for civil liberties: 77.1.[15] This was the Court that had the task of interpreting the scope of civil rights legislation.

Issue Evolution. The Kennedy administration presided over few real efforts at pushing the frontiers of *Brown*. Cox preferred the incremental approach. In the public/private cases, the solicitor general and the Court did not move doctrine significantly. The passage of the Civil Rights Act gave the solicitor general the opportunity to expand policy across a number of issue areas, reinforce existing doctrine, and move into second-generation cases.

During the Kennedy and Johnson terms interesting patterns were developing outside the race area. The most intriguing changes occurred in issue areas that were philosophically related, but structurally different from civil rights.[16] Indeed, some of the most significant freedom of speech, press, and association decisions in this era resulted from cases with strong civil rights components. Some states attempted to harass the NAACP, hoping that precedents that placed limits on freedom of association rights of alleged communists could be imposed on the group.[17] In *NAACP v. Alabama,* the Court decided unanimously that the requirement that the organization disclose its membership lists violated freedom of association.[18]

The scope of the civil rights movement expanded to the grassroots level.[19] Southern cities reacted by jailing protesters, often for breach of the peace. A central aspect of the Legal Defense Fund's strategy in response to the jailings was to assert First Amendment freedom of speech protections.[20] More than a dozen cases were decided on free speech grounds and helped reconfigure doctrine in that area. Libel law is perhaps the best example. The *New York Times v. Sullivan* landmark arose from a civil rights issue.[21]

Brown's connection to criminal procedure was less direct. Innovations in *Brown* created an environment for individual landmarks. To protect blacks against state procedures, the Court radically altered the constitutional provision dealing with *habeas corpus* (*Fay v. Noia*). State defendants could launch collateral attacks on their convictions. If an individual was convicted, exhausted state appeals, and unsuccessfully petitioned for certiorari to the Supreme Court, that defendant could seek a writ of *habeas corpus* to have the case retried in federal court.

In *Mapp v. Ohio,* the Court extended incorporation to the exclusionary rule. Within a few years, the Court incorporated the Fifth and Sixth Amendments.[22] None of the landmark incorporation decisions (*Mapp, Gideon v. Wainwright,* and *Miranda v. Arizona*) involved civil rights, but nationalizing the law would protect southern blacks. Samuel Walker considers the ACLU's role in the due process revolution and the incorporation cases as the organization's most significant contributions to the civil rights movement.[23]

The Johnson Solicitors General

Three solicitors general served under Johnson: Cox, Thurgood Marshall, and Erwin Griswold. Under Johnson, they were involved in nineteen civil rights cases. In each of the cases, the solicitor general argued successfully in favor of the civil rights claimant. As Figure 4-1 shows, the factors considered important in influencing the solicitor general were mutually reinforcing. The president strongly supported civil rights. The Court was the most liberal of the twentieth century. Congress passed strong legislation that demonstrated support for the expansion of civil rights. In the decade after *Brown,* there were few major decisions, but the unanimity of decisions sent a strong signal. The Civil Rights Act provided the impetus for spillovers to a variety of other issues.

The Johnson solicitors general tilled some old ground and broke new ground. They participated in five desegregation cases, continuing the work of their predecessors, fulfilling the roles of tenth justice, to help the Court write doctrine, and attorney general as law enforcement officer. Congressional action pushed them into new areas: they defended the constitutionality of the Civil Rights Act and the Voting Rights Act, sought ways to link them to past civil rights acts, and tried to get the Court to expand Congressional intent.

The solicitor general was a key component in the development of civil rights doctrine. There was an evolution in the scope of the solicitor general's position across the Johnson administration. The obvious explanation is that the identity of the solicitor general changed. Cox submitted his resignation and Johnson accepted it. Specifically telling Marshall there was no guarantee of a seat on the Supreme Court, Johnson enticed him off the Court of Appeals.[24] Cox's moderate positions gave way to Marshall's more aggressive approach. Respect for traditional judicial restraint was replaced by a willingness to exploit a rising tide of judicial activism. Marshall, past director of the Legal Defense Fund, was more liberal and had a greater stake in civil rights than Cox.

Ultimately, the explanation is more complicated and reflects the dynamics of the institutional and policy environment. Marshall served a president who was more publicly committed to civil rights than Kennedy. Marshall's brief term was coincident with a more sympathetic Court that continued to expand the boundaries of civil rights. Marshall was also backed by Congressional power that Cox did not possess. On the other hand, issue evolution suggests that cases were getting more difficult over time. While the solicitor general invariably supported civil rights, there was variation in the scope of the briefs and arguments.

Eight of the nineteen were cases in which the U.S. government was

---

FIGURE 4-1

ENVIRONMENTAL CONSTRAINTS ON THE SOLICITOR GENERAL:
JOHNSON ADMINISTRATION

SG`

SGw	SGp	SGc

Liberal————————————————————————————Conservative

Supreme   President   Congress
Court
Precedent

SGp: Position Solicitor General would adopt if doing the president's bidding
SGw: Position Solicitor General would adopt if winning was the sole goal
SGc: Position Solicitor General would adopt to avoid Congressional response
SG`: Actual position the Solicitor General adopted

a party, ten involved voluntary *amici* briefs, and the solicitor general was invited to participate in one. In most circumstances, voluntary *amici* briefs represent the best opportunity for major policy intervention because the solicitor general has the most discretion and the fewest constraints. The office can advance the president's agenda in such cases. Yet, the Johnson solicitors general, particularly Cox, did not use the *amici* to full advantage.

Typically, cases in which the government is a party are not effective vehicles for advancing policy goals. The solicitor general is constrained by the need to defend legislation. The case normally involves an interpretation of the statute before the Court. During the Johnson administration, the most important cases involved the government as a party in challenges to the Civil Rights Act and Voting Rights Act. The distinctions between the roles that solicitors general play and the constraints they face are tied to the form of participation. For the Johnson administration, however, they tended to blend together. The second Warren Court was willing to expand civil rights. Thus, as the tenth justice, solicitors general could argue for broad extensions of doctrine, as if they were playing the role of attorney general for policy making. In addition, the Civil Rights Act and Voting Rights Act provide the Justice Department with extensive authority, thus the solicitor general would argue some cases as attorney general for law enforcement. Once again, the scope of the arguments did not need to deviate from one role to another.

In *Heart of Atlanta Motel v. United States* and *Katzenbach v. McClung,* Cox argued that the Fourteenth Amendment should not be construed as a limit to Congressional power under the Commerce Clause.[25] During construction of the Civil Rights Act, Cox led the chorus arguing for use of the Commerce Clause, rather than the Fourteenth Amendment. He felt that the existence of the *Civil Rights Cases* (1883) made the Fourteenth Amendment a risky proposition.[26] According to Burke Marshall, using the Commerce Clause caused no problems for Cox: "*Wickard v. Filburn* provided the basis for this. John and Robert Kennedy wanted to know why we were using the Commerce Clause as the basis, rather than the Fourteenth Amendment."[27] Assistant Attorney General Nicholas Katzenbach recalled that civil rights groups also wanted to use the Fourteenth Amendment but that "we felt that the Commerce Clause, by far, was constitutionally the safest clause to use in terms of moving legislation." Katzenbach conceded that he would have used both the Commerce Clause and Fourteenth Amendment: "I felt that would even be stronger. Using the belt and the suspenders was fine." He could not understand why civil rights groups failed to embrace the Commerce

Clause, considering its genesis. He felt that it would be a marvelous irony for the protection to come under the Commerce Clause, when that provision was added to the Constitution as a compromise for recognizing the right to own slaves.[28]

In *Heart of Atlanta Motel,* Cox claimed that he was seeking no extension of doctrine, just a reiteration of familiar principles concerning the Commerce Clause. Cox argued that Congress had the power under the Commerce Clause and necessary and proper clause to regulate local activities that had "a close and substantial relation to commerce" to foster and promote commerce or relieve burdens and obstructions on commerce. He maintained that racial discrimination burdened commerce, thus prohibiting discrimination was a legitimate exercise of power. Cox argued that discrimination was a national problem and the importance of any individual establishment and its link to commerce must be judged as part of a complex and interrelated national problem.[29]

The broad questions concerning the Civil Rights Act's application were narrowed considerably in *McClung,* a case involving a restaurant that refused to serve blacks. Cox invoked the same legal principles he had asserted in *Heart of Atlanta Motel.* He argued that discrimination in restaurants had a real effect on commerce. Cox alluded to the effects of demonstrations against public eating places that discriminated. He pointed to the reduction in the number of customers caused by the discouragement of black patronage, which reduced the quantity of goods purchased through interstate channels.[30]

The Court agreed with the solicitor general that the harmful Civil Rights Cases were without precedential value because the Reconstruction statutes were not based on the Commerce Clause. The Court unanimously ruled that the Civil Rights Act of 1964 was within Congressional power. The Court ruled that Congress had ample basis to pass the restaurant portion of the act. Congress had assembled an impressive array of information to show that discrimination in restaurants had a direct and highly restrictive impact on travelers and, as a result, interstate commerce.[31]

In *United States v. Guest* and *United States v. Price,* Solicitor General Marshall argued for a very broad view of section 1983 of the Reconstruction era civil rights acts. Some opposition to civil rights took violent forms. The problem was the reluctance of some state courts to bring those accused of murdering blacks and civil rights activists to justice. The federal government felt compelled to apply the terms of the Enforcement Act of 1870 and intervene in such cases. Section 2 of the 1870 Act (18 USC section 241) forbade private interference with the rights of citizens as provided within the privileges and immunities clause of Fourteenth Amendment. Under section 17 (18 USC section 242) a state officer who interfered with the civil rights of citizens could be punished for denying privileges and immunities and violating the due process and equal protection clauses of the Fourteenth Amendment.[32]

Price and *Guest* gave the government the chance to test the scope of those statutory provisions. These were important cases involving provisions that had been fallow for decades. The Justice Department wanted to know the extent of its power to implement civil rights initiatives. The Court needed to act in a way that was consistent with Congressional intent and would not mitigate the need for additional legislation. In addition, there were questions whether the Civil Rights Act of 1964 placed limits on Reconstruction era provisions.

Price involved the murder of three civil rights workers. Three local officials were implicated along with private citizens who were charged in the conspiracy. *Guest* was more difficult because no state or local governmental officials were involved. The Justice Department wanted to pursue the case to determine whether the Court considered the law "adequate for control of this type of terrorism."[33]

The department did not feel that it could press Congress for new legislative authority until existing judicial remedies were exhausted. Despite his reservations, Cox wanted to establish the scope of the department's authority under sections 241 and 242 in a single round of litigation. The cases might also provide hints as to whether the political branches had the constitutional power to correct the deficiencies of Reconstruction laws. Between the time the cases were filed and heard, Cox resigned and Johnson named Marshall the first African American solicitor general.[34] By announcing that Marshall would argue *Price* and *Guest,* the administration demonstrated how important it considered the cases.

The government was constrained by the fact that the Fourteenth Amendment did not reach private action. This was particularly problematic in the *Guest* case. The government agreed that only a state could deprive a person of rights, but argued that a private individual could "interfere" with the exercise of such rights or privileges once they had become vested. Marshall argued that the Court had held in *Monroe v. Pape* and *Burton v. Wilmington* that illegal conduct on the part of private persons acting in concert with state officials constituted state action which was punishable under federal law.[35]

In *Guest,* Marshall argued that there was state action in the case. The government claimed that the Equal Protection Clause required states to make equal rights available to all their citizens, imposed an obligation on states to take action against private conspiracies directed at depriving citizens of the use of public facilities, and allowed federal intervention if a state violated this duty. Marshall argued that private individuals were subject to punishment for conspiring to interfere with the use of public facilities by others not because they themselves violated the Constitution, but because they perpetuated a denial of equal protection by the state.

The government tried to link Reconstruction statutes with the Civil Rights Act of 1964. Marshall claimed that section 241 could be used against those who conspired to deprive others of rights created by Title II of the Civil Rights Act. He disputed the claim that Congress had explicitly excluded those rights from the protection of the 1870 conspiracy statute in passing the Civil Rights Act. The government argued that when private citizens joined hands with state officials to carry out a plan to deprive citizens of their constitutional rights, they lost their claim to be treated as private citizens and acted under the color of law.

The Court confined its decision to statutory grounds thus avoiding constitutional interpretation. The Court accepted the government's position that the actions of private citizens took place under the color of state law, but did not endorse the contention that section 241 protected rights created by Title II. The Court strategically sidestepped that question to avoid a potential conflict with Congress over whether it had removed Title II from the protection of section 241.[36] Legislation to expand the protection of the Reconstruction era statutes was pending in Congress and the Court did not want to make a decision that might hinder its prospects.

As solicitor general, Marshall participated in three cases dealing with voting rights. With passage of the Voting Rights Act, Congress authorized direct action by the Justice Department to register voters, ensure they were not prohibited from going to the polls, and make certain that ballots were correctly counted.

Attorney General Katzenbach argued in *South Carolina v. Katzenbach* that the Voting Rights Act was a legitimate exercise of the Fifteenth Amendment. The brief departed from typical procedure: rather than wait for individual violations to create cases that might take years to litigate, the government asked the Court to consider a range of broad and narrow questions concerning the Voting Rights Act.[37] The brief argued that Congress was not limited by its expressed powers merely to allow the courts negative authority to strike down state laws in violation of the amendment, but that Congress could take positive action as well. Katzenbach argued that no parts of the Constitution give states absolute authority to grant or withhold franchise on any conditions they choose.

In particular, the brief argued that the Constitution expressly forbade withholding voting rights on the basis of race. The Court unanimously dismissed South Carolina's contention that the act was unconstitutional, ruling that Congress had not usurped the reserved powers of states.[38] For the Court, Warren claimed that the "burden of time and inertia" should be shifted to the states and supported the act's relatively automatic remedies.[39] According to Stephen Pollak, then a deputy in the division, "*South Carolina v. Katzenbach* was the most important vindication of voting rights."[40]

Johnson created an historic precedent when he appointed Thurgood Marshall to the Supreme Court. To fill the vacancy of solicitor general, he nominated Erwin Griswold, dean of Harvard Law School and a former member of the office. In the *amici* briefs, Griswold encountered a problem that periodically affects lower court judges and solicitors general. Lower courts often cannot anticipate when the Supreme Court is going to accelerate the development of doctrine or launch a retreat. Similarly, if the solicitor general is contributing to the long-term evolution of doctrine, the office is unlikely to be prepared for a dramatic change in the nature of the Court's decisions. The later Warren Court stood as a "high-water mark in [its] jurisprudential histories . . . the hard core liberal wing of the Court had acquired its fifth vote."[41]

Most of the voluntary *amici* briefs filed by Griswold involved second-generation school desegregation cases to combat southern intransigence. In *Green v. County School Board of New Kent County,* the Court made an important change in desegregation policy. The cases involved another attempt by southern states to thwart desegregation: pupil assignment laws. Griswold argued that these plans would perpetuate segregation.

The government's brief was moderate and circumspect. This may have been a function of the retreat by Congress, the moderation of Griswold, or the increasing difficulty of the cases. The solicitor general, playing the role of tenth justice, failed to anticipate doctrinal change. This is not surprising in that the solicitor general normally fashions arguments within the context the Court has established.[42] The solicitor general was asked about busing, but Griswold demurred, claiming that the government was not prepared to argue for that remedy.[43] The Court changed the constitutional rule from a prohibition against compelled segregation to an affirmative duty to desegregate by dismantling all dual systems.[44] According to Pollak, "*Green* was a great turning point for our desegregation efforts. The South had used grade-by-grade gradualism. The Court finally threw that out. We had been living and dying by that plan. It was choking our efforts at desegregation."[45]

In the most important voluntary *amicus* case, *Jones v. Alfred Mayer,* the government argued for a broad construction of past civil rights acts and for defining the private/public distinction in housing discrimination. Attorney General Clark played a central role in getting the solicitor general to intervene as *amicus* on behalf of Jones, who was denied a house.[46] The case was an extension of *Shelley v. Kraemer,* but involved exclusion from an entire community rather than a single dwelling. According to Pollak, who signed the brief, "The arguments in *Jones* were hard to make because of past Supreme Court decisions. The Solicitor General must respond to Court precedents and the precedents were negative. The decision in *Jones* was a great victory and not expected at all. . . . It was a radical decision."[47]

According to Hugh Davis Graham, the decision "signalled the intention of the mature Warren Court to read into legislative history the policy preferences of the Court's majority." The opinion by Justice Potter Stewart was "a revolutionary reading of the statute." The Court ruled that the 1866 Civil Rights Act barred private discrimination in housing. Unlike the other decisions, though, the authority stemmed from the Thirteenth Amendment, which banned slavery and provided Congress with positive authority to enforce it. The Court ruled that the amendment was also designed to remove "the badges and servitudes of slavery." Stewart provided a broad reading of the amendment to include "the freedom to buy whatever a white man can buy, the right to live wherever a white man can live. If Congress cannot say this much, then the Thirteenth Amendment made a promise the Nation cannot keep." According to Pollak, "*Jones* was a very significant interpretation of section 1982. The Court breathed new life into the dormant provision. The decision was obscured by the Fair Housing Act, which came around the same time, but the Act was less necessary because of *Jones.*"[48]

Griswold filed briefs in second-generation voting rights cases, most notably, *Allen v. State Board of Elections.* The case, brought by private litigants with the help of the NAACP, involved changes in Mississippi electoral laws that were designed to hinder minority voting and representation. The government was invited to express its position on whether the changes required preclearance by the attorney general under section 5 of the Voting Rights Act, which was designed to apply to changes in registration and voting procedures. The question concerned whether the attorney general could review annexations, the drawing of new district lines, and changes that involved minority voting strength.[49] In response to the Court's invitation, the solicitor general argued for an expanded view of section 5.

The Court expanded the notion of preclearance, providing more authority for the attorney general. More importantly, the Court began to change the focus from the denial of the right to vote to questions regarding potential dilution of voting power. Section 5 would now be applied broadly to all types of election laws, rather than just registration and voting.[50]

The Court examined issues that were not before it, expanded the relief sought by the parties, and broadened its interpretation of the Voting Rights Act.[51] In its decision, the Court held that voting included all action necessary to make a vote effective. When districts were malapportioned, the Court ruled that an individual living in a larger district had a diluted vote. The Court took the concept of voting dilution that it had developed in reapportionment cases and extended it to include dilution of a definable group's voting power.[52] The decision had broad spillover effects, shifting the focus of civil rights from individual to group remedies. This would eventually culminate in affirmative action programs.

The Court expanded the notion of vote dilution in *White v. Regester* (1973), a case in which the solicitor general did not intervene. Vote dilution is defined as "the practice of reducing the potential effectiveness of a group's voting strength by limiting its ability to translate that strength into the control of (or influence with) elected public officials." There are a number of devices that could be used to achieve that: at-large elections, a decrease in the size of legislative bodies, racial gerrymandering, and a change of offices from elective to appointive. The problem for the solicitor general and the Court was how to define vote dilution and what standard to use to attack it.[53]

In constructing the Voting Rights Act, Congress did not require the attorney general to prove intent to challenge state voting procedures. The negative effects of voting procedures were enough to force change. In *Allen,* the Court took a step toward changing the definition of harmful effects. By changing the focus from questions of disenfranchisement to an investigation of whether changes in voting procedure would dilute minority voting strength, the Court reinvented the Voting Rights Act. The "effects standard" would soon be transplanted to other issues, most notably employment law.

Conclusion

The Johnson administration marked the transformation of civil rights to the administrative stage and from constitutional to statutory cases. Much as the Truman solicitors general set the context for the litigation phase, the Johnson solicitors general established the framework that would dominate the administrative phase.

The Kennedy and Johnson years demonstrated a wide variance in the work of the solicitor general. The solicitor general's positions always favored civil rights, but the breadth of the arguments varied with the position and strength of the president and rise and decline of Congressional support for civil rights. The Johnson solicitors general took fuller advantage of the institutional and policy environments than any of their predecessors. Cox and Marshall emphasized the political over the legal perspective. For the first time, solicitors general had a full arsenal of weapons at their disposal to continue the development of civil rights.

Attorneys general were aggressive and willing to use the solicitor general as a resource. Under Johnson, the solicitor general recast its institutional role, becoming a dominant actor in civil rights litigation. The dramatic expansion of arguments and doctrine was the result of the confluence of all the factors in the solicitor general's environment. The president was a strong proponent of civil rights and the CRD reflected those priorities. Congress was a positive force for the first time. Congressional support encouraged Cox to abandon restraint and did not constrain Marshall's activist tendencies. Cox and Marshall acted strategically to expand the Civil Rights Act and the Voting Rights Act, pushed desegregation, and linked those statutes to Reconstruction legislation. The later Warren Court was willing to write a virtual blank check for civil rights. Not only were favorable precedents proliferating, but the Civil Rights Act and Voting Rights Act provided extensive authority for the executive branch.

Because of this confluence, the roles of the solicitor general were reinforcing. The government was a party in many cases, but the solicitor general went beyond the role of tenth justice, asking the Court to go beyond the statutory authority. The Court was a willing participant in expanding doctrine. In that sense, the solicitor general treated the briefs as if they were *amici* with widespread discretion and played the role of attorney general as policy maker. The solicitors general used their briefs as vehicles for breathing life into statutes passed during Reconstruction. In expanding the authority of the Justice Department, the solicitor general also served in the role of attorney general as law enforcement officer.

There were significant changes in the solicitor general's institutional environment and capacity. Instead of arguing that cases should be narrowly construed, confined to specific questions, and designed to avoid confronting antagonistic precedents directly, solicitors general asked for expansive interpretations of the legislation. Even Cox was willing to try to extend the Civil Rights Act. Marshall, more of a politico than a legalist, tried to push the envelope and take advantage of the Court's judicial activism. He sought to extend the Civil Rights Act by linking it with post–Civil War statutes. In *South Carolina v. Katzenbach,* the government asked the Court to address a number of questions that were not on the docket. The return of a legalist, in this case Griswold, was a portend. He failed to anticipate further activism and the policy direction of the Court in desegregation, but sought expansions in voting rights and housing.

As Johnson increasingly shifted his attention to Vietnam and his public support and professional reputation waned, the solicitor general began to adopt more moderate, less activist positions. This was a consequence of decreased Congressional and presidential support, a more moderate solicitor general, and the advent of more difficult cases. The one factor that did not change was the Court. The Court was willing to accept the broadest arguments the solicitor general or the NAACP would proffer. When the solicitor general made narrow arguments, the Court was often willing to use its initiative to expand them.

With the universe in proper alignment, did the solicitor general act on sincere or strategic preferences? The solicitor general stayed the course in desegregation and used the Civil Rights Act to push the boundaries of policy into other areas. There was evidence of policy making to pursue sincere goals. With the arrival of the second Warren Court, the solicitors general went beyond Congressional intent in a number of areas. First, the solicitors general were successful in reinvigorating the legislation of the Reconstruction era and linking it to the Civil Rights Act of 1964, thus expanding the Fourteenth and Fifteenth Amendments. Second, they were able to expand the Thirteenth Amendment to cover modern forms of discrimination. Third, they treated the Civil Rights Act and the Voting Rights Act as a foundation to build on, rather than boundaries to work within. In *McClung,* Cox successfully argued for a very broad view of the Commerce Clause. In *South Carolina v. Katzenbach,* the government asked for and received expedited answers to a series of questions regarding the Voting Rights Act. In *Allen,* the solicitor general responded to an invitation by the Court to consider changing the focus from the denial of the right to vote to questions regarding potential dilution of voting power. Section 5 would now be applied broadly to all types of election laws, rather than just registration and voting. A major advance came in voting rights, when the solicitor general recommended the use of the disparate impact standard, which would soon spread across other civil rights domains.

The Johnson solicitors general had an important impact on policy evolution. They helped expand civil rights into a number of areas outside of education. The passage of the Civil Rights Act and the Voting

Rights Act thrust the solicitor general into the center of race litigation. Both acts spread civil rights terrain well beyond desegregation, increasing the range of the solicitor general's activities. At the same time, Griswold did not seek to push the boundaries. He failed to see the Court's issue expansion and changes in doctrinal development. Despite the solicitor general's reluctance to take a firm position, the Court made a decisive move in school desegregation in *Green*. Indeed, in referring to the new precedent Earl Warren sent a memo to William Brennan, saying, "When this opinion is handed down, the traffic light will have changed from *Brown* to *Green*."[54]

RICHARD NIXON: CIVIL RIGHTS V. THE SOUTHERN STRATEGY

The goals of the Nixon administration were bound to differ from those of its predecessor. Yet, Nixon did not replace Johnson's solicitor general. It is difficult for a new solicitor general to change positions in a case or on an issue. It would seem to be that much more onerous for Griswold to reverse field on a case or an issue simply because a new party controlled the White House. This would constrain an administration that wanted to move more deliberately or retreat in civil rights.

The Nixon solicitors general faced a strategic environment and institutional rules and norms that favored civil rights. Congress had passed the Civil Rights Act and seemed intent on being a positive force. The CRD had expanded authority. The Court had been extending positive precedents into other areas. The OSG under Johnson had been increasingly active, constraining successors who might want to move more cautiously.

Executive. The election of Richard Nixon threatened a disjuncture in race relations. Nixon did not want to be a leader on civil rights. But while there were changes, there was not a wholesale retreat. According to Stephen Ambrose, Nixon passed on his best opportunity for greatness: civil rights. Nixon was quoted as saying, "I will do what the law requires and not one thing more."[55] He repeatedly said that he would ask Congress for no further civil rights legislation.[56] As part of his southern strategy to enhance Republican power, Nixon ran and governed on planks of law and order, opposition to busing to achieve school integration,[57] and in support of the freedom of choice plans the Court had rejected as a means of delaying integration. Ultimately, Nixon tried to achieve with legislation what he failed to get from the courts, a moratorium on busing.[58] Congress allowed the bill to die in conference committee. A similar measure was killed by liberals with a filibuster, a weapon normally used against civil rights. Critics claimed that the administration had no coherent civil rights program and was largely motivated by political goals.[59]

John Mitchell was the consummate example of an advocate attorney general.[60] To implement the southern strategy, the Justice Department reversed a number of policies. Mitchell announced that the department would slow school desegregation,[61] urging the solicitor general to break with past litigation policies. Failing that, the department pursued a strategy of nonenforcement by the CRD, which prompted a revolt and mass resignations by careerists.[62] During the proposed extension of the Voting Rights Act, the department supported lifting mandatory preclearance requirements. Mitchell was caught in the net of scandal and forced to resign. A procession of less partisan neutrals followed.[63]

The Civil Rights Act of 1964 gave authority over desegregation policy to the Departments of Health, Education, and Welfare (HEW) and Justice. HEW could cut off federal funds to school districts that failed to dismantle dual systems. Nixon appointed Robert Finch, a liberal, to head HEW. It was thought that Finch was committed to a strict enforcement of civil rights law and a rapid end to segregation in the South.[64] But while Finch wanted to enforce the laws and press forward, Mitchell wanted to slow the process.[65] Ultimately, the administration announced a shift in the policy-making locus to the Justice Department. Mitchell and Finch announced that HEW would rely less on holding funds hostage and more on using the federal courts.[66] This would enhance the position of the solicitor general but also potentially increase pressure on the office.[67] There were good practical reasons to avoid cutting funds. After all, such a policy harmed victims of discrimination as well as the perpetrators.[68] There was a political benefit also, if funds were slashed, the administration would be blamed.[69] The litigation strategy, on the other hand, was time consuming. A judicial strategy would shift the onus away from the president to the courts. Meanwhile, Nixon could placate the South by promising to appoint strict constructionists to the judiciary.[70]

The administration was interested in furthering judicial restraint, but the CRD had pushed well beyond the statutory provisions for almost a decade. It would be hard for a new head of the division to come in and alter the dynamics. That task initially fell to Jerris Leonard. As Leonard said, "Mitchell told me to be sure I was right and not to push the envelope. . . . I knew my mandate: enforce the law, don't expand it."[71] Leonard's task was complicated by the fact that civil rights groups distrusted the administration. There were frequent clashes between political advisors and careerists. Leonard struggled to balance the organizational ethos with commandments from above.

When Leonard left the division, he was replaced by Stanley Pottinger. According to David Rose, who served in the employment section at the time "Stanley Pottinger was very sympathetic to civil rights. He pushed hard . . . he felt strongly about civil rights laws."[72] The leadership of the division got more liberal as the solicitor general and the Court were getting more conservative and issue evolution was posing more difficult questions.

Congress. Support for civil rights in Congress began to flag as the Johnson presidency was ebbing. Indeed, the aggregate liberalism of Congress declined significantly.[73] Congress tried constitutional amendment, threats to the authority and appropriations of HEW, and to the jurisdiction of the Court if busing continued.[74] Nixon opposed virtually all major civil rights legislation pending in Congress.[75] Any new initiatives would need to come from Congress, but with a presidential veto as a threat, such proposals would be modest. Still, Congress served as a counterweight to executive gambols in the judicial branch and to block attempts by Nixon to pass legislation that would limit civil rights. Arguments by the Justice Department in favor of narrow or conservative interpretations of statutes would run the risk that Congress would retaliate though the veto would make that less likely. Congress did pass the Equal Employment Opportunity Act of 1972, which transferred power to sue from the attorney general to the EEOC.[76]

Supreme Court. Nixon campaigned on the promise that he would put strict constructionists on the Court to reverse or limit the activism of the Warren Court. The Nixon Court was born with the retirement of the chief justice. In a short period of time, Nixon was able to change the leadership and composition of the Court, appointing the so-called "Minnesota Twins," Warren Burger and Harry Blackmun, as well as Lewis Powell and William Rehnquist, replacing among others, Fortas and Hugo Black. The result was a sharp decline in the Court's adjusted support for civil liberties to 59.9 and then to 50.5. By no means did the Burger Court initiate a "constitutional counter-revolution," but certainly the environment was not propitious for the expansion of civil rights.[77]

Issue Evolution. Civil rights cases before the Court reached another level of evolutionary development. The Court had bequeathed a deep reservoir of favorable precedents in light of constitutional challenges to the Civil Rights Act and Voting Rights Act. The Court breathed new life into Reconstruction era statutes as well. In *Jones,* the Court attacked private discrimination. But the notion of issue evolution is that cases become more difficult over time. In no issue area was that as clear as in civil rights. With *de jure* segregation prohibited, cases involving extraordinary remedies and *de facto* segregation were working their ways through the lower courts. Segregation patterns in the North would soon be on the Court's agenda. Changes in executive leadership and the composition of the Court would alter the course of issue evolution.[78]

The Nixon Solicitors General

The decision not to replace Johnson's solicitor general suggested the nonpolitical nature of the OSG, but it may have constrained a president who was not committed to his predecessor's policies. It is difficult enough for a new solicitor general to come to office and change the government's position to reflect a new administration's priorities. That task would be even more difficult when the new solicitor general is the old solicitor general.

The relationship between the CRD and the solicitor general changed over time. Griswold was more liberal than Leonard, though both were fairly moderate. Robert Bork, who eventually succeeded Griswold, was considerably more conservative than Pottinger, head of the CRD from the end of the Nixon administration through the Ford presidency. According to Bork, "His views may have been a little out of step with the Administration's. The question was not acute until the Ford Administration and it arose particularly on the question of busing."[79]

Griswold and Bork participated in twenty-eight civil rights cases. Despite the perceived reluctance of the president to push civil rights, his solicitors general continued to support existing principles. In the aggregate, the Nixon solicitors general filed on behalf of civil rights claimants in twenty-two cases. In a number of cases, the solicitors general took a moderate position that supported principles of civil rights, but asked the Court to impose some limits. Playing the role as tenth justice required solicitors general to help construct doctrine and meant that they did not want to argue aggressively against civil rights and risk rebuke.

Griswold participated in twenty-one civil rights cases during Nixon's tenure. He was successful in fourteen of these cases. Those cases were dominated numerically by desegregation and cases defining the lines between public and private facilities. Those issues shared substantive importance with a pair of important employment discrimination cases. Bork only participated in six civil rights cases during the Nixon administration and was successful in five.[80] One northern desegregation case and one employment case were most noteworthy.

Figure 4-2 is a spatial representation of the factors that influenced the solicitor general. Griswold served under presidents of different parties, which limited his partisan ties. He often argued similar cases for the Nixon administration and sought consistency. This does not mean that he did not ask the Court to slow the spread of discrimination remedies or clash with the Justice Department. With a Democratic Congress and strong precedents, it would have been foolhardy to attempt a full scale retreat in civil rights. Bork faced similar constraints that tempered his ideology. With the wealth of precedents and a Court not yet ready to limit desegregation, he was constrained in the type of arguments that would attract favorable judicial attention. Bork argued most cases for the civil rights claimant. He did, however, argue to limit the extent of remedies and urged the Court to halt expansion in some areas. Issue evolution provided opportunities to limit the spread of civil rights.

The Nixon administration was constrained in its initiatives in school desegregation cases by the *Green* decision, which had stiffened the Court's resolve to deal with the issue. The Johnson-Nixon years were the formative period for enforcement policy, just as the Truman-Eisenhower years had been the formative period for the normative rule of *Brown*. The Nixon administration's general position enunciated support for *Brown*, while trying to limit its applicability and the remedies used to further its principles.

The administration opposed busing to achieve desegregation, a position it continued to discuss as it enforced decisions that contradicted its

---

FIGURE 4-2

ENVIRONMENTAL CONSTRAINTS ON THE SOLICITOR GENERAL:
NIXON ADMINISTRATION

SG`

	SGw	SGc	SGp	
Liberal				Conservative
	Precedent	Supreme Court	Congress	President

SGp: Position Solicitor General would adopt if doing the president's bidding
SGw: Position Solicitor General would adopt if winning was the sole goal
SGc: Position Solicitor General would adopt to avoid Congressional response
SG`: Actual position the Solicitor General adopted

desires.[81] The Justice Department shared the view of Nixon's political advisors who wanted the desegregation issue put to the rest before the 1972 election. Nixon was committed to local solutions. As he said, "I felt that to the greatest extent possible, plans for desegregation should be made by school boards, local communities, and the courts in each area or region, rather than by bureaucrats in HEW in Washington."[82]

Griswold argued eleven desegregation cases during the Nixon administration. Most involved second-generation questions. Griswold made important practical and symbolic arguments on behalf of the administration. In six cases, Griswold argued that the South had not discharged its responsibilities. While the solicitor general never argued that districts had fully met their responsibilities, in four desegregation cases the government opposed the requests of civil rights groups.[83] These cases represented the first exceptions from the solicitor general's unbroken support for desegregation. The retreat was partially a function of a Republican administration pressing a "Southern strategy"[84] and partially because of the more difficult nature of the cases.

In its initial case, the administration was compelled to support the principles enunciated in *Green*. Soon, however, the administration seemed to strike a retreat.[85] Politics impinged on the solicitor general in *Alexander v. Holmes County Board of Education*. Secretary Finch was asked to submit desegregation plans for Mississippi schools. Under direct orders from the president, HEW sought delays in submitting the plans.[86] HEW argued that prompt compliance with the dictates of *Green* would create "chaos, confusion, and a catastrophic educational setback."[87]

Griswold could not unequivocally support the government's position, so he assigned the argument to Leonard. Griswold did sign the petition because he thought a reasonable argument could be made for the position[88] and failure to sign the brief would have sent a strong message to the Court. Arguing for HEW, the government opposed the position of the NAACP for the first time. Also, for the first time, the justices rebuffed the government, holding that the time for "all deliberate speed" in implementing desegregation had passed.[89] According to Leonard, "The Court did not want to show any signs of slowing desegregation down. The Court wanted to send a clear signal to the school boards and people in the White House. We understood that."[90]

After some hedging, the administration complied with *Alexander*. As James Turner noted, "To its credit, the Nixon Administration upheld its end of the bargain." This point was illustrated by Leonard, "I never had a clue whether Richard Nixon and John Mitchell truly supported civil rights, but they supported the law." The administration had practical political reasons to do so. According to Leonard, "Nixon wanted the desegregation issue gone before the next election." Still, Nixon wanted to comply on his terms. He was leery of the consequences of the decision. "One thing I was determined to ensure was that the many young liberal lawyers in HEW and in the Justice Department's Civil Rights Division would not treat this decision as a carte blanche for them to run wild through the South enforcing compliance with extreme or punitive requirements they had formulated in Washington."[91]

Perhaps the two most important desegregation cases Griswold argued during the administration were *Swann v. Charlotte Mecklenberg School District* and *Keyes v. School District No. 1*. Each case involved a first: in *Swann,* the question concerned remedies for a densely populated urban district; in *Keyes,* questions of desegregation came North.

Swann was a case that received heavy administration attention. Griswold filed an *amicus* at the certiorari stage, urging the Court to avoid a determination on the merits.[92] The Court disregarded the suggestion and decided to consider the issue. Griswold recognized that this was a politically sensitive case. He instructed his staff to compile presidential speeches about busing and neighborhood schools and incorporated those positions into the government's brief.

Griswold was summoned by Mitchell, who wanted to see the brief. Though he viewed this as an unusual request, Griswold considered it within the attorney general's authority. Griswold assumed that the brief was sent to the White House for review. The brief was returned with requests for four changes that he considered minor.[93] Griswold filed a cautious brief on the merits.[94] While the solicitor general did not part with the requirements of *Green,* he urged the Court to tailor the remedy narrowly to fit the violation. The extent of the violation was unclear, Griswold argued, because *de facto* and *de jure* discrimination were intertwined. The solicitor general rejected the use of strict ratios for the racial composition of the schools and did not call for the abolition of every all-black school.[95]

Griswold argued for an incremental policy toward integration and opposed the broad use of busing. For the first time, the solicitor general supported a local school district and opposed judicial authority to force integration.[96] During oral arguments, Griswold widely quoted Nixon in arguing for neighborhood schools.[97] The Court rejected the government's position and applied *Green.* The majority established a strong precedent for widespread busing to dismantle dual school systems. In response, the division filed a series of motions to compel compliance with *Swann.*[98] At the same time, though, Nixon instructed the Justice

Department to draft a constitutional amendment opposing busing. *Swann* marked a watershed. After a decade of thwarting southern attempts to circumvent *Brown,* the Court ruled that if there is *de jure* segregation, the sole question was the extent of the remedy.[99]

Keyes became the most important burden of proof case in school desegregation policy.[100] Griswold filed an *amicus* brief, but did not state a formal position that sided with either the school district or the NAACP. As the solicitor general noted in his *amicus* brief, this case raised, for the first time, questions involving the application of the Equal Protection Clause in the context of racial concentration in a northern urban area with no history of compulsory segregation. The government argued that some school boards had taken official steps to cause or promote segregation, but some of the worst concentrations of single race schools were not caused by official actions. Griswold argued that the adoption of neighborhood schools, Nixon's preference, could not be said to be racially discriminatory. Griswold argued again that remedies should be narrowly tailored to fit the extent of the discrimination.[101]

The Court disagreed with the solicitor general's conclusion that discrimination in the central city was not attributable to official action. The Court ruled that a school district could not escape responsibility for policies that kept a large percentage of black students racially isolated. Because of past policies, the Court ruled that the city was obligated to go beyond making future policies race neutral.[102]

Griswold had disputes with the Justice Department over some desegregation cases. In one, Griswold refused to sign a brief requesting a stay from implementing a desegregation order. The Court denied the case. Griswold argued that if he signed the brief, it would be a capitulation to political pressure and would have undermined his effectiveness with the Court.[103]

Just after the 1972 election, Nixon accepted Griswold's resignation, replacing him with the more conservative Bork.[104] Griswold left after presiding over important changes in the solicitor general's approach to desegregation. Those changes had not been manifested in the Court's opinions, but helped establish a new context for these cases.

What factors explain Griswold's retreat from his predecessors and his own work under Johnson? The most obvious explanation would be the change in administration. Nixon won the election in part because of his challenge to massive desegregation and its remedies. The combined vote percentage of Nixon and George Wallace suggested that this position resonated with the electorate. Griswold frankly admitted that he tailored the government's position on desegregation to fit Nixon's policies. To be sure, Griswold stayed within the context of existing precedent, but the solicitor general took a more restrained position. Part of the perceived retreat by the government may have been a function of the growing conservatism of the Court. Nixon had promised to choose strict constructionists and it appeared at the outset he was succeeding.[105] The other important factor was issue evolution. Many of the desegregation cases Griswold argued during Nixon's first term were more complicated issues than his predecessors faced. Questions of broad remedies and what to do about northern *de facto* discrimination broke the consensus on the Court.

The most important case Bork argued before Nixon resigned, *Milliken v. Bradley,* marked another significant symbolic retreat in the solicitor general's position. *Milliken* represented the most complex northern desegregation case to date. There had been clear evidence of *de jure* segregation in the Detroit school system. The district court ruled that governmental action and inaction at all levels had created and perpetuated a dual system. Any potential remedy was limited by the fact that a Detroit-only plan would not work given the racial homogeneity of the city and patterns of white flight to the suburbs. The NAACP was caught on the horns of a dilemma: should the organization risk a negative precedent by asking for a "remedy of unprecedented size and scope"?[106] Ultimately, the NAACP decided any remedy must include the suburbs.

The case posed no such problems for the administration. Bork argued that the remedy had to be tailored to fit the violation. Bork noted, "There were some strong feelings about the case in the Civil Rights Division, but Pottinger did not strongly argue for the other side."[107] Bork argued that the remedy could be extended only where the violation had directly altered the suburbs and only to the extent necessary to eliminate the segregative elements of the violation. The brief maintained that where only one district was involved, there was no constitutional requirement that relief include balancing the racial composition of city schools with those of suburban districts.[108] The administration had made a calculated decision to limit the breadth of busing plans.[109] The solicitor general had been arguing from the outset of the administration for limiting remedies and finally found the appropriate case in front of the properly constituted Court.

In a 5-4 decision, the Court refused to countenance a multidistrict remedy. If, as some argued, there were no significant differences between the facts of *Keyes* and *Milliken,*[110] then the Court was announcing a major retreat. Even if the distinguishing features are recognized, *Milliken* was a symbolic statement that the expansion that began with *Brown* was no longer inexorable. As Stephen Halpern wrote, "*Milliken* was a turning point. It was one of the first nonunanimous Supreme Court decisions in a school desegregation case, and the first time that the Court had over-ruled a desegregation decree in the three years since its *Swann* decision endorsing the broad remedial powers of district courts."[111] The decision was important in structuring the subsequent course of desegregation policy and empowered the Nixon and Ford administrations to limit their efforts in northern desegregation cases.

There were two other areas of civil rights that dominated concerns during the Nixon administration: employment and distinctions between the public and private spheres. In the employment realm, the adminis-tration was active in pushing the frontiers. The dominant theory in em-ployment law focused on group rather than individual rights.[112] The ad-ministration supported equal employment opportunity, advocating the controversial Philadelphia Plan.[113] The Justice Department worked hard to limit the distinction between public and private forms of discrimi-nation. Only public discrimination could be attacked under the Four-teenth Amendment, so the administration sought a broad definition of what was considered public.

Griswold participated in five facilities/public accommodations cases as *amici*. Griswold had an advantage Cox had lacked, the backing of the Civil Rights Act. The cases involved whether parks, pools, and recre-ation centers, which were closed to blacks, were considered private or public. In each of the five cases, Griswold argued that the discrimination could be attacked under civil rights laws. He was successful in three cases.

In two cases with similar facts, *Sullivan v. Little Hunting Park*[114] and *Tillman v. Wheaton-Haven*,[115] Griswold successfully argued that a neigh-borhood recreational facility and a pool, respectively, were not private fa-cilities. In each case, a black family was denied access to facilities that white families could utilize. Griswold argued that neither the recreation facility or the pool was a private club. If black families who rented or owned houses in the community could not use the pool or the recreation facilities, then they were deprived of full use of their property. In each of the cases, the Court agreed, following virtually every part of the solici-tor general's briefs.[116]

In the two most difficult cases, the Court decided that there was no legal recourse to combat discriminatory policies. In one, *Palmer v. Thompson,* the city closed its public pool, rather than permit integration. Griswold argued that the closing was for the expressed purpose of pre-venting blacks from using the community pool. The Court disagreed, claiming that the pool was closed for everyone so there was no discrim-ination.[117]

The expanding nature of civil rights litigation pushed the Nixon solicitors general into a wide variety of employment discrimination cases. There were two significant cases in which Griswold filed *amici* briefs. In *Griggs v. Duke Power,* the solicitor general was invited to participate to state the government's position concerning the use of standardized tests and education requirements that were unrelated to the job, but used to discriminate against blacks. The Justice Department felt that this case provided a weak vehicle for examining the propriety of using employment tests and advised plaintiffs not to appeal the decision. An adverse decision could have limited Title VII law.[118] The objective facts of *Griggs* did not suggest that this case would merit Supreme Court interest. It was a dissent by Court of Appeals Judge Soboloff, the former solicitor general who argued *Brown,* that attracted the Court's attention. He argued that disparate impact was the only means of fully implementing Title VII.[119] The government's brief borrowed heavily from his dissent.

The government's stance "stemmed from an amalgam of litigating precedent, core values, views of the Labor Department and EEOC, and presidential policy." The Department of Justice had begun formulating a position on disparate impact during the Kennedy administration. The EEOC's position on the use of aptitude testing dated back to Johnson's presidency. The refined position and the focus on disparate impact was consistent with Nixon's support for the affirmative action directives of the Philadelphia Plan.

When the case got to the Supreme Court, the solicitor general urged the justices to accept it to review the use of aptitude tests that disqualified a high percentage of blacks and did not predict job performance. The department had, in a series of voting rights cases, developed the position that policies that appeared neutral on their face, but perpetuated the effects of past discrimination were unlawfully discriminatory. Doctrine was transplanted first to desegregation cases and then to *Griggs* and Title VII.

While the government's position was built on prior positions in employment cases and other areas, the eventual brief was an acceleration from the normal progression of cases.[120] The brief argued that such tests do not measure ability, but serve to limit employment and promotion opportunities. The brief maintained that though the policies appeared neutral, they were no different from practices found illegal. The solicitor general urged the Court to defer to EEOC guidelines. Although it was a contested point, the solicitor general maintained that Congress contemplated the use of job-related tests only. The brief argued that a test that accurately predicted success or was related to the skills required to fulfill the job would be allowable, but in this case, that relationship did not exist.[121]

The Court unanimously followed the government's position, holding that selection processes that appear neutral on their face "cannot be maintained if they operate to 'freeze' the status quo of prior discriminatory employment practices."[122] According to William Eskridge: "Although the legal world was stunned by the Supreme Court's unanimous adoption of a disparate impact approach in *Griggs,* careful observers should not have been too surprised by the Court's opinion, which closely followed the analysis suggested by the nation's two most eminent Republican lawyers (Sobeloff and Griswold), the leading civil rights group, and the agency charged with implementing the statute." He added:"*Griggs* represented a policy more vigorous than that which Congress would have wanted in 1971." The committee with gatekeeping power on the issue, the House Education and Labor Committee, was more liberal than the House as a whole, giving it the ability to thwart potential overrides.[123]

Wasby argues that "the Title VII campaign was probably larger in scope than the *Brown* campaign, but it received less attention because it had to compete for attention with many other litigation efforts and did not lead to a single Supreme Court ruling of *Brown's* stature, although *Griggs v. Duke Power Co.* was very important."[124] The decision in *Griggs* "paralleled *Brown* in its importance in its area of law." In both cases the government was invited to participate by the Supreme Court and its response in each case was not neutral or nonpartisan. Rather, the government staked out a firm position favoring civil rights. Each case occurred under Republican presidents and solicitors general. Both decisions were landmarks. Indeed, the extraordinarily broad ruling in *Griggs* "encouraged a whole bunch of cases testing selection devices."[125]

Congress did not override *Griggs,* even though the business community wanted the decision limited or overturned. The political changes of the 1970s, the Court moving to the right as Congress moved to the left, canceled each other out on Title VII issues. The long-term impact of *Griggs* would be consequential. Once it was relatively easy to demonstrate discrimination, via disparate impact, the question of remedies was the next logical issue. The prospects for affirmative action were much brighter after disparate impact became the standard.[126]

In *McDonnell Douglas v. Green,* the solicitor general filed a voluntary *amicus* brief. The government argued for a formula for alleged victims to demonstrate a *prima facie* case for discrimination. Griswold argued that a number of issues dealing with the final determination of the matter were not yet ripe for review and thus, the Court should dismiss the petition for certiorari as improvidently granted.[127] The Court agreed with the solicitor general on the criteria for a *prima facie* case and for employer rebuttal, but went beyond the solicitor general's advice to explore the merits of the claims. The case became the basic framework for burden of proof in employment discrimination cases.[128]

The Nixon administration did not achieve all or most of its litigation goals during the truncated presidency. The administration laid the groundwork for slowing or reversing Court-mandated integration. In employment cases, the EEOC and solicitor general were responsible for a monumental expansion of employee rights, paving the way for the battle over affirmative action and helping define the line between the public and private realms.

Conclusion

I will assess the Nixon and Ford administrations together, but consider the former briefly at this point. The Nixon administration may have wanted its solicitors general to adopt a political perspective, but it was forced by circumstances to move toward the legal end of the continuum. Strategically it was difficult for the administration to retreat at the outset. The Johnson administration had committed the government to a general position and specific positions in pending cases. All new administrations face that. Keeping the same solicitor general constrained the new administration.

The Johnson solicitors general presided over the high watermark for civil rights. In that respect, any successor would appear to retreat and Griswold and Bork did in desegregation. The environment did not favor a wholesale reversal, but as cases got more difficult, involving remedies, northern desegregation, and public-private issues, retreat was possible. In other areas, most notably employment doctrine, the solicitors general exercised activism that rivaled their predecessors. They supported the broad policy positions of the EEOC and CRD.

The goals of the solicitors general were moderated by strategic interaction and rules and norms. Griswold and Bork had to pay attention to a Congress that was relatively liberal and increasingly important because many decisions were based on statutory grounds and a still activist Court that was unsympathetic to significant retreats. The rules and norms, most notably precedent and agency policy, generally supported staying the course. More complicated cases were emerging, suggesting room for retreat.

The Nixon solicitors general were affected by the political and legal realms, but on balance, the latter dominated the former. The administration may have wanted to move more decisively to limit desegregation, but its hand was stayed by doctrinal development. Griswold and Bork filed briefs that were more liberal than might be expected, partially as a response to a Court that was still activist. Griswold freely admitted trying to incorporate some of Nixon's positions in briefs. Bork moderated certain arguments to conform more closely to the political forces. But those arguments were largely shaped by legal considerations. Nixon used political resources to change the legal realm through his Supreme Court appointments.

For the early part of the administration, the solicitor general fulfilled the role of attorney general as law enforcement officer when filing *amici* and tenth justice, trying to help the justices impose consistency on the law when the government was a party. But as desegregation cases came North, and focus turned to remedies, the solicitor general used *amici* briefs to pursue the role of attorney general as policy maker.

Gerald Ford: Continuity in the Short Term

There would be consistency in the goals of the solicitor general in the Ford administration. Strategic interaction with Congress would pose difficulties, given the political fallout from Watergate. The Court was more conservative, but while it generally supported civil rights, it did issue the first negative decisions. Institutional rules and norms did not favor a wholesale retreat. Precedent was still strongly pro-civil rights, but issue evolution was presenting the solicitor general and the Court with increasingly difficult questions.

Executive. Congressman Gerald Ford had a mixed record on civil rights. He supported the Civil Rights Act of 1964 and the Voting Rights Act, but as the Johnson administration wound down and civil rights initiatives were seen as threatening business, Ford opposed open housing initiatives.[129] President Gerald Ford did little more than continue the work of Richard Nixon. He instructed the Justice Department to look for cases that could be used to limit busing.[130] Like Nixon, he introduced legislation to restrict busing. Weakened by the midterm election and the backlash of Watergate, the administration accepted the extension of the Voting Rights Act. In the end, Ford did little of a positive nature to extend civil rights, but he did little harm to existing policy.[131]

The Justice Department was headed by Attorney General Edward Levi, a distinguished legal scholar, who was characterized as a neutral. According to Ford, the Justice Department had the most lasting scars of

Watergate. Levi was a natural choice in the wake of Watergate, though many Republicans were critical of his nonpartisanship, with critics noting that law and politics are so closely related.[132]

The Justice Department did not try to dismantle the machinery for enforcement of civil rights.[133] But there were disputes between the CRD and the solicitor general. According to Brian Landsberg, head of the Appellate Section for Civil Rights, "Stan Pottinger was fairly liberal—pro-integration, busing, affirmative action, bilingual education. Bork was skeptical. There was a great deal of interchange, debates, and discussion. They often needed to bring the attorney general in to settle the disputes." As Bork noted, "Levi and I disagreed with him. The ultimate decision belonged to the Attorney General and, if it was important enough, to the President."[134]

Congress. President Ford paid a major price for Watergate. First, Congress used Nixon's vulnerability to invade executive power, "taking more authority than Congress could handle." Then, in the 1974 elections, "the voters swept aside tradition" while punishing the Republicans.[135] A liberal Congress became even more ideological.[136] Electoral backlash against Republicans brought a huge class of Democratic freshmen to Congress. The bottom line was that Ford was constrained on his initiatives. He was forced to use a veto strategy to protect his goals and limit Congressional policies he opposed.[137] Ford achieved some success running government with one-third plus one in one house of Congress, the margin needed to sustain his veto.

Supreme Court. Ford had only one Supreme Court appointment, John Paul Stevens, thought to be a moderate-conservative.[138] He has been more liberal on the Court to be sure, but he could hardly replace Justice William Douglas, arguably the most liberal justice. Thus, the aggregate liberalism of the Court declined to a twenty-five-year low 45.5.[139] Thus, as the cases were getting more difficult, with affirmative action on the horizon, the Court was increasingly becoming more conservative and approaching a critical mass.

Issue Evolution. The Burger Court did not reverse existing precedents and in some areas, it actually expanded the rulings of its predecessor. Indeed, according to Ronald Kahn "the Burger Court, not the Warren Court, made *Brown v. Board of Education* a reality."[140] Still, as desegregation came North, the Court put brakes on the growth of civil rights. Certainly, part of the reason can be attributed to a more conservative Court, but issue evolution was also responsible. More difficult cases continued to reach the Court's docket, raising questions of *de facto* segregation, spreading to employment and private discrimination and affirmative action.[141] There were now precedents in place that could be used to limit the expansion of civil rights and the solicitor general was increasingly willing to utilize them. But there were constraints on potential retreats, most of the cases involved employment discrimination and the ink on strong positive precedents was still drying.

The Ford Solicitor General

Bork had a remarkably unsuccessful record in civil rights during Ford's tenure. Bork argued eight cases in which the government was a party, five on behalf of civil rights claimants. He lost seven of the cases in which the government was a party. Three of the cases involved employment discrimination and required statutory interpretation. In the *amici* cases, Bork entered on behalf of civil rights claimants in four of six cases. Bork had more success with these six briefs, joining the winning side four times. He was invited to participate in one case.

Bork attempted to follow precedent, even when he disagreed with it. The increasingly conservative Court was willing to depart from precedent and limit the reach of civil rights. A liberal Congress was a counterweight to how far the solicitor general could go to limit precedents or statutory provisions, but the president could veto those initiatives and Ford showed a willingness to wield the veto stamp.

In employment discrimination, Bork argued for broad remedies for victims of discrimination. In *Albemarle Paper Co. v. Moody,* Bork filed an *amicus* brief, arguing that district courts can order back pay. The solicitor general argued that Title VII was not only designed to root out causes of discrimination but to make victims whole again. The government charged that the employment tests were unrelated to job qualifications and had a disparate impact on blacks.[142] The Court agreed, supporting the use of back pay as a remedy for past discrimination and ruling that Congress intended Title VII to deal with the consequences of employment practices, not simply the motivations.[143]

In *Franks v. Bowman Transportation,* the government filed an *amicus* to argue that back pay alone was not sufficient. The OSG supported seniority credit for people denied employment on the basis of race. To deny seniority credit would create permanent disfavor for victims. Back pay or front pay would provide financial compensation, but the government argued that victims could only catch up by having seniority restored as if they had been hired in the first place.[144]

The Court's decision echoed the government's brief. The Court ruled that an award of seniority retroactive to the date of the job application was an appropriate remedy. The Court ruled that Title VII vested broad equitable discretion in the federal courts to order affirmative relief including reinstatement or hiring of employees, back pay, and any additional relief the court deemed appropriate. The Court argued that merely to require the employer to hire the victim would fall short of a "make whole" remedy. Without an award of seniority credit dating from the time when the victim was denied employment, individuals could never gain their rightful places in the hierarchy of seniority that determines the distribution of employment benefits.[145]

The solicitor general stayed the course in *Washington v. Davis,* adopting the role of tenth justice, arguing on the basis of *Griggs* and *Albemarle Paper* that tests employed to choose Washington D.C. police officers disproportionately discriminated against black applicants. The Justice Department had relied on *Griggs* in subsequent cases in drafting the "Uniform Guidelines on Employee Selection Procedures." The solicitor general represented the Civil Service Commission, which had formulated the test, as a party in the case.

The solicitor general's brief was circumspect. It argued that the evidence showed a *prima facie* case of adverse impact on minorities. The brief argued that the evidence was unclear concerning whether the test was job related, which would make it acceptable. If the brief was reluctant to take a firm position on the bottom line, it was clear that the solicitor general was relying on the Title VII decisions.[146]

During oral arguments, Justice Powell raised a different issue: whether the standard in constitutional cases, like this one, should be equivalent to statutory grounds under Title VII. The government argued that the standards should be the same. As Landsberg maintained: "There can be no doubt that the prior strong position of the department in support of plaintiffs in *Griggs* and *Albemarle Paper* influenced the solicitor general to make this response despite its adverse implications for the client agency."[147]

The Court rejected the argument, claiming that there had to be intent to discriminate. The majority ruled that the Court of Appeals erred in resolving the Fifth Amendment issue by applying standards applicable to Title VII cases. The Court ruled that the rigorous statutory standard of Title VII involved a more probing judicial review and less deference to the acts of administrators than is appropriate under the Constitution. In this case, the Court ruled that there was an apparent racial impact, but no discriminatory purpose was claimed. The majority argued that any extension of statutory standards required legislative prescription.[148]

The Court's decision marked an important change in discrimination law. The Court had used the *Keyes* decision to draw a distinction between *de facto* and *de jure* segregation, requiring a demonstration of intent in the former. In employment, while *Griggs* had made disparate impact enough to demonstrate discrimination, *Washington* required disparate treatment or intent, a much more difficult standard to meet.[149] There was a distinction between the constitutional and statutory grounds, but the seeds were sown for the future demise of that distinction. Indeed, the solicitor general shifted its position in the wake of *Washington,* allowing federal agencies to defend against constitutional suits by insisting that alleged victims prove intentional discrimination.[150] Just as the Court transplanted doctrine from one area to another in an effort to expand doctrine, it was using a similar process to contract rights.

Bork argued one major case, *Runyon v. McCrary,* which focused on whether the Civil Rights Act of 1866 extended to private schools that discriminated in their admission policies. The case brought together a number of doctrinal streams. First, it involved private schools, tying it to the public/private cases. Second, because schools were involved, desegregation was a subtext. Third, the case was based on 42 USC 1981, a post–Civil War act that was created as an exercise of Congressional power under the Thirteenth Amendment, like *Jones v. Alfred Mayer.* The precedents from those streams largely moved in the same direction and suggested that the government should argue that these schools were not private. There was also a liberal Congress that could react to a restrictive decision. On the other hand, the administration was unlikely to support a narrow interpretation of what was considered private and the Court was increasingly conservative.

Bork filed a forceful brief that built on two of the three streams. As tenth justice, Bork tried to fill doctrinal gaps, basing part of his argument on the *Sullivan* and *Tillman* precedents. Drawing parallels, Bork argued like the pools, the schools were not strictly private. It was not enough that students who were discriminated against could go to another school, just as it was not enough to go to another pool.[151] The Court had extended *Jones* in a few cases that the OSG had not entered. Bork supported its further extension to private schools.[152] He argued that the schools advertised and created a contractual relationship that was covered under 42 USC 1981. The brief argued that Congress had the power to determine what are badges of servitude and incidents of slavery and to combat them through legislation.[153]

The Court reaffirmed *Jones,* closely following the script laid out by the solicitor general. The Court held that section 1981 prohibited private, commercially operated, nonsectarian schools from denying admission to prospective students because they were black. The Court ruled that racial discrimination practiced by purportedly private schools was a classic violation of section 1981: the parents of minority students sought to enter into a contractual relationship with the schools, but the school did not offer services on an equal basis to white and nonwhite students. Section 1981 constituted a legitimate exercise of Congressional power to enforce the Thirteenth Amendment. The decision was also consistent with the Court's desire to short-circuit attempts to avoid desegregation.[154]

Eskridge cites *Runyon* as the best example of a civil rights decision that suggests the Court adjusted its preferences to reflect those of the sitting Congress, rather than the Congress that enacted the legislation. The decision was "expressly premised upon the Court's belief that Congress in 1971–72 had signaled its approval of the application of *Mayer* to section 1981." In addition Justices Powell and Stevens stated in concurring opinions that they considered *Jones* wrongly decided, but precedent backed by expressions of Congressional preferences compelled them to support this interpretation.[155]

Bork argued two voting rights case during the Ford administration, *Richmond v. United States* and *Beer v. United States.* While the Court had strictly enforced section 5, in these two cases the justices limited the authority of the attorney general. In *Beer,* New Orleans implemented a redistricting plan that changed the districts to run north–south. The government claimed that this had the effect of diminishing black voting strength. Bork tried to transplant the *Griggs* precedent, arguing that the Court should consider the effects of the changes.[156] The argument combined elements of three roles of the solicitor general: tenth justice in filling doctrinal gaps, attorney general as law enforcement officer in protecting the authority of the department, and attorney general as policy maker in pushing the division's priorities.

The Court was not swayed and parted company with the solicitor general, adopting a new interpretation of section 5, distinguishing redistricting from annexation cases. The Court ruled that the new plan did not diminish black voting strength. Thus, the Court was moving to a relative standard of retrogression and vote dilution, rather than an absolute standard. As Abigail Thernstrom noted, "A scheme that provided no black districts when none had existed before would presumably be precleared, although one that provided five when there had been six would not." The decision was modified by the Voting Rights Act of 1982.[157]

Conclusion

The Nixon-Ford solicitors general were constrained by the activities of their predecessors. Under Johnson, the OSG had argued for and received broad interpretations of civil rights legislation. The fruits of that expansion, enhanced power for the attorney general in voting, HEW in school desegregation, and the Justice Department for enforcement, ensured that the government would be an active partner in litigation. In addition, the government now had the power to intervene as a party, increasing the opportunities for acting strategically.

The tenures of Griswold and Bork demonstrate many of the constraints that the solicitor general faces. Griswold tempered his positions in a number of cases to reflect the differences between serving a Democrat and a Republican. Bork had no such conflict; he was a conservative serving conservative presidents. The record shows that Bork filed more briefs that stretched civil rights than restricted them. There were a number of reasons for that: Congress was liberal, especially late in the Ford administration and willing to flex its institutional muscle, many cases involved statutory interpretation, the Court, while more conservative, had not initiated the predicted counterrevolution, and most precedents supported civil rights.

Certainly, Griswold and Bork acted on strategic rather than sincere preferences. The Nixon administration tried to convince the Court to slow desegregation and was rebuffed. Griswold and Bork faced a series of third-generation cases, involving desegregation in the North and remedies like busing. The solicitors general urged the Court to oppose busing and to draw distinctions between *de facto* and *de jure* discrimination with mixed success. Outside school desegregation, Griswold and Bork continued to press for civil rights protection. In cases defining distinctions between public and private, the solicitors general took a view that arguably went beyond the requirements of the Civil Rights Act. They also pushed the frontiers in employment discrimination. Still for the first time, the government opposed the Legal Defense Fund, breaking a three-decade alliance.

Throughout the Nixon administration, there was a visible tension between the legal and political realms. Griswold and Bork were often compelled by judicial and internal office precedent to gravitate toward the legal end of the continuum. During the Ford administration, Bork began to move toward the political end of the spectrum in some areas. Part of it was a function of the changing nature of the legal environment and part because of the increased difficulty of the issues before the Court.

Bork had less success when he took a political stance. Part of this was a function of the institutional environment that the unelected Ford faced and part was due to the policy environment. Ford faced a strong, recalcitrant Congress that might retaliate for a narrow decision. The Court was more conservative, but did not show a willingness to reverse doctrine. The policy environment was not conducive to retreat either.

Many of the cases involved employment and voting rights, areas that the administration generally favored. In those areas, Bork took a more legal perspective and had more success. In his activities, Bork acted more as the attorney general as law enforcement officer in deciding voting rights cases, protecting the authority of the Justice Department. In employment cases, the solicitor general served as the tenth justice, helping the Court fill in some of the doctrinal holes left in the wake of *Griggs*. In busing and desegregation, Bork tried to exert more policy-making influence.

The Nixon and Ford solicitors general had a significant impact on the development of civil rights doctrine. They helped guide the Court through the expansion of employment doctrine and the contraction of desegregation policy as the cases came North. The solicitor general's position on busing was rejected by the Court. Griswold and Bork played a significant role in helping the Court define the line between public and private discrimination. Bork successfully argued for the application of the Thirteenth Amendment to modern civil rights questions. He also tried to transplant the expansive *Griggs* holding to voting rights. The Court rejected that position, but Congress legitimated it by overturning the decision.

JIMMY CARTER: THE DEMOCRATS RETURN

The goals of the solicitor general moved to the left under Jimmy Carter. The problem is that goals are tempered by strategic interaction and institutional rules and norms. The strategic environment and norms posed constraints and opportunities. Congress was fairly liberal. The Court was more conservative and issues were getting more difficult, suggesting retreats could be in the offing. Precedent generally supported civil rights, but prospects for further advances were not encouraging.

Executive. Jimmy Carter demonstrated a two-pronged commitment to civil rights. First, he strengthened the enforcement mechanisms of the CRD and the EEOC. Second, Carter made great strides in diversifying the courts by selecting more women and blacks than all previous presidents combined.[158] "Together," according to Norman Amaker, "these developments reinvigorated the civil rights enforcement effort that had been listless in the Ford years."[159] At the same time, Carter presided in a period when the political climate did not support the extension of civil rights. The Carter presidency, for all its purported goals, was not marked by impressive domestic achievements.[160]

Carter chose Griffin Bell as attorney general. Continued disillusion-ment with Watergate, a theme of the 1976 election, convinced Carter to choose a neutral. Carter tried to depoliticize the Justice Department and exempted Bell, a former judge, from reelection duties. Bell presided over more aggressive enforcement of civil rights and was instrumental in opening up the judicial nomination process.[161] He was also protective of the OSG. After an incident in which he felt that the administration had interfered with the solicitor general, Bell asked the Office of Legal Coun-sel to prepare a memo outlining the solicitor general's relationship to the president and the attorney general.[162] There was also a departure from tra-ditional selection patterns for the assistant attorney general for civil rights. Carter chose Drew Days, a former member of the Legal Defense Fund. Democrats had typically selected individuals who had not been associated with the civil rights movement to avoid southern opposition.

Congress. Carter had the benefit of a Democratic Congress, but the gulf between the executive and legislative parties was large enough to en-sure that relations would not be smooth. Light argues that Carter was un-prepared for the rigors of the presidency, thus ceding agenda leadership to Congress.[163] Institutional reform had decentralized Congress, making any president's job more difficult. In the wake of Watergate, the presi-dency was weaker and Congressional power was more diffuse. Carter could not deal with these institutional realities.[164] Overall, the Stimson-MacKuen-Erikson scores show that Congress was relatively liberal, but the Democratic majorities displayed "incoherence and divisiveness."[165] Its reluctance to expand civil rights was a signal to the Court that Con-gress might not interfere with narrow decisions.

Supreme Court. Carter was the first president since Andrew Johnson to serve without having the opportunity to appoint a justice. Even James Garfield who served only six months had the chance to nominate a justice. Thus, although Carter returned the Democrats to power and was willing to extend civil rights, he was facing a Court that was retrenching (a score of 45.5, the most conservative since 1952).[166] The Court would pose problems for an administration interested in pushing liberal posi-tions.

Issue Evolution. Two decades of almost exclusively positive civil rights decisions had built an array of precedents, but there were exceptions. The Nixon-Ford solicitors general argued for limits on existing precedents and, occasionally, the Court agreed. With a conservative Court in place and increasingly difficult cases on its docket, opportunities for retreat were present. Still, the administration felt the judicial environment was propitious enough to make litigation part of its civil rights strategy.[167] Issue evolution was potentially a major factor as the CRD pushed harder. The administration was more aggressive in pursuing voting rights cases and reinstituting desegregation cases. *Griggs* spawned more employment cases and created the conditions for affirmative action. Thus, the administration was bringing more difficult cases in a less favorable institutional environment.

The Carter Solicitor General

The return of a Democratic administration to the Justice Department was reflected in the priorities of Solicitor General Wade McCree, a former judge. The environment had changed as Figure 4-3 shows. The president and Congress supported civil rights. For the first time since the Truman administration, the Court was less sympathetic to civil rights. Precedent was still favorable, but there were exceptions for the first time. Issue evolution was bringing increasingly difficult cases, complicating McCree's task.

McCree and Acting Solicitor General Friedman, who ran the office until McCree was confirmed, participated in twenty-six civil rights cases and in each case, the OSG supported the civil rights claimant. Friedman was involved in four cases, two in which the government was a party, one

---

FIGURE 4-3
ENVIRONMENTAL CONSTRAINTS ON THE SOLICITOR GENERAL:
CARTER ADMINISTRATION

SG`

	SGc	SGp		SGw	
Liberal———————————————————————————————Conservative
	Precedent	Congress	President	Supreme Court	

SGp: Position Solicitor General would adopt if doing the president's bidding
SGw: Position Solicitor General would adopt if winning was the sole goal
SGc: Position Solicitor General would adopt to avoid Congressional response
SG`: Actual position the Solicitor General adopted

involving voting rights and one reapportionment, and two desegregation cases as *amicus curiae*. All four had begun during the Ford administration. In one desegregation case, the government changed sides, in the other it changed emphasis. McCree argued seven cases in which the government was a party. He participated in fourteen cases as a voluntary *amicus curiae* and was invited to participate in one case. Of the twenty-two cases he was involved with, there were ten employment discrimination, one housing, one criminal procedure, three voting rights, and three desegregation cases. McCree is best remembered for the first three Supreme Court cases addressing affirmative action.

McCree and Friedman were successful in eighteen of the twenty-six cases. They were successful in seven of the nine cases in which the government was a party and backed the winning side in ten of the sixteen cases in which they filed *amici* briefs. In the most important cases involving affirmative action, voting, and desegregation, McCree was on the winning side in eight of nine.

Most of the ten employment discrimination cases involved statutory interpretation and filling gaps in existing policy. With a Democratic Congress in place, it was rational for the solicitor general to seek a broad interpretation of legislation and that was typically the office's position. Even though the Court was conservative, it had expanded precedents in this area. The solicitor general appeared to play the role as tenth justice, helping the Court fill doctrinal holes left in the wake of *McDonnell Douglas.*

Despite eight years of Republican policies directed at limiting remedies for school segregation, Bell announced that the administration would not reverse the government's position on busing. But the division viewed consistency more broadly: the government's position had been to comply with precedents. Thus, the administration did not explicitly break from its predecessor's position, but "brought a new perspective to the facts and a more expansive view of how the legal standard should apply."[168]

In *Dayton v. Brinkman* and *Columbus v. Penick,* the solicitor general argued that Columbus and Dayton had long-established dual systems and had done little to dismantle them. Across a range of activities that included teacher assignment, location of schools, and creation of attendance zones, the cities "made the black schools blacker and the white schools whiter."[169] Later neutral policies only froze old patterns of segregation. The government argued that because the extent of the violation was systemwide, the remedy had to be systemwide as well.

The solicitor general's brief was virtually a blueprint for the Court's opinion. The Court's retreat in desegregation policy had been temporarily stayed. While the decision seemed out of line with other northern cases, segregation in Columbus and Dayton had clear *de jure* elements, justifying the remedy.

The government argued three cases under the Voting Rights Act of 1965. The Court had begun to retreat on voting rights issues. Still, Mc-Cree opted for a broad interpretation and was successful in two of the three cases. In *City of Mobile v. Bolden,* plaintiffs argued that changes in procedures had the effect of diluting black voting strength. The solicitor general filed an *amicus* brief, arguing that there was intent to discriminate behind the change in the electoral system. This was narrower than the argument of the NAACP that purposeful intent need not be demonstrated to find discrimination. In other words, the litigants were arguing that disparate impact was sufficient, as in employment discrimination. The government urged the Court to adopt this revised, more forgiving definition by arguing that disparate impact was a sign of discriminatory intent.[170]

The Court concluded that the Voting Rights Act of 1965 pertained only to intentional discrimination, abandoning past interpretations, which did not require intent.[171] In addition, the Court rejected the solicitor general's suggestions for proof of intent. After initially extending the Voting Rights Act to cover minority vote dilution, the Court made it more difficult to provide a remedy for such dilution. A plurality for the badly divided Court held that the Fifteenth Amendment prohibited only formal barriers to voting, not dilution of voting strength. The decision "gravely damaged section 2."[172]

The vote dilution cases changed the focus of litigation from the right to vote to the right to representation. Jurisdictions that sought to limit black participation could move from denying them the right to vote to "more sophisticated schemes developed to dilute the impact of their voting strength." The *Bolden* intent standard made it almost impossible for plaintiffs to challenge discriminatory electoral systems. The decision galvanized civil rights groups, who viewed it as catastrophic. They marshaled their resources for a battle on Capitol Hill to construct a "statutory bypass around it."[173] The lobbying campaign was designed to replace the intent standard with an effects or result standard.

In the end, Congress would grant the NAACP what the Court did not, extending the Voting Rights Act to cover disparate impact.[174] Congress revised section 2, dictating a results standard in dilution cases. Instead of extending the Voting Rights Act for five or seven years, as in 1970 and 1975, respectively, Congress extended the provisions for twenty-five years. In *Rogers v. Lodge,* which was announced two days after President Reagan signed the extension into law, the Court retreated from the intent standard of *Bolden*.[175]

The legacy of McCree's tenure is largely defined by the affirmative action cases. The central case was *Board of Regents of the University of California v. Bakke,* which symbolized the pressures that can affect the office. Carter essentially decided that the government would enter the case.[176] He publicly announced that the secretary of HEW, Joseph Califano, and Attorney General Bell would prepare the government's position. The initial brief, produced in the Justice Department, argued that the university's plan was unconstitutional and that Bakke should be admitted.[177] According to Landsberg, "McCree had reservations about affirmative action programs and how to approach them."[178] He supported general principles of affirmative action, but opposed the California plan as a quota.[179] Substantively, McCree was set to argue that a race-based plan, even a remedy, must meet the high standards of strict scrutiny. Califano and proponents of affirmative action tried to influence the president and restructure the brief. Califano expressed concern that two holdovers in the OSG from the Nixon administration controlled the early formulation of the brief.[180] The Congressional Black Caucus notified Carter that it attached the same significance to *Bakke* as to *Brown*.[181]

Given the respect the Court holds for the solicitor general, such an initial brief was bound to be influential. Part of the reason that the solicitor general does not get involved in early cases is that positions have not been developed. The solicitor general can wait until the Court has set boundaries and then help construct the emerging doctrine. There are practical considerations, as well, in waiting to take a position. The administration was sharply split over affirmative action.[182] Had the Court staked out a position, it may not have been easier to come to a consensus over these issues, but it would have placed constraints on available alternatives. It would have provided doctrinal cover for proponents of a position proximate to the Court's. McCree understood the influence the decision would have, but was sensitive to the limitations of the case. Without existing doctrine, the justices would rely on the facts of the case and they were not particularly favorable in McCree's view. Thus, he wanted to ask the Court to tread lightly and remand the case, rather than make a sweeping pronouncement. This would eventually be the government's position.

Battle lines were drawn over broader notions of affirmative action. But underlying the conflict was the tension over what is law and what is politics.[183] McCree wanted to argue as tenth justice, while others wanted him to play the role of attorney general as policy maker. Bell felt that the White House staff was trying to extend its influence. He had no doubt that if the staff had its way, "every major issue that naturally fell to the Justice Department would be considered a policy issue rather than a legal matter." Califano took a different position: "The Justice Department should no more have exclusive rights to formulate positions on seminal constitutional law than the Treasury Department has to prepare tax legislation or formulate economic policy, without broad involvement of the interested government agencies."[184]

Bell instructed McCree and Days to develop the government's position. In formulating the policy, Bell had confrontations with the White House over the appropriate scope of the brief. Vice President Walter Mondale and the president's staff favored a sweeping position supporting affirmative action. Mondale and Califano prevailed on Carter to modify the brief. Carter instructed Bell to order McCree to rewrite the brief.[185] Bell tried his best to insulate the solicitor general. McCree said that he never received, either directly or indirectly, a statement that the White House wanted him to adopt a certain position. Rather, Bell would synthesize the suggestions and carry them to McCree without disclosing their source. Eventually, Bell provided McCree with a list of the principles that the government should advocate in the case.[186]

The eventual product was a brief supporting affirmative action, but opposing rigid quotas.[187] In the ultimate brief, the government supported neither the university nor Bakke. The brief rejected the notion of strict scrutiny or a standard of presumptive unconstitutionality and distinguished between quotas and goals. The Court's narrow 5-4 decision reflected the divisions in the administration and vindicated the moderate position the government adopted. Had the government argued the position urged by Califano,[188] the chances of holding Powell's decisive vote would have diminished. Indeed, the final decision looked to Bell a lot like the first brief McCree had written, the one that touched off the firestorm.[189] For shifting majorities, the Court ruled that Bakke should be admitted, that the university's plan was an impermissible quota that violated Title VI, that affirmative action plans were not per se unconstitutional, and that race conscious plans should meet the standard of strict scrutiny, but that if the government had a compelling interest in adopting an affirmative action plan, it could outweigh the heavy constitutional burden.[190]

The decision opened the door to other affirmative action cases. *United Steelworkers v. Weber* involved a voluntary consent decree between a company and a union. The agreement included a plan that granted preferences to black employees over whites with more seniority in admission to crafttraining programs until the percentage of black craftworkers in a plant was commensurate with the percentage of blacks in the labor force. Brian Weber challenged the program as a violation of Title VII. The Court of Appeals had found the plan suspect, claiming that such programs were permissible only if there was a clear showing of past discrimination.

In its petition for a writ of certiorari, the government argued that upholding this ruling would chill voluntary affirmative action programs.[191] The solicitor general argued that Title VII permitted affirmative remedial action by employer and union where the union could show *prima facie* discrimination.[192] Attorneys for Weber argued that actual disparate treatment must be proved to justify the affirmative action program. The government argued that a demonstration of disparate impact was sufficient, a standard that would be much easier to meet. The government maintained that its position was structured by the Court's employment decisions, most notably *Griggs, Albemarle,* and *Franks,* which stood for the principle that victims of alleged discrimination could receive seniority credit to redress an injustice. Thus, the solicitor general reasoned that affirmative action, particularly if it was voluntary, was an appropriate remedy. Further, the solicitor general conceded that the Court may have pushed Title VII beyond its original intent, but Congress had the opportunity to overturn the decisions or tighten Title VII and did not do so. If anything, the Equal Employment Opportunity Act of 1972 revised Title VII to bring it in line with expansive Court decisions.[193] The Court agreed with the solicitor general's position that Title VII prohibitions against racial discrimination did not condemn all private, voluntary affirmative action plans.

Eskridge argues that *Weber* is another example of a response to the sitting Congress, rather than the one that passed Title VII. While the justices conceded that the decision could not be squared with the original intent of Title VII, a number of justices "were sensitive to the pressures for affirmative action created by *Griggs* and to the approval of *Griggs* voiced by the gatekeeping committees in 1971. For this reason, a Court critical of affirmative action in constitutional cases interpreted the Civil Rights Act of 1964 to allow a broader range of preferential programs than one would expect." Apparently, the solicitor general found similar distinctions, arguing for a broad view of affirmative action in *Weber,* after offering a narrower view in *Bakke.*

In Eskridge's view, the Burger Court made more conservative decisions in constitutional cases, where there was little chance of an override than in analogous cases of statutory interpretation. "[T]he Court seems, perhaps unconsciously, to have molded its preferences in statutory cases (but not so much in constitutional cases) to accommodate the more liberal preferences of Congress and the President in the late 1970s."[194] This was similar to the relationship between *Griggs,* a statutory decision acknowledging disparate effect, and *Washington v. Davis,* a constitutional decision, requiring intent or disparate treatment.

In *Fullilove v. Klutznick,* McCree had political cover, supporting policy that had provided for assistance to minority businesses. The Public Works Employment Act of 1977 established Minority Business Enterprises (MBE) to help minority contractors obtain federal contracts. The act set aside 10 percent of the money for federal contracts to go to minority-owned business. That policy was justified on disparate impact grounds.[195] Nonminority contractors sued, claiming MBE provisions violated Title VII and the Fifth Amendment.[196] They argued that any race-based law, whether harmful or benign, must meet the standard of strict scrutiny. Under that formula, such laws must be struck down unless they serve a compelling governmental interest.

The solicitor general argued that the MBE was an appropriate remedy for an intractable social and economic problem. McCree urged deference to the Congressional policy. The government denied that the remedy was a violation of the Fifth Amendment. The brief maintained that Congress had broad authority through its spending power and under the Thirteenth and Fourteenth Amendments. In addition, the solicitor general argued that many statutes, including the Civil Rights Act and the Voting Rights Act took race into account. These measures had failed to solve this particular problem, so the MBE was designed. To answer claims that the MBE violated Title VI, the brief stated: "There is no inherent inconsistency between a requirement that contracting be done without discriminatory consideration of race and a requirement that every good faith effort be used to achieve minority participation pursuant to legislative mandate in grant funding."[197]

The Court agreed with the solicitor general. The Court ruled that Congress' use of racial criteria as a condition attached to a federal grant was a valid means of accomplishing its objectives, and the MBE provision did not violate the equal protection component of the Due Process Clause of the Fifth Amendment. To achieve the goal of equality of economic opportunity, Congress had latitude to try techniques such as limited use of racial criteria to accomplish remedial objectives, especially in programs where voluntary cooperation is induced by placing conditions on federal expenditures. The Court held that the MBE program was not constitutionally defective because it might limit opportunities for non-minority firms who were innocent of prior discrimination. When creating a limited and properly tailored remedy to cure the effects of past discrimination, "a sharing of the burden" by innocent parties was not impermissible.[198]

Conclusion

While every administration wrestles with legal and political perspectives, the Carter administration went through a more visible conflict than most. There was an institutional change that may have influenced the eventual balance. Wade McCree was the first of a number of solicitors general who did not have the independent reputation to insulate the office. The president was a supporter of civil rights, but relatively moderate. The CRD was aggressive in trying to recoup some of the losses from the Republican administrations. The Justice Department tried to insulate the solicitor general from the political forces. Congress was relatively liberal and would serve as a counterbalance to the more conservative Court in statutory decisions. There was pressure from civil rights groups to counter retreats after eight years of Republican rule.

The policy environment provided a mixed range of factors for the solicitor general to consider. Employment cases arose in the context of past decisions and did not raise new issues. The solicitor general could provide a legal response and serve the function of the tenth justice and the attorney general as law enforcement officer. In desegregation, the solicitor general was more aggressive and political. In these cases, the solicitor general was much closer to the attorney general as policy maker. The affirmative action cases created contentious battles between those arguing from a legal perspective and those who supported a more political position.

To return to the central question: what impact did McCree have on the development of civil rights? The solicitor general supported civil rights, but argued more centrist positions. McCree wanted to establish some consistency in the desegregation decisions. That was a problem because the northern *de facto* precedents were unfavorable. McCree also tried to expand voting rights, with mixed success. The Court had begun to retreat during the previous administration, but McCree shouldered forward with expansive arguments. The solicitor general suffered one consequential loss that was overturned by Congress. With the blessing of the president and Justice Department and without opposition from Congress, McCree urged broader extensions in the area of employment discrimination. The solicitor general continued to play an important role in building doctrine.

McCree's tenure is best remembered for legitimating affirmative action, a logical extension of employment doctrine. The Court's decisions, particularly in *Bakke,* closely paralleled the solicitor general's arguments. The conflict over construction of the *Bakke* brief was the quintessential example of the legal/political struggle. McCree, who had doubts about affirmative action, was prepared to argue a narrow position. The broad interpretation in *Weber* continued the process of seeking expansive readings of the Civil Rights Act. While the Court was not overly conducive to broad remedies, precedents favorable to civil rights constrained the justices. *Griggs,* in particular, set the context for affirmative action. Given the forces in the solicitor general's environment, it was not surprising that the OSG adopted positions supporting extensions of civil rights.

The affirmative action cases represented a departure from previous cases and emblematic of their difficulty was the division in the administration about the position the government should adopt. Because Mc-Cree was relatively unknown, he lacked the independent stature that most of his predecessors possessed. The interference that the solicitor general faced prompted Bell to commission a memorandum from the Office of Legal Counsel concerning the role of the solicitor general. The memo reflected the delicate balance between law and politics and the place of the solicitor general within the shifting constraints. The memo stated that legally the solicitor general is responsible to the attorney general, but the independence of the office must be jealously guarded. In politically sensitive cases, the attorney general needs to shield the solicitor general. To preserve the independence of the office, the solicitor general should decide when to seek the advice of the president and the attorney general.[199] In the wake of *Bakke,* the memo seemed to be a necessary reminder. As Ronald Reagan took office, the memo seemed to assume an ironic tone.

CONCLUSION: THE SOLICITOR GENERAL IN THE ADMINISTRATIVE PHASE

As in the Truman administration, the Johnson solicitors general moved forcefully on their sincere preferences and presided over significant advances in civil rights. This created the context that dominated civil rights litigation for the next fifteen years and constrained Republican solicitors general. The confluence of factors meant that the political and legal forces were in alignment for Cox and Marshall. Subsequent solicitors general who served during the administrative phase faced a number of constraints, had to sacrifice sincere preferences, and opted to move toward the legal end of the continuum.

The litigation phase was marked by the early stages of civil rights policy. During the transition to the administrative phase, more subareas, most notably employment law, began to emerge. *Green* ended one stage of desegregation policy. Questions of remedies, like busing and northern *de facto* segregation, spawned subsequent generations of development. The passage of the Civil Rights Act took questions of public/private discrimination to the next stage. In *South Carolina v. Katzenbach,* voting rights doctrine moved through the early stages in one case. Questions of vote dilution ushered in a second generation of voting cases.

The administrative phase formally introduced Congress to civil rights policy construction. The passage of the Civil Rights Act and Voting Rights Act had a dramatic effect on the Court and the solicitor general. Taking advantage of the policy window that Congress had opened, the solicitor general proposed and the Court supported a broad conceptualization of the Civil Rights Act and a linkage between the current act and Reconstruction era measures. The solicitor general treated the provisions of the Civil Rights Act and Voting Rights Act as a floor rather than a ceiling. The Court supported most of those extensions. The impact of Congress could be seen in expansive statutory decisions like *Griggs* and *Weber.* For its part, Congress could have overturned or threatened Court decisions that were too broad, but its silence was considered a signal of its assent.

The administrative phase saw a broader range of activities for the solicitor general. Large Congressional majorities passed strong legislation to empower the executive branch to protect civil rights. The president was committed to advancing civil rights. The Supreme Court reached its liberal zenith. The confluence of these factors made the job of the solicitor general relatively easy and Cox and Marshall took advantage. For the first time, they had the legislative authority to file cases and they sought to enlarge the scope of authority Congress had provided. With the external factors in alignment, the role of the solicitor general changed perceptibly. The solicitor general became more of a facilitator, following the recommendations of the CRD and pushing the envelope.

As the Vietnam War intensified and claimed the Johnson presidency as a casualty, public opinion and Congress turned against further civil rights programs. Nixon began the process of transforming the Court as desegregation cases moved North and involved more controversial remedies. Conditions appeared ripe for a retreat by the solicitors general. For the first time a solicitor general opposed a civil rights group before the Supreme Court. That retreat was predicated on issue evolution and complexity. Strategically, it would have been difficult to break with policies that the office and the division had constructed for a generation and ask the Court to reverse past precedents.

The prevailing judicial context, the preferred position doctrine, had been well-established, even if the emerging Burger Court was less inclined to extend its boundaries. Thus, a solicitor general who might want to reverse or limit existing precedents was facing a jurisprudential and policy context that was stacked against his interests. The success of the solicitor general during the litigation and early administrative phases had a downside: it expanded the terrain of civil rights and made it vulnerable if a hostile Court or a solicitor general interested in curbing its growth was appointed.

Under the surface, however, changes were beginning to develop. As cases got more difficult and the Court got more conservative, the justices began to limit civil rights. The Warren and Burger Courts had stretched the provisions of the Civil Rights Act and Voting Rights Act beyond the original intent in employment and voting. The Court countenanced affirmative action and voting dilution. With the blessing of the solicitor general, the Court changed the requirement that individuals prove intent to discriminate to the mere existence of disparate effects in employment and voting. Over the protests of the solicitor general, the Court retreated on disparate impact. This would trigger Congressional reaction and open the door for the Reagan administration to redefine civil rights issues. Maybe most significantly, the personality of the solicitor general changed. McCree followed well-known independent solicitors general like Cox, Marshall, Griswold, and Bork. As issues reached the later stages and the political stakes were raised, the OSG would increasingly be pressured. It would be harder for anonymous solicitors general to buck this rising tide.

CHAPTER 5

The Solicitor General in the Redefinition Phase

1981–2000

REDEFINING ISSUES IS one of the most difficult tasks in American politics. Issues are largely path dependent. They take on a certain tone and do not normally deviate. The first three Republican successors to Franklin Roosevelt did not try to reverse the New Deal or the context of American politics. Ronald Reagan was willing to buck the odds. In civil rights, the Reagan administration tried to redefine the central questions. Issue evolution had pushed affirmative action to the center of the Court's concerns. The administration drew a line in the sand on the issue, but its policies did not stop there. The administration made attempts to reverse or limit other precedents. Years of Republican rule made the Court a more favorable forum for possible redefinition.

Redefining issues is particularly difficult for the solicitor general. Part of the role of the solicitor general is to help the Court establish doctrinal equilibrium across issue areas. Yet, the redefinition phase entails the opposite: trying to get the Court to revisit and reverse existing precedents. In these circumstances, the solicitor general must balance the demands of competing masters. The administration can tip the balance by packing the Court. The litigation strategy was critical for the Reagan administration because of divided government.

If the administration did not succeed in getting many issues redefined, it helped change the context for decision making. The Bush administration was the one to profit, continuing the policies of its predecessors. The Clinton administration wanted to return to pre-Reagan interpretations, but found its task complicated by recent reversals. The solicitors general largely followed the lead of the presidents who appointed them, but their strategies were confounded by the aggressive stances that Congress adopted to reverse Court decisions.

Table 5-1 shows the support for civil rights claimants and success on the merits for each administration during the redefinition phase. The table breaks down support and success by the form of participation. The remainder of the chapter examines the most important cases in the Reagan, Bush, and Clinton administrations.

RONALD REAGAN: THE ATTACK ON AFFIRMATIVE ACTION

Decision making by the solicitor general is a function of his goals, tempered by strategic interaction and the impact of institutions. The goals of the Reagan solicitors general were clear: they sought to further the administration's agenda. Their ability to achieve those goals was dependent on the other actors in their environment. Divided government posed constraints. Congress was increasingly aggressive in protecting civil rights. The Supreme Court was increasingly sympathetic to the administration. Institutional norms and rules were not operating in the administration's favor. Precedent was not generally supportive, agency positions supporting civil rights had been long established, and previous solicitors general had argued in favor of civil rights for a generation. In effect, the Reagan administration was asking its solicitors general to

TABLE 5-1

SOLICITOR GENERAL'S SUPPORT FOR CIVIL RIGHTS AND SUCCESS
BY TYPE OF PARTICIPATION DURING THE REDEFINITION PHASE

Support for Civil Rights
Type of Participation

	Party		Invited		*Amicus*		Total	
President	*Pro*	*Con*	*Pro*	*Con*	*Pro*	*Con*	*Pro*	*Con*
Reagan	9	5	2	3	9	8	20	16
Bush	3	1	0	0	4	3	7	4
Clinton	9	1	2	0	6	0	17	1

Success on the Merits
Type of Participation

	Party		Invited		*Amicus*		Total	
President	*Won*	*Lost*	*Won*	*Lost*	*Won*	*Lost*	*Won*	*Lost*
Reagan	11	3	3	2	10	7	24	12
Bush	2	2	0	0	5	2	7	4
Clinton	4	6	1	1	4	2	9	9

assume the task of destabilizing the law. The administration tried to re-structure these norms and its environment. Part of that entailed insti-tutional reorganization: adding a political appointee to the OSG and creating new mechanisms to further its agenda.

Executive. Ronald Reagan presided over the politics of reconstruc-tion.[1] One of the most visible targets was civil rights. Rather than cycli-cal patterns of expansion and decline caused by issue evolution, this rep-resented a fundamental change in policy. If the expansion of civil rights was based on policy spillovers across a variety of areas, retreat followed a similar pattern. The administration attempted to limit desegregation and housing initiatives, attacked affirmative action passionately, and opposed the extension of the Voting Rights Act.[2] Like Johnson, the Reagan ad-ministration was animated by its civil rights policies, but in the opposite direction.[3]

Reagan wanted to reverse trends by redefining the terms of the debate.[4] Abortion changed from the rights of women to the rights of the unborn. Affirmative action was now defined as reverse discrimina-tion. Policies were dominated by the premise that individuals should be treated as individuals, rather than as members of a group.[5] Remedies needed to be narrow and strictly tailored. Affirmative action was wrong because it used discrimination to remedy discrimination. The notions of a colorblind Constitution and the provisions of the Civil Rights Act were used by liberals to justify desegregation. Now they were employed by conservatives attempting to eradicate affirmative action.[6] Traditional civil rights advocates, defending existing definitions, argued that the ad-ministration had launched a frontal assault on civil rights.

The task of redefining civil rights was difficult, given entrenched defi-nitions, active civil rights groups, and precedents. The administration was accused of turning back the clock on existing rights. According to W. Bradford Reynolds, the head of the CRD and the most visible target of criticism: "I felt a great deal of frustration at being unable to communi-cate what we were trying to achieve. . . . We argued strenuously from the beginning. . . . We needed to hone the arguments in ways that were care-ful and forceful. Early, it was more important to say it and say it carefully."

As issues and fact situations in individual cases got more difficult, the administration could have attempted to distinguish the case of the mo-ment from existing precedents. But Reynolds knew that the conse-quence of such a strategy was to lend support to the precedent that the administration would prefer to undermine. Rather, broader arguments would be advanced to reconfigure the underlying theory the Court used in deciding civil rights cases.[7]

Most civil rights initiatives came from a Justice Department headed by William French Smith and Edwin Meese. Smith and Meese forcefully propounded a new theory of jurisprudence and a revised view of the appropriate role of the judiciary, favoring judicial restraint.[8] The CRD accrued significant power under Smith and Meese. The division traditionally pursued a course of incremental progressive and nonpolitical law enforcement regardless of administration. As Joel Selig, who served in the CRD, noted: "The Division's preference has always been for the middle ground; its approach has been neither maximalist as advanced by more militant civil rights advocates, nor minimalist as advanced by those committed to the narrowest possible interpretation of the civil rights laws. As a result, Division attorneys rightly consider themselves in a position to criticize approaches that partake of either extreme."[9] Under Reagan, the division was charged with a radical departure from this tradition. The authority of the division was strengthened when the administration weakened the authority of the EEOC, a potential rival.

Opponents charged that Reynolds led "the Reagan Administration's assault on civil rights."[10] Reynolds reversed past Justice Department policies, opposed Supreme Court precedents, fought further school integration, argued for narrow interpretations of statutes, and reversed voting rights policies.[11] There were charges that Reynolds attempted to pressure the solicitors general into carrying the administration's agenda cases before the justices.[12]

Reagan also sought to pack the federal courts with conservatives faithful to his legal goals.[13] Control of the lower courts carried a number of benefits. First, most cases end in the lower courts. Second, those cases heading for the Supreme Court get shaped in the lower courts. Lawyers sympathetic to the administration could begin to fashion cases before conservative federal judges, preparing briefs to move into the appellate courts.

The results provided opportunities for the OSG. According to Reynolds, "The greatest accomplishment of the Department of Justice and the Administration was the judicial appointments at all levels. There was a real sea change . . . in judicial attitudes beginning in the second term. The appointments explain in large measure how we were able to move the Administration's agenda."[14]

Congress. The conservative Court and administration faced a liberal House wary of their activities. Republicans controlled the Senate for Reagan's first term, but never got a majority in the House. Still, control of one house was enough to ensure that Reagan's veto could be sustained and attempts to overturn conservative Supreme Court decisions could normally be thwarted.[15] The Stimson-MacKuen-Erickson measures show that ideologically, the Senate in 1981–86 was the most conservative of the 1956–90 period.[16]

Despite presidential attempts to undermine it, Congress strengthened the Voting Rights Act in 1982. The administration opposed the extension of the act because it contained a provision that forbade state action, which had the effect of diluting minority representation. This looked like disparate impact, a target of the administration's litigation strategy in employment cases. The administration's ultimate strategy was not to oppose extension of the act, but to weaken its enforcement.[17] Once Democrats took back the Senate, Congress was willing to reverse the Court and presidential priorities and did so with the Civil Rights Restoration Act (1988).[18]

Supreme Court. One of the most telling editorial cartoons of the 1984 campaign showed nine justices who looked exactly like Ronald Reagan sitting on the Supreme Court bench chanting "forty more years."[19] Like Nixon, Reagan had the opportunity to remake the Court in his own image. Reagan appointed three new justices and promoted Rehnquist to chief justice. The Baum adjusted scores showed the lowest support for civil liberties (44.1) in three decades. With Reagan facing a recalcitrant House, the ideological composition of the Court suggested that this was the most favorable venue for his social agenda.[20]

More importantly, perhaps, the Court was beginning to reconfigure its institutional role, rejecting the preferred position doctrine. The "new" philosophy, a return to past doctrine, advocates attention to the intent of the framers of the Constitution and a stricter construction of the document. In practical terms, a majority desires to balance individual rights and competing social interests on a more equal footing than the preferred position doctrine. This theory is complemented by a willingness to defer to the elected branches in civil liberties and civil rights, thus rejecting the liberalism that had guided judicial policy making.[21] This new role was much more conducive to the administration than the preferred position doctrine.

Issue Evolution. The administration had a number of factors in its favor as it attempted to recast civil rights policy. Many of the cases presented difficult issues for the increasingly conservative Court. Despite some reversals, though, existing civil rights precedent was not conducive to the wholesale changes the administration was seeking. Affirmative action, the primary object of the administration's scorn, was entrenched.[22] The Burger and Rehnquist Courts largely adhered to precedent and did not fully join the war the administration was waging. In fact, in significant ways, the Burger Court made the task more difficult by expanding the definitions of gender discrimination, casting the net of equal protection more broadly, and insulating civil rights precedents.[23]

The Reagan Solicitors General. The Court was certainly the most favorable institutional environment for the administration. According to David Rose of the employment section of the CRD, "The Reaganauts made a conscious effort to use the courts as in the sixties. Courts would lead the way. It was better than using Congress or administrative regulations. The Administration grabbed hold of the appellate process in the OSG and in the Appellate Section. They tried to control the flow of litigation."[24]

The relationship between political appointees and staff attorneys in the OSG and the CRD was noteworthy. For decades, the office and the CRD supported a broad view of civil rights. The civil rights decisions created supportive precedents that Reagan solicitors general tried to limit or undermine. This caused problems for staff attorneys who had helped establish and buttress those precedents. According to Lincoln Caplan, staff attorneys viewed the political appointees as "social revolutionaries with no regard for the law," while the Reagan appointees viewed the careerists as "intransigent holdovers."

The Justice Department tried to reassign some of the division's attorneys because of a fear that they would undermine its agenda. There were charges that the OSG had become politicized and a number of attorneys left the office.[25] Reynolds claimed that "for a number of years, we rewrote briefs in the front office. We reviewed every brief. Many late nights we reworked and rewrote the briefs. The crew in the office was pretty darn good attorneys. . . . They did not sabotage the briefs. At the same time, the briefs were not written with passion or enthusiasm. I edited them to put heart into them. It was not their fault—they did not believe in our position, but they were professionals."[26]

Ideologically, Rex Lee and Charles Fried reflected the administration they served.[27] Lee and Fried were involved in thirty-six civil rights cases. In fifteen of those cases, Lee and Fried filed briefs or argued for the civil rights claimant. In the other twenty-one cases, they argued against the civil rights claimant. They were successful in twenty-three of the thirty-six cases. The data lend credence to the argument that Fried pushed a more conservative agenda than his predecessor. Lee filed briefs or argued eleven cases in favor of civil rights and ten against. Fried argued just four cases for the civil rights claimant, while he opposed those claimants in eleven cases. This translated to different levels of success: Lee won fifteen of his twenty-one civil rights cases, while Fried won just eight of his fifteen cases.

Figure 5-1 shows the array of forces that faced Rex Lee during Reagan's first term. The president, Department of Justice, and the CRD had moved decisively to the right. The House was liberal, but a Republican majority in the Senate produced the potential for stalemate. The Court was shifting to the right, but was still moderate on civil rights. Issue evolution provided opportunities and constraints. In northern desegregation cases, the Court had limited remedies. In constitutional disputes, the Court was less inclined to support a broad interpretation of civil rights, providing an open window for the administration. On the other hand, the administration was constrained by sweeping employment decisions and precedents recognizing affirmative action.

There were differences between the positions taken by Lee based on the type of the participation. In the nine cases in which the government was a party, Lee filed three cases on behalf of civil rights and six against. In ten voluntary *amici* briefs, Lee did the opposite, filing six briefs in favor of the civil rights claimant and four opposed. The other two cases handled during Lee's tenure involved invitations from the Court.

In some cases, Lee was obligated to support legislation the administration probably opposed. The majority of the cases in which the Lee supported civil rights occurred in cases involving the authority of the EEOC and the attorney general. Lee had a mixed record on employment discrimination and did not actively pursue EEOC cases.[28]

Figure 5-1
Environmental Constraints on the Solicitor General: First Term Reagan Administration

$$SG`$$

	SGc	SGw	SGp
Liberal———————————————————————————Conservative			
	Precedent	Congress	Supreme President Court

SGp: Position Solicitor General would adopt if doing the president's bidding
SGw: Position Solicitor General would adopt if winning was the sole goal
SGc: Position Solicitor General would adopt to avoid Congressional response
SG`: Actual position the Solicitor General adopted

There were substantive differences in the cases that explain the apparently counterintuitive positions that Lee took. Some of the cases presented clear violations of civil rights. In five cases, one as party[29] and four as *amici*,[30] Lee filed briefs supporting the EEOC. Though the cases involved procedures that were critical to the agency and did not yield groundbreaking decisions, there were differences between the cases. In two of the four *amici* cases, the briefs were filed for the United States and the EEOC. In the other two *amici* cases, the EEOC went forward without the solicitor general's blessing. Although the OSG helped construct the briefs, they went forward without the support of the solicitor general and the president.[31]

Lee was also involved in four cases concerning the Voting Rights Act of 1965. In two cases, the government was a party[32] and in the other two, the solicitor general filed *amici* in response to invitations.[33] Each of the cases involved questions about preclearance requirements. Often, voting rights cases involve complicated issues and the justices invite the solicitor general in hopes of getting some assistance. In addition, the Court is often seeking nonpartisan information from the solicitor general. In the voting rights cases, Lee supported the position that changes under the Voting Rights Act needed preclearance, maintaining the authority of the Justice Department. Congress was an important constituency and the solicitor general acted as the attorney general for law enforcement. Thus, there were reasons for the solicitor general to adopt the pro–civil rights position.

In general, Lee was successful before the Court winning 77 percent of his cases, above the average solicitor general success rate of 67 percent. Lee was convinced that this was a function of his willingness to exercise restraint when campaigning for the administration's agenda. Although he was concerned about the need to preserve standing with the Court, Lee acknowledged that there were times when he should stand for principles the Court was not prepared to embrace. Lee reasoned that there could be long-range objectives, but there were large costs and it was rarely advisable to make this choice. Lee argued that you could "dip your bucket into the well of principle once or twice a year."[34]

Reynolds was more inclined to battle for principles and damn the short-term consequences. Lee did his best to hold out arguing that if he had done what Reynolds wanted and brought cases to further the president's agenda and lecture the Court, he would lose those cases and the Justices would not take him seriously.[35] Reynolds maintained that "our differences were not philosophical but how to say what we want to say and to have the greatest impact on the Court. Rex brought to the table considerable background and expertise on how to get five votes. I brought a passion and vigor without modulating it too much." According to Richard Wilkins, an assistant in the office: "Rex would not allow the most terrible stuff to go forward. Brad had control over the final briefs in the lower courts—he often made extreme arguments. In the Southern courts, there were judges who had risked their lives and careers on behalf of desegregation who were being asked to do some extreme things."[36]

The majority of cases in which Lee filed a brief against civil rights claimants involved the so-called "agenda cases." Despite his success and a record that was far from ideologically pure, Lee is most associated with these cases, advancing the administration's legal strategy. Lee was less inclined to use *amici* than either his predecessors or Fried. The office seemed to get more politicized after Lee left, but his tenure was not free from controversy.

In *Bob Jones University v. United States,* the issue of tax exemptions for a religious institution that discriminated on racial grounds was complicated by politics. The Carter administration was set to file against the university when the 1980 election turned it out of office. Deputy Lawrence Wallace was going to continue that position.[37] In the initial petition responding to the request for certiorari, Wallace agreed that the revocation of tax exempt status was consistent with Congressional intent.[38] Justice Department lawyers objected however, claiming this was contrary to Reagan's election promise. Reynolds argued that Congress did not intend to deny tax exempt status to such private schools. After weighing various positions, Smith informed the White House that he favored Reynolds's position.

The administration failed to understand the symbolic nature of its decision to support Bob Jones. This became a public issue and raised a storm of criticism and protest from attorneys in the CRD.[39] Because Lee had recused himself because of involvement in a similar case as counsel for the Mormon Church, Acting Solicitor General Wallace was asked to sign the brief, but he refused. In discussing his reluctance, Wallace said: "I had the responsibility to represent the United States in the Supreme Court. It was my case. I cannot remember another occasion during my 14 years in office when we've changed position in a case after taking a position with the Supreme Court."[40] A compromise was effected, Wallace would sign the brief, but he "dropped a footnote," saying that "this brief sets forth the position of the United States on both questions presented. The Acting Solicitor General fully subscribes to the position set forth on question two only."[41] In effect, this "tied a tin can" to the brief, alerting the Court to dissension within the office. The brief argued that the government did not condone discrimination, but it was the responsibility of Congress to remedy this situation.[42]

Reynolds argued for the government, but the OSG asked the Court to "appoint 'counsel adversary' to Bob Jones University to defend the Treasury Department's earlier position."[43] The Court complied with the unusual request and invited former cabinet member William Coleman to defend the IRS policy. Coleman argued that there was a long-standing government attempt to end discrimination and that the IRS regulation was based on public policy choices made by Congress.[44]

The decision was widely considered to be a defeat for the president and the Justice Department. According to Reynolds, "We were probably right on the law in *Bob Jones,* but Rex felt it was too late in the day. Too much water had been over the dam. He felt we would have to undo a lot of precedents and that was unlikely. He thought we would take a considerable hit and we did."[45] According to Selig: "By refusing to avail itself of the moderating influence of career Department attorneys, the administration failed to take advantage of the institutional strengths at its disposal and instead set itself up for an embarrassing defeat."[46]

The Court's decision looked like a rebuke and suggested damage to the relationship with the OSG. The decision fueled a chain reaction. Inside the office, Wallace, who had been in charge of civil rights, was relieved of those cases. To take charge of civil rights, the administration established the position of principal deputy, a political appointee.[47] Career attorneys in the CRD lost faith in the administration and the Reagan appointees lost confidence in the careerists they felt were out to undermine their agenda.[48] Reynolds and the political appointees increasingly turned to other mechanisms to circumvent this entrenched bureaucracy.[49]

There were five other agenda cases for Lee: two desegregation and three affirmative action cases. The desegregation cases, *Washington v. Seattle School District* and *Crawford v. Board of Education Los Angeles,* involved amendments to state constitutions seeking to limit busing. Reynolds announced at the outset of the administration that the Justice Department "was not going to compel children who don't choose to have an integrated education to have one."

The desegregation cases arose under the Carter administration and in the lower courts, the CRD successfully argued that the state amendments, passed overwhelmingly by the voters, were unconstitutional. Carter's Justice Department argued that the Washington initiative was conceived and sponsored with discriminatory intent.[50] The Reagan administration, however, changed sides. Landsberg argued that a defensible argument could be made for the Los Angeles case, but that the Seattle plan "simply had to be affirmed, prior case law dictated it."[51]

Wilkins, who was involved in the cases, claimed that the CRD took an extreme position that was very different from that advocated by the OSG: "In a draft brief, Reynolds wrote that this Court has never said that busing was a legitimate remedy. I fell off my chair, what about *Swann v. Charlotte Mecklenberg?* I filed a reply memo saying we cannot file this brief in this form. We needed to say while busing has been a legitimate remedy, it is a troublesome remedy. Busing categorizes children on racial grounds and sends them across school districts, sometimes for hours, simply to achieve some balance. Are there other ways to go about achieving the same ends?" Wilkins reasoned that Reynolds was too polemic and engendered unnecessary ill will: "We needed calm, rational arguments that were appropriate fine tuning for these difficult issues and remedies. We were busing for wrong reasons, not to improve education, but strictly to change racial balance. The Constitution does not demand this. In fact, it forbids it. . . . We had veered off course instead of combating this, we reinforced racial thought."[52]

The administration did not escape criticism. Selig charged that "on the one hand, the administration asserts that the Supreme Court has held only that busing is one permissible tool of desegregation, not that desegregation ever requires busing. On the other hand, the administration argues more or less explicitly that the cases in which the Court has endorsed busing were wrongly decided and unabashedly advances its own policy reasons why it would have decided these cases differently." According to Selig, "The Reagan administration's policy of refusing to seek mandatory busing remedies in any circumstances, even if busing is the only way to achieve the greatest possible degree of actual desegregation in a case where unconstitutional segregation exists, is flatly inconsistent with the governing law as dictated by the Supreme Court."[53]

Washington Initiative 350, a statewide ballot, was passed by voters to prohibit busing children to districts outside their neighborhood. The issue was whether a state could prevent local school boards from making decisions about issues of a racial nature. California Proposition 1 was similar in that it was designed to end extensive busing, but had one distinctive feature: the amendment said that busing was not to be used as a remedy unless mandated by the federal courts.

Lee argued that the amendments were colorblind, neither Proposition 1 or Initiative 350 created "an impermissible racial classification."[54] or imposed special burdens on racial minorities. The briefs argued that the states showed no intent to discriminate in constructing the amendments and thus did not violate the Equal Protection Clause of the Fourteenth Amendment. Lee argued that the Constitution did not mandate local educational policy in the Washington case.[55] In the California case, Lee argued that states should be allowed to experiment with remedies short of busing.[56] The stance was consistent with the administration's overriding goals of avoiding the use of racial classifications, however benign, and limiting the scope of remedies.

Though the differences between the two plans appeared to be relatively minor,[57] the Court found them to be consequential, declaring the Washington amendment unconstitutional, but upholding the California amendment. In rejecting the Washington amendment, Justice Blackmun held for a 5-4 majority that there was discriminatory intent and the amendment created special burdens for minorities. In *Crawford,* however, the Court approved Proposition 1, ruling that there was no discriminatory intent. California had required more of its school under the state constitution than the federal Constitution. The Court refused to support the argument that once a state chooses to do "more" than the Fourteenth Amendment requires, it may never retreat to federal requirements because that interpretation would undermine a state's democratic process.

Concurrently, Reynolds was trying to redefine the notion of affirmative action. Reynolds argued that *Weber* was "wrongly decided" and announced that he would seek test cases to challenge the ruling.[58] He argued that remedies must be specific and tied to the violation. He wanted to change the focus from groupthink and racethink to focus on individuals. Reagan had been successful at attacking such programs with the buzzword "quota." Reynolds's briefs in the lower courts made frequent use of the term and relied on legislative intent: Congress had denied that the Civil Rights Act required "hiring, firing, or promotion of employees in order to meet a racial 'quota' or achieve a certain racial balance."[59]

Reynolds raised the stakes, arguing on constitutional grounds that affirmative action programs were violations of the Equal Protection Clause.[60] Traditionally, the Court had struck down virtually every law that discriminated on racial grounds as unconstitutional. For centuries, the vast majority of those laws were directed at blacks and other minorities. Government-sponsored affirmative action was designed to remedy past discrimination and granted preferences to minorities and women. Reynolds argued if discrimination is wrong, then it is wrong no matter who benefits. If the Court is going to hold discrimination against blacks to strict scrutiny, then the standard for discrimination against whites should be the same. Justice Powell had suggested this in *Bakke.*[61]

The CRD, which had "been a powerful engine in the drive toward a race- and gender-conscious interpretation of civil rights statutes and the Constitution" seemed to be limiting those initiatives.[62] The administration did not trust the career attorneys to follow its agenda. Reynolds created a shadow CRD, circumventing the normal machinery. There were advantages to this arrangement for the administration, most notably a responsiveness to its agenda. The costs of maintaining this shadow division were inefficiency and low morale.[63] For one former member of the division, Irving Gornstein, the perceived retreat created a dilemma: "I had to decide if I was going to be a government servant or part of the movement." Gornstein stayed, but he moved to the Voting Rights section because he perceived it as being more aggressive in implementing its directives.[64]

Lee's most notable *amicus* brief was the attack on affirmative action in *Firefighters Local Union 1784 v. Stotts.* The question of victim specificity had been the subject of a battle between Reynolds and Lee regarding the position that the solicitor general would take in *Stotts.* Reynolds wanted to use the case to establish the proposition that relief, even for specific violations of the Civil Rights Act, must be victim specific. Career members of the OSG argued otherwise as did the EEOC, saying that there were many programs that had such consent decrees. Lee eventually argued Reynolds's stance, but opted for a more tentative position, qualifying the argument for a completely colorblind Constitution.[65]

Lee argued that under Title VII courts were limited by the general policies and objectives of the Civil Rights Act. Lee argued that one policy of overriding importance under Title VII was the preservation of seniority systems. Lee's argument turned on the fact that the minority firefighters themselves were not victims of past discrimination. He sought to change the focus of the Court's attention to the individuals in the case, rather than a group remedy. The government argued that the courts unnecessarily caused a difficult constitutional question regarding the scope of Congressional power to authorize the courts to provide race-conscious remedies.[66]

It was an argument designed to win the case, but more importantly, perhaps, to prepare the Court for a broader stance down the road. The Court's opinion seemed to go beyond the solicitor general's argument to the core of the administration's position. According to Raymond Wolters, "Large parts of the opinion were cribbed from the arguments of Rex Lee and William Bradford Reynolds." A majority ruled that the District Court had erred in barring Memphis from implementing its "last hired, first fired" seniority system. Justice White accepted the government's argument that the stated purpose of the decree was to rem-edy past discrimination in hiring and promotion and "that remedy did not include the displacement of white employees with seniority over blacks."[67] The opinion accepted an argument that Reynolds had ad-vanced that narrowed remedies to "identifiable victims."

Lee was effusive about the victory, saying, "If you want to attribute to me the statement that this is one of the greatest victories of all time, I won't dispute you."[68] The decision suggested that indeed this was more than a mere extension of the special protection for seniority plans.[69] Reynolds hailed the decision claiming, "*Stotts* may well represent the most significant victory for civil rights in the Nation in many years." In-deed, according to Brian Landsberg, who was the chief of the division's appellate section: "After *Stotts,* Reynolds took the position that all affir-mative action programs were suspect. He tried to read *Stotts* for much more than it was worth." According to James Turner, a career deputy in the Department of Justice, "Reynolds put out an all points bulletin to stop affirmative action programs."[70]

Reynolds also made attempts to exert a measure of control over the OSG. Caplan referred to Reynolds as the "Shadow Solicitor." Accord-ing to Reynolds, "There were cases that I felt we should take to the Court. Rex felt they were not the right vehicles. We discussed it among ourselves. In the end, the Attorney General made the call. We each won our share."[71] In some of the agenda cases, Reynolds or a deputy would write an alternate brief when the solicitor general's brief was deemed un-satisfactory. Caplan charged that Reynolds tried to usurp the role of the solicitor general.[72]

Lee was successful in drawing the antipathy of liberals and conserva-tives. His name was on briefs seeking to arrest or reverse a number of civil rights precedents and attacks on *Roe v. Wade,* earning the enmity of lib-erals. Lee also infuriated the most conservative members of the presi-dent's team because he tried to rein in the most extreme briefs.[73] He was criticized for winning too often, evidence that he was not pushing the president's agenda forcefully enough.[74] But according to Carter Phillips, "Lee generated enormous good will with the Court. The Court would relax when Lee took the podium." Wilkins added that "Rex Lee always got it just about right. He always made what I considered the appropri-ate legal arguments."[75] Caplan argued that Lee resigned because of in-creasing attempts by Meese and Reynolds to politicize the OSG, which he feared would damage the relationship between the solicitor general and the Court.[76]

Charles Fried, who had been principal deputy, was given the title acting solicitor general. The conventional wisdom is that Fried had to pass an abortion litmus test before he was nominated to be solicitor general.[77] Figure 5-2 shows the environment that Fried faced. The president, attorney general, and CRD were still conservative, but if anything, more aggressive. Fried faced a different Congress: Democrats controlled both houses and were quite willing to respond to Reagan's proposals. The Court had been reshaped to a degree—it was a bit more conservative. Most importantly, there was new leadership and an emerging philosophy that was favorable to the administration's designs. Issue evolution seemed to be drifting in the administration's direction. Lee had won some impressive victories, but had notable defeats, as well. The battle for control of the Court had been joined and the administration was trying to encourage a growing conservative majority.

Reynolds and Fried clashed frequently. Reynolds maintained that "I was much closer to Rex than to Charles. He was less comfortable with the policies the administration was advancing and the arguments pressed on the Court. My differences with Rex were over how to present the case, not what to present. But with Charles, the differences were substantive." While Lee and Reynolds had disputes that Smith had to resolve, the differences between Fried and Reynolds were more numerous. As Reynolds said, "With Charles more things would go to Attorney General Meese. Ed almost always sided with me. I think that stuck in Charles' craw."

According to Reynolds, "One of the problems Charles had was that he was very adamant and vocal that he was fully on board on these

---

FIGURE 5-2

ENVIRONMENTAL CONSTRAINTS ON THE SOLICITOR GENERAL:
SECOND TERM REAGAN ADMINISTRATION

SG`

SGc SGw SGp

Liberal————————————————————————————Conservative

Precedent Congress Supreme President
Court

SGp: Position Solicitor General would adopt if doing the president's bidding
SGw: Position Solicitor General would adopt if winning was the sole goal
SGc: Position Solicitor General would adopt to avoid Congressional response
SG`: Actual position the Solicitor General adopted

issues before he was confronted with the need to stand and deliver on them. . . . He was not as committed to the Reagan agenda as Rex was." Part of that was a function of Fried's position. As Lee knew, the solicitor general often had to moderate positions and balance the designs of the president with the need to argue before the Court. Some of it may have been a function of the issues on the agenda as Reynolds conceded: "Of course, timing is part of this. Many of the cases percolated to the Supreme Court during his term. The cases had come through the lower court levels. The agenda was teed up a little better at that time."[78]

For his part, Fried wrote that "working with Brad Reynolds was the toughest part of my job." He claimed that "along with the browbeating he would threaten that if he did not get his way, then 'the attorney general' would hear about it. At first I found this a little terrifying."[79] According to David Rose, "Fried was more compliant than Rex Lee. It was clear that Brad Reynolds and Ed Meese were calling the shots on policy. The independence of the OSG was taken away under Fried. Fried had to go along with that."[80] Reynolds gave credence to this view, "Charles was an adequate mechanic to do what we wanted once we wound him up and pointed him in the right direction." Rose noted that there were visible signs of the relationship: "I saw Charles Fried waiting in the outer office for Reynolds' to talk to him. It was a symbol of Reynolds' influence. I never saw the Solicitor General sitting in the outer office of the Assistant Attorney General. The Assistant Attorney General would normally go see the Solicitor General."[81]

Reynolds argued that Fried was not ideologically pure on the central issue: "He was not completely there on affirmative action. Charles felt that the ends justified the means. He felt that some affirmative action programs should be given more time. He was willing to continue some of the programs."[82] During Fried's tenure, the OSG was involved in eight cases that raised affirmative action and employment discrimination questions. In three of the cases, the government was a party, in the other five, the solicitor general entered as *amicus.*

Some cases, such as *Local 93 Firefighters v. Cleveland* and *Local 28 of the Sheet Metal Workers v. Equal Employment Opportunity Commission,* were terrible vehicles for efforts to limit affirmative action. The Supreme Court could have adopted narrow grounds for the decisions. Instead, the majority cut a wider swath, allowing racial preferences for nonvictims under some circumstances.[83] In *Local 93,* Brennan's opinion specifically refuted many of the solicitor general's positions and sharply criticized Fried's "misguided" arguments.[84] Fried considered the decision one of the biggest disappointments of his tenure and offered his resignation to Meese.[85]

The *Local 28* decision was particularly troubling for the administration. First, six justices reaffirmed the *Weber* decision. Second, the Court specifically dismissed the solicitor general's argument that even consent decrees were involuntary. By rejecting the argument, the Court used the more forgiving *Weber* standard for consent decrees.[86] In response to the decisions and in contrast to the reaction to *Stotts*, Reynolds announced that "the Justice Department was abandoning its efforts to eliminate numerical quotas from state and local affirmative action programs."[87]

Fried was particularly interested in *Wygant v. Jackson Board of Education*. In implementing layoffs, white teachers with seniority were adversely affected. The case involved a program to protect minority teachers with less seniority. Rather than questions concerning hiring or promotion, the case involved the loss of jobs. The CRD had sided with the white teachers and argued for the same victim-specific approach that the Court adopted in *Stotts*. To Fried this was the right question with an appealing set of facts.[88] There was no evidence of past discrimination by the Board of Education. The program was established to remedy "societal discrimination" that had led to a limited number of black teachers. The layoffs were based on the notion of keeping minority teachers as role models for students. While *Local 28* and *Local 93* were statutory challenges under Title VII, *Wygant* was a constitutional challenge.[89] Among other things, this meant Congress was largely helpless to respond to the decision. The solicitor general entered *Wygant* as an *amicus curiae,* but the Court refused the office's request for time to argue.

Indirectly, Fried advocated use of strict scrutiny regardless of who the beneficiary was or how benign the remedy. He argued that any remedy must be narrowly tailored to fit the alleged violation. He was able to persuade the Court. Justice Powell advanced the position that racial discrimination should be judged by the strict scrutiny standard, whether whites or blacks were the victims. Powell found the claim that there was "societal discrimination" too diffuse to provide a compelling rationale for racial preferences, particularly when layoffs could result.[90] Fried remarked that "Powell came closer to getting it right than we had."[91] But in dicta, Powell seemed to suggest that *Stotts* did not signal the decisive shift in policy that Reynolds had argued.[92] With *Wygant* and *Stotts,* the administration had some favorable precedents and some success in structuring affirmative action policy, but it was apparent that the solicitor general had not convinced the Court to effect a wholesale change in the theory underpinning affirmative action. Indeed, supporters of affirmative action could put a positive spin on the decisions, claiming the decisions did not repudiate any existing precedents and merely found that these programs, imposing layoffs, had gone too far.

These doctrinal advances were coupled with institutional changes. The CRD became involved in a number of disputes with the EEOC over the position the government would take in some important cases. The EEOC had been created with clear institutional weaknesses and though the agency had some litigating authority, there were limits to that power. The EEOC needed clearance from the solicitor general to enter a case.[93]

The EEOC lost important battles for power within the Justice Department. The EEOC pleaded its position to the solicitor general, but was told that it would have to accept the Justice Department's opposition to affirmative action.[94] According to Rose, "The Reagan Administration pre-empted the EEOC, rather than attack it directly. It was clear that the Department of Justice was calling the shots."[95]

Institutionally, the emasculation of a rival would give the Justice Department more authority to speak with one voice. Politically, weakening the EEOC would remove a voice that might oppose the division's interpretation of civil rights. The EEOC was powerless to resist these impulses and Congress failed to come to its rescue.[96] Reagan appointees began to reconstruct a potential ally, the Civil Rights Commission, as well as the EEOC itself.[97]

In *Watson v. Fort Worth Bank,* which Fried regarded as an important transition case for a frontal reconsideration of *Griggs,* the Court invited the solicitor general to participate. The question was whether *Griggs* applied only to objective criteria, like test scores, education requirements, height, and weight or whether it applied to subjective criteria like supervisors' recommendations and interviews. Fried argued that only objective criteria should be covered and argued that when objective measures are used, then disparate impact should be the standard. But when subjective criteria were the basis for promotion, intent should be the standard. Fried argued that if the Court was going to use the *Griggs* criteria for subjective measures it would lead to quotas and undermine other parts of Title VII. The Court rejected his argument, but O'Connor's opinion gave the solicitor general a cue to bring further cases and which arguments to advance.[98]

In *Watson,* Fried asked the Court for time to participate in oral arguments. The Court refused the request. In three other civil rights cases, including *Wygant,* the Court refused to allow Reagan solicitors general to participate in oral arguments. It is considered unusual for the Court to refuse the solicitor general's request for time to argue a case. The Court turned down requests of the Reagan solicitors general to argue fourteen times in the 1984–87 terms.[99]

On the eve of the end of Reagan's second term, Fried argued two affirmative actions cases: *Martin v. Wilks* and *Ward's Cove Packing v. Atonio.* Fried viewed *Ward's Cove* as a chance to "tame" *Griggs.* Fried argued that the case was an ideal opportunity to show how "once the redistributive, social-engineering mentality takes hold, law and logic are swamped."[100] Using cues that O'Connor suggested in *Watson,* Fried's *amicus* brief tried to move the Court from an effects test to an intent test. Under the test Fried advocated, plaintiffs would have to identify the process that led to hiring, thus showing intent to discriminate. Under traditional disparate treatment and effects tests, the employee had to show that an alternative plan was available to employers. Fried argued that employees must show that the alternatives are just as efficient and effective as the existing program, a more difficult standard.

White's opinion in *Ward's Cove* paraphrased and endorsed the points made by Fried's brief and shifted the burden from employers to employees in such cases.[101] The Court ruled that the existence of disparities was not proof of discrimination in and of themselves. Workers had to show that companies had no legitimate need for the challenged practices. The opinion disposed of the language of *Griggs* that pressured employers to use quotas.[102]

Fried's victory was short-lived. Congress passed the Civil Rights Act of 1990 to nullify the Court's interpretations. President Bush vetoed the bill, claiming it would lead to quotas. The Senate failed by a single vote to override the veto. The Civil Rights Act of 1991 was passed with a few compromises.[103] Bush's hand was forced by a number of events and a calendar that showed an election less than a year away made it impossible for Bush to veto this version. According to James Simon, "Most of the conservatives' narrow victories in civil rights cases were blunted by the Civil Rights Act of 1991."[104] The legislation not only repudiated the *Ward's Cove* reinterpretation of *Griggs,* but it struck more deeply, providing opportunities to challenge discrimination in seniority systems.[105] Even if one does not go as far as Robert Smith, who wrote, "the seniority system is the most pervasive form of institutional racism,"[106] this was important because such systems could be used to insulate a plan from affirmative action.

Reynolds and Fried wanted to challenge set asides under Minority Business Enterprise (MBE) provisions. Fried wanted to attack *Fullilove* directly, but without the groundwork he felt it would have been "a kamikaze mission." *City of Richmond v. J.A. Croson* was the perfect case in his view. Richmond constructed a large set aside program, even though there was no evidence of overt past discrimination.[107] Fried argued that the Court should adopt strict scrutiny to review the set aside. He distinguished the Richmond program from *Fullilove*. First, the program in *Fullilove* provided for 10 percent of the contracts to go to minority contractors compared to 30 percent in the Richmond program. Second, Congress had broad authority under the Thirteenth and Fourteenth Amendments to set up the program in *Fullilove*. Fried argued that the Court had recognized that there might be "overriding national interests to justify selective federal legislation that would be unacceptable for an individual state."[108] Third, the federal program was narrowly tailored. The solicitor general's briefs typically asked for narrow tailoring and proof of discrimination. That strategy was an indirect attempt to distinguish a current case from existing precedent. This time, the solicitor general tried to attack the precedent, rather than seeking an exception to it. The brief did not insist on victim specificity or prior discrimination. It was a winning strategy and a major victory in reformulating affirmative action, at least in the context of set asides.[109]

O'Connor's plurality opinion borrowed heavily from the solicitor general's brief. O'Connor applied strict scrutiny, saying that racial classifications, even if benign, must be "strictly reserved for remedial settings."[110] Discrimination against whites would be treated the same as discrimination against blacks. Under strict scrutiny, the program must serve a compelling purpose to survive constitutional muster. O'Connor distinguished between general "societal" discrimination and "identified" discrimination.[111] Only the latter could be remedied and the program had to be narrowly tailored to achieve that. In the Court's view, past discrimination in Richmond did not support the use of such a rigid remedy. O'Connor further supported the solicitor general's view that Fourteenth Amendment rights adhere to individuals, thus making membership in a group irrelevant to the considerations.[112]

While the affirmative action cases raised the ire of civil rights groups, Fried was not ideologically pure enough to escape criticism from the right. The heaviest criticism was tied to *Patterson v. McLean Credit Union*. The case caused great anxiety for the civil rights community. Brenda Patterson sued under section 1981 for racial and sexual harassment. In Fried's view, the extension of the statute to private activity was a terrible stretch. But in the original brief, Fried wrote that the interpretation of *Runyon v. McCrary* though distorted, was well-established.[113]

In this instance, the Court was the cause of Fried's problem. Civil rights proponents and the liberal justices were shocked when a majority ordered reargument on the question of whether the Court should reconsider *Runyon*.[114] Symbolically, coming just four days after Anthony Kennedy had replaced Powell, it seemed to be a portend of a judicial turn to the right. In practical terms, this was a threat "to one of the foundation decisions in civil rights."[115] At a meeting with the attorney general, some argued that the administration needed to help stiffen the resolve of its allies on the Court.[116]

Fried felt that the case was a trap and decided not to file a brief: "I saw no reason to bait the various bears a second time. I did not think a reconsideration of *Runyon* was a good idea. I did not think that the Court would overturn it."[117] Further, he argued: "Our silence now would be an eloquent but respectful way of saying to the five members of the Court who had asked for reargument that this was a misconceived enterprise."

Despite pressure, Meese did not overrule Fried. There were good reasons for this strategic discretion. First, Bork, one of Fried's predecessors, had supported the precedent and argued for a broad interpretation. In addition, in previous cases and an earlier version of this case, Fried had supported the precedent. To argue otherwise now, he felt, would look like the last gasp of a departing administration.[118] It was not lost on Fried that 66 senators, 119 representatives, 47 states attorneys general, and 112 civic groups joined in briefs supporting *Runyon*.[119] Given the widespread support for the precedent, if the Court overturned it, Congress would undoubtedly respond by restoring the status quo. Finally, Fried felt that urging the Court to overturn *Runyon* would be a futile gesture that would jeopardize his attempts to overturn *Griggs* and succeed in the *Croson* case.

Conservatives excoriated Fried, with one saying he was "running a renegade operation that looks more like a Dukakis solicitor general's office." To make matters worse, the Court unanimously upheld *Runyon* but Kennedy went to great lengths to reject the solicitor general's position that the old civil rights act could extend beyond discrimination in initial hiring to cover harassment. Indeed, the Court did not extend *Runyon* or the Civil Rights Act of 1866, the position the administration favored. Fried considered it "odd to get a judicial scolding reminiscent of *Sheet Metal Workers*."[120]

Fried participated in two voting rights cases. In the most important of the two, the solicitor general did not support the civil rights claimant. The case occurred in the context of a struggle over the Voting Rights Act. With Reynolds as the point man, the administration fought its extension.

The Court invited the solicitor general to participate in *Thornburg v. Gingles,* which the Justice Department considered the most important voting rights cases of the 1980s. In *Mobile v. Bolden,* the Court had ruled that the government must prove discriminatory intent in voting dilution cases. Congress reversed the decision with a 1982 amendment to the Voting Rights Act holding that proof of discriminatory effects is sufficient. The case involved the amendment that the administration had actively opposed.[121] Under Reynolds's direction, the Justice Department sided with a southern state for the first time in a voting rights case. The legal question was how to interpret the new amendment. The practical question for the solicitor general was whether at large elections were a surreptitious form of racial discrimination. According to Fried, the case presented real problems: "The statute made no sense. The 'good guys' were lined up against us. It was an uphill fight from the word go."[122]

The brief argued that the lower court interpretation of the Voting Rights Act was "fundamentally flawed." If invited briefs are supposed to be more neutral and less partisan, the solicitor general ignored that norm.[123] Robert Dole and nine other senators filed a brief arguing that the administration misinterpreted Congressional intent. In essence, the case permitted the Court to revisit debate between disparate impact and intent, this time in the context of voting rights. The solicitor general was again arguing for intent, but the Congressional brief argued that disparate impact was sufficient.

The Court's decision followed the lines that Dole's brief had suggested.[124] Justice Brennan's opinion established a three-prong test to establish vote dilution. First, the minority group must be large and geographically compact. Second, the minority must be politically cohesive. Third, bloc voting by the white majority must be sufficient to defeat the minority's preferred candidate.[125] The opinion seemed to rebut the solicitor general's argument point by point.[126] Reynolds claimed that "we were surprised by the decision in *Thornburgh.*" These cases would return in an altered form and the administration's position would be vindicated. According to Reynolds: "The post-*Gingles* voting cases were close to our arguments. This was due, in part, to the fact that we rewrote internal guidelines in the Voting Rights Act. We wanted to make damn sure that the 'effects' did not overtake enforcement."[127]

Conclusion. Reagan solicitors general set the context for the redefinition phase and provided opportunities for their immediate successor and constraints for the Clinton administration. As with the Truman and Johnson solicitors general who defined their eras, Lee and Fried acted more decisively on the administration's goals and had a major impact in altering the context for civil rights policy.

The solicitors general acted in a different fashion from their Republican predecessors. When Griswold and Bork argued against extensions of civil rights, it was often due to issue evolution. The issue had reached a difficult stage and the solicitor general would try to distinguish the case of the moment from the existing precedent. Lee and Fried tried a different tack. Distinguishing a case would reinforce the odious precedent. Instead, they attacked the existing precedent, not because of issue evolution, but because their policy goals dictated that result.

The administration made a conscious effort to redefine the questions and approaches that had dominated civil rights for over a generation. Redefining issues puts the solicitor general in a difficult position. A major role of the solicitor general is to help the Court impose doctrinal equilibrium and continue the path of issue evolution. Redefinition flies in the face of these designs: trying to get the Court to reinterpret precedent and change prevailing views regarding a certain issue.

The administration changed sides in a number of pending cases. The solicitors general attacked affirmative action and desegregation doctrine. They launched an assault on the effects standard in voting rights and employment, trying to overturn *Allen* and *Griggs,* urging the Court to replace them with more stringent intent tests. In some areas, Lee and Fried did not press the position the administration favored. Most notably, Fried held to precedent in *Patterson.*

There is no doubt that political considerations dominated legal ones in the Reagan administration and this was increasingly the case as time went on. Typically, the solicitor general acts strategically, with legal positions tempering political stances coming from the administration. The administration tried to free its solicitors general to act on its sincere preferences. Regardless of the prospects for victory, the solicitor general shouldered on, trying to get the Court to revisit a number of precedents. While they were not entirely successful, they moved the office more toward the political sphere. There were institutional changes in the OSG, most notably the creation of the principal deputy.

Lee and Fried tried to avoid the normal constraints that confront the solicitor general. Typically, the discretion provided through the voluntary *amici* briefs permit the solicitor general to serve as attorney general as policy maker. In the EEOC cases and areas of clear discrimination, Congress and the agency were the primary constituencies and the office adopted the role of solicitor general as attorney general for law enforcement.

When the government was a party, the solicitor general often acted as if it was a discretionary *amicus* brief to maximize policy making. The solicitor general argued as if it was the tenth justice and that limits to voting rights and desegregation were consistent with emerging doctrine.

The conventional wisdom is that there was a disjuncture in the role of the solicitor general during the Reagan administration. The attorney general exerted greater control than normal. The administration also redefined the relationship between the CRD and the solicitor general. Over time, Reynolds increasingly gained power and influence over the agenda issues and wielded enormous authority over the solicitor general. Though the Court was conservative, the stridency of the solicitor general in the agenda issues seemed to cost the administration the key votes of moderate justices. Congress mobilized to counter the administration's conservative gambols. The solicitors general were not overly concerned with the position of Congress because the president could veto any legislation directed at Court decisions they liked.

The policy environment was a problem for the administration. It wanted to destabilize precedent and doctrine. But the Court was not ready for a wholesale reversal and the administration, on a finite clock, did not have the time to do the background work necessary to distinguish precedents and undermine them in an incremental fashion.

The goals of the solicitors general were clear: to maximize the Reagan agenda in the courts. The attorney general and the CRD tried to push the solicitor general to go even further. Lee tried to moderate the positions of the political operatives with mixed success. Fried was not as fortunate. Like McCree, Lee and Fried were the newer brand of solicitor general. They lacked the independent base of authority that would permit them to withstand the political winds. Still, in a number of cases, Lee, in particular, supported civil rights claimants suggesting that legal concerns were not absent from the office's consideration.

Issue evolution, an increasingly conservative Court, and a few precedents were favorable to Lee and Fried. They struggled, with mixed success, to avoid alienating the Court as they pursued attempts to change disparate impact into intent, reverse affirmative action, limit desegregation, and overturn *Roe.* The evidence suggests that they went too far. While solicitors general normally attend to the Court to build up a reserve, Lee and especially Fried borrowed against that. It is a rational strategy for a president on a finite calendar. The future relationship would be a problem for the next president.

The attack on affirmative action and disparate impact yielded some success, but coupled with attempts to overturn *Roe,* it opened the solicitor general to charges of politicization and cost the office some legitimacy. While some claim that the OSG has always been politicized to a degree, Fried conceded that this was a broadly held perception: "It may have affected our success before the Court. It may have influenced Powell and Stevens a little."[128] Toward the end of the administration, Congress became an active participant in civil rights and reversed decisions it opposed.

Of the competing forces in its policy environment, precedent was not favorable when Ronald Reagan took office in 1981. During the last elected Republican administration, disparate impact and busing were read into the law. During the Carter administration, affirmative action was legitimated by the Supreme Court. These were primary targets of the Justice Department and solicitors general. Precedents were recent, suggesting that excising them would not be easy. Reagan did have the chance to continue restructuring the Supreme Court. As the second term unfolded, the administration was increasingly bolder. If the solicitors general did not really get the Court to adopt a new theory, they managed to get the Court to take a careful look at some issues. The cases began to question notions of "groupthink" and "racethink."[129]

While litigation seemed to be the best avenue, the administration was trying to achieve a revolution through an office that is not constructed for such purposes. According to William Bryson, "At the beginning of every Administration, there are a new group of eager, energetic lawyers, who feel 'we finally have our chance, and want to change everything.' There is a great pent up demand. But the impetus for change and the fervor die down. The OSG is characterized by incrementalism and a huge amount of inertia. This is not satisfying to the political appointees who are on limited time clocks." The Reagan operatives did not retreat. According to Selig, "The fundamental difference between the Nixon and Reagan administrations in the school desegregation area is that the Nixon administration recognized its responsibilities to the rule of the law."[130] The Reagan administration continued to pursue its notions of public policy and to use the courts and the OSG. This caused problems as Wilkins noted: "They were so intent on fixing in seconds a problem that had developed over 25 years. It took 30 years to get to *Brown,* we could not fine tune it in a few months."

Proponents of the administration's policies lamented some lost opportunities. According to Wilkins, "The Court, with the best of intentions, reinforced groupthink. We needed to break that cycle of thinking. But we had to do it slowly and not overreach. There was a window of opportunity for the careful fine tuning necessary for these issues. But

Reynolds was like a bull in a china shop. We missed the opportunity to develop reasonable positions." Wilkins maintained that "Reynolds was overzealous in his arguments. He pushed too far, too fast. He was perceived as mean spirited."[131]

The policies and apparent fervor of the administration raised red flags for Congress, the courts, and among career attorneys in the Justice Department. According to Deputy Solicitor General Kneedler, "The Civil Rights Division wanted to enforce civil rights law, but there was a perception that Reynolds did not. There was a perception during the Reagan years that the Civil Rights Division's protector role was being cast off." Kneedler summed up the perception: "When the government seems to be arguing against long-standing institutional positions, it gives the Court some pause."[132]

Landsberg said that there were differences in the way that the administration attacked litigation: "There is always some argument that could be made to reverse a previous decision. The Reagan Administration was more aggressive in pushing these arguments."[133] The question is whether this harmed the relationship between the office and the Court and hampered the efforts of the administration to achieve its goals. According to Bryson:

> The common wisdom is that the political cases threaten the relationship between the Solicitor General's Office and the Supreme Court. My view is different. The Office does nothing to its credibility by bringing these cases. The Court expects the Administration to enter and advance politically sensitive cases. The Office loses credibility if it is not honest and scrupulously correct in citing the facts and the law. The Office risks its credibility if it produces briefs in a . . . manner that suggests overreaching. You can never misrepresent the facts, or precedents, or the fact that you are pushing the envelope. It is appropriate to push the envelope. But even if you are candid you cannot push the envelope too many times. Rex understood that.[134]

A number of analysts and members of the OSG charged that Reynolds did not.

Reynolds lamented the apparent lack of success: "We thought probably naively that with two terms we could be successful in getting the affirmative action train turned around, getting the legal approach to desegregation turned around, and getting *Roe v. Wade* reversed. We fell short on all these fronts. You can't turn the ship of state on a dime."[135] At the same time, if the final results were not evident, there were manifestations. As Simon noted, "For more than three decades, the modern Supreme Court has served as the crucial national institution that had encouraged the civil rights movement by broadly interpreting the Constitution and federal laws to protect racial minorities. The 1988 Court term, in which *Patterson* was decided, marked the end of that historic judicial era. With the advent of the conservative Rehnquist Court majority, Congress, not the Court became the channel for civil rights activism." It extended beyond the Court as Reynolds noted: "There were more and more places to shoot the cannon as time went on. There were more places to go that were receptive. More doors were open to advance our arguments." And if the administration left without accomplishing its goals, success was imminent. As Reynolds noted, "At the end of the second term and Bush's years, the courts were very receptive to our ideas. A great deal of our agenda eventually got through."[136]

If the administration did not succeed in getting many issues redefined, it helped change the context for decision making. The major advance may have been the steady reduction of the institutional barriers that had constrained the solicitors general. The Bush administration was the one to profit, continuing the policies of its predecessors. The Clinton administration would face a monumental task in its efforts to reverse the policies.

George Bush: A Kinder, Gentler Reagan?

The goals of Bush's Justice Department and solicitor general were not significantly different from their predecessors. Congress was not sympathetic to Bush's civil rights agenda, but the Court was increasingly conservative. The rules and norms provided some opportunities and imposed some constraints on the solicitor general. If the Reagan administration did not achieve many of its goals, it laid the groundwork necessary to remove some institutional obstacles. The Reagan administration reinvented the civil rights machinery, created a shadow CRD, and placed a layer with a political appointee in the OSG. The Reagan solicitors general did not achieve a number of landmark decisions, but they chipped away at some precedents and succeeded in redefining some concepts. The Bush administration had the opportunity to take advantage.

Executive. Ronald Reagan's was a defining administration that laid out a broad context for change; George Bush's role was to fill in some of the gaps and implement some of the agenda. Skowronek called him the "faithful son" of the Reagan legacy who wrestled with questions about his political identity.[137]

There was a decided ambivalence to Bush's civil rights policies. Bush had been a moderate, who in a previous life as a member of Congress, had supported civil rights and affirmative action. But as the successor to an administration that made affirmative action its target, Bush did not depart much from Reagan.[138] The Justice Department opposed passing a civil rights bill. Bush worked to get a version passed that was more palatable to conservatives. He vetoed a bill that he felt went too far. His veto was sustained by one vote.[139] Eventually, his hand was forced by the success that David Duke had as a Republican candidate and the fallout from the Clarence Thomas nomination, and he signed a revised civil rights bill.[140]

The Civil Rights Act of 1991 was an example of the interaction of the legislative, executive, and judicial branches. The act nullified nine Supreme Court rulings, restoring legal standards that placed the burden of proof in anti-discrimination suits on employers. The legislation instructed courts to follow *Griggs,* which held employers responsible for justifying employment practices that were seemingly fair but had an adverse impact on women and minorities.[141]

The controversy over the Reagan Justice Department seemed to push Bush into a less partisan, more neutral stance with the retention of Attorney General Richard Thornburgh. But Cornell Clayton argues that the changes from the Reagan Justice Department were more of degree than kind. Power over legal policy shifted from the attorney general to White House Legal Counsel C. Boyden Gray. Gray, a conservative, established regular contact with Solicitor General Kenneth Starr. He helped get Thornburgh's successor, William Barr, appointed. Gray, Barr, and Starr worked closely to establish and direct legal policy.[142] According to James Turner, deputy attorney general, "The Bush Administration's tone in civil rights was more moderate, but only in tone. Starr pursued the same kind of policies."[143]

After the position remained vacant for the first year of the administration, Thornburgh chose a friend, John Dunne, state senator from New York, to head the CRD. Dunne had a different set of priorities than Reynolds: "I made some efforts to slow down the changes the Division had been making. The Civil Rights Division was perceived as not being supportive of the principles of civil rights. I wanted to change that. I wanted to pull the Division more toward the center. I was not pushing to reopen matters that had been settled. But I wanted to take a different approach to emerging matters."[144] This approach created conflicts between the solicitor general and the division.[145]

Congress. President Bush had to face some unrequited wrath left over from battles between Reagan and Congressional Democrats. The presidential veto was an important component of Bush's legislative strategy.[146] He needed a tool to combat a Congress that was, according to aggregate measures, quite liberal.[147] Civil rights issues were quite salient as the Court's decisions in *Martin* and *Ward's Cove Packing* angered Congress, which eventually passed a law overturning them.

Supreme Court. There was great symbolism tied to the Bush appointments to the Supreme Court. David Souter and Thomas replaced Brennan and Marshall, respectively. This deprived the Court of its most liberal members and the last two proponents of the "preferred position" doctrine, which had been the dominant philosophy of the Court for a half-century. Souter was considered a moderate conservative, while Thomas was characterized as very conservative.[148] The changes seemed to create the critical mass for conservatives and finish the job that Nixon and Reagan had begun. Certainly, a wide-open window of opportunity was available for the administration to pursue its agenda.

Issue Evolution. In general, the work of the Reagan solicitors general arrested the expansion of civil rights in many areas and created retreats in others. The administration did not have the impressive landmark decisions, but its efforts had planted seeds that would bear fruit. Civil rights was on the presidential and Congressional agenda because of the Court's affirmative action decisions.[149] The failure to impose doctrinal equilibrium on the issue kept it on the agenda. The Court did establish the position that affirmative action should be narrow and specific and that strict scrutiny would be the standard.

The Bush Solicitor General. With the retirement of the two most liberal justices and a more favorable set of precedents, Kenneth Starr, Bush's solicitor general, seemingly had more room to maneuver. Starr was left the task of repairing the apparent damage done by the Reagan solicitors general and to decide whether to continue the initiatives of his predecessors. According to Richard Seamon, "Ken Starr was highly sensitive to the Court. When arguing for changes in the Court's jurisprudence, we were not as confrontational as under Charles Fried."[150] Starr had aligned himself with conservatives during his years as a judge and was a strong supporter of Reagan's civil rights agenda.[151] As Roger Clegg, a member of the OSG before moving to the CRD, "Ken Starr, from my perspective as a conservative, was a rock of integrity and right minded-ness on these issues. I never had any doubt that he would do the right thing."[152] Lee and Fried had presided over important changes in policies, but Starr would fill in the details.

Figure 5-3 shows the constellation of forces that influenced Starr. The executive branch was still far to the right, though Bush was willing to compromise on occasion. The Justice Department moderated a bit under Thornburgh, but returned to the right under Barr. The CRD moved toward the middle. Congress was a potentially important part of the solicitor general's calculus. Democrats controlled both houses and were anxious to check gambols that threatened civil rights. The Court had been moving to the right and Bush would abet that transition by appointing Souter and Thomas. Issue evolution was increasingly favor-able to a continuation of the Reagan administration's policies: third-generation cases were typically beyond the Court's support. The Court also showed signs of support for attempts to redefine issues.

The OSG argued four civil rights cases in which the government was a party, entered six cases as voluntary *amici,* and was invited to enter one case by the Court. Perhaps in deference to a Congress controlled by Democrats, Starr argued three of the four direct cases on behalf of civil rights claims. In the six voluntary *amici* cases, which are usually more im-portant and provide greater discretion, Starr filed three briefs in favor of civil rights claimants[153] and three against such claims. The OSG won seven of the eleven civil rights cases during Starr's tenure.

Four of the pro–civil rights briefs (one direct, two voluntary *amici*

FIGURE 5-3
ENVIRONMENTAL CONSTRAINTS ON THE SOLICITOR GENERAL:
BUSH ADMINISTRATION

$$SG`$$

	SGc			SGw	SGp	
Liberal——————————————————————————————Conservative
	Congress	Precedent		Supreme Court	President	

SGp: Position Solicitor General would adopt if doing the president's bidding
SGw: Position Solicitor General would adopt if winning was the sole goal
SGc: Position Solicitor General would adopt to avoid Congressional response
SG`: Actual position the Solicitor General adopted

briefs, and one invited brief) were voting rights cases. Such arguments protected the authority of the attorney general, which may explain the pro–civil rights positions. In addition, despite perceived retreats in some areas of civil rights, the administration continued to enforce voting rights.[154] In voting rights, the solicitor general typically assumed the role of attorney general for law enforcement.

Two cases concerned whether section 2 of the Voting Rights Act covered statewide judicial elections. According to Dunne: "I felt very strongly about the voting rights cases. I pushed very hard in those cases. Ken was a little reluctant to pursue the cases. We had some heated discussions. Ken finally went ahead with them."[155] In *United States v. Roemer* and *Houston Lawyers Association v. Mattox,*[156] the solicitor general argued that the Voting Rights Act covered such elections. Starr argued that the amended version of section 2 was passed in 1982 to reverse the *City of Mobile v. Bolden* decision, thus it did not shorten the reach of the act. Starr argued that the attorney general had long considered judicial elections to come under the purview of section 2. Starr argued that the word "representatives" covered judges who won popular elections.[157]

The Court agreed that the 1982 amendments covered judicial elections and that it was appropriate to characterize election winners as representatives of the districts in which they campaigned. The Court held that legislative history provided no support for the claim that the term "representatives" meant only legislative and executive officials or that Congress would have chosen the word "candidates" had it intended to apply the vote dilution prohibition to judicial elections.[158]

In the most important cases, Starr normally adopted positions that were less favorable to civil rights. Part of it was attributable to the composition of the Court, part to the willingness of the solicitor general to countenance redefinition, and part was a function of issue evolution: the cases were getting more difficult.

In *Board of Education of Oklahoma City v. Dowell,* Starr argued that the school board was under no obligation to combat unintentional resegregation. He urged the Court to provide structure and guidance for the end of court supervision. Starr framed the broader questions: "We had to ask what is the meaning of desegregation and what does it mean to have a unitary system?" Starr argued that if Oklahoma City had established a unitary system, then the school district should be relieved of the desegregation decree. Starr argued that in the absence of a continuing violation, there was no need for continuing judicial relief. The government claimed that court-ordered desegregation was supposed to be a process with a beginning and an end and strictly a temporary remedy.

Starr claimed that "we were satisfied that the school board had met its obligation. The 10th Circuit approach was unduly rigid and ill-suited for federal control of local institutions. By the standard of the 10th Circuit, the consent decree could become an instrument of oppression."[159] The solicitor general sought to have the Court define what it meant to be a unitary system and to determine when a district had achieved that status. To demonstrate this, Starr suggested that the lower court pay attention to the length and quality of compliance, faithfulness to the decree, and elimination of vestiges of past *de jure* discrimination. The solicitor general urged the Court to use the "*Green* factors" from *Green v. County School Board.* The surest evidence of a dual system would be racial stratification of students, faculty, services, physical plant, and operations. Once vestiges of the *de jure* system have been eliminated, Starr argued that the standards of evaluation for ripple effects should be lowered significantly.[160]

According to Starr: "Issues of local control, values of federalism, and the like weighed heavily in the balance of jurisprudence and policy. We believed in local control and federalism. The 10th Circuit seemed insensitive to those types of concerns. They were using antitrust principles, but these were fact intensive cases, as civil rights cases tend to be."[161] The government sought and received a lenient standard for determining when court supervised desegregation should end. The Court ruled 5–3 that the 10th Circuit standard for dissolving a desegregation decree was more stringent than required by previous decisions or the Equal Protection Clause. The Court ruled that a school district attained unitary status when it satisfied two conditions. First, the district must comply, in good faith, with the desegregation decree for a "reasonable period of time." Second, it must eliminate, "as far as practicable," the remnants of unlawful desegregation.[162]

In *Freeman v. Pitts,* Starr argued for reduced supervision over the DeKalb, Georgia, school system, thus asking the Court to relax the standards even further. Starr maintained that a school district should be released from court supervision even if it has not removed all vestiges of discrimination from all facets of the system. In *Freeman,* there were still disparities in faculty assignments and expenditures per pupil, but Starr argued that remaining imbalances or inequities were not evidence of past unlawful actions.[163] The Court agreed with the government, ruling that a district court has the authority to relinquish supervision and control of a school system in incremental stages, before full compliance had been achieved in every area of operations.[164]

In *Dowell* and *Freeman,* the Court followed the blueprint that Reynolds had constructed and labored to legitimize. The turning point for these decisions had been set in motion by the Nixon administration as second-generation cases began to emerge in the North.[165] Judicial supervision of the schools was necessary only during the transition period when public schools were ridding themselves of discrimination. The Court ruled that judges exceeded their authority if they tried to use remedies to counteract demographic trends, residential patterns, and social conditions.[166]

While the Court was lowering the standards in primary and secondary schools, the justices considered the case of segregated public colleges. In *United States v. Fordice,* Starr resisted the opportunity to extend the retreat to segregation in colleges. He was constrained by the fact that this was a federal policy that he was obligated to defend. A long history of racial segregation in Mississippi colleges was the subject of the case.

Throughout the genesis of this case, which began in 1975, the government supported the argument that to remedy discrimination in colleges, the state must pump resources into historically black colleges. As the case got to the Supreme Court, however, Starr reversed position on one critical issue. While the administration and the Justice Department were sharply criticized for the reversal, the government still supported the plaintiffs, parting over the remedy. Thus, attacks on the administration were muted to avoid losing its support altogether.

In the petition for certiorari, the solicitor general claimed that there was no constitutional obligation to correct disparities in funding, programs, and facilities. According to Starr: "We were of the view that the dual system had not been dismantled—that was straightforward—there was no disagreement about that. The differences revolved around what to do as a remedy." Starr wrestled with the bottom line: "We needed to conceptualize the extent of the wrong and what to do as a remedy. There were very different positions on that issue."[167]

The campaign to get the government to reconsider its reversal reached the White House as a presidential advisory board on historically black universities expressed concern over the position the Justice Department had adopted. Bush claimed that he was unaware of the change in position and vowed to help. Despite the maneuvering, Starr made no changes in the brief. Bush intervened directly, ordering the Justice Department to reverse its position on funding. Just before the deadline for filing, Starr reversed position in the Reply Brief.[168]

As Starr noted: "We came to our views and the opening briefs stated those. In the reply brief, we stated that we changed our position on the remedy. The president's views were reflected in the reply brief." Starr argued that the president felt strongly about not injuring the historically black colleges. Starr took the extraordinary step of adding a footnote, set off by an asterisk, claiming that the position adopted in the opening brief was no longer the position of the United States. The case provided the classic dilemma for the solicitor general. As Starr noted, "Could I embrace this, in good conscience, or could not, in good conscience, accept those views? It was not the sort of fundamental disagreement that would cause me not to sign the brief or to resign."[169]

Ultimately, Starr argued that Mississippi had not satisfied its constitutional obligation to dismantle a dual system that violated the Equal Protection Clause and Title VI of the Civil Rights Act. The government argued that a state must not only adopt policies that are race neutral, it must also eliminate vestiges of past discrimination. The brief claimed that Mississippi was not fulfilling its obligations under *Brown v. Board of Education*. The government presented evidence to support its contention: use of standardized test scores to segregate students, duplication of programs, discrimination in services, salaries, faculty, and facilities. These policies in the solicitor general's view effectively endorsed and encouraged continued segregation. The arguments and evidence looked very much like those the Court had heard a generation earlier in cases involving elementary schools in southern states.

The solicitor general rejected the argument that *Brown* was not applicable because elementary students were assigned to schools. The state had attributed the existence of single race public colleges to individual choice. The government claimed that free choice was not enough. Past discrimination had constrained choices. Starr argued that the state would fulfill its obligation to dismantle the dual system when a high school graduate's choice of college was "wholly voluntary and unfettered."[170]

By an 8-1 majority, the Court ruled that Mississippi had not met its obligation to dismantle the segregated system. While admission to any university was theoretically open to all, there were subtle mechanisms that fostered segregation. The Court ruled that if a state perpetuated policies or practices that could be traced to past *de jure* discrimination and lacked sound educational justification, then the state was in violation of the Equal Protection Clause. The Court ruled that public colleges must go beyond merely establishing racially neutral admissions policies.[171]

For the first time, the Court applied *Brown* to higher education. The Court held the state to an affirmative duty to rid itself of the vestiges of past segregation. It was not enough to demonstrate that the state had abandoned its past discrimination.[172] The Court decided that public colleges must eliminate *de facto* discrimination if those practices lacked clear educational purposes and resulted from *de jure* discrimination.[173] The Court relied on *Dowell* and *Freeman,* asking whether existing racial identifiability is attributable to the state and examining a wide range of factors to determine whether the state had perpetuated segregation. The Court concluded that the state had failed across a variety of the *Green* factors.[174]

The OSG continued its predecessor's attempts to dismantle affirmative action. *Metro Broadcasting v. Federal Communications Commission* involved policies to promote minority ownership of broadcasting stations. Since *Fullilove,* state and local programs had been found to be wanting constitutionally. Thus, the FCC program seemed vulnerable. As Neal Devins noted: "The case was a political battlefield because Congress had statutorily mandated the FCC to defend its preference policy in the wake of efforts by Reagan appointed commissioners to reexamine those affirmative action programs."[175] The case was complicated by the fact that Bush appointed three commissioners who favored the preference policy. Thus, the case represents another example of the inherent tensions the solicitor general faces.

Initially, the FCC and solicitor general papered over their differences by agreeing to oppose the granting of certiorari in hopes of passing the issue back to Congress and the D.C. Circuit. When the Court granted the petition, the rift became apparent. The FCC tried a power play, claiming that the commissioners would file a separate brief with or without the solicitor general's authorization. The OSG filed a brief that was contrary to Congressional policy and the position of FCC. Starr recused himself because the issue had been before him when he served on the Court of Appeals. The OSG did permit the FCC to file a brief stating its position. According to Devins, this may have been a function of a sensitivity to the FCC's position with Congress, a fear that the FCC would ignore the OSG, claim its independent authority, and file on its own, or that the political fallout was not worth the risk of denying the FCC access to the Court's docket.[176]

Principal Deputy John Roberts, who argued the case, said, "We felt that we could not defend the FCC's position. The Court would be better served by letting us present our views. The FCC's position was different from the Solicitor General's. It is rare to air linen in public like this, but because the FCC is an independent agency, we had no control over the development of the litigation in the lower courts."[177] The office filed *amici* in the cases regarding FCC policies.

Roberts argued that the FCC's policy of awarding "qualitative enhancement for minority ownership" in granting licenses violated the equal protection component of the Fifth Amendment. The OSG argued that the policy used race as a classification and was therefore constitutionally suspect. The brief relied on *Croson,* arguing that strict scrutiny should be required in evaluating the program. The Court had distinguished state programs from federal, which were held to a lower standard. Roberts asked the Court to bring the standards for federal policies into line with state policies. The brief argued that if strict scrutiny was required, then the government's program must be narrowly tailored to achieve a compelling rationale. Roberts argued that programming diversity was not a sufficiently compelling interest, nor narrowly tailored. Roberts maintained that neither Congress nor the FCC had tried less drastic means of achieving their desired ends, nor had they established the factual evidence to support the use of racial classifications.[178]

The Court upheld FCC regulations that reserved television and radio licenses for minority owners, distinguishing between "benign" and "invidious" racial classifications. The 5-4 majority held that the former should not be subject to the same level of scrutiny as invidious classifications.[179] The majority held that classifications were benign because they did not harm minorities and only incidentally burdened whites. The dissenters, who had struggled to equate all forms of discrimination, claimed that no discrimination was benign. They supported the solicitor general's argument that all racial classifications must satisfy strict scrutiny. O'Connor argued that the FCC's goal, promotion of broadcast diversity, was too diffuse and amorphous and unrelated to any legitimate basis for employing racial classifications.[180]

Conclusion. To return to the questions that guide this research: how did the solicitor general balance forces and what impact did the OSG have on the development of civil rights doctrine? The Bush administration was perhaps closest to the Johnson administration in that many of the political and legal forces were in alignment. The president and the attorney general kept pushing the Reagan agenda. The CRD was more moderate leading to some battles with the solicitor general. The Court was more conservative and more willing to consider the extreme arguments that it had rejected two years earlier. Only Congress, which reversed some civil rights decisions, was not sympathetic to the administration's positions. Indeed, Congress put the Court and the solicitor general on notice in affirmative action. The policy environment was more favorable also, as the Reagan administration's modest success in getting some precedents limited and attracting votes portended an emerging majority.

Like Lee and Fried, Kenneth Starr tried to expand the role of the solicitor general. Starr moved toward the political end of the spectrum in civil rights. He was responsible for creating exceptions to affirmative action and creating a blueprint for terminating desegregation. In the voluntary *amici* cases, the solicitor general tries to assume the role of attorney general as policy maker. Starr was able to play that role when the government filed an *amicus,* but his attempts to assume that role when the government was a party were often frustrated. In voting rights, Starr had disagreements with the assistant attorney general for civil rights and adopted the role of attorney general as law enforcement agent. After presidential pressure, he opted for a legal interpretation in the Mississippi universities case. This pushed the solicitor general into the less political role as attorney general as law enforcer and tenth justice.

The rules and norms that had constrained Reagan's solicitors general had been reduced over their two terms. Starr was able to take advantage and achieve some of the victories that eluded his predecessors. This permitted Starr to act on the administration's sincere preferences and continue the agenda that Lee and Fried had launched. The Bush political appointees largely wanted to continue the work of their predecessors. They had the opportunity because the legal environment was more propitious. The nominations of Souter and Thomas seemed to provide a critical mass for conservatives. Doctrinal trends and issue evolution had been moving in their direction.

The relationship between the CRD and the OSG changed. In virtually every administration, the solicitor general moderated the positions of the CRD. But under Starr, the OSG often pushed for more extreme stances. Dunne tried to move the division more to the center, but Starr sought to continue the policies of the previous administration. Dunne won his share of battles over voting rights when Thornburgh was attorney general, but when Barr replaced him, Starr's authority increased. The impact of the solicitor general was evident in that Starr was able to overcome the opposition of the CRD in a number of cases. Starr also appeared to repair some of the damage that occurred in the Reagan administration.

Starr's impact should not be underestimated. He won a number of campaigns launched by Reynolds. The administration was able to capitalize on the foundation that the Reagan solicitors general had established. Its success would constrain the new Democratic administration. Favorable decisions in *Dowell* and *Freeman* achieved the goal of reversing long-standing desegregation policies. The office argued against set asides in the *Metro Broadcasting* case, but the Court narrowly upheld the policy.

BILL CLINTON: THE NEW DEMOCRAT?

The ability of the Clinton solicitors general to achieve their goals was dependent on overcoming constraining rules and taking advantage of favorable institutional norms. The deck was stacked against them. There were periods of divided government and the Court was significantly more conservative. Norms and rules were increasingly unfavorable to civil rights. Over the previous twelve years, Republican administrations had reconstructed the OSG, changed the ethos of the CRD, and contributed to a number of precedents limiting civil rights.

Executive. Bill Clinton's arrival in Washington held out the promise of ending two decades of actual gridlock and four years of virtual gridlock during the Carter administration. Clinton had majorities in both houses, an activist agenda, and the rhetorical skills to fulfill the promise. But his agenda was left of the median member of the House and right of his party.[181] In addition, his mandate was challenged even before he took the oath of office. Clinton received only 43 percent of the total vote and ran behind most Democratic representatives. Thus, both parties felt free to test his resolve and authority.[182]

Clinton was a self-proclaimed new Democrat. Whatever that label meant, there was a commitment to civil rights. The harsh policies of the Reagan-Bush administrations provided a foil for candidate Clinton. After a rocky two years, Democrats lost control of the House for the first time in forty years. As a result, Clinton made a decided turn to the right. Still, in the course of his re-election campaign, Clinton supported affirmative action using the slogan: "mend it, don't end it."[183]

The Department of Justice had trouble gaining traction. Clinton's first choice for attorney general, Zoe Baird, met resistance.[184] The president's choice to head the CRD, Lani Guinier, was a target for her views on minority representation in voting districts.[185] The administration withdrew her nomination. Clinton went the neutral route for attorney general with Janet Reno.[186] Reno had a tempestuous first term and was rumored to be a casualty of the president's second-term strategy, but she survived. The administration eventually selected Deval Patrick, former counsel for the Legal Defense Fund, to head the CRD. Patrick left after the first term and a firestorm followed the nomination of his successor, Bill Lann Lee. Like Guinier, Lee was a victim of his past views, this time on affirmative action. The Republican-led Senate blocked consideration of his nomination. Clinton used an end run, appointing Lee as acting assistant attorney general.

Reno did not interfere with Solicitors General Drew Days and Seth Waxman and Acting Solicitor General Walter Dellinger in civil rights. She spent more time on crime issues, leaving civil rights to Deputy Attorney General Jamie Gorelick. According to Principal Deputy Paul Bender, "She would ask to review politically sensitive cases. She would make recommendations and exert influence in some cases. Influence occurred very frequently. It was rare to veto a position or decision outright, but not all that rare to have some influence." According to Patrick, head of the CRD, "Most of the work we did involved no discretion. Only when there was discretion was there concern and interference. . . . It was up to the White House, the Attorney General, and her Deputy to make the political calculations."[187]

Bender argued that Days struggled to insulate the office: "There was a constant tug of war to keep the office independent of the interference." According to Patrick: "Jamie thought of herself as making the political calculations."[188] Gorelick's effect was to moderate the initiatives of the division and the solicitor general. This was a departure from past Democratic administrations, where a more liberal Justice Department was often restrained by moderate solicitors general.

Congress. Clinton's majority was neither large nor cooperative. According to one member, "A lot of Senators don't know how to act with a Democrat in the White House."[189] While he started with a sympathetic Congress, it was lost in the midterm election. Clinton seemed to lose his focus and control of the agenda, abdicating leadership on domestic issues.[190] By nationalizing the election, running on a platform called the Contract with America, and taking control of the House, Republicans believed they had a mandate for change. Clinton proved to be resourceful and resilient and was able to scramble to middle ground.[191]

The class of 1994 was not overtly sympathetic to civil rights, leaving open the question of whether it would retaliate if the Court imposed limits. Congress had specific interests according to Deval Patrick: "Congress was most interested in the church burning and affirmative action cases. The response in the church burning cases was forceful and positive. But in the affirmative action cases, it was negative and completely out of proportion to the number of cases and the scope of the issues in those cases."[192] Despite his re-election, Clinton had no coattails, so Congress remained an antagonist force. This was significant because since 1988, it had been Congress not the Court that was the forum for civil rights.[193] The president's party made unprecedented gains in the 1998 election.

Supreme Court. It had been a generation since Thurgood Marshall was appointed, the last successful nomination by a Democratic president. Clinton replaced Byron White and Harry Blackmun with two moderates Ruth Bader Ginsburg and Stephen Breyer. Given the former support of White for civil rights and the increasingly liberal voting of Blackmun, the net effect has not been dramatic.[194]

Issue Evolution. The Rehnquist Court resisted the repeated invitations of the solicitor general to begin a wholesale retreat in civil rights during the Reagan and Bush administrations. While the Court threatened a number of precedents, it often stopped at the brink. The new philosophy arguing for judicial restraint and deference to the elected branches did not augur well for pushing civil rights in the courts. The Clinton administration was also constrained by the fact that almost all of the civil rights cases before the Court were difficult, next generation employment questions and a series of emerging voting rights cases that involved the question of minority districts, which combined elements of affirmative action and redistricting.

The Clinton Solicitor General. Drew Days, former assistant attorney general for civil rights under Carter and member of the Legal Defense Fund, was named solicitor general. When Days resigned in the waning days of the first term, Clinton selected Walter Dellinger to serve as acting solicitor general.[195] After Dellinger returned to the faculty at Duke University law school, Clinton nominated Seth Waxman, who served as principal deputy under Dellinger to become solicitor general. According to Dellinger, "Drew had substantial, but not the complete, confidence of the Attorney General." Days ran into a number of problems resulting from switching position in a number of cases, some very liberal stances in civil rights cases, claims that the Court did not fully trust the solicitor general and did not seek the office's input, a relatively low rate of success, and a controversial stance in one visible case. Dellinger, who seemed more willing to adopt moderate positions, maintained, "I had a considerable amount of running room. No one had as much leeway as I had as Solicitor General. . . . I had the confidence of the President and the Attorney General. I had been a senior advisor in the Administration. I had served in the Office of Legal Counsel and earned trust. I had an unusual degree of freedom within the Administration and the Department of Justice."[196]

The most activist political appointees of the OSG and the CRD were very critical of the administration's record in restoring the rights they felt had been neglected during a dozen years of Republican rule. According to Bender,

The Clinton Administration did not have broad range plans
like the Reagan Administration had in its attack on *Roe v.
Wade* and race conscious affirmative action. The Administration worked more day-to-day, reacting to cases and issues.
The general attitude was not to look too liberal. The Administration wanted to retain race conscious affirmative
action in some form. The Administration generally seemed
to want to keep things the same as they had been in the
Reagan–Bush Administrations. I was frustrated by the slow
movement toward any change. It was a blown opportunity
to make needed corrections. It will have been eight years
and very little will have occurred.[197]

Patrick echoed these sentiments: "The White House was nervous about
politics of many of the issues. It was not a goal oriented White House
from the point of view of the development of precedents. I never heard
from the White House until it heard from the *Wall Street Journal* and the
New York Times. I came in and asked what do you want? I was told our
agenda is vigorous enforcement. Then after some complaints and edito-
rials, they said 'well, not that vigorous.'"[198]

Bender expressed disappointment, accusing the administration of
having "a complete lack of principle." He said, "The attitude is that there
is nothing worth fighting for. Everything is pragmatic, everything is
'How are we going to look in the newspapers.' Very rarely were you told
that it was your job to do the right thing. The message was always 'Don't
get us in trouble.'" "But," as Dellinger said, "not on race. You can't say
we did not try on race."[199] Those efforts were often rejected by a conservative Court.

Figure 5-4 shows the forces that the Clinton solicitors general faced
after the 1994 midterm election. It was not a propitious environment.
Once the Republicans took control of the House, the safety net for civil
rights was threatened. The Supreme Court was not favorable to the types
of reversals the office would seek. Issue evolution presented a significant
constraint: the civil rights questions of the period arose in the context of
difficult, multidimensional cases. A dozen years of aggressive attacks on
civil rights had undermined some important precedents further con-
founding the task for the Clinton solicitors general. Even within the administration, there was division. The CRD was very anxious to reverse
recent Court decisions, but the Justice Department was less committed
and tried to place brakes on the solicitor general and the division.

The empirical results reflect the constraints the office faced. Clinton solicitors general entered twenty civil rights cases and supported civil rights claimants in nineteen. Their success level in civil rights was not impressive, winning just nine of the twenty cases. Their civil rights agenda was dominated by second-generation Voting Rights Act issues and the complex minority district cases. Days and Dellinger supported affirmative action and racial gerrymandering. But the cases were litigated in an environment that was unfavorable to civil rights and with a diminished threat of Congressional retaliation. The Court seemed intent on banning affirmative action altogether in favor of a color-blind Constitution.

Given the problems in staffing the highest positions in the Justice Department, it took the administration a while to get a solicitor general appointed and confirmed. As Richard Seamon noted: "There was a period early in Drew Days tenure when things were happening slowly. Things were backing up. We spent time reexamining the positions the previous Administration had taken to determine what different decisions might be needed."

During the interim period, William Bryson, who served as acting solicitor general, presided over two civil rights cases. The government took the side of the civil rights claimants in both cases and lost both. One was a voting rights case, *Holder v. Hall.* Less than two weeks before Clinton was inaugurated, lame duck Solicitor General Starr filed briefs in *Holder* and another voting rights case. Starr defended the position saying he was trying to clear the dockets to help the new administration. Lani Guinier attributed the move to baser political motives: "The Justice Department

---

FIGURE 5-4
ENVIRONMENTAL CONSTRAINTS ON THE SOLICITOR GENERAL:
CLINTON ADMINISTRATION

SG`

	SGp		SGc		SGw	
Liberal—————————————————————————————Conservative
	President		Congress	Precedent	Supreme Court	

SGp: Position Solicitor General would adopt if doing the president's bidding
SGw: Position Solicitor General would adopt if winning was the sole goal
SGc: Position Solicitor General would adopt to avoid Congressional response
SG`: Actual position the Solicitor General adopted

is acting gratuitously in its rush to file these briefs. The deadline they were apparently trying to meet is Inauguration Day."[200] Seamon claimed: "It appeared to be an attempt to box the new Administration in on a specific issue."[201]

The Clinton administration changed position in the case. As Robert Long noted, "The new Solicitor General has to weigh the policy versus the legal arguments. The previous Administration may have taken a position that is difficult either legally or politically. It is easy to change positions in a case like that. If the arrows are both pointed in that direction, it makes the decision an easy one."[202] What made this case more difficult, as Long noted, was that Bryson, a career deputy, was the acting solicitor general. Some of the difficulties inherent in changing position were mitigated by the fact that John Dunne, the head of Bush's CRD, backed the side the Clinton administration supported.[203]

During his tenure, Days argued or entered eleven civil rights cases. In ten cases,[204] Days supported the civil rights claimant, but he was on the losing side in six. Five of Days's cases involved minority voting rights and racial gerrymandering, another three involved other Voting Rights Act issues. In *Shaw v. Reno* (and *Shaw v. Hunt*), *Miller v. Johnson,* and *Bush v. Vera* the Court limited reapportionment to create minority districts despite attempts by the solicitor general to ensure the protection of minority voters. The arguments that the Reagan administration advanced that programs to enhance the opportunities afforded minorities are just as discriminatory as those that hurt minorities had been brought to bear in these cases.

The minority district cases proliferated as a function of a confluence of political and legal factors. The Court had upheld the effects test in *Gingles,* creating an environment for such cases. In *Gingles,* the Court interpreted the 1982 revisions of the Voting Rights Act to mandate the creation of the maximum number of minority districts. Democrats favored the creation of black majority districts because it would enhance the party's power. Republicans favored the policy because the concentration of black voters in minority districts would whiten neighboring districts, making them more Republican. Civil rights groups were unwavering in their support.[205]

Shaw v. Reno involved the infamous 12th District in North Carolina, created to enhance minority voting power. The district was 160 miles long, included parts of twenty-eight different counties, and snaked its way along Interstate 85. One state legislator claimed that if "you drove down the interstate with both car doors open, you'd kill most of the people in the district."[206] The solicitor general began with the argument that past precedents allowed the state to take race into account when drawing the districts. The government argued that the fact that the 12th District was neither compact nor aesthetically pleasing did not undermine the constitutionality of the decision to draw the district. The solicitor general was constrained by recent precedents outside the voting rights area requiring strict scrutiny. The solicitor general urged the Court not to require strict scrutiny in these cases, arguing that it was legitimate for the state to take race into account to avoid violations of Voting Rights Act.[207]

In the majority opinion, Justice O'Connor transplanted the color-blind standard of affirmative action that argued for strict scrutiny to the majority-minority voting districts, thus limiting the use of benign race-based classifications.[208] She argued for the narrow tailoring of remedies, again borrowing directly from the affirmative action decisions. As Abigail Thernstrom noted, the Court held that "race-based districting is no different than other forms of discriminatory state action."[209]

The decision seemed to be confined to the unusual nature of the district. Lawyers in the Justice Department and the OSG and analysts felt that the decision did not appear to lay "the foundation for a major attack on the Voting Rights Act."[210] But the Reagan administration had attempted to shift the focus from group rights to individuals. *Shaw v. Reno* suggested the Court might be amenable to that in voting rights.

It was unclear where the Court was heading doctrinally in the wake of *Shaw*. According to Patrick, "There were so many cases and they came so fast. . . . I feel for people in the voting section—there was no real guidance from the Court." The OSG did not initially consider the decision to be a clear limitation to minority districts. According to Bender, the principal deputy responsible for civil rights cases, "My only regret is that maybe we should have asked the Court to overrule *Shaw v. Reno* directly. I don't think the Court would have done that. We tried to find some new grounds, a way to distinguish the cases. We explored every possible avenue, they were all dead ends."[211]

Subsequent cases seemed to be appropriate vehicles for constraining the damage of *Shaw*. According to Days: "We looked for the best cases. The Louisiana and Georgia cases looked promising based on O'Connor's visual test in *Shaw v. Reno*. The Louisiana Attorney General, who was pro-minority districts, made a good effort to defend districts. Georgia made a half-hearted defense of its own districts."[212] The decisions led Days to settle other redistricting cases.

The character of the dynamic relationship between the solicitor general and the Court was evident in the majority-minority district cases.

There were a number of cases arising quickly, limiting the ability of the solicitor general to adapt to emerging doctrine. The decisions were negative, but not broad enough to provide guidance. The decisions continually undercut the ground of the solicitor general. The office tried, with little success, to distinguish each case from the previous decision.

In *Shaw,* the Court did not say that majority-minority districts were always subject to strict scrutiny. Rather, the government argued that the Court held that districts were suspect if they departed dramatically from traditional districting practices (compactness, contiguity, and respect for subdivisions). In *United States v. Johnson,* the government argued that the 11th District in Georgia was not so irregular that it could be construed as an effort to segregate the races for purposes of voting. Days had a fall back position: in case the Court required strict scrutiny, this district satisfied that. The state had a compelling reason, compliance with section 2 of the Voting Rights Act, and the remedy was narrowly tailored.[213]

In *Miller v. Johnson,* a companion case, the Court broadened its previous decision, holding that the bizarreness of the district was no longer a necessary condition for finding redistricting suspect. The Court ruled that allegations that race was the dominant and controlling rationale in drawing district lines were sufficient to state a claim under *Shaw.* The Court ruled that the 11th District was drawn with the explicit purpose of creating safe black constituencies and thus rejected the district on the grounds that it constituted unconstitutional racial gerrymandering.[214] The decisional trend was becoming clear.

In *Johnson v. DeGrandy,* the government charged that reapportionment of Florida legislative districts had diluted minority voting power. In *Johnson* and *Holder,* the Court tried to develop a standard for evaluating vote dilution. The Court ruled that there was no violation of the Voting Rights Act if minority voters' share of the voting population reflected the population even if additional minority districts could be created. Despite the solicitor general's arguments, the Court loosened the *Gingles* standards. The Court adopted a more forgiving "totality of circumstances" approach, which makes "substantial proportionality" the standard for determining whether vote dilution exists.[215]

In these cases, the solicitor general tried to fulfill the roles of attorney general as policy maker and as law enforcement officer, appearing to err on the side of the former. Meanwhile the Court was trying to impose stability on these cases and probably needed the solicitor general to play the role of fifth clerk or tenth justice.

Walter Dellinger, was involved in four civil rights cases, all as a party. Dellinger supported civil rights claimants in each case and was successful in two of the four. Three of the cases involved interpretations of the Voting Rights Act and the fourth continued the development of minority district doctrine. The Court continued to limit the creation of minority-majority districts because of an overriding concern with race that violated strict scrutiny.[216]

There were other civil rights issues for the Clinton solicitors general. In *Adarand Constructors v. Pena,* the administration sought to protect a federal affirmative action program. Days argued that the Department of Transportation program was consistent with *Fullilove* and *Metro Broadcasting.* Though these precedents supported the position the president favored, the Court rejected the solicitor general's argument and held that the Fifth Amendment required strict scrutiny of all race-based actions by the federal government in the same way that the Fourteenth Amendment required strict scrutiny when the state or local laws had race-based distinctions. O'Connor's opinion carefully documented the evolution of affirmative action decisions. She held that *Metro Broadcasting* was a "surprising turn" that was out of line with other decisions. In that decision, the Court adopted the use of intermediate scrutiny for benign classifications, like affirmative action.[217]

The Court had regularly upheld affirmative action programs that had been Congressionally designed and supported even when it was finding state policies wanting. But the Republicans seized control of Congress in 1994. Without the protection of Congress, the Court's majority was free to impose its view of minority business enterprises. According to Bender: "*Adarand* was a dismal defeat. The Court decided a different issue—an issue that no one raised in the case. The Court wanted to overrule *Fullilove.* We argued that federal and state programs were different. But the Court disagreed. It was a 5-4 decision. O'Connor opted for strict scrutiny. The other four opposed any race based affirmative action. The case was a disaster for us."[218]

The affirmative action and minority district decisions suggested the potential demise of race-based remedies. Strategically, opponents of affirmative action sought to get the issue on the Court's docket. After a school district in Piscataway, New Jersey, dismissed a white teacher to meet budget constraints, a suit ensued. The Bush administration entered the case on behalf of Sharon Taxman, the white teacher. Taxman won in the lower court and the school board appealed.

The case was controversial and divided the Clinton administration. Paul Bender noted: "I approved the decision of the Civil Rights Division to get involved and reverse the government's position in the case. I knew it would be touchy, but we were on the wrong side in the previous administration."[219] According to Dellinger, who had to deal with the case later, "The Civil Rights Division and Paul Bender decided at the last minute, without telling anyone, to change sides in the case. It was done without consultation. The President and Jamie Gorelick were on vacation. By announcing the decision, it put the Administration in a difficult position. Because it was a public event, if we changed position again it would look like we were backtracking. . . . The decision to change sides caused distrust for the rest of Drew Days' tenure." Dellinger added, "The Solicitor General sought to file as *amicus* in the Court of Appeals. The Court of Appeals was so outraged that it refused to accept the brief."

Dellinger said, "This was a ticking time bomb. Someone needed to decide what to do with it." Some argued that the school board should accept the decision, rather than risk an adverse Supreme Court decision, which would create a harmful precedent and perhaps sound the death knell for affirmative action.

The concern for the administration was that if it reversed position again, the move would look politically motivated. This was not a problem for Dellinger: "I was surprised that people thought it was impossible to do a double back flip and reverse the government's position again. I thought we needed to get it right." Dellinger wrote a memorandum to Attorney General Reno claiming that the school board's position was indefensible and the Court of Appeals decision was right on that point. Dellinger argued that the government should support Sharon Taxman. In the end, the president supported his position.

Dellinger reasoned that "the defense of any affirmative action program had to be very carefully done. The Court was clear that you cannot justify the use of race for just any purpose. Affirmative action must be tied to some operating goal of the enterprise not just for race itself." Further, according to Dellinger, "The use of layoffs could be defended only if there was no less burdensome tools that could be used as a remedy. The Court had been clear on that point: the remedy must be narrowly tailored. There was no showing by the school board that this was narrowly tailored."[220]

Responding to the Court's invitation to state a position, Dellinger argued that the Court of Appeals was wrong in prohibiting all affirmative action, but he urged the justices to deny certiorari because the facts of the case were so unusual.[221] Dellinger said, "We did not address the underlying merits on this case, but just focused on the sweeping language of the Third Circuit's opinion. . . . We would have no credibility if we tried to defend the firing of Sharon Taxman. Nothing else we could say would be defensible. The Court would reject our position and the conservatives on the Court would tell the moderates that the Administration would argue race as the sole grounds and that the Court should decide that no race can be used at all."[222]

Jeffrey Toobin argued, "As a matter of legal strategy, it's hard to quarrel with Dellinger's handling of the case. It's always better to dissuade the Supreme Court from reviewing a case that's likely to hurt your long-term political goals." But not everyone agreed with that assessment. According to Bender, "The Court invited the government to participate at the cert stage. The Office of the Solicitor General told them not to take the case. The waffling was based entirely on politics."[223] In the end, the Court ignored the solicitor general's advice and accepted the case, providing the potential for a landmark ruling. According to Dellinger, "The Third Circuit's view was very strong in rejecting the government's position. The reaction to a bad case and a bad defense was that the Circuit Court might well throw the baby out with the bath water. The Court of Appeals issued a scorched earth ruling that you can't use race at all. If you try to defend the indefensible uses of race, you run the risk of a very negative decision. If the Third Circuit had been upheld, it would have crippled affirmative action."

After Dellinger left office, the Justice Department helped broker a deal to settle the case and avoid a possible harmful precedent. He felt that this was the best possible solution: "Fortunately, it was not decided by the Court. Our brief helped the school board see the light and they decided to settle the case." Dellinger felt "it was wrong as a matter of good civil rights policy. It had the possibility of harming civil rights policy. Defending every possible affirmative action program made it impossible to defend any affirmative action program."[224]

The task of restoring civil rights created tensions. The issues were visible, the stakes were high, and the odds were not favorable. The relationship between the OSG and the CRD was not without some friction. A dozen years of Republican leadership and attempts to create new theories of civil rights had important consequences. The division and the solicitor general under Reagan and Bush had reversed some previous decisions and limited others. The new leadership of the division and the civil rights community were anxious to have their voices heard after twelve years of perceived neglect.

The solicitor general, however, was under a different set of constraints. The preceding decade had seen increasingly narrow civil rights decisions. Going forward with a vigorous civil rights agenda seemed like a self-defeating proposition. Days, however, was a past head of the CRD. He referred to Patrick as "the immediate successor that I never had."[225]

Days's selection of Bender placed an unabashed liberal and a strong proponent of civil rights in charge of these issues. According to Days, "The Civil Rights Division was overzealous in some circumstances, but that happens with many agencies. I was sympathetic to the Civil Rights Division." Dellinger was more pointed: "The Civil Rights Division was sometimes sloppy in its enthusiasm. The attorneys were not as candid as they needed to be. They seemed to play hide the ball. Many of the cases had a strong political interest and the Division didn't want to look at the countervailing arguments. The Civil Rights Division was overruled a lot."[226]

The tension between the division and the OSG was palpable in a number of cases and in general approach. As Patrick said, "There were routine complaints about the Solicitor General's Office interference in rewriting briefs." His other criticisms were more to the point of specific differences: "The Solicitor General's Office was comprised of very smart people, but they were often caught up in the game of predicting where the Court was going. They got involved in abstract questions and intellectual puzzles. They often took the lifeblood out of the briefs. They focused on intellectual puzzles that involved a combination of Court precedents, how law was evolving, and the political sensitivities of the justices on the Court. The facts get pushed out of the case. The real problems are obscured by the puzzles." Dellinger concurred in that judgment, "The Solicitor General's Office was seen as bloodless, highly technical and insufficiently committed to the purpose of the Division."[227]

In Patrick's view, the voice of the solicitor general was an echo of the Court. The Court was moving in a certain direction and the OSG was well aware of those predilections. Patrick wanted to ground cases in reality, while he felt the solicitor general and the Court were working on a different plane. "I was not interested in litigating abstract issues. Real problems in real people's lives, that was our goal. So much of the Supreme Court's interest in civil rights is in remedies that it has lost sight of the real people in the cases. There is an astonishing lack of interest in the facts. There was a real failure of the solicitor general's office to consistently engage the Court on all but highly rarified and intellectual grounds. By not raising the facts, the solicitor general let them off the hook. You need to rub their noses in the facts and real life problems."[228]

The careerists in the OSG could argue that the division was out of step with the administration and more importantly, the Court. They could point to the record; the Court rejected the solicitor general more often than not in civil rights. Bender was well aware of this. Regarding the administration, he said, "The Attorney General's Office wanted to take more moderate positions. I agreed with the Civil Rights Division in most cases." He also recognized that liberal arguments had a consequence: "Our lower success rate in the Supreme Court was simply a matter of a conservative Court and our more liberal positions."[229]

Conclusion. Bill Clinton presided over the first Democratic administration to serve two terms in a generation. Clinton solicitors general had the least success in civil rights. It was not unusual to see the goals of the solicitors general diverge somewhat from the administration, but the direction of the divergence was unprecedented. Typical roles were reversed: the political forces were applying the brakes, while the legal actors were trying to accelerate the engines. The solicitor general wanted to pursue an activist agenda and halt the damage that the Court had done to civil rights or restore past precedents. The solicitor general adopted the "political" position, while operatives in the Justice Department opted for the "legal" position. Days wanted to push the frontiers and follow the position adopted by the CRD, but was reined in by political appointees who claimed they were "new" Democrats. Dellinger and Waxman were more circumspect in their approaches.

The Clinton solicitors general adopted the role of the attorney general as policy maker. The problem was that they were constrained by the minority district cases that combined the issues of voting rights and affirmative action. In retrospect, the solicitor general probably should have assumed the role of the tenth justice, trying to find some grounds on which to limit the emerging negative precedents.

The lack of success was not surprising: the institutional and policy environments were the most unfavorable since the Nixon administration. Almost every factor in those environments was negative. The administration was split between those trying to hold the line and those who wanted to be aggressive. There was no safety net for solicitors general interested in pursuing civil rights. In the past, negative Court decisions would have incurred the wrath of Congress. With a Republican majority and constitutional grounds, the prospects of reversal were remote. The Court, exercising its new restraint, was unlikely to return civil rights to its previous prominence. The Court was quite conservative although Clinton's two appointments stemmed the tide to a degree.

During the redefinition phase of civil rights policy, the work of the Reagan solicitors general set the context for their successors. The Clinton administration attempted to return civil rights doctrine to the pre-Reagan period, but it was constrained. The OSG found itself enmeshed in the minority district controversy. The solicitor general supported the creation of minority districts. Incrementally, the Court dismantled the districts on the grounds of racial gerrymandering. Days supported federal set aside programs similar to ones that the Court had supported in the past. But the Rehnquist Court claimed that they violated strict scrutiny.

In the end, the Clinton solicitors general left a negative legacy because the Court rebuffed their position and created hostile precedents. The minority district cases were a downward spiral of increasingly broader negative decisions. These decisions and *Adarand* suggested the potential demise of affirmative action. The case that could have sealed its fate, *Taxman,* was settled before it could create a devastating precedent. That appeared to be a wise strategic decision, particularly in view of the fact that pursuing sincere preferences was a futile gesture.

CONCLUSION: THE SOLICITOR GENERAL IN THE REDEFINITION PHASE

Has the solicitor general become more politicized? The question became salient during the Reagan administration. There is a natural tension between law and politics. How they get balanced is the task that confronts the solicitor general on a daily basis. Through the litigation phase, the legal realm dominated the political in the calculations of the solicitor general. The balance between the political and legal changed somewhat in the administrative phase, but legal considerations still generally held sway. That seemed to change in the redefinition phase. The legal inertia in the office had to be overcome to elevate political considerations. That took personnel and institutional changes. The changes in the office were a function of the nomination of less powerful men to be solicitor general, the perception that there was more politicization in hiring in the ranks, and changes in the institutional mechanism. This led to increasingly pitched battles between the solicitor general and the CRD.

In part, the perceived politicization was a function of attempts to redefine issues. The solicitor general was asked to destabilize law, encouraging the Court to reconsider past precedents and upset policy equilibrium. No one would argue that the office has ever been completely free of political impulses, but some have argued that the differences in the Reagan administration were of kind, rather than degree. The redefinition phase represented a disjuncture. In civil rights, there was a palpable sense that the solicitor general has moved decisively toward the political end of spectrum. Solicitors general seemed willing to do the administration's bidding. Power over litigation shifted from the legal to political end of the spectrum. Part of this, of course, is a function of the controversial nature of civil rights as an issue. The redefinition phase was marked by almost uninterrupted divided government, meaning that Congress and the president were on opposing sides.

Solicitors general were willing to depart from existing precedent and established patterns of civil rights policy. This was a departure from past presidents who might have wanted to draw a line on civil rights, but whose solicitors general did not do their bidding. In the past, when solicitors general retreated, it was not because they were trying to reverse past decisions, it was because issues had gotten too difficult. There were practical reasons for the Reagan administration's changes, though. First, issues had evolved to the point where they were very complex. Second, the Court signaled its willingness to reconsider past precedents.

Like the Truman and Johnson solicitors general, Reagan solicitors general helped shape the role their successors would play. Lee and Fried created opportunities for Starr and constraints for Days, Dellinger, and Waxman. In the litigation and administrative phases, solicitors general were able to take positive precedents in one area and transplant them. A number of principles had guided the expansion in the administrative phase: the use of disparate impact as the standard for judging discrimination in employment and voting, affirmative remedies that would not freeze the effects of prior discrimination, the consideration of race in devising remedies for past discrimination, and voluntary affirmative action plans even when no prior discrimination existed. The desire to reverse them was the guiding principle of the redefinition phase.

Lee, Fried, and Starr achieved some measure of success, though Congress had the final say on a number of issues. They were able to take precedents they supported and transplant them to other areas. They were able to turn the negative northern desegregation back into the South to begin to end court supervision of school districts. They were also able to take the limitations that they suggested and the Court imposed on affirmative action to use to limit *Griggs* and transplant them to voting rights.

The solicitors general of the redefinition phase more frequently acted as the attorney general as policy maker than the tenth justice or the attorney general as law enforcement officer, even when the form of participation suggested they should operate otherwise. The Reagan solicitors general had clear targets, but they were constrained by a Court not willing to undermine precedents and a Congress that was vigilant on civil rights matters. In cases in which the government was a party, Lee had to be more of a law enforcement officer than a policy maker. When discretion permitted, Lee exercised more policy-making prerogatives. Fried and Starr moved further along the spectrum to political. The Clinton solicitors general tried to reverse the policies of their predecessors, again elevating the political perspective over the legal.

It is tempting to think that the Reagan solicitors general altered the nature of the office and that the genie cannot be put back in the bottle. The Clinton administration was not immune from charges that its solicitors general were political. In a sense, the power and authority of the office may have changed during the battle over the New Deal or after *Brown*. Judicial activism certainly encouraged the solicitor general to tip the political/legal balance. And it may be that a new judicial restraint is needed to restore the legal realm to primacy.

Part III

THE SOLICITOR GENERAL AND GENDER DISCRIMINATION AND REPRODUCTIVE RIGHTS

THE TREATMENT OF PEOPLE has often been based on certain immutable characteristics, such as race, age, and sex. In using these characteristics, law reinforces social customs. Gender has been an important factor in defining legal rights and responsibilities.[1] Sex discrimination resembles race discrimination, but differs in important respects. Both were typically based on stereotypes and prejudice. But while racial discrimination in statute was often regional in scope, statutory sex discrimination was more pervasive, being found across the nation. Indeed, as Fisher and Devins argue, "Discrimination against women has remained entrenched for centuries because of tenacious cultural beliefs and practices."[2]

The Supreme Court showed little concern for gender issues until *Reed v. Reed* in 1971. Prior to that, the Court upheld state laws that stereotyped women as weak and needing protection. The Court denied legal recourse for gender discrimination issues at the exact time that it began emasculating the Fourteenth Amendment. The day after it had, in effect, read the privileges and immunities clause out of the Fourteenth Amendment in the *Slaughter House Cases* (1873), the Court upheld an Illinois law that forbade women from practicing law. Just two years later, the Court upheld a law barring women from voting.[3] A decade later, the Court had changed the nature and meaning of the Fourteenth Amendment and foreclosed it as a source of legal protection for women's rights. As late as 1948, while the Court was beginning to outlaw some forms of racial discrimination, the Court was upholding state laws banning women from certain jobs.[4] Even the liberal Warren Court allowed the exemption of women from jury duty in *Hoyt v. Florida*.

Race and gender issues shared some common constitutional and statutory grounds: the Fourteenth Amendment and the Civil Rights Act of 1964, respectively. But these similarities were more symbolic than practical. Indeed, the differences between the two explained why gender took so much longer to develop than race. The Fourteenth Amendment was constructed to ameliorate racial discrimination. It was thought, later, to include prohibitions against gender discrimination, but the amendment is gender specific, referring only to males. The Civil Rights Act of 1964 had explicit prohibitions against gender as well as race discrimination, but the former were added in an attempt to make the bill unpalatable in hopes of precipitating its ultimate defeat. The role of the Supreme Court could not have been more different. Beginning in the 1930s, the Court began to attack racial discrimination, culminating in the *Brown* decision that set a context for the Civil Rights Act.

There was no major substantive or symbolic victory for women's rights advocates.

The civil rights victories of the decades leading up to *Brown* and bridging the gap between the landmark decision and the landmark legislation were a function of the work of a dedicated policy entrepreneur, the Legal Defense Fund of the NAACP. Its victories energized the movement and continued the momentum. The work of the solicitor general and the Department of Justice in lending critical symbolic and practical support cannot be overstated. There was no such external or governmental support for gender equality until much later.

In subsequent chapters, I examine the work of the solicitors general in gender discrimination and reproductive rights under different institutional conditions. To establish the context for the next two chapters, I examine some of the aggregate analysis of the solicitor general's support for gender equality and success on the merits and the contribution to reproductive rights litigation.

THE EMERGENCE OF GENDER ISSUES AND REPRODUCTIVE RIGHTS

Women's rights have passed through three overlapping stages in the Supreme Court. The first stage, 1965–77, involved the constitutionalization of reproductive freedom. The second stage, 1971–82, was the constitutionalization of gender equality. The final stage, which began in 1978, involved statutory construction, as the Court interpreted civil rights legislation passed by Congress.[5]

Gender discrimination and reproductive rights policy evolved in different ways from different constitutional foundations. Yet, the two issues were linked symbolically. Women's groups considered them necessary parts of a full spectrum of rights. Recognition of reproductive rights in the Supreme Court occurred at about the same time as recognition of gender equality. The abortion issue did not arise directly from gender, but equal protection cases raised the sensitivity of litigants and some justices to symbolic connections between these issues.[6]

Women's rights have been divided into two doctrinal streams. Gender discrimination was attacked under the Fourteenth Amendment while reproductive rights were part of privacy doctrine created by the Court in *Griswold v. Connecticut* from the shadows and penumbras of the First, Third, Fourth, Fifth, and Ninth Amendments.[7] Privacy created the environment for abortion, but the new policy window could only be opened by the emergence of gender equality as a viable independent issue. The use of privacy as a basis for reproductive rights constrained the development of the issue and threatened its viability. Many argued that reproductive rights would be on firmer grounds if they were based on the Fourteenth Amendment.[8]

The separation of issues hurt women's rights in two ways. First, by dividing the sources of rights between two sets of constitutional provisions and bodies of precedents, the Court ensured that favorable decisions would not necessarily be mutually reinforcing. Thus, while a favorable Fourteenth Amendment decision might have symbolic spillover effects for reproductive rights, it would not directly contribute to the development of that doctrine. Expansive gender equality precedents could not prevent limitations on reproductive rights. Second, ultimately the Court retreated in each area. While the Fourteenth Amendment is a potentially strong vehicle, the Court refused to use strict scrutiny to ensure gender equality.[9] Similarly, the Court held that privacy was a fundamental right that triggered strict scrutiny, but in practical terms, reproductive rights have seldom been granted that level of protection. The separation of the constitutional bases gave the solicitor general the opportunity to pursue the president's agenda in the abortion cases without undermining gender doctrine and incurring the wrath of Congress.

Many gender discrimination cases were not argued or decided on constitutional grounds, but involved interpretations of statutory provisions. In some ways, this appeared to make the Court's job easier.[10] Much of the ground had been paved by race cases and Congress had passed a number of provisions. The statutory basis for many gender cases is the Civil Rights Act of 1964, most notably Title VII, which prohibits employment discrimination. The Civil Rights Act also created the EEOC. Even before the Civil Rights Act, Congress passed the Equal Pay Act. In 1972, Congress amended Title VII and added Title IX, which prohibited sex discrimination in educational programs receiving federal funds.[11] Reproductive rights, on the other hand, typically involved state laws that had to pass constitutional muster.

TRENDS IN GENDER AND REPRODUCTIVE RIGHTS CASES

Gender issues, though similar to race in substance, looked different across many dimensions. First, the solicitor general was less likely to get involved in gender cases, taking part in just fifty-seven of the ninety-two cases on the Court's docket. The solicitor general was less likely to support the position that would expand rights, supporting gender rights in thirty-four of fifty-seven cases. The success rate was also lower in gender than in race cases. The solicitor general was on the victorious side in thirty-eight of fifty-seven cases. Most of the government's involvement took place in the Carter and Reagan administrations, thirty-four of the fifty-seven cases.

Partisan support and success in gender cases resemble race cases. In the aggregate, solicitors general in Democratic administrations were significantly more likely to support gender rights claimants than their Republican counterparts. Table III-1 shows that Republican solicitors general supported gender discrimination claimants in fewer than half the cases, while Democrats supported gender equality in eighteen of twenty-two cases. Table III-2 shows that Democrats had much more success than Republican solicitors general.

Table III-3 shows the type of participation and levels of support for gender equality across administrations. One item is particularly noteworthy: in the race cases, the solicitor general filed ninety-four *amici* and sixty-three cases as a party. While the dominant mode of participation in race cases was the voluntary *amicus* brief, which gives the solicitor general greater discretion, in gender policy, the solicitor general filed similar numbers of *amici* and direct party briefs. That suggests Congress

Table III-1
Support for Gender Discrimination Claimants by Political Party in Cases Involving the Solicitor General

	Political Party of President		
Gender Rights Position	*Democratic*	*Republican*	*Total*
Favor Gender Equality Claimants	18	17	35
Oppose Gender Equality Claimants	4	19	23
Total	22	36	58

Table III-2
Success of the Solicitor General by Political Party in Gender Discrimination Cases

	Political Party of President		
Success on the Merits	*Democratic*	*Republican*	*Total*
Win	17	21	38
Loss	5	15	20
Total	22	36	58

played a large role in gender cases and that solicitors general were less likely to enter cases involving state laws.

The Ford administration appeared most resistant to gender claims, but all five briefs it filed against claimants came when the government was party and Bork had to defend legislation. The Carter administration supported gender equality in eleven cases, but the three exceptions were much more noteworthy.

Reagan solicitors general made the deepest inroads, opposing gender rights in five of eight *amici* briefs, both invited cases, and half the ten cases in which the government was a party. The attack on affirmative action and disparate impact in race cases spilled over to gender cases. For their troubles, Congress reversed a number of the Court's decisions.

There is evidence of early doctrinal confusion. In the early stages of issue development, solicitors general supported gender rights claimants as often as they opposed them. The success rate was marked by an even number of victories and defeats. Part of this was a function of the fact that the early cases occurred on Republican watches. Once the Court established some doctrinal clarity, solicitors general supported gender equality in more than two-thirds of the cases during the later stages. The success rate during that stage was 72 percent.

The pattern of solicitor general activity in reproductive rights looked quite different than either race or gender litigation. Solicitors general maintained a safe distance from reproductive rights cases. Only when the government was forced to confront the issue by a Congressional statute or a Supreme Court invitation did the Nixon, Ford, or Carter administration participate. When their solicitors general did participate, it was in cases that did not involve the core rights, but the exercise of those rights.

TABLE III-3

SOLICITOR GENERAL'S SUPPORT FOR GENDER RIGHTS
AND LEVELS OF SUCCESS BY TYPE OF PARTICIPATION

Type of Participation

	Party		Invited		*Amicus*		Total	
	Pro	*Con*	*Pro*	*Con*	*Pro*	*Con*	*Pro*	*Con*
Support	14	13	3	3	18	7	35	23

	Party		Invited		*Amicus*		Total	
	Won	*Lost*	*Won*	*Lost*	*Won*	*Lost*	*Won*	*Lost*
Success	18	9	4	2	15	10	37	21

That changed when the Reagan administration targeted abortion, attacking *Roe v. Wade* directly and indirectly and using the issue as a litmus test for its judicial nominations. Indeed, the widespread perception that the Office of the Solicitor General had become politicized was a function of the attack on *Roe.*

Chapter 6 examines the emergence and early evolution of gender and reproductive rights litigation, concentrating on the Nixon, Ford, and Carter administrations. Chapter 7 concerns the later development and redefinition of gender and reproductive rights litigation and the activities of the Reagan and Bush administrations and the attempts of the Clinton solicitors general to redress the balance.

The Solicitor General and the Emergence and Definition of Gender and Reproductive Rights Policy

W HILE THEY WERE NOT unsympathetic to gender equality, the primary interest of solicitors general was to help the Court reach a standard and impose equilibrium on doctrine. The solicitor general served as the tenth justice when the government was a party. The achievement of goals was tempered by the need for strategic interaction. There was legislation on the books, so Congress would be a participant. The Court showed a willingness to address these issues, even if the justices could not settle on a standard. Rules and norms were problematic for the solicitor general. There was no direct precedent supporting gender equality. Groups used analogies from other areas, most notably race. The span of issues that initially confronted the Court was dramatic, ranging from state laws that were patently unconstitutional to statutes that provided benefits to compensate for past inequalities. This impeded efforts to impose consistency on doctrine. Two other constraints were noteworthy. One involved the competing interests that had to be balanced against gender equality. This sometimes placed the solicitor general into multidimensional cases arguing for judicial deference to the countervailing interest. Second, the solicitor general had to argue on behalf of Congressional policies that often provided unequal treatment.

As in civil rights, the solicitor general has to balance the designs of the president and the executive agency with Congressional interests. The solicitor general has to operate with the proclivities of the Supreme Court and doctrine in mind, as well as considering the evolution of the issue. Still the calculations that the solicitor general followed in gender and reproductive rights were different from those used in civil rights.

Presidents were not as interested in gender issues as civil rights. Early in the evolution of gender policy, few presidents considered it salient.

Reproductive rights, on the other hand, was a campaign issue that presidents cared a great deal about. Many considered abortion a litmus test for judicial appointments and an important determinant in choosing some solicitors general. At the outset, though, solicitors general kept their distance from the issue, forfeiting the chance to use *amici* to fulfill the role of attorney general as policy maker. Rather, they served as fifth clerk or Congress was a primary constituency. This would change with the Reagan administration.

Gender rights were dominated by statutory law. This had the potential to constrain the influence of the president and the Court. The solicitor general and the Court would be called on to interpret statutory provisions in a number of factual situations. Congress was a central actor. There has been a volatility to this separation of powers dynamic, however. In interpreting statutory intent, the solicitor general and the Court needed to respond to the current Congress, rather than the one that passed the legislation.[1] After all, it is the current Congress that can respond to a solicitor general's interpretation or a Court decision. Indeed, Congress passed legislation strengthening gender equality and civil rights in response to Court decisions it opposed.

In reproductive rights, the dynamics looked different. The main issues were constitutional, which because of the extraordinary majorities needed to overturn decisions, limited the influence of Congress. A number of Constitutional amendments were proposed to no avail. There were attempts to strip the Court's jurisdiction, which failed. Congress did have the authority to pursue blocking legislation or make the exercise of reproductive rights more difficult. Some of these measures passed.[2] The Court's role was more central in these areas and the president's influence over the government's legal position was more direct. Despite this, solicitors general successfully avoided the early cases because presidents wanted to avoid the issue. Congress tried to limit funding when it was unable to attack the right directly. When solicitors general went to Court, it was at the request of the justices or to defend legislation. Thus, they were constrained in their arguments. Rules and norms for the issue were established without the solicitor general's assistance.

The shape of gender rights and abortion policy is a function of the composition of the Supreme Court. The ideological and doctrinal predilections of the Court provide a context for the strategies, tactics, and issue analogies used by the solicitor general and groups litigating gender rights issues.[3] The OSG could not push cases or arguments that were out of line with the ideological tenor of the Court.

For almost the entire history of this litigation, changes in the composition of the Court have created an increasingly negative environment for gender and reproductive rights.[4] Of the Republican appointments since *Reed,* only Justice John Stevens has supported civil liberties and civil rights in more than half the cases he decided.[5] Two decades of conservative appointments appeared to create a critical mass with the votes to dismantle many of the precedents that expanded civil rights. Yet, as the Court got more conservative and cases got more difficult, judicial support for gender equality did not decline.[6] At the same time, reproductive rights were sharply curtailed.

The increasing conservatism of the Court was not without consequences. Strategically, a solicitor general who was a proponent of gender equality would be advised to narrow the scope of cases, avoiding constitutional issues. On the other hand, the composition of the Court encouraged the solicitor general to expand the review of abortion cases, in hopes of overturning *Roe.* This chapter examines the roles that Erwin Griswold, Robert Bork, and Wade McCree played in structuring the developmental phase of gender and reproductive rights issues.

GENDER RIGHTS POLICY

Policy construction is done by analogy and is an evolutionary process. In the Supreme Court, a new issue typically results from an ancillary issue often as the conscious effort of litigants or justices seeking to transplant success from an existing area. New issues carry baggage, positive and negative, from related precedents and existing interpretations of relevant constitutional provisions until they ultimately emerge on their own. This constrains their pattern of growth to a degree but also provides opportunities to expand favorable precedents. Gender issues have been affected by the race paradigm. Gender doctrine was a result of a legal analogy from race under the Fourteenth Amendment. Yet, reliance on the race paradigm, which was also used by the solicitor general, could not capture the complexities of gender.[7]

Though race was a prologue, gender did not follow the same progression. Normally, the solicitor general is less likely to get involved in the early stages. Indeed, the solicitor general was absent from more of the early cases than in race. This meant that the office was less able to stamp its imprint on the development of doctrine.

There were trends that suggested an expansion of gender rights if it was linked to race doctrine. Solicitors general under Johnson and Nixon (in employment) had participated in expanding the scope and coverage of the Civil Rights Act and linked it to the Reconstruction acts. The Warren and Burger Courts had shown a propensity for expansive decisions. On the other hand, there was uncertainty tied to the constitutional basis of gender rights. The Fourteenth Amendment pertained to race, but would the Court extend that to gender issues and what level of scrutiny would emerge?

Each of the branches contributed to the emergence of gender policy. Congress passed the Equal Pay of 1963, Title VII, and Title IX of the Educational Amendments of 1972. President Johnson provided support with an executive order that required federal contractors not to discriminate in employment practices and to adopt affirmative action measures. The Supreme Court joined the fray in 1971. Unlike civil rights, progress did not initially come from the courts; it was primarily derived from the legislative and executive branches.[8] As a result, the solicitor general played a more supportive role. According to Stephanie Seymour, "The birth of gender equality was less a product of the Court . . . than a product of the times."[9] The Burger Court had to make difficult choices that were not clearly covered by the Fourteenth Amendment, such as discrimination based on age, gender, illegitimacy, or disabilities.[10]

Title VII was designed to deal with discrimination on the basis of race, sex, national origin, and religion. Constitutional provisions pertained specifically to public discrimination. Title VII was designed to extend protection against discrimination to the private sector. The ban on sex discrimination was inserted with little discussion to clarify legislative intent. Hearings on the Civil Rights Act contained almost no reference to sex discrimination. Compounding the problem was that these provisions were added in an attempt to defeat the Civil Rights Act.[11] The courts had to define who was covered by the statute. In addition, the EEOC had more problems clarifying and applying the definition of gender discrimination than in other areas. Bans on discrimination allow an affirmative defense that the requirement in question was a bona fide occupational qualification (BFOQ). Courts have interpreted this broadly, allowing employers to argue that a legitimate BFOQ exists.[12] Among the BFOQs allowed were veteran's preferences, seniority, merit systems, and professional ability. This has presented the greatest threats to Title VII[13] and made the job of an solicitor general interested in pursuing equality more difficult.

Title IX was a law requiring gender equality in educational programs that receive federal assistance. A violation of the law would result in the denial of federal funds.[14] Title IX cases would arrive on the Court's docket about a decade after the emergence of gender doctrine.

Balancing Law and Politics in Gender Discrimination Cases

There were differences between the trends in cases in which the government was a party and those the solicitor general voluntarily entered as *amici*. Many of the early cases were relatively easy. States often had old laws that patently discriminated against women. It was no stretch for the solicitor general to oppose those laws or the Court to declare them unconstitutional. Part of the reason that the solicitor general did not get involved in many early cases was the ease of the factual situations. Issue evolution suggests that cases get more difficult over time and this occurred in the *amici* cases. In the direct party cases, however, the issues were difficult from the outset. Some federal laws favored women. Did this constitute gender discrimination?

Statutory provisions were of two types: early statutes offered benign forms of discrimination to help women, later statutes were designed to root out discrimination. The development of gender policy was not linear. There were structural and institutional barriers to the development of gender equality. Policy development was constrained by the timing of decisions, a conservative Court, and the lack of early statutory and Constitutional authority. The Fourteenth Amendment makes no mention of gender. This was important for some justices. Thus, the litigation environment for the solicitor general was more constrained than it was for race.

In every case, the policy that discriminated, whether against women or men, is balanced against a competing interest. A problem for gender litigation was the governmental and economic nature of the activities. When those activities involved criminal law or the military, the Court was asked to defer to the governmental interest.[15] Most cases involved some economic benefit. Under the preferred position doctrine, the Court typically treats economic issues with judicial restraint. This created a barrier to a broad expansion of equality.

Compounding the problem was that some policies favored women, ostensibly to remedy past discrimination. There was a distinction between laws that provided benign and invidious discrimination. The latter looked like laws that discriminated on racial grounds, the former like affirmative action programs.[16] As Judith Baer wrote, the treatment of women included both "the cage and the pedestal."[17]

In some ways, emerging doctrine seemed to provide a win–win situation for women. The Supreme Court was poised to strike laws that discriminated against women. At the same time, the Court was willing to countenance laws that preferred women or corrected for past discrimination.[18] The problem was that some of the "helpful" laws were predicated on paternalistic stereotypes. Upholding those laws may have helped women in some tangible ways, but perpetuated other inequalities. Controversy over whether to support these so-called "benign programs" divided the women's rights movement. Some feminists and women's groups advocated the "asymmetrical approach," arguing that it is crucial to recognize women's unique needs and differences. Others argued that women are best served by making gender irrelevant and treating the sexes equally.[19] The divisions caused problems for the agencies in formulating policies and the solicitor general in deciding which policies to defend.

The Women's Rights Project of the ACLU was trying to get the Court to construct a new theory or adapt race theories to meet different factual situations. Feminist groups argued that state-sponsored or aided discrimination against women should merit the same level of protection as race. Like race, sex discrimination seemed to meet the criteria for strict scrutiny: it burdened a politically powerless group on the basis of a visible, immutable characteristic.[20] There was a deliberate strategy to aim first at programs that discriminated against men as a means of expanding the notion of gender discrimination. The question was whether the solicitor general would help these groups like the office helped the NAACP.

The positions and arguments adopted by the solicitor general in gender issues varied on three dimensions. First, there was variation by president and policy goals as the OSG got more conservative. Second, the arguments of solicitors general varied relative to the type of case and the evolution of the issue. As issues evolved from first-generation cases involving overt discrimination to more difficult second-generation cases involving compensatory programs, the solicitor general used different arguments. Finally, the position varied by the type of participation: whether the office argued the case because the government was a party, was invited to participate, or voluntarily filed an *amicus* brief. While the composition of the Court is normally a major factor in the solicitor general's decision making, it seemed less important in gender policy.

Table 6-1 reflects the three differences. The Nixon-Ford administrations supported gender equality in just half the cases they entered. But there were significant differences because of the type of involvement. The Republican solicitors general supported gender equality in only one of the seven cases they entered as a party, many of which involving programs to help women, but all of the cases in which they filed *amici*. The Carter solicitor general was more consistent, opposing gender rights in two of six cases in which the government was a party and two of seven in which he filed an *amicus* brief. Three of the four were very significant cases. The levels of success, shown in Table 6-2, do not reveal such clear patterns. Griswold and Bork were a little less successful in the discretionary *amicus* cases than in defending benign legislation. McCree, Carter's solicitor general, had success in both types of cases.

Gender cases fit a few different categories. There were old state laws that discriminated against women. The solicitor general entered some of these cases as *amici* to support attacks on those statutes. Another category involved federal laws, often social security and other benefits, in which women were beneficiaries to compensate for past inequalities. The line between benign and invidious discrimination was certainly blurry.[21] In these cases, the solicitor general was obligated to support the provision. A third category included cases in which the EEOC (or the Department of Labor) filed a complaint claiming discrimination against women in working conditions or remuneration. The solicitor general normally filed a brief on behalf of the EEOC.

TABLE 6-1

SOLICITOR GENERAL'S SUPPORT FOR GENDER RIGHTS
AND TYPE OF PARTICIPATION BY PRESIDENTIAL ADMINISTRATION
IN THE EARLY STAGE OF ISSUE EVOLUTION

Type of Participation

	Party		Invited		*Amicus*		Total	
President	*Pro*	*Con*	*Pro*	*Con*	*Pro*	*Con*	*Pro*	*Con*
Nixon	1	1	0	0	3	0	4	1
Ford	0	5	0	0	2	0	2	5
Carter	4	2	1	0	5	2	10	4

TABLE 6-2

SOLICITOR GENERAL'S SUCCESS ON THE MERITS AND TYPE OF
PARTICIPATION IN GENDER RIGHTS CASES BY PRESIDENTIAL
ADMINISTRATION IN THE EARLY STAGE OF ISSUE EVOLUTION

Type of Participation

	Party		Invited		*Amicus*		Total	
President	*Won*	*Lost*	*Won*	*Lost*	*Won*	*Lost*	*Won*	*Lost*
Nixon	1	1	0	0	2	1	3	2
Ford	3	2	0	0	0	2	3	4
Carter	4	2	1	0	6	1	11	3

TENTATIVE BEGINNINGS: THE NIXON-FORD ADMINISTRATIONS

Richard Nixon supported the Equal Rights Amendment (ERA), but there was little in his campaign to suggest support for gender issues.[22] Congress did not rush to add any protection for gender rights or equality for women. Ultimately, in 1972, Congress added Title IX to deny federal funds to educational programs that discriminate on gender grounds. As with Title VII, the provisions were brief and vague and carried the potential for advancing equality, but the courts would determine whether its promise would be realized.[23] In the aftermath of Watergate, a liberal Congress failed to take advantage of the open policy window, passing but a few minor acts.

As Nixon came to power, the Warren Court was sitting. Its activism had spawned a constitutional revolution and created the expansion of civil rights. Precedents in the race domain were favorable, but there was a question of whether the Court would transplant them. As far as gender was concerned, precedents were dated, but hostile to equality.

Reed v. Reed opened the Court's agenda to gender cases. An 1864 Idaho law gave men preference over women in serving as administrators of wills. The Court ruled that there was no legitimate justification for the law. Because of the arbitrary nature of the law, the Court did not need to consider the appropriate level of scrutiny. The law failed even the forgiving minimum scrutiny standard.

In many new areas, the solicitor general does not participate in the first case, unless invited. Rather, the OSG waits for the Court to set a context and then begins to operate within the framework. The solicitor general did not enter the *Reed* case, but it was not long until the office was thrown into the maelstrom. Many of the cases involved government programs, necessitating the participation of the solicitor general.

During the Nixon-Ford administrations, the OSG was involved in twelve gender cases. An additional nine gender cases were on the Court's agenda, but the solicitor general refused involvement. As befitting the emergence of a new area, Erwin Griswold and Robert Bork were involved in some novel cases that did not recur, such as cases involving the First Amendment, the Immigration and Naturalization Service (INS), and military policies. In addition, they filed briefs in one employment case, three pregnancy cases, three cases involving social security benefits, and two additional benefits cases, issues that would become staples of the gender agenda. Griswold was involved in two gender rights cases, one as an *amicus* and one as a party. Bork was involved in nine gender cases, five as a party and four as a voluntary *amicus.* One *amicus* brief was filed by the office without Bork's signature.

The first time the solicitor general registered a view in a gender case was in *Phillips v. Martin Marietta,* the first Title VII case to reach the Supreme Court. The company refused to hire women with preschool children, although it would hire men who had preschool children. Griswold filed an *amicus* at the certiorari stage urging the Court to accept the petition. On the merits, the government argued that this was not a bona fide occupational qualification and thus a clear violation of Title VII.[24] The Court issued a *per curiam* decision, finding that the policy was flawed. But the Court was tentative and left room for companies to use stereotyping in employment decisions. The Court refused to exclude the possibility that stereotyping about women's roles could justify a BFOQ defense.[25]

Phillips represented the type of traditional law that discriminated against women and was easy for the solicitor general to oppose. The next Supreme Court case to attract the solicitor general's attention, *Frontiero v. Richardson* (1973), involved the type of "benign discrimination" that would trouble the solicitor general and the Court for the next generation and hinder efforts to impose stability on doctrine. The pathbreaking case was brought by the Women's Rights Project.[26]

In *Frontiero,* Griswold was obligated to support Congressional and military policies regarding differential benefits for servicemen and servicewomen. Most importantly, the solicitor general played a role in structuring consideration of the underlying standard. Griswold argued that the Court should uphold the provision and adopt the lowest level of scrutiny. He argued that the provision represented a reasonable exercise of Congressional power. Griswold claimed that because this involved an economic benefit, the Court should use the rational basis to evaluate the statute. He argued that sex classifications were different from race and did not merit the same level of scrutiny. The government's brief claimed that racial classifications were based on social contempt and required the highest level of scrutiny. Gender classifications, on the other hand, could be justified because they were often based on objective physiological and sociological differences.[27] Griswold argued that such classifications did not stigmatize women or imply inferiority.

Griswold urged the justices to wait for the outcome of ERA and legislation that was pending in Congress. He argued that the legislative branch, rather the judiciary, should determine policy aimed at social change.[28] The Court rejected the government's argument, but could not agree on an overriding standard. In a plurality opinion, Justice Brennan argued that gender analysis merited strict scrutiny, but could not attract a fifth vote. According to Ruth Bader Ginsburg, the use of heightened scrutiny meant that the Court had taken a giant step beyond *Reed* and moved farther and faster than anyone would have guessed.[29]

The majority preferred to wait for ERA, which looked inevitable at the time, to make sex a suspect classification.[30] In a concurrence, Powell argued that "the Court should not usurp the democratic process" while states were considering the ERA.[31] According to Kirp, Yudolf, and Franks, "Although the *Frontiero* plurality opinion was meant to chart the course of gender litigation, it did not begin to comprehend the varieties of legislation it would reach."[32] The Court ultimately decided on the middle-level standard in a case the solicitor general did not participate in, *Craig v. Boren* (1976). But there were exceptions to this general approach. The Court would use minimum scrutiny to evaluate gender-based distinctions to compensate women for past discrimination and in pregnancy cases.[33]

Bork did not support the use of heightened scrutiny for gender cases, arguing, "Race was a guide for the gender cases, but not support for strict scrutiny. I did not think that it should be treated like race." That middle standard was not a satisfying alternative for Bork: "There was a real mess in the law. We were advocating the rational basis in our briefs. The Court could not decide. The idea of an intermediate standard added unnecessary confusion to that body of law."[34]

The government was a party to five cases during Bork's tenure. In these cases the solicitor general argued on behalf of an administrative agency, the EEOC, or Congressional policy. In some senses, the solicitor general and the Court were constrained by Congress. The solicitor general normally urged deference to the elected branches and avoided constitutional grounds, even when the other party attempted to expand the issue. As a consequence, few of these were landmark decisions.

Many of the statutes involved in these cases were designed to help women. The solicitor general supported these policies and the Court often accepted the arguments. Many of the challenged policies, designed to overcome past discrimination, were rooted in stereotypic views and paternalistic attitudes toward protecting women.[35] In its brief in *Craig v. Boren,* the ACLU argued that seemingly benign classifications were part of a cultural message that distinguished men from women. The harm of stereotyping and the malevolent effects of benign classifications have not been adequately captured in the arguments of the solicitor general, the Court's decisions, or traditional equal protection analysis.[36]

Four of the five cases that Bork argued involved programs that were challenged because they discriminated against men. One case, *Schlesinger v. Ballard,* involved the military's "up or out" policy. Under regulations a male officer had to be promoted within nine years or would be asked to leave the service. Women, who were banned from combat, were given thirteen years because they had fewer opportunities to earn promotions. Bork argued that the different time periods reflected practical needs, sound personnel decisions, and important public policy considerations. Bork argued that for military matters, the Court should adopt the rational basis test. He argued for traditional deference to the military.[37] Agreeing with the government, the Court "reaffirmed its commitment to the separate spheres ideology."[38] Brennan argued in dissent that rather than advantage women, the policy would harm them.[39]

Other benign classifications were also challenged as discriminating against males. These cases involved social security provisions that gave preference to widows over widowers and to women over men in calculating pension benefits. Before *Craig* established moderate scrutiny, the solicitor general argued for the rational basis standard and minimum scrutiny. In *Weinberger v. Wiesenfeld* and *Califano v. Goldfarb,* Bork argued that the policy of providing social security benefits to widows with children, but not to widowers with children, was rational because it recognized the difficulties that widows traditionally face. Bork maintained that this preference fulfilled a legitimate, compassionate objective of ameliorating harsh economic realities. He argued that Congress had consistently rejected attempts to extend benefits to widowers.[40] The Court disagreed in both cases. A majority argued that the laws were based on "archaic and overbroad" generalizations that males are always the primary wage earners. In *Weisenfeld,* the Court held that children were the intended beneficiaries and a denial to men with children was flawed policy. In *Goldfarb,* in a 5-4 decision, the Court ruled that forcing widowers to show financial dependence to get benefits was discriminatory.[41]

The policies of the INS were the subject of *Fiallo v. Levi.* INS regulations allowed mothers to claim preferential immigration status for their illegitimate children, but refused the same privilege to fathers. Bork argued that this was a political question best left to Congress and the INS. Bork opined that what might be suspect in domestic policy should be constitutional in international affairs.

Bork did add one argument about gender differences: fathers were less likely than mothers to keep close relationships with their children.[42] The Court agreed with the solicitor general, deferring to the INS policies and Congress' role in international affairs. The Court also accepted the solicitor general's argument about differences between fathers and mothers. As Susan Gluck Mezey argues, "The Court upheld statutes in which the biological reality of women bearing children was intertwined with the cultural role of women assuming primary care for children. By not probing the cultural biases behind the law, the Court accepted the government's assertion that the sexes were not similarly situated."[43]

In *Corning Glass Works v. Brennan* the solicitor general supported gender equality. This was the first case involving the Equal Pay Act to reach the Supreme Court. The company had traditionally paid higher wages to night inspectors than day inspectors. Inspectors' jobs were considered "women's work" and "demeaning," thus men were paid more to compensate.[44] The brief for the Secretary of Labor argued that the differences in wages had their origins in gender distinctions. The company tried to correct the problem by hiring women to the late shift. The solicitor general argued that this did not remedy the problem. Instead, legislative history and *Griggs* suggested that would merely freeze existing disparities.[45] The Court held that the company violated the Equal Pay Act and agreed that moving women to night positions was not a sufficient remedy.[46] For the majority, Justice Marshall accepted the government's argument that time of day should not be considered a working condition, like surroundings and hazards.

The arguments in the direct party cases were in marked contrast to the four *amici* briefs Bork filed. Three of the four briefs involved questions of pregnancy, the center of great controversy. In one additional pregnancy cases, Bork did not sign the brief. The OSG supported gender rights in the five cases in which *amici* were filed. They were successful in just two.

In each of the *amici,* Bork argued that the state law was constitutionally suspect because it represented discrimination. The first two cases, *Pittsburgh Press v. Pittsburgh Commission on Human Relations* (1973) (designations in want ads by sex, raising freedom of press concerns)[47] and *Cleveland Board of Education v. LaFleur* (1974) (mandatory leave for pregnant teachers), represented relatively clear discrimination, typical of early cases in issue evolution. The Court responded positively, but in each case, the solicitor general's argument and the decision was based on alternative constitutional grounds. By deciding cases on the bases of the First Amendment and privacy respectively, the Court limited the reach of the positive precedents for equal protection cases.

The first two pregnancy cases, *LaFleur* and *Turner v. Department of Employment Security* (the solicitor general was not involved), were struck down on the basis of due process. Due process analysis permitted justices to avoid holding that discrimination against pregnant women was gender based.[48] Thus, the Court was able to avoid subjecting pregnancy to the more rigid equal protection analysis adopted in *Craig*. The EEOC had shown little concern for pregnancy initially, but later reversed its position, arguing that there was a Title VII violation.[49] The Court had not ruled on the constitutional question (whether Equal Protection forbade discrimination) or whether it turned on a reading of the statute.[50] That would change and lead the Court into a dynamic relationship with Congress and the solicitor general.

In *Geduldig v. Aiello* (1974), Acting Solicitor General Daniel Friedman filed an *amicus* brief on behalf of the EEOC, arguing that a California policy providing disability insurance for virtually every disability except those arising from pregnancy was discriminatory.[51] The EEOC had supported strict scrutiny in gender cases, against Bork's wishes. Friedman's brief argued that the policy failed both strict scrutiny and the rational basis tests. The brief charged that pregnancy had been singled out for special treatment and the policy discriminated on the basis of sex.[52]

The case forced the Court to confront a gender issue on constitutional grounds for the first time. A majority ruled that there was no constitutional requirement that states cover all disabilities. The Court determined that the state had a legitimate interest in fiscal responsibility and could exclude some conditions. The majority focused on the fact that it was an economic policy, traditionally evaluated by the rational basis standard. Eva Rubin surmises that the justices may have assumed that ERA would soon be passed and that it would be preferable to have a constitutional amendment settle this controversy, rather than an interpretation of the Equal Protection Clause.[53] In the meantime though, according to Laura Otten, the decision said, "If you do not opt for parenthood, we will treat you the same as we treat males . . . however, if you wish to be a parent, you are on your own."[54]

When pregnancy cases shifted from constitutional to statutory grounds, Bork participated in *General Electric v. Gilbert* (1976), a Title VII case involving a denial of disability benefits for pregnant women. In *LaFleur,* the Court adopted one of Bork's arguments, deciding the case on privacy grounds. The majority held that this mandatory leave policy was an unconstitutional burden on a woman's choice whether to bear a child.[55] The decision to view this in the context of privacy limited its precedential value.

The previous decision that was most relevant to *Gilbert, Geduldig,* created a harmful precedent for women's rights. *Geduldig* was based on constitutional grounds, while *Gilbert* was statutory. In *Gilbert,* Bork argued the administration's position that disability benefits should cover pregnancy. The brief was considered weak and may have hurt the case, thus structuring the construction of doctrine.[56]

The Court ruled that Title VII did not give the EEOC authority to promulgate rules in this area. The Court chided the EEOC for changing its position on pregnancy.[57] The Court, split on ideological grounds, justified its decision on the grounds that pregnancy was a special physical disability. As in *Geduldig,* the majority held that the policies created a distinction between pregnant and nonpregnant people, rather than a gender-based distinction.[58] The Court suggested that only if pregnancy was explicitly used to discriminate would it be suspect. Even more problematic, the decision created an adverse precedent that would affect subsequent pregnancy cases and spill over to other gender cases.

Reaction to the decision was pronounced. The EEOC lobbied for change because the Court's interpretation conflicted with its position. Congress passed an amendment to Title VII, the Pregnancy Discrimination Act, expanding the definition of sex discrimination to cover pregnant workers. Congress explicitly rejected *Gilbert* and *Geduldig* and the Pregnancy Discrimination Act rejected the uniqueness approach adopted by the Court, mandating that pregnancy must be treated like other conditions.[59] While the new act protected pregnant workers, it did not remove the negative precedent.[60]

Conclusion. The solicitor general typically has to weigh a variety of factors in deciding which cases to enter and what arguments to make. The calculations in gender rights were different from civil rights. Gender policy was not an agenda issue for Nixon or Ford. Congress was not in the forefront of the issue. The Court was less liberal and activist than the Warren Court, but it had not sounded a full retreat in civil rights. Direct precedent was unfavorable, but analogies from race were promising. Griswold and Bork, however, refused to advocate that approach. The proposed Equal Rights Amendment seemed to play a role like the pending Civil Rights Act of 1964 for race. The solicitor general and the Court did not want to launch initiatives that might undermine ERA. Passage of the Civil Rights Act legitimated the strategy in civil rights, but failure to ratify ERA meant that proponents of gender equality had lost at both ends.

In the end, it is unclear whether the solicitor general's reluctance to support heightened scrutiny was part of the reason that it took the Court a while to enunciate a clear standard or whether the solicitor general's reluctance stemmed from a strategic estimate that the Court would not be willing to go that far. The Nixon solicitors general were constrained in civil rights, limiting their ability to retreat. In gender, however, there was no structure to guide the solicitors general and they acted in a manner closer to the perceived position of the administration, more conservative and restraintist.

What accounts for the differences in the government's position in *amici* and direct cases? In the latter, the solicitor general argued against gender equality in six of seven cases. In the former, the office argued for equality in all five cases. In the cases in which the government was a party, Congress and the agency were the primary constituents and the solicitor general urged deference to their positions. Because of the statutory nature of gender policy, Griswold and Bork showed great concern for Congress in formulating their arguments. The solicitor general played the role of tenth justice trying to help the Court to impose consistency and a standard of evaluation for the cases. In the voluntary *amici* cases, the solicitor general acted less like the attorney general as policy maker and more as the attorney general as law enforcement officer.

A major factor contributing to the differences was the evolution of gender policy. Cases involving "benign classifications" presented difficult issues. It was not women who were the victims of the discrimination, it was men. There was a conscious effort by women's groups, often with Ruth Bader Ginsburg as lead counsel, to challenge these programs as violations of gender equality. Gender policy was just emerging at the time, so there was uncertainty for the OSG as well as the Court.

The confusion for the solicitor general can be traced to the novelty of the issue, the emergence of different issues simultaneously, and the failure of the Court to define standards. The range of legislative activity that confronted the Court and solicitor general was staggering. From old state laws that were clearly discriminatory to federal laws that tried to protect women and compensate for past inequalities, the Court and the solicitor general had to try to impose consistency on a vast terrain. The confusion of the Court and the solicitor general helps explain the evolution from no defining standard to evaluate gender to two standards: in cases involving discrimination against women, the Court used moderate scrutiny, but in evaluating laws that favored women, the Court seemed to use minimum scrutiny.

The solicitor general's influence in these early cases was not dramatic. The OSG was often constrained by the policy positions of Congress. But one should not dismiss the impact of the office. Its arguments helped shape doctrine and precedent. If most of the cases did not create landmark decisions, they did buttress and structure the evolving gender doctrine. Ultimately, the influence of the Nixon and Ford solicitors general in gender litigation was important because the cases were part of an emerging issue, but upholding benign classifications reinforced stereo-types that could be used to create harmful precedents in other cases.

CARTER'S SOLICITOR GENERAL: VICTIM OF THE TIMES?

With women's rights issues on the public agenda, it was difficult for presidential candidates to ignore the issue. Jimmy Carter was pro-choice and a proponent of women's rights, but Joan Hoff claimed that "under his lackluster administration both legislation and litigation improving the legal status of women began to slow down."[61] Carter selected Eleanor Holmes to revitalize and expand the authority of the EEOC. One of the major changes was to move from individual cases to pattern and practice and class action suits.[62]

The Congress that Carter faced was one of the most liberal in history, coming on the heels of Watergate. Congress passed the Pregnancy Discrimination Act to overturn *Gilbert,* but did little else to buttress women's rights. Eight years of Republican control of the White House had moved the Supreme Court to the right. This was not an auspicious development for an issue that would require the Court to extend statutory and constitutional interpretation. Issues were advancing to secondary stages as the Court got more conservative. The Court had drawn a line in the sand on state laws that discriminated on gender grounds. But moderate scrutiny suggested that there would be a ceiling on protection. The Court, abetted by the confusion of the solicitor general, was still trying to reconcile its position on laws that favored women.

Though Wade McCree was solicitor general for an administration that was more supportive of women's rights than its predecessors, his record in gender discrimination cases was mixed. There were twenty-nine gender cases on the docket, but the solicitor general was involved in only fourteen. The administration was the only one to enter fewer than half the gender cases granted certiorari. McCree's tenure was dominated by seven employment cases, most of a second-generation nature. Of the other significant cases, there were two benefits cases as well as one that involved pensions. Two multidimensional cases involved criminal law. Perhaps his most important case involved the male-only draft.

In the six cases in which the government was a party, McCree filed two briefs supporting Congressional legislation that was antithetical to gender equality. When McCree was invited to file an *amicus* by the Court, he supported a broad interpretation of equality. McCree filed seven voluntary *amici* briefs, five on behalf of gender equality. In the end, the greatest legacy that McCree left was negative. In the most important cases, the solicitor general opposed gender equality and left unfavorable precedents.

As a party, five of the six cases involved social security benefits or EEOC procedures. McCree contributed to the expansion and emergence of EEOC procedures. The early social security cases involved some programs that discriminated against women and others that discriminated against men by providing compensatory benefits for women.

In the most important case, *Rostker v. Goldberg,* McCree defended the male-only draft from charges of sex discrimination. McCree urged the Court to follow traditional deference to the elected branches and the military. He argued that it was inappropriate to use a standard of review that would substitute the Court's judgment for that of Congress. Even conceding the use of a higher standard, McCree argued that the government had a compelling interest.[63] The solicitor general's brief reflected paternalistic attitudes and stereotypes that were written into law.

The Court's decision reflected the solicitor general's arguments about gender and judicial restraint. Justice Rehnquist's opinion was very deferential to Congressional prerogatives in military affairs. Indeed, as Kirp, Yudolf, and Franks argued, "There is good reason to wonder whether gender has any significant meaning in the decision."[64] The Court sustained the exclusion of women without regard to the underlying justifications and implications. Nancy Levit maintained that the justices accepted the stereotypes without questioning or probing.[65] The opinion made no reference to gender differences, but the dissenters accused the majority of stereotyping and said that the differences were a subtext for the decision.[66]

The solicitor general contributed to the decision by offering the Court a blueprint for judicial restraint. The case represents a classic example of the difficulties of tracing the causal arrow in the dynamic relationship between the solicitor general and the Court. Was the argument so persuasive that it helped an undecided Court reach consensus or did McCree advocate judicial restraint because he knew the Court would decide the case in this fashion? As Deborah Rhode claimed, "The Court's political capital is not without limits, and its members might have well assumed that most women did not place conscription high on their list of social priorities."[67]

In most instances, McCree supported positions to further equality. *Cannon v. University of Chicago* and *General Telephone v. EEOC* involved procedures for pursuing gender rights claims. *Cannon* concerned whether a private person could sue a recipient of federal assistance under Title VI to enforce Title IX. This was a "timebomb" left in the wake of

Bakke. The Department of Health, Education, and Welfare was a defendant, but McCree supported the plaintiff in the brief. He argued for a linkage between Title VI and Title IX. McCree based his argument on previous decisions that allowed private attorneys general to help the government enforce civil rights. The Court ruled that individuals have a private right of action. The decision opened the courthouse doors to increasing numbers of discrimination cases.[68]

In *General Telephone,* the question involved whether the EEOC had authority under Title VII to seek relief from discriminatory practices for a class of people without certifying the class. The solicitor general argued that this was not a traditional class action and that the EEOC as a public agency need not be certified as a class representative.[69] The Court agreed, providing additional support for the government in gender discrimination cases. The solicitor general served as the tenth justice filling holes in doctrine.

One can understand why solicitors general who support gender equality might file a contrary brief when the government is a party. They may be forced by Congressional or agency policy to adopt such positions. The *amici* provide solicitors general with the opportunity to pursue their goals or the president's. Although McCree filed five voluntary *amici* in favor of gender rights and was on the winning side in four of those cases, his contribution to gender issues is best remembered for two *amici* he filed against gender equality. The Court agreed with McCree in both cases. The cases, *Personnel Administrator of Massachusetts v. Feeney* (1979) and *Michael M v. Sonoma County Court* (1981), like the male-only draft case, had multidimensional components leading McCree to downplay discrimination in favor of competing interests.

In *Feeney,* the question was whether the Court would opt for *Griggs* or *Washington v. Davis.* In *Griggs,* on statutory grounds, the Court decided that disparate impact was enough. But in the constitutional decision, *Davis,* the Court required intent. In *Feeney,* state law provided employment preferences for Vietnam veterans. The law, neutral on its face, provided a generous program of benefits.[70] The law had the effect, unintended according to McCree, of discriminating against women, in that the vast majority of veterans were males. The solicitor general maintained that only purposeful discrimination violated the Equal Protection Clause. He used analogies to argue that farm programs overwhelmingly favored whites and males and welfare programs tended to favor blacks and Hispanics. McCree argued and the Court agreed that the statute discriminated between veterans and nonveterans not between men and women.[71] The solicitor general argued for an intent standard, rather than disparate impact. This argument highlighted the negative influence of the *Gilbert* precedent. The Court had used similar reasoning to justify classifications between pregnant and nonpregnant people (rather between women and men, which would be semi-suspect) in *Gilbert*. The lack of strict scrutiny and disparate impact were fatal for proponents of gender equality. The Court ruled that those challenging a statute that was facially neutral, but had a disparate impact, had to show intent to discriminate, which was much more difficult to prove, thus opting for a standard closer to *Davis* than *Griggs*.[72]

Michael M involved a statutory rape statute that imposed criminal sanctions on males who had intercourse with underage females, but did not punish females who had sexual relations with underage males. The solicitor general argued that the differential treatment was justified by biological differences between men and women. McCree argued that the California law furthered a compelling interest, the deterrence of teenage pregnancy and prevention of injury to prepubescent girls.[73] The Supreme Court, in a plurality opinion authored by Justice Rehnquist, took the analysis even further. One of the Court's justifications was based on the argument that only women could get pregnant. The solicitor general's brief and the Court's opinion assumed that the "harmful consequences of pregnancy are 'by nature' only visited upon women."[74] That distinction seemed to contradict the Court's analysis in pregnancy cases. According to Levit, pregnancy which did not make a difference in *Geduldig* and *Gilbert,* was determinative in *Michael M*.[75] The Court ruled that the state's interest was sufficient enough that it need not meet the more difficult *Craig* standard. The dissenters argued that upholding the distinction tended to reinforce stereotypes of male aggressiveness and female vulnerability.[76] The latter provided support for policies and precedents that perpetuated harmful stereotypes, but were in accord with the motivation of protective legislation.

In most cases, McCree supported equality, but few rose to the prominence of the negative landmarks. One case had the potential to be a landmark, but fell short. In *County of Washington v. Gunther* (1981), a case brought by female prison guards who were paid less than male guards, McCree offered the Court a broad interpretation of the Equal Pay Act. The case was thought to be a prelude to consideration of comparable worth policy.[77] The Court decided the question on the narrowest grounds, holding that the Equal Pay Act went beyond Title VII in attacking intentional gender-based wage discrimination, but stopped short of comparable worth.[78] The *Gunther* precedent seemed to provide a foundation for a favorable comparable worth decision, but it has consistently been narrowed by the Court. The Reagan administration refused to lend regulatory support to the decision and its solicitors general refused to follow it up. Indeed, operatives in the administration labeled pay equity and comparable worth "the looniest idea since Looney Tunes."[79]

In three other cases, McCree filed *amici* on behalf of gender equality. *City of Los Angeles Department of Water Power v. Manhart* raised the question of whether employers could deduct more money from women's pay because actuarial tables suggested that women lived longer and would draw retirement benefits for a longer period. The practical question was "Does Title VII bar employment discrimination if the distinctions are based on true generalizations?"[80] McCree argued that this was explicit discrimination and a violation of Title VII and the Equal Pay Act. The city argued that the policy was similar to the exception for pregnancy benefits. Like pregnancy, longevity was a physical condition of women. McCree disagreed, distinguishing *Gilbert* and arguing that there was no rationale for these distinctions.[81] The majority agreed and decided that Title VII focused on individual cases, downplaying the role of generalizations.[82] Justice Stevens claimed that the classifications in *Gilbert* were based on disability, but in this case, distinctions were based on gender.[83]

One case, *Great American Federal Savings & Loan v. Novotny,* was similar to race cases decided in the wake of the Civil Rights Act of 1964. The case involved an attempt to link Title VII to Reconstruction legislation. Griswold and Bork had argued repeatedly that the Civil Rights Act did not repeal sections 1981, 1982, 1983, and 1985. In *Alfred Mayer* and *Runyon,* solicitors general were successful in strengthening the present Civil Rights Act and resuscitating moribund Reconstruction acts. McCree used these precedents to argue that section 1985 could be used in conjunction with Title VII. He argued that the aggrieved should be vested with all possible remedies.[84] The Court ruled that plaintiffs could not use section 1985 to bypass the administrative scheme set up under Title VII further separating race and gender doctrine.[85]

Conclusion. To return to the questions that structure this analysis, how did the solicitor general balance the various forces in his environment and how did the office contribute to the development of doctrine? For McCree, the answers are complicated. The aggregate support points in one direction, but the office's positions in the important cases suggest a different result.

The factors facing McCree seemed to portend a dramatic expansion of gender rights. The president supported gender rights, Congress was very liberal, and the Court had provided some favorable precedents and moderate scrutiny. At first glance, McCree did not seem to take full advantage of the opportunity. But he faced complex cases that seemed to arrive relatively early in the evolution of gender issues. McCree was constrained by issue evolution and a Court that was less likely to create or expand rights.

McCree came to office just after the Court had decided on moderate scrutiny. This appeared to open a window for decisions that would protect equality. That was enough for cases of clear discrimination, but as issues got more difficult the standard was considered wanting. The Court appeared to use a minimum standard when it was dealing with programs designed to help women. The solicitor general played the role of tenth justice, helping the Court build doctrine and recognizing in the most difficult cases involving national security and criminal law that the justices were loathe to exert activism.[86]

In a sense, the administration presided over a holding pattern. In the aggregate, the administration looked like a strong defender of gender equality and McCree had high levels of success. But the doctrinal footprints McCree left were relatively negative. *Roskter* and *Michael M* were short reach precedents, but they had significant symbolic implications. *Feeney* had practical and symbolic consequences. Attempts to link Title VII to Reconstruction Era remedies did not gain Court support as in the race cases. McCree had some success in a number of employment discrimination cases. In general, the Court struck most classifications based on stereotyping and upheld programs designed to redress the secondary economic position of women.[87]

The Solicitor General and Reproductive Rights Doctrine: Keeping a Safe Distance

Reproductive rights were a political minefield for an office that prides itself on making legal calculations and leaving political judgments to others. As Kristen Luker asks, "What is it about abortion—of all the myriad of issues we face daily—that makes it so troubling, so hard to deal with in reasoned tones?" A large part of the problem she feels is that "the two sides share no common premises and very little common language."[88]

With the issue in the judicial arena and part of the dialogue in presidential elections, it is not surprising that the president and Court would be the dominant actors in the solicitor general's environment. Because most abortion laws were state policies, the solicitor general's means of getting involved in cases was through the *amicus curiae* brief. The *amicus* provides the solicitor general with the most discretion, the fewest constraints, and is the best vehicle for pursuing the president's goals. Reproductive rights were constitutional issues, meaning that the extraordinary majorities necessary for Congressional retaliation were unlikely, creating a different calculus for the solicitor general and the Court.

As a consequence of the controversy and the fact that the federal government was not directly involved, solicitors general under Nixon, Ford, and Carter were reluctant to enter cases either in the lower courts or the Supreme Court. In fact, during these administrations, the OSG entered only two cases, one as the result of an invitation and one as a party. In neither case was the right to abortion itself involved and each time the solicitors general did not support the pro–reproductive rights side.

The position in reproductive rights cases was significantly different from the office's activities in sex discrimination cases. Despite its opposition to abortion, the Nixon administration had no interest in getting involved in the issue, according to Bork.[89] Thus, the issue evolved without the government's input. This would constrain the positions that the solicitor general could adopt in the short run and prospects for success later. The Court defined the right in *Roe v. Wade* and set the context for doctrinal development. Normally, the Court announces an important decision and then lets the issue percolate in the lower courts for a few years before it wrestles with second-generation cases. The Court adopted this stance in reproductive rights. As questions of viability, parental consent, and the regulation of doctors and hospitals began to emerge in the lower courts, the Supreme Court kept a distance. When the next major case reached the Court's docket, *Planned Parenthood v. Danforth,* the solicitor general avoided participation.

When the solicitor general did get involved, it was in an indirect fashion and at the Court's request. Bork was invited to address the question of whether states could restrict funding for abortions in a trilogy of 1977 cases, *Beal v. Doe, Maher v. Roe,* and *Poelker v. Doe.* According to Epstein and Kobylka, the presence of the government was "significant." Bork argued: "The fact that a women has a qualified right to an abortion does not imply a correlative constitutional right to free treatment." Bork attacked the trappings of the right, rather than the right itself. His argument structured debate in conference and became the basis for the Court's opinion. Thus the solicitor general's position was important in moving the Court along the path of retreat from *Roe.*

Without a request from the Court, Bork opted to keep the government out of abortion cases for the rest of his tenure. The next opportunities came during the Carter administration under a president who was more sympathetic to reproductive rights. The first case, however, did not bode well for pro-choice forces and constrained the solicitor general.

The Hyde Amendment, which prohibited the use of Medicaid funds for abortion, brought the solicitor general back to the Supreme Court. Passage of the amendment represented the only major legislative victory for the right-to-life movement during the 1970s. A district court found the amendment unconstitutional, a victory for the pro-choice forces, but it was threatened when McCree asked the justices for an expedited review. In the lower court, in addition to the reproductive rights issue, there were establishment and free exercise of religion arguments. Pro-choice groups argued that the Hyde Amendment would excessively involve government in religion and placed a burden on women in following the dictates of their conscience.

In *Harris v. McRae,* McCree urged the Court to uphold the amendment because it was his job to argue for a federal law. He dismissed the freedom of religion claims. He argued that the Hyde Amendment was compatible with decisions in the trilogy of cases that first involved the solicitor general. McCree argued that Congress only needed a rational basis for treating abortion differently from other medical procedures. Representative Henry Hyde, author of the amendment, and the right-to-life group Americans United for Life (AUL) did not trust the administration to argue for the law so they intervened and submitted an *amicus.* Indeed, the AUL brief was more thorough and raised additional arguments in support of the law.[90] By a narrow 5-4 margin, the Court upheld its constitutionality in a decision that closely reflected the position of the solicitor general. Justice Stewart's opinion was legalistic like the solicitor general's brief, avoiding the policy arguments that groups on both sides preferred to offer. The Court rejected the freedom of religion claims. The Court followed the rationale of the *Beal, Maher,* and *Poelker* decisions. The Court and the solicitor general were partners in creating and sustaining the standards for review of abortion funding.

Conclusion. The solicitor general forfeited the opportunity to help the Court construct doctrine. There were practical reasons to take this tack. First, the solicitor general typically does not get involved in new issue areas. Second, the solicitor general abided by the adage that hard cases make bad law. Finally, there was simple political expedience. The volatility of abortion meant that presidents would rather avoid the issue.

When the solicitor general did get involved, it was during the later stages when the trappings of the issue rather than the right itself were in question. Thus for a decade, no administration had to take a stand on the issue of reproductive rights before the justices. In the initial cases, the solicitor general's positions were constrained by an invitation to file a brief or legislation. When it could have adopted the role of attorney general as policy maker, the office refused, opting instead to be the fifth clerk and tenth justice in the two cases.

CONCLUSION: THE SOLICITOR GENERAL AND THE EMERGENCE OF GENDER AND REPRODUCTIVE RIGHTS

The solicitor general was constrained by a number of factors at the outset. First, the office often had to defend statutes that discriminated against men, a form of gender discrimination. Second, strict scrutiny was virtually unprecedented except for race, and moderate scrutiny had not been created. Thus, it would be difficult for the solicitor general, who needs to react rather than lead the Court, to ask for an extraordinary standard. Third, while statutory language is normally vague, creating problems for the solicitor general and the Court, gender provisions were even more problematic. Legislative intent was missing and provisions were often added as an afterthought. Finally, gender precedents while old, were quite hostile.

Gender was not an agenda issue like civil rights or reproductive rights. The political environment and existing precedent suggested judicial restraint in gender policy. The groups most responsible for structuring litigation wanted to define gender discrimination like race. The solicitor general did not support that construction. The OSG took a passive role in the early stages, letting the Court define the boundaries. The factors in the environment were dynamic and more compressed than in civil rights. The Court was becoming more conservative and less willing to exert activism for the expansion of rights. At the same time, the solicitor general was getting involved as more difficult cases were winding their way to the Court. This posed constraints for the office.

Because the issue was less salient to presidents, a change in administration did not necessarily mean that the new solicitor general would adopt a different legal position or change sides in a particular case. Early in the development of the issue, as the Court wrestled with the appropriate standard for evaluating gender claims, the solicitor general fulfilled the role of the tenth justice trying to help the Court impose some stability on doctrine.

This meant that gender would look more like typical issues than civil rights in that legal concerns would dominate political ones. In addition, the opportunities and constraints solicitors general faced were significantly different in gender cases. Civil rights was initially constitutional, limiting Congressional impact. In gender, statutory construction was the dominant mode of the cases, meaning that Congress would be a part of the environment. The influence of Congress was passive and negative until passage of the Pregnancy Discrimination Act. The Congressional acts that were being interpreted tended to involve programs that discriminated in favor of women.

As an issue, reproductive rights looked like civil rights because of the constitutional provisions, the political nature, and the visibility of the issue. In reproductive rights, the political forces crowded out the legal ones. The political strategy meant nonparticipation by the OSG. Although there were a variety of state laws on the Court's docket that the solicitor general could have joined via an *amicus curiae* brief, the Nixon, Ford, and Carter administrations kept a distance.

With most of the cases coming from the states, the solicitor general could have used the *amicus,* with a wide range of discretion, to serve as the attorney general as policy maker. Instead, the solicitor general acted as the fifth clerk and tenth justice, waiting for a CVSG or for the government to be a party. The solicitor general seemed to argue for consistency in doctrine rather than for particular policy goals. When it entered those cases, it was to deal with secondary issues involving funding, rather than the right itself.

The solicitor general faced particular difficulties in the way that gender issues spread out. The evolution of race developed in a more systematic fashion and at a more leisurely pace than gender issues. Gender cases involved both benign and discriminatory programs and a wide range of substantive issues. Almost immediately, second-generation stage cases crowded the docket before the Court had filled in the details. This stripped the Court of the opportunity to let those issues percolate through the system and forced the solicitor general to assume the role of tenth justice.

The percentage of Supreme Court cases that the solicitor general did not enter was considerably higher than in civil rights, particularly at the emergence of the issue. The role of the solicitor general intensified as the issue developed and the office was drawn into cases by statutes. In addition, *amicus* activity expanded as gender evolved.

The Solicitor General and Gender and Reproductive Rights Policy

Retrenchment and Recovery

REDEFINITION WAS NOT a central goal of the Reagan administration in gender policy, but the process was underway in civil
rights and had spillover effects. Reagan was the first president to
oppose ERA.[1] The administration's attack on affirmative action and the
disparate impact standard had implications for gender policy. The administration was best known for its assault on *Roe v. Wade*. Just as gender
reinforced reproductive rights when the two issues were emerging, limitations on one set of rights could be used as a symbolic means of limiting the other.

The goals of solicitors general in gender were far from dominant concerns. Goals are tempered by strategic interaction and a need to adapt to
institutional rules and norms, which can impose constraints or provide
opportunities. When policy goals are not primary, legal goals may take
precedent. If the Reagan solicitors general decided to recreate the script
of the race cases, they faced constraints. Congress, which had asserted itself in civil rights, was likely to do the same in gender issues. The Court
was increasingly conservative, but gender precedents were more recent,
suggesting that justices might not be willing to reverse them. Other
norms were also relevant. First, the administration was attacking precedent in civil rights, which might influence gender cases. In addition,
changes in institutional mechanisms, such as the creation of the principal deputy, the shadow CRD, and weakening EEOC would have implications for gender policy.

In the area of reproductive rights, goals were clear and the Reagan
and Bush administrations tried to use legal arguments to attack a profoundly political issue. When the administrations were criticized for advocating judicial restraint while encouraging the Court to overturn *Roe*,

Attorney General Meese and Justice Scalia argued that two wrongs made a right. Scalia argued that using judicial activism to overturn a decision created from previous activism was, in effect, an act of judicial restraint. Strategic interaction would not be as much of a factor because reproductive rights was a constitutional issue and Congress could not muster the extraordinary majorities necessary to overturn decisions. The presidents did their parts, putting opponents of abortion on the Court, to alter the strategic environment. The primary norm, recent precedent, was not favorable.

Table 7-1 shows the support for gender claimants in the Reagan, Bush, and Clinton administrations. The Reagan administration was not very supportive of gender equality, while the Clinton administration was unanimous in its support. The Bush administration had limited opportunities for involvement. Table 7-2 shows the success of the different administrations. The Reagan administration had success as a party, but split the cases it entered as *amici*. There was variation by solicitor general in

TABLE 7-1

SOLICITOR GENERAL'S SUPPORT FOR GENDER RIGHTS AND
TYPE OF PARTICIPATION BY PRESIDENTIAL ADMINISTRATION IN
THE LATER STAGE OF ISSUE EVOLUTION

	Type of Participation							
	Party		Invited		*Amicus*		Total	
President	*Pro*	*Con*	*Pro*	*Con*	*Pro*	*Con*	*Pro*	*Con*
Reagan	5	5	1	2	3	5	9	12
Bush	1	0	0	1	1	0	2	1
Clinton	4	0	1	0	3	0	8	0

TABLE 7-2

SOLICITOR GENERAL'S SUCCESS ON THE MERITS AND TYPE OF
PARTICIPATION IN GENDER RIGHTS CASES BY PRESIDENTIAL
ADMINISTRATION IN THE LATER STAGE OF ISSUE EVOLUTION

	Type of Participation							
	Party		Invited		*Amicus*		Total	
President	*Won*	*Lost*	*Won*	*Lost*	*Won*	*Lost*	*Won*	*Lost*
Reagan	7	3	2	1	4	4	13	8
Bush	1	0	0	1	0	1	1	2
Clinton	3	1	1	0	2	1	6	2

both levels of support and success within the Reagan administration. The Clinton administration had more success in gender cases than in the race cases. The remainder of the chapter examines the trends through the most important cases.

Only the Ford and Reagan administrations supported gender rights in fewer than half of the cases they entered. Reagan solicitors general supported gender equality in only nine of their twenty-one cases. When reproductive rights is included, the image is more stark with Lee and Fried attempting to undermine and overturn *Roe*. There was significant variation between Reagan's two terms. Rex Lee supported gender rights in eight of thirteen cases, while Charles Fried was supportive in but one of eight. When the administration was a party, support was evenly split, but as *amici,* the solicitor general supported gender rights in just three of eight briefs. When there were constraints on the office, Lee, in particular, was more likely to file a brief supporting gender equality.

THE REAGAN SOLICITORS GENERAL: PURSUING AN AGENDA

The Reagan administration targeted reproductive rights in formulating its legal strategy. Efforts to limit gender rights were less premeditated, but represented extensions of attacks on civil rights and reproductive rights. While their tenures were dominated by second-generation employment discrimination cases, Lee and Fried presided over the emergence of some new issues: Title IX, sexual harassment, and affirmative action in a gender context. They also revisited pregnancy in three second-generation cases involving the Pregnancy Discrimination Act.

Under Lee, the OSG argued eight gender cases in which the government was a party, five on behalf of equality. Given the opportunity to expand or contract the interpretation of Titles VII and IX, the solicitor general normally opted for the interpretation favored by the EEOC. In most of these cases, the solicitor general adopted the role of tenth justice. Lee was invited to file a brief in one case. Lee filed voluntary *amici* briefs in four gender cases. In three of the four cases, Lee argued a position that favored broader gender rights.

In *Newport News Shipbuilding and Dry Dock Co. v. Equal Employment Opportunity Commission,* the solicitor general argued a second-generation Title VII case involving pregnancy benefits. The question was whether a company was discriminating against male employees in violation of the Pregnancy Discrimination Act of 1978, by providing medical insurance for workers that covered spouses' maternity costs less favorably than costs resulting from other spousal illnesses or injuries. In *Gilbert,* the Court ruled that the denial of pregnancy benefits did not constitute gender discrimination, but Congress overturned the decision by passing the Pregnancy Discrimination Act. The question was whether this act protected the spouses of workers. The EEOC took the broad view, holding that the Pregnancy Discrimination Act covered spouses as well as workers. Lee argued that the EEOC's construction of the provision for insurance coverage for spousal pregnancy should be accorded great weight. The brief argued that judicial deference was particularly appropriate because the head of EEOC informed Congress of the agency's construction of the statute while the Pregnancy Discrimination Act was pending, and that construction was not challenged.[2] The solicitor general argued that Title VII prohibited employers from discriminating against males in providing benefits for spouses and that the Pregnancy Discrimination Act applied to all claims involving pregnancy.

While the preferences of the solicitor general and the Court were to the right of Congress, Lee's argument and Justice Stevens's opinion took note of the history of the issue. Stevens noted that Congress had decisively rejected *Gilbert* when it amended Title VII. He claimed that the committee report in support of the Pregnancy Discrimination Act showed that the dissenters in *Gilbert* had correctly interpreted Congressional preferences.[3] While this case raised a different question, the Court could be reasonably certain that Congressional preferences had not changed. Thus, the Court ruled that the company could not give male employees less protection for their spouses than it gave female employees. The Court avoided further reversal by Congress and "recanted its earlier approach to pregnancy discrimination."[4]

A pair of Title IX cases raised controversy. In *North Haven Board of Education v. Bell,* two school districts challenged the authority of the Department of Health, Education, and Welfare (HEW) to issue regulations prohibiting sex discrimination in the employment practices of educational institutions operating federally assisted programs. North Haven argued that Title IX employment regulations exceeded the authority conferred on HEW. It sought to enjoin HEW from attempting to terminate federal assistance to the school district on the grounds of noncompliance with employment regulations.

Lee argued that two basic objectives of Title IX were to assure that federal funds did not support programs and activities marked by discrimination on the basis of sex and to provide protection for individuals against discriminatory practices. The brief argued that the legislative history of Title IX demonstrated that Congress intended to prohibit sex discrimination in employment in federally assisted education programs.[5] The solicitor general reasoned that this question was called to Congress' attention and it did not modify the statute. The Court held that examining employment records was within HEW's authority. But there were concerns that the Court would limit the regulations to funding specific programs.[6] That became a reality when Bradford Reynolds announced that Title IX did not apply to the institution as a whole, but only to federally funded programs.[7]

That was the subtext in Lee's most significant gender case, *Grove City College v. Bell* (1984). There was a great deal of discussion concerning how the administration should proceed.[8] The college itself received no funds, but its students got federal aid. The question before the Court was whether this made Grove City a recipient of "federal financial assistance" under Title IX. If Grove City was considered a recipient, then the practical question concerned whether the college would lose all its federal assistance or just funds targeted at the program that was the subject of the discrimination. In this case, the "education program or activity" that received federal grants was the college's financial aid program.

Lee argued that the question of whether the penalty was program specific or institution wide was beyond the scope of the case and urged the Court not to address it in the respondent's brief on certiorari.[9] On the merits, Lee supported the position of the Secretary of Education that Title IX regulations were program specific.[10] This reversed the position that the Carter administration had taken in the lower courts. A bipartisan group of forty-nine Senators and Representatives filed an *amicus* brief opposing the government's position. Their brief argued that Congress had intended the institution to lose all federal funding, not just that targeted at the individual program.

The Court, rejecting Congressional intent, ruled that providing federal funds to some programs or activities did not permit civil rights regulation of the entire institution.[11] The decision limited the scope of Title IX, weakened the enforcement of sanctions against gender discrimination, and spilled over to other civil rights enforcement.[12]

In the wake of *Grove City*, Congress sought to restore Title IX. For two years, Senate opponents successfully filibustered the Civil Rights Restoration Act. The act passed Congress, but was vetoed by President Reagan, who adopted the narrow position of the Court. Both houses of Congress were able to muster the votes to override the veto and overrule *Grove City*, restoring the intended force of Title IX. Under the Civil Rights Restoration Act, if a college receives any federal funds, the entire institution is covered.[13]

A variety of cases raised issues the Court had been wrestling with since gender emerged. In *Califano v. Webster,* the Court addressed the question of whether women could exclude three more lower earning years than men. The solicitor general defended the policy as a means of compensating for the economic disparities between men and women. The Court accepted the government's position, but continued to grapple with moderate scrutiny. The Court ruled that "a benign, compensatory purpose is not an automatic shield which protects against any inquiry into the actual purposes underlying a statutory scheme."[14] The Court was willing to countenance programs that were designed to compensate for past discrimination, even if they appeared to violate moderate scrutiny. In effect, the Court used minimum scrutiny for "benign" programs.[15]

None of the gender cases in which Lee filed an *amicus* brief was a landmark, but all contributed to building doctrine. During his tenure, significant gender cases were not percolating through the lower courts.[16] In three of the four cases, Lee argued a position that was not entirely compatible with the policies of the administration, but more closely aligned with the position of Congress. Lee played the role of attorney general as law enforcement officer, rather than policy maker, in filing these briefs.

Charles Fried filed voluntary *amici* briefs in five gender cases. In four of the five, Fried pushed the conservative social agenda through the briefs he filed and met resistance from the Court in each case. *Meritor Savings Bank v. Vinson* (1986) was not initially one of the agenda cases, but some attorneys in the Justice Department thought it important enough to advance it to Fried's attention. The case involved an employee who charged that she was sexually harassed repeatedly by her boss. *Meritor* was the first sexual harassment case under Title VII to reach the Supreme Court. The question was whether unwelcome sexual advances by a supervisor toward a subordinate employee, which created an intimidating, hostile, or offensive working environment, constituted employment discrimination in violation of Title VII.

The case involved claims of a "hostile environment" rather than *"quid pro quo"* sexual harassment. Guidelines to deal with sexual harassment had been developing in the EEOC and the lower courts. *Quid pro quo* harassment is defined as a requirement of sexual relations for some employment benefit. Such harassment becomes, in effect, a condition of employment. The more difficult questions surround harassment that creates a so-called hostile work environment. In such circumstances, conduct or verbal abuse of a sexual nature creates an intimidating, offensive, or unbearable working environment.[17] The issue of *quid pro quo* harassment was not present because Vinson, the victim, received promotions based on merit, and her boss's conduct had no effect on her salary, bonuses, or the economic terms and conditions of her employment. Various courts of appeals had held *quid pro quo* sexual harassment to be a violation of Title VII, but the law was vague as to a hostile environment. The EEOC had previously issued guidelines specifying that "sexual harassment" was a form of sex discrimination prohibited by Title VII, even if the harassment led to noneconomic injury.[18] Fried argued that unwelcome advances that created a hostile working environment violated Title VII, but that Vinson failed to prove a claim of sexual harassment.

Fried urged deference to the lower court holding in determining whether there was sexual harassment or consensual relations. On the question of whether an employer could be held strictly liable for an offensive working environment created by a supervisor's sexual advances, Fried argued that an employer should not be liable unless it knew or had reason to know of the sexually offensive atmosphere. Fried argued for a narrow interpretation of sexual harassment, which the Court, in a surprisingly broad unanimous opinion written by Justice Rehnquist, firmly rejected.[19] The Court ruled that a Title VII violation may be established even though the victim of sexual harassment establishes no tangible economic loss. The Court ruled that it was enough that the harassment created an abusive environment. While *Meritor* was compared to *Reed* as a path-breaking decision that altered perceptions about women, the behavior in the case was so awful there was a question whether the precedent would have applicability to grayer shades of activity.[20] Congress supported the decision by providing further remedies in the Civil Rights Act of 1991, though it avoided defining sexual harassment.[21]

In perhaps the most important of his cases, Fried filed a brief in *Johnson v. Transportation Agency, Santa Clara County* (1987), an affirmative action case. Most affirmative action cases had been based on race. This was the first plenary consideration of a Title VII gender claim. The CRD was anxious to get involved in the case. Fried, however, was not pleased with the case, claiming that it had terrible facts: Diane Joyce was the first woman to hold such a position, the program was voluntary, and she was qualified.[22] Fried would have preferred a mandatory affirmative action program where an obviously less qualified woman was promoted over a man. That would allow the office to make a legal argument that was consistent with the administration's goals. Fried claimed that attorneys in the Justice Department looked for ways of making the case "go away."[23]

The conservative public interest groups decided that they did not want to allot part of their time to the solicitor general, so Fried's partic-ipation was limited to an *amicus* brief. Strategically, Fried felt that only a moderate position could carry a majority. Fried argued that no barri-ers had been erected to keep women from working or being promoted, therefore there was no discrimination. The case revisited a question from the race cases: should the Court require proof of intent to discriminate or was disparate impact enough? The government had traditionally ar-gued for the latter; the Reagan administration sought the former. Fried provided an exit strategy for the Court, arguing that the justices should remand the case to determine whether there was purposive discrimina-tion.[24]

Fried argued that the case presented difficult issues that could be an-swered only by extrapolation from past decisions. The solicitor general had played a central role in limiting and reversing affirmative action and was anxious to protect those precedents. This presented difficulties for Fried: because this involved a gender issue, it might not need to survive strict scrutiny. Thus, Fried had to argue that there was no reason to con-clude that Congress, in enacting Title VII, intended employers to be freer to discriminate on gender grounds rather than race. Fried dismissed the distinction: regardless of the constitutional difference between the two forms of discrimination, they must meet the same level of justifica-tion if the employer is to escape liability.

Fried argued that the impermissibility of utilizing "societal discrimi-nation" was, if anything, even more compelling in the Title VII context. If societal discrimination cannot serve as a justification, then only the employer's own actions can serve as a predicate for remedial action. Fried continued his arguments from past race cases that no affirmative action plan is permissible if it is not narrowly tailored to protect the interests of innocent parties while trying to remedy prior discrimination. Fried ar-gued that the plan should be rejected because it was neither remedial nor narrowly tailored.[25]

The Court upheld the program, with a majority arguing that an affirmative action plan created by a public employer to remedy a lack of women on the job force did not violate Title VII even where there was no showing of prior discrimination. Justice Scalia wrote a forceful dis-sent supporting the administration's position that intent to discriminate must be proven and that innocent people, like Paul Johnson, the man passed over for promotion, were victims of a new brand of discrimina-tion.[26] Scalia argued that the decision turned Title VII into a potential tool for discrimination.[27]

The solicitor general was also involved in a number of second-generation employment cases. *Price Waterhouse v. Hopkins* was a so-called "mixed motive" case. In *McDonnell Douglas v. Green* and *Texas Department of Community Affairs v. Burdine,* the Court had established standards for cases in which an employee charged that intentional discrimination was the sole basis for an adverse employment decision. *Price Waterhouse* involved the more common occurrence, the proper treatment of Title VII cases involving "mixed motives" in which evidence shows that both discriminatory and nondiscriminatory motives played some role in reaching a particular employment decision.[28] The case raised a number of questions: Did Title VII require a causal link between a discriminatory motive and an employment decision? If so, how would "cause" be defined? Did Title VII impose a different analysis of causation in mixed motive cases than in single motive cases? Who would bear the burden of proving causation? And could a defendant limit the plaintiff's remedy if the defendant proved that, in addition to an illegal cause, an independent and wholly valid motive explained the employment decision? Because virtually every disparate treatment case would, to some degree, entail multiple motives, this was a critical case.

Fried maintained that Title VII disparate treatment cases should be resolved under the *McDonnell Douglas–Burdine* framework. The analysis should not depend on whether the case was categorized as involving "mixed" or "single motives." Fried argued that since causation was a necessary element of Title VII liability, then under *Burdine,* it followed that the plaintiff would bear the burden of persuading the court that she had been the victim of intentional discrimination. He held that the plaintiff is a "victim" only if the employer's illegal motive caused the adverse employment decision. Part of the reason for refusing to promote Ms. Hopkins was based on stereotypes. But Fried argued that stereotyping, without more, did not constitute a violation of Title VII. Fried concluded that a defendant could limit the plaintiff's remedy by showing that the employment decision would have been the same without the illegal cause.[29]

The solicitor general's brief was consistent with arguments from race cases. Fried was interested in attacking disparate impact, which was raised in *Price Waterhouse.* The Court confined its decision to the issue of which side should bear the burden of proof. The Court disagreed with the solicitor general, holding that once the plaintiff proved that gender was a factor, the burden of proof shifted to the employer to demonstrate that it would have made the same decision on legitimate grounds. But the Court ruled the company had an affirmative defense if it could demonstrate that its decision was based solely on legitimate grounds.

Failure to do so would permit the lower court to conclude that sex was a factor in the decision and the company violated Title VII.[30] The decision provoked Congressional resistance and was overturned by the Civil Rights Act of 1991. Unlawful employment practices would be established when there was discrimination on the basis of race, gender, religion, or national origin even if legitimate factors were involved.[31]

The lack of support by the solicitor general was partially a function of the increasing difficulty of individual cases. Many employment and pregnancy cases fit this profile. The Pregnancy Discrimination Act overturned some decisions, but it raised other legal questions. While the Pregnancy Discrimination Act did not allow women to be treated at a disadvantage, did it forbid special treatment for pregnancy? *California Federal Savings and Loan Association v. Guerra,* a classic later-stage case, was a reverse of previous pregnancy benefit cases. Past cases involved laws that excluded pregnancy from disability benefits. California law did the opposite: it forced employers to provide benefits and job guarantees for women who were on maternity leave. The company claimed that the California law was preempted by the Pregnancy Discrimination Act, which required that pregnancy be treated the "same" as other disabilities. The case was important because other states had similar measures that went beyond the Pregnancy Discrimination Act.[32] The Court had invited the solicitor general to express the views of the government in a related case *(Miller-Wohl Co. v. Commissioner of Labor & Industry)* that presented essentially identical preemption questions, but in this instance, the office filed a voluntary brief.

While Congressional action forbade discrimination, it was silent about preferences. Fried argued that while the law shared the same goals as the Pregnancy Discrimination Act, the manner of achieving its purposes violated Title VII's nondiscrimination mandate. The California law singled out pregnant employees for special treatment by requiring that employers guarantee disability leave and reinstatement rights, regardless of disability policies toward other employees. Thus, the solicitor general claimed that the state law conflicted with the "preeminent principle of equal treatment of male and female employees generally announced by Title VII and specifically extended to pregnancy-based classifications by the PDA."

Fried argued that Title VII, as amended by the Pregnancy Discrimination Act, preempted the California law. Fried claimed that while the state law furthered legitimate and important health and safety goals, it did so in an impermissible manner. By singling out the disability of pregnancy for special treatment, the law invited employers to discriminate on the basis of pregnancy, albeit favorably.

The brief argued that a state requirement that an employer must grant benefits to pregnant employees that it need not provide other employees violated the requirement that pregnant employees "be treated the same" as other persons "for all employment-related purposes." Because the Pregnancy Discrimination Act equates pregnancy-based discrimination with gender discrimination, California's policy "does not pass the simple test of whether the evidence shows 'treatment of a person in a manner which but for that person's sex would be different.'"[33]

If the Court held that the state law was preempted, all state preferential treatment laws were in jeopardy. The Court rejected the position of the solicitor general, claiming that Congress was aware of preferential treatment and manifested no intention to ban those preferences. For the majority, Justice Marshall argued that Title VII was designed to remove barriers that kept women from participating fully and equally in the workforce. The Court appeared to recognize that the Pregnancy Discrimination Act permitted special pregnancy-based policies.[34]

In general, Fried was remarkably unsuccessful in his *amici* in gender cases, joining the losing side in four of the five cases he entered. Fried seemed out of step with the Court in gender cases. In some cases, Fried, playing the role of attorney general as policy maker, tried to stretch precedents from race cases and keep the arguments consistent. The problem for Fried was that he was trying to use fourth-generation precedents from one area to cover second-generation cases in another area.

Conclusion. The goals of the Reagan administration did not include a frontal attack on gender, but affirmative action and employment decisions in race necessitated arguments to that effect. In terms of issue evolution, gender was a decade behind race. Affirmative action and disparate impact questions eventually took a gender tone. Gender cases arose in a different institutional context. The Court was more conservative, the solicitor general was less supportive, and the moderate scrutiny standard the Court used was less conducive to advancing gender equality.

On the other hand, the statutory basis of the rights meant that Congress was a force for the Court and solicitor general to reckon with. Initially, many Congressional acts involved benign programs that sought to help women, but reinforced traditional stereotypes. After passage of the Pregnancy Discrimination Act, Congress became a positive force, counteracting limiting Court decisions. Congress became an important constituency and forced the office to adopt the role of tenth justice, rather than permitting the solicitor general to play the role of attorney general as policy maker.

Issue evolution played a dual role. Some second-generation pregnancy and employment cases allowed the administration to pursue its goals. Other issues obligated Lee and Fried to adopt positions that supported equality, particularly after Democrats reassumed control of the Senate. Some cases involved overt discrimination or issues that seemed to be settled. Others involved the interpretation of Congressional acts expanding rights. To attack those would invite judicial rebuke. Indeed, a number of Court decisions were modified or reversed by Congressional action. The composition of the Court led the administration to believe that it could aggressively push its agenda. Reagan's appointments seemed to create a critical mass that would provide the votes to enact his social policies through the courts. The president was willing to use his veto to blunt opposition to Court decisions the administration favored.

There was more of a balance between the legal and political forces. Perhaps the most important factor was the OSG itself. The Reagan presidency was a time of great controversy for the office. Analysts feel that the solicitor general tested the traditional comity that existed between the office and the Supreme Court, risking its relationship for the sake of a social agenda that ultimately failed to be enacted. Solicitors general attempted to pursue the president's agenda through the courts, but their impact may have been counterproductive. Their open attempts to overturn *Roe* may have done more harm than good and may have cost the administration the votes of conservative justices like Powell, O'Connor, and Kennedy in other areas.[35]

The ultimate question is what impact did the Reagan solicitors general have on gender doctrine? On the whole, the direct effect appeared to be negative. Lee and Fried often argued, sometimes successfully, for limiting the extension of gender equality. They argued for limiting Title IX, the reach of the Pregnancy Discrimination Act, affirmative action, and a narrower conceptualization of employment discrimination. In some cases, the Court rebuffed the solicitor general, appearing to react to the position Congress supported. A number of decisions were reversed by a Congress that became the primary institutional defender of gender equality. Even in supporting gender equality, the solicitors general argued narrowly.

Fully Joined: The Attack on Reproductive Rights

Though no president had actively supported reproductive rights, none had sent a solicitor general into Court to try to reverse *Roe*. For the Reagan administration, reproductive rights was the dominant agenda issue. Because of the constitutional nature of the issue, the Court was the primary forum. This increased the pressure on the OSG. Once again, the concepts of law and politics were in tension. The position of the political appointees, who desired change, was on a collision course with tenured members of the OSG and Justice Department whose long-term relationship with the Court is predicated on respect for precedent. *Roe* was less than a decade old, suggesting that the Court might be reluctant to undermine or reverse it. On the other hand, some of the *Roe* majority was beginning to retire and opposition to abortion was a litmus test for their replacements.

The issue moved to the center of American politics when Justice Powell, a force in the center of the Court, resigned. The administration nominated former Solicitor General Bork to take his place. The nomination touched off a firestorm of controversy and a battle between pro-choice and right-to-life groups that ended with Bork's defeat.[36]

Rex Lee was acceptable to right-to-life groups who carefully scrutinized the Reagan appointments. Once in office, however, Lee was tortured by the need to balance law and politics. He was widely criticized by pro-choice activists for attacking *Roe* and by right to life groups for not attacking it vigorously enough. Lee wanted to carry the banner for the administration, but he realized that a strident position might offend the Court and cost him in other cases.

In *City of Akron v. Akron Reproductive Health Services* (1983), the government became directly involved in abortion litigation that did not involve funding for the first time. The Akron ordinance had a mandatory waiting period for women seeking an abortion and consent requirements. Lee not only filed an *amicus* brief, but asked for time to argue as well. Although some members of the administration wanted him to attack *Roe* directly, Lee did not take the extreme path. Rather, he argued that the Court had never really applied the sweeping language of *Roe* in first-trimester abortions. He argued that since the *Planned Parenthood of Central Missouri v. Danforth* (1976) decision, the Court had been making exceptions to reproductive rights. The Court permitted restrictions unless they unduly burdened the right to an abortion. Lee argued that in determining whether something was unduly burdensome, the justices should defer to the state legislatures.[37] Even though he did not ask the Court to overturn *Roe,* his proposed solution would have that effect.

During oral arguments, the justices, most notably the author of *Roe,* Harry Blackmun, trained their attention on Lee. In response to questions, Lee denied that he sought the reversal of *Roe.* He claimed that question of whether to reverse *Roe* was not before the Court. Lee admitted that was an issue for another day. Blackmun responded that Lee either wanted the reversal of *Roe* or *Marbury v. Madison,* which created judicial review.

The close questioning was a portend of the decision to strike the Akron ordinance in its entirety. The Court gave pro-choice groups their strongest victory since *Roe.* Powell's opinion implicitly, but completely, rejected Lee's arguments. Powell dismissed the argument that the justices had misinterpreted the Constitution and wrote that *stare decisis* demanded respect. The decision was seen as an embarrassment for the administration. But Lee did not consider it a complete loss. Indeed, Justices O'Connor, White, and Rehnquist adopted some of the points made by Lee. In particular, O'Connor began to advocate the undue burden argument offered by Lee.[38]

Right-to-life forces stepped up their efforts and pro-choice groups were stirred to action by the aggressiveness of the administration. Attorney General Meese placed the issue under the auspices of Reynolds and the CRD. Under his direction, the administration redoubled efforts at overturning *Roe.* The division availed itself of the opportunity in the first abortion case during its watch, *Thornburgh v. American College of Obstetricians and Gynecologists* (1986).

In *Thornburgh,* the solicitor general took the opportunity to ask the Court to overturn *Roe* directly. The Pennsylvania law was not very different from the law struck down in *Akron.* During the genesis of the case, Lee left office. It is unclear whether he was fired or resigned, but apparently Lee did not want to go through with the case. Charles Fried was named acting solicitor general. According to accounts, Meese would agree to remove the "acting" designation only after Fried filed an *amicus* brief in *Thornburgh* requesting that *Roe* be overturned. Fried did just that, abandoning the undue burden standard and claiming *Roe* violated the intent of the framers of the Constitution and introduced instability into the law. He argued that the Court's opinion in *Akron* was a significant departure from doctrinal development since *Roe.* Fried argued that "the textual, doctrinal, and historical basis for *Roe v. Wade* is so far flawed" that the Court should reconsider and abandon it. Fried concluded that the trimester approach and attempts to establish viability were arbitrary.[39]

The brief was roundly criticized. Former Solicitors General John Davis, Archibald Cox, Erwin Griswold, and Wade McCree condemned it as too strident. Some claimed it was the most polemic brief the office ever filed. Even Lee claimed that the solicitor general should not tell the Supreme Court it has made errors of constitutional doctrine. More than two hundred lawyers in the Department of Justice protested the administration's brief.[40] Blackmun remarked that it was "an amazing brief."[41]

Fried requested time to argue the government's position, but Pennsylvania refused to share its allotted time and the justices denied his request. The Court's decision was a stinging rebuke of Fried's position. In his opinion for the Court, Justice Blackmun refuted the solicitor general's position by emphatically upholding *Roe*. In dissent, Rehnquist and White agreed with the solicitor general's bottom line that *Roe* should be overturned. O'Connor refused to go that far. Instead, she returned to the undue burden standard in *Akron,* but went a little further noting the problems caused by *Roe.*

President Reagan tried to shield Fried from some of the criticism, claiming that he had personally approved of the brief.[42] Fried admitted raising issues and rationales to provide allies on the Court with ammunition to insert new arguments into the debate in hopes that support would be forthcoming.[43] He did not put a positive spin on the decision, calling the ruling a defeat. He publicly announced that he would not make a "pest" of himself before the Court by pressing the issue again, hoping to avoid damaging the relationship between the OSG and the Supreme Court.[44]

Conclusion. The Reagan administration was widely criticized for politicizing the OSG. Much of that criticism was a result of activities in the abortion cases. Clearly, the political factors dominated the legal in this area during Reagan's tenure. According to Andrew Frey, who resigned as a deputy during Fried's tenure: "The Solicitor General normally has a moderating effect on policies of other parts of the government. But operatives in the Reagan Administration felt that the overriding responsibility should be carrying out the policies of the Administration. They viewed Rex Lee as a captive of his staff, they did not trust him, he was too moderate. The Administration was much more comfortable with Charles Fried."[45]

Because reproductive rights was a constitutional issue, the solicitors general dedicated to the reversal of *Roe* could safely keep Congress at a distance. Because this was the quintessential agenda case, the president was the primary constituency. Lee and Fried had to measure whether the Court would permit them to launch a frontal attack. The Court seemed more conducive to arguments limiting reproductive rights, but the bottom line was that the solicitor general would be arguing that doctrine should be destabilized.

Lee, acting strategically, tempered the arguments the administration would have advanced. Even in his abortion case, Lee would not directly request that *Roe* be overturned. He left office as the next abortion cases were pending and his principal deputy, Fried, took the ultimate step, asking the Court to overturn *Roe.*

Whether there was any long-term or permanent damage in the relationship between the Court and the OSG, it seems clear that the administration lost some of its capital with the Court. Fried conceded as much.[46] Through its judicial appointments, the administration tried to change the institutional context and seemed to be on the verge of creating the critical mass necessary to excise *Roe.* In the end, the administration had little tangible success to show for its efforts. But those efforts were not wasted. They provided the ground work for the Bush administration.

THE BUSH ADMINISTRATION: CONTINUING TRENDS

George Bush came to the White House promising to lead a kinder, gentler administration. He pursued the general policies of his predecessor. Bush placed a not-so-subtle emphasis on family values. The subtext of that stance was a rejection of feminist principles.[47] Bush opposed affirmative action, vetoing the Civil Rights Act of 1990 and doing his best to undermine the 1991 bill that was passed in its wake.[48] Like his predecessor, Bush did not use the EEOC and administrative agencies to pursue employment equality. Bush also vetoed the Family and Medical Leave Act, claiming that he opposed mandated leave policies.[49] Bush faced an active, hostile Congress that was chafing after eight years of Ronald Reagan.

As president, Bush proposed a constitutional amendment to ban abortions and provide legal rights for the fetus. In addition, Congress passed a bill to provide federal funds for abortions in cases of rape and incest. Bush vetoed the bill, reportedly because he feared that some women might falsely claim rape or incest to get an abortion.[50]

There were not many gender cases on the docket during the administration. Solicitor General Starr filed *amici* briefs in two gender discrimination cases. In addition to an employment case, Starr dealt with a case at the intersection of sexual harassment and Title IX as well as the first case involving fetal protection laws. *United Automobile Workers v. Johnson Controls* (1991) provided the OSG with a difficult balancing task.[51] Johnson Controls had a fetal protection policy banning all women, except those who could prove infertility, from jobs involving exposure to lead. The Civil Rights Act of 1991 had made it easier to attack such policies.[52] Did this constitute a BFOQ? There was a safety risk, but it was to the unborn. The administration had a stated objection to reproductive rights and considered whether to support the policy for its protection of the unborn. In the end, Starr argued that the policy was discriminatory because it did not consider possible effects on men exposed to lead. A number of the *amici* supporting Johnson Controls, most notably the brief filed by the U.S. Catholic Conference, focused on the rights of the unborn. The Court largely adopted the solicitor general's analysis, recognizing the difficulty of the office's position in balancing the rights of the unborn and those of the workers.[53] The Court ruled that the company's policy did not constitute a BFOQ because it did not depend on the ability to perform the task in question.[54] The decision reinforced the use of the disparate impact standard.[55]

Starr was invited to file a brief in *Franklin v. Gwinnett County Public Schools* (1992), a Title IX case involving sexual harassment of a student by a teacher. The question was whether Title IX provided a cause of action for harassment by a teacher. The Court asked the solicitor general to assess whether an alleged circuit conflict was on point and to obtain the views of the executive branch on the potential extension of the law. The case was a follow-up to the *Grove City* case, which Congress had reversed by passing the Civil Rights Restoration Act of 1988.[56]

Starr's brief was the only one that sided with the school district. One question concerned whether Title IX was designed to deal with harassment. The solicitor general argued that Title IX did not reach such cases. The brief cautioned against judicial activism and reading too much into the Civil Rights Restoration Act. Starr argued that the Court should not find an implied remedy for an implied right to sue. Rather, the brief argued that Congress should determine the appropriate remedy.

The Court unanimously rejected Starr's arguments. Under Title IX, students who had been victims of sexual harassment could sue the school board. Thus the Court expanded Title IX to extend protection from sexual harassment. In the opinion, Justice White maintained that there was a long history "of allowing the federal courts to use any available remedy for a legal wrong." White held that "if a right to action exists to enforce a federal right and Congress is silent on the question of remedies, a federal court may order any appropriate relief."[57] White reasoned that Congress had a number of opportunities to restrict the scope of the right to sue and refused. He noted that Congress had overturned a number of restrictive Court decisions in recent years. Indeed, the Court seemed to act strategically and almost overcompensate, by expanding the right to sue. In doing so, the Court opted for an interpretation close to the position of the sitting Congress.

Continuing the Battle against Reproductive Rights

Just two days after the election of George Bush, Fried filed an *amicus* brief for the government in *Webster v. Reproductive Health Services* (1989) urging the Court to reconsider *Roe*. Fried deliberately waited until the election had passed to avoid interjecting the case into the campaign. Because the government had no direct stake in the case, it looked like a purely political move by a lame duck administration.[58] Attorney General Thornburgh approved continuing the case and aiming directly at *Roe*.[59] Changes in the composition of the Court seemed to favor the administration's position. *Webster* involved a range of provisions including viability, public funding, and restrictions on public employees who could not perform abortions or counsel women seeking an abortion. It was the case that right-to-life advocates had been seeking and that pro-choice forces had feared.

Fried was not solicitor general at the time of oral argument, but the Bush administration requested that he argue the case. It has been asserted that no one in the new administration wanted to deal with the case.[60] After *Thornburgh,* Fried had publicly stated he would not ask the Court to overrule *Roe*. Freed from his position as solicitor general, Fried rejoined the battle with broader leeway to argue the extreme position.[61]

Fried, officially listed as a special assistant to the attorney general, argued that *Roe* was based on two premises: that there is a fundamental right to an abortion and a state does not have a compelling interest in prenatal life. He dismissed both and urged the Court to "abandon its efforts to impose a comprehensive solution to the abortion question."[62]

During oral arguments, Fried claimed that *Roe* could be safely excised like a "single thread" without tearing at the fabric of constitutional law that had been constructed from privacy and abortion precedents. He tried to cover his political goals with legal arguments. A number of justices, particularly O'Connor, seemed skeptical.[63] In the decision, the Court upheld the Missouri law, but did not overturn *Roe*. O'Connor, who cast the decisive vote, advocated the undue burden standard that Lee had advanced.[64] *Roe* survived in name, but it had been weakened significantly and seemed to be on the brink of extinction. The administration could tip the balance with one appointment.

On the day that the Court issued the *Webster* decision, it announced that it had accepted three abortion-related cases. Solicitor General Starr had his first chance to intervene with an *amicus* brief in *Hodgson v. Minnesota* (1990), a parental consent case. Starr argued that the regulation did not infringe on a fundamental right and served a legitimate state interest. Although it was not relevant to the case, Starr argued that there was uncertainty about the proper standard of review in assessing the constitutionality of abortion regulations.[65] Thus, Starr took the unusual step of urging the justices to go beyond the question of parental consent to the core issue of abortion itself. The Court declined the invitation to expand the issue, although it upheld the parental consent provisions with all six Reagan and Bush appointees supporting the law.[66]

In *Rust v. Sullivan*, the solicitor general again weighed in against reproductive rights. The Secretary of Health and Human Services had promulgated regulations that forbade expenditures of any federal funds to programs that advocated or counseled women about abortions. The government was a party when the regulation was challenged as a violation of the First Amendment and a women's right to an abortion and inconsistent with Title X of the Public Health Act. On the basis of *Harris v. McRae*, Starr argued that the government could prohibit doctors in federal clinics from advising patients about the availability of abortion.[67] The brief for Health and Human Services argued that the regulation did not violate the First Amendment. In addition, Starr argued that though abortion was legal, the government was under no obligation to fund, promote, or encourage abortion. For good measure, the brief argued that *Roe* should be overruled.[68]

The environment was perfect for this brief. The resignations of Justices Brennan and Marshall threatened the viability of *Roe*. Indeed, as Mark Graber notes, "No longer content to weaken judicial protection for abortion rights, the justices began engaging in pro-life policy making." A 5-4 majority held that federal funds could be denied to any organization that even mentioned abortion as a possible option.[69]

Starr filed an *amicus* brief in *Planned Parenthood of Southeastern Pennsylvania v. Casey* (1992). He argued that the government had abandoned the undue burden standard in *Webster* and *Hodgson*. Starr claimed that the standard begged the central question, whether there was a fundamental right to abortion, and did not provide a meaningful guide for weighing competing interests. Starr pressed the argument that *Roe* was wrongly decided and should be overturned. He argued that a fundamental right could only occur with a historically protected right. Abortion, Starr argued, had been criminal activity as late as 1973.[70] If the Court was unwilling to overturn *Roe*, Starr asked the justices to clarify the standard of review for abortion regulations and make clear that the liberty interest did not rise to the level of a fundamental right, triggering strict scrutiny.[71]

While there appeared to be enough votes to overturn *Roe*, the Court did not provide the solicitor general with the result the office had been seeking for a decade. The opinion written by O'Connor, Kennedy, and Souter was the quintessential example of judicial restraint. They wrote that "liberty finds no refuge in a jurisprudence of doubt." With constitutional and political considerations in mind, they held that "after considering the fundamental constitutional questions resolved by *Roe,* principles of institutional integrity, and the rule of *stare decisis,* we are led to conclude this: the essential holding of *Roe v. Wade* should be retained and once again reaffirmed."

While a majority refused to overturn *Roe,* the Court continued to allow state regulations that limited abortion rights. More importantly, the Court continued to lower the standard of protection for reproductive rights. In his dissenting opinion Justice Blackmun praised O'Connor, Kennedy, and Souter for "an act of personal courage and constitutional principle" in refusing to overrule *Roe,* but argued that the Court should be an issue in the 1992 election. Blackmun wrote: "I fear for the darkness as four justices anxiously await the single vote necessary to extinguish the light. . . . I am 83 years old. I cannot remain on this Court forever and when I do step down, the confirmation process for my successor may well focus on the issue before us today."[72]

Another case, *Bray v. Alexandria Women's Health Clinic,* involved the intersection of abortion rights and gender discrimination. The clinic sued Operation Rescue, claiming that its protests reflected an animus against women, which could be attacked under the Civil Rights Act of 1871. If the clinic could establish that opposition to abortion was gender based, this would link reproductive rights to the Fourteenth Amendment and call into question the Hyde Amendment and restrictions on federal medical assistance. That was unlikely because the pregnancy precedents were so limited.[73]

Starr filed a brief opposing the clinic. He argued that the protests were not directed toward women, but against abortion activity. He supported this contention by reminding the justices that they had repeatedly held that different treatment for pregnancy did not necessarily represent gender discrimination.[74] The Court ruled that the protests were not directed toward women as a class, but were intended to halt the practice of abortion and reverse its legalization.[75] The Court held that women seeking an abortion were not a protected class.

Conclusion. Abortion was one of the agenda issues for the Reagan and Bush solicitors general. If the symbol of *Roe* remained after their attacks, it was a shell of its former self. In an ironic way, the path was paved for dismantling *Roe* by the Court's crabbed interpretation of the pregnancy decisions. If pregnancy was not considered a distinctive attribute of women, then the right to reproductive freedom could be undermined. Unable to reverse *Roe,* the symbol of abortion rights, solicitors general attacked abortion directly and indirectly. In general, it is clear that the OSG damaged reproductive rights. This was not without costs. The office became much more visible and some argue politicized to an unprecedented degree. There were concerns that relations between the OSG and the Court had been damaged.

The political forces dominated the legal and Starr tried, as Fried had, to expand the issues to get the Court to reconsider *Roe.* With what they considered a bad precedent on the books, there was little reason for the administration to act strategically. The solicitor general could pursue the administration's agenda. Of course, extreme arguments could hurt the solicitor general in other areas. In the end, though the office elevated political over legal concerns, Justices O'Connor, Kennedy, and Souter opted for a legal interpretation. Despite reservations, they argued for the norm of settled jurisprudence.

BILL CLINTON: TRYING TO RESTORE GENDER EQUALITY AND REPRODUCTIVE RIGHTS

Bill Clinton was arguably the first real proponent of women's rights and reproductive rights elected to the White House. Unfortunately for proponents, Congress and the Court were more conservative, doctrine had become less favorable, and the questions were more difficult. Further, the Court continued to argue that it was redefining its institutional role. The practical effect was that the Court would be less likely to take the type of cases that would alter doctrinal development. The question was whether the administration would launch an activist counterthrust to its predecessors. Given the administration's position in civil rights, there was no guarantee that it would exercise the full extent of its authority.

In the gender area, the CRD and the OSG were active and did not run into the same barriers that the administration placed in front of them in civil rights. Given the development of the issues, the number of questions before the Court was limited. There were no direct chances to buttress *Roe* and only a handful of gender cases. In the latter, though, the OSG did its best to expand doctrine. The work of the Clinton solicitors general in gender policy was dominated numerically by five sexual harassment cases. There were additional important cases involving all-male military academies and the reach of the Commerce Clause.

The sweeping decisions concerning sexual harassment, particularly

Meritor, created a number of second–generation questions considering the standards for demonstrating harassment. The *Meritor* decision did not address the standard of employer liability in harassment cases.[76] Neither Title VII nor the Civil Rights Act of 1991 had defined harassment in any tangible way. Congress had not reacted negatively to past decisions. It was left to the Clinton solicitors general to play the role of tenth justice and help the Court continue doctrinal development.

The administration filed an *amicus* brief in a second–generation sexual harassment case, *Harris v. Forklift Systems.* The lower court determined that Harris needed to demonstrate psychological injury to obtain relief under Title VII. Acting Solicitor General Bryson argued that Title VII did not require such a showing and sought more objective measures.[77] The justices agreed unanimously that a plaintiff need not prove adverse psychological effects to show that there was a hostile work environment. Rather, courts should consider a broader objective standard: the frequency of offensive behavior, whether it was threatening or humiliating, and whether it interfered with the plaintiff's work performance.[78]

Three more sexual harassment decisions were announced within days of each other. *Gebser v. Lago Vista Independent School District* was brought under Title IX, rather than Title VII. Gebser was a high school student who had sexual relations with a teacher. The question was whether the school district, which received federal funds, was liable for the teacher's actions, which constituted sexual harassment. Solicitor General Waxman filed an *amicus* brief arguing that Title VII agency principles relating to supervisor harassment and case law governed Title IX harassment cases as well.[79]

The Court disagreed, claiming that a school district was not liable unless it was notified of the behavior and demonstrated indifference. In a 5–4 decision, the Court ruled that the liability principles of Title VII do not control Title IX. The majority ruled that Title IX did not discuss the scope of available remedies and could not be implied from Congressional intent. The justices invited Congress to change the statute if it wanted to provide such relief.[80] The majority appeared to be responding to a more conservative Congress that would be less likely to reverse its holding.

The other cases were brought under Title VII and raised questions of the standards of liability in hostile work environment cases. Hostile environment cases were more difficult to prove and thus, the threshold for liability was presumably higher. *Faragher v. City of Boca Raton* and *Burlington Industries v. Ellerth* raised the issue of whether the city and company, respectively, were vicariously liable for the behavior of supervisors who harassed the petitioners and created a hostile work environment. The government filed *amici* briefs arguing for a broad interpretation of agency principles. The briefs argued that the company and the city were liable when the employer knows or should know about a supervisor's harassment.[81]

The Court ruled that under Title VII, an employee who refuses unwelcome sexual advances may recover without showing the employer was negligent or having to demonstrate adverse consequences from her refusal. More importantly, the Court ruled that the labels *quid pro quo* and hostile work environment were not controlling for a determination of liability.[82]

In the end, the Court appeared to issue contradictory decisions. The Court broadened the definition of Title VII liability. But the school district, which had more knowledge of the teacher's sexual harassment than the city or the company had, was found not to be liable. The difference turned on the statutory provisions: there was liability under Title VII, but not Title IX.

At the end of the 1995 term, the Supreme Court announced its decision in the much anticipated *United States v. Commonwealth of Virginia* case. The issue was whether the state can maintain single-sex military academies. Virginia sought to create a separate and almost equal military program at Mary Baldwin College, a women's college. Most interestingly, Principal Deputy Paul Bender asked the Court to use strict scrutiny, rather than moderate scrutiny, which had been the standard for two decades, though that issue was beyond the purview of the Court.

According to Bender, "We talked about the VMI case at great length. The Attorney General and the Assistant Attorney General did not really seem to care about the position we took with respect to strict scrutiny." Strategically, the decision seemed curious. The Court had rejected strict scrutiny and was getting more conservative. Still, Bender shouldered on, "If the Court was ever going to adopt strict scrutiny, we felt this was the time. We put it right up front in our brief." Part of the impetus came from litigants in the area, according to Bender: "There was much discussion about it from the women's groups. They were very interested. I had no feelings about whether we could win with that argument." Bender argued that "our primary interest was in the symbolic nature of strict scrutiny."

During oral arguments, Bender abandoned the position: "I was afraid too much of the argument would be taken up by the issue. I needed to get it resolved straight out. Justice O'Connor started with the questioning, asking if we were indeed advocating strict scrutiny. I responded that it was left open in past cases. She responded that we never supported that. Thus I retreated right at the start." Bender claimed that "the women's groups were angry that I did not push it more strongly, but I felt that Justice O'Connor was a fifth vote that we needed. If she was not ready to adopt strict scrutiny, there was no point."

There were potential costs if the argument succeeded. Getting the Court to recognize strict scrutiny could jeopardize gender-based affirmative action. Bender acknowledged that possibility: "We thought about it. It could crap up gender based affirmative action. The women's groups wanted it despite that potential problem. The standard was symbolic to women's groups." Still, he dismissed the possibility that achieving a strict scrutiny standard would necessarily doom affirmative action, saying, "In the end, the Court does what it wants." In essence, Bender thought the two could coexist.[83]

The process of doctrinal construction took a symbolic turn when the OSG argued for strict scrutiny. The office had begun the process by arguing for minimum scrutiny when the doctrine was in its nascent stages. Now, in the face of well-developed doctrine, the solicitor general asked the Court to reconsider standards it had used for a generation. Not surprisingly, the Court rejected arguments that it should elevate gender issues to strict scrutiny, but the justices ruled that the Virginia Military Institute (VMI) must admit qualified women or forfeit state funding. Justice Ginsburg authored the majority opinion declaring that the alternative military program did not provide an equal education for women and was a "pale shadow" of the VMI program.

Since 1995, there have been threats to Congressional power and policies and gender has not been immune. In *United States v. Morrison,* the constitutionality of the Violence Against Women Act was before the Court. Waxman argued that the law was an appropriate exercise of Congressional power under the Commerce Clause. Waxman argued that violence against women placed a substantial burden on commerce and the national economy. The solicitor general urged the Court to defer to Congress on the issue. Even though the act was not tied to traditional commercial activities, this was a legitimate exercise of Congressional power.[84] The problem for the solicitor general was that a number of recent Supreme Court decisions had been carving out exceptions to the Commerce Clause power of Congress.

By a narrow 5-4 majority, the Court ruled that the law was beyond the commerce powers of Congress. Chief Justice Rehnquist's opinion claimed that gender-based violence, like the gun-free zones in *United States v.*

Lopez, had no connection to economic activity. Thus, the Violence Against Women Act, like the Gun-Free Zone Act, was unconstitutional because it violated the police powers of the state. The decision continued the process of limiting the reach of the Commerce Clause. In dissent, Justice Souter chided the majority for judicial activism and noted that the 1964 Court upheld the use of the Commerce Clause to attack racial discrimination in *Heart of Atlanta Motel* and *McClung.*[85] Whether this doctrinal trend will threaten future civil rights legislation is an open question.

Conclusion. The Clinton administration had hoped to reestablish some of the precedents that the Reagan and Bush administrations had weakened. They had very little success in civil rights. Generally, the Clinton period will be seen as a holding pattern for gender policy. The opportunities for change were limited. First, the retreats were not as pronounced. Second, the Court had a more confined agenda. The Clinton solicitors general only had a handful of cases available to them and most involved sexual harassment. The Court expanded, with the solicitor general's blessing, the definition of harassment and made it easier to prove. This did not mean that the administration did not elevate political concerns when it had the opportunity. Painting with the broadest strokes, the solicitor general used the one case available to argue that the Court should revisit the use of moderate scrutiny.

The goals of the president and the solicitor general were the most dominant factor in explaining why so-called New Democrats who argued for moderation in civil rights were willing to push the envelope in gender cases. The argument for strict scrutiny seemed to ignore one critical factor: the Court. The composition of the Court, despite recent appointments, did not portend a sympathetic hearing on that issue. One factor appeared to change dramatically over the course of the two terms: Congress. Republican gains in 1994 and 1996 suggested that Congress might no longer serve as a check on negative Court decisions. In addition, decisions limiting the reach of Congressional authority under the Commerce Clause were not a positive harbinger for civil rights.

Trying to Reclaim *Roe*

After Bill Clinton was elected, the threat to *Roe* appeared to diminish. The administration would not send its solicitor general into Court to continue dismantling reproductive rights. Clinton was able to replace the author of *Roe* (Blackmun) and one of its two original opponents (White) with pro-choice justices.[86] At the same time, the Court largely avoided abortion cases, preferring to let lower courts deal with the issue. Thus, the administration had few opportunities to address the merits of the issue.

Given the interrelationships between issues, solicitors general had a number of chances to affect abortion policy in cases that did not directly involve abortion rights, but had related facts. The briefs provided the solicitor general with the opportunity to take a public stand on the issue. In a handful of multidimensional cases involving free speech with reproductive rights as a backdrop, Drew Days filed *amici* briefs that supported pro-choice advocates.

Days filed briefs in three cases involving right-to-life protestors. In *NOW v. Scheidler,* the solicitor general supported the use of Racketeer Influenced and Corrupt Organizations Act (RICO) as a means to stop abortion protestors. Days encouraged the Court to expand the scope of the statute.[87] The Court agreed with the solicitor general, holding that although the primary rationale for passage of RICO was economic enterprises, the laws may be applied to organized criminal activity inspired by noneconomic motives.

In *Madsen v. Women's Health Center,* Days argued that the buffer zones to keep anti-abortion protesters at a distance were reasonable time, place, and manner restrictions on the exercise, rather than the content of the speech.[88] The Court allowed restrictions within 36 feet of the clinic, but parted with the solicitor general in *Schenck v. Pro-Choice Network of Western New York,* refusing to allow a "floating buffer zone" that followed patients and staff going to and from the clinic.

Waxman presided over the only case in eight years that involved abortion rights. *Stenberg v. Carhart* involved a Nebraska law that banned the controversial late-term "partial birth" (dilation and extraction) abortions. The solicitor general argued that the Nebraska law was vague and so overbroad that it could prevent legal second-term abortions. The government argued that the law, while permitting partial birth abortions if the mother's life was in danger, did not include exceptions for the health of the woman, rape, or incest.[89]

The Supreme Court declared the law unconstitutional, in a fractured 5-4 opinion because it did not provide an exception to protect the health of the mother. The Court agreed that the statute was overbroad in that it would impose an undue burden on women seeking a D&E, dilation and extracation, the most common abortion procedure. Three of the four dissenters argued that *Roe* and/or *Planned Parenthood* were wrongly decided and should be overturned. Scalia argued that the decision should reside with the people because the Constitution is silent on the issue.[90] The division on the Court promises to keep the issue at the center of presidential concerns.

Conclusion. The Clinton administration made no secret of the fact that it supported the pro-choice position, but had few opportunities to bring that position to the Court. In this instance, institutional norms constrained the administration. The Rehnquist Court, as a part of its emerging role, decided not to take cases that involved the core of the reproductive rights issue. Given the interrelationships between issues, solicitors general had a number of chances to affect abortion policy in cases that did not directly involve abortion rights, but had related facts. The briefs provided the solicitor general with the opportunity to support pro-choice forces in ancillary cases. Clinton used executive orders to rescind Bush's gag order on doctors in clinics that receive federal funding. He also vetoed a bill that would ban all partial birth abortions. Thus it was no surprise that the solicitor general would file an *amicus* brief to attack the Nebraska law.

CONCLUSION: RETREAT IN GENDER AND REPRODUCTIVE RIGHTS

Eventually, the solicitor general played a central role in reproductive rights. In the previous period, solicitors general tried to define the political issue in legal terms. Now, the political forces dominated the legal. Redefinition was a pronounced goal of the Reagan administration in reproductive rights. Lee and Fried had little tangible success, incurring the enmity of justices in the center of the Court. One of the constraints on solicitors general is that they argue on behalf of just one client. Thus, if solicitors general incur the ire of the Court, it may be translated to other cases. If Lee and Fried did not succeed in having *Roe* overturned or significantly weakened, they were able to move the debate and introduce the notion of an undue burden. They also helped create the conditions that Starr could exploit more successfully. The Clinton administration did not have the opportunity to litigate on the core issue, but had worked on the peripheries.

The battle over reproductive rights continues to be waged in state legislatures and lower courts. The variety of restrictive laws in many states seems to ensure that future questions will work their way through the judicial hierarchy. Some may attract the four votes required to grant *certiorari* and the attention of the president and the solicitor general. With future appointments, a judicial nominee's stance on abortion should continue to be a crucial factor.

Legal considerations were elevated over political for the most part in gender rights. Some redefinition in gender policy was a result of spillovers from civil rights. Questions of remedies and standards for determining discrimination were fought on racial grounds. Reversing affirmative action and disparate impact were parts of the Reagan solicitor general's agenda. When similar cases came in a gender context, Fried argued for consistency. Some of the administration's success in limiting affirmative action and disparate impact was overturned by Congress. Clinton solicitors general did not have much of an opportunity to stem the redefinition in gender. Most of the gender cases filled in details on sexual harassment. They tried, unsuccessfully, to revisit strict scrutiny.

In the end, the role of the solicitor general was less significant in gender than in civil rights or in abortion. The solicitor general played a passive role in defining gender policy and a less direct role in its redefinition. Gender rights were not as central to presidential concerns and the Court was favorably disposed and used civil rights doctrine as an analogy.

Congress was a major factor because solicitors general had to argue statutory interpretation in many cases. Congress served as a bulwark for gender equality. When the Court interpreted a provision too narrowly, more than occasionally with the solicitor general's blessing, Congress served as a check and overturned a number of decisions.

CHAPTER 8

The Solicitor General

Law in a Sea of Politics

THIS BOOK BEGAN with the aphorism that law and politics cannot truly be separated. While the solicitor general is proof of that, members of the office often refer to law and politics as competing conceptions. The tensions between law and politics are well recognized by those who have served in the OSG and external actors who have working contact with them. Those tensions were certainly prevalent in civil rights and reproductive rights and they were precisely the issues that were responsible for the perception that the solicitor general has become more enmeshed in the political sphere. The notion that the Reagan administration politicized the office is widely shared, but the infusion of politics is nothing new. There were cases in every administration that had political overtones and external pressure.

The question is how pervasive those elements have become. Solicitors general are chosen for their legal acumen and expertise but also because their views reflect those of the administration. The legal realm suggests continuity in staying within the framework bequeathed by one's predecessor, respecting precedent, and acting within the boundaries constructed by the Supreme Court. Those factors may constrain a solicitor general who wants to pursue the administration's goals. It can also provide opportunities for a solicitor general who wants to keep the political forces at bay. The political realm suggests a dynamic and provides the solicitor general with some freedom to break from legal constraints. It invites more voices and views into the calculations. That may provide conflict with the solicitor general's institutional goals, especially the desire to maintain a strong relationship with the Supreme Court and preserve the independence of the office.

These tensions are manifested in questions about the definition of policy making. One of the recurring remarks of members of the OSG was that policy decisions were formulated elsewhere. In the case of civil rights, gender policy, and reproductive rights, policy priorities were set in the CRD. But the OSG has to approve the brief before the case can be appealed to the Court of Appeals or the Supreme Court. This potential veto has direct and indirect effects. First, the agency could be expected to modify its position preemptively to surmount this possible obstacle. More directly, the OSG may reject the brief or modify it to make it more palatable to the Court. This may not constitute the construction of a policy position, but it is policy making by any definition.

The solicitor general is a gatekeeper in a manner reminiscent of the Supreme Court. For government agencies, the OSG makes the first decision involving certiorari.[1] Similar to the justices, though, it is more than a simple binary decision to accept or reject. The justices may expand or contract the issues in the litigants' briefs. In many instances, the justices are only interested in one or two questions in a multifaceted brief, so they will excise unwanted questions and perhaps narrow remaining issues, a process of "issue suppression." Less common, but more interesting, is "issue expansion" whereby the justices take the petition and expand the questions, often changing the very nature of the case.[2]

The OSG can be expected to make use of similar processes when it permits a brief to go forward. The normal expectation is that the office will temper briefs coming from the agencies and suppress issues, which seems to be more related to the legal end of the continuum. This is reflected in the fact that the solicitor general seldom reverses positions in cases.

The process of issue expansion speaks more to the political dimension that influences the office. Issue expansion can occur in a couple of circumstances. First, the OSG may decide that the agency has not been aggressive enough. Second, the office may decide to change positions when a new administration comes to power. Both of these are relatively rare phenomena, but to the extent that they occur, they are more likely in controversial areas like civil rights and reproductive rights. Notions of issue expansion are more likely in the voluntary *amici* briefs where the solicitor general has more freedom and discretion. In civil rights and reproductive rights, it was not uncommon for solicitors general to file briefs that asked the Court to go beyond the issues in the case at hand. At different times, for instance, solicitors general asked the Court to expand civil rights acts or to end affirmative action or abortion.

There are a number of factors that limit the ability of solicitors general to change positions in a case. New solicitors general have to argue cases that were in the pipeline before they took office. In such instances, the previous solicitor general has committed the office to a position. Second, the solicitor general has to follow the agency's directives, which have been honed and established over time. Finally, it is difficult to argue a policy that represents a sharp break with the Court, which normally values precedent. In most areas, a new solicitor general would stay the course. In civil rights, at least recently, it has not been unusual for a change in administration to yield a change in position.

SHAPING THE CONTEXT?

Solicitors general since the Truman administration have run the gamut from legal to political, well-respected to barely known, legal giants to mere mortals. All were strategic actors who needed to balance an array of forces. The environments they faced varied. The ability of the solicitor general to shape the office's environment is dependent on a number of conditions and factors. First and foremost, is the nature of the issue. Second, there is the history of the issue and related issues. Third, issue evolution plays a role. Finally, there are the institutional factors arising from other actors in the solicitor general's environment. Some solicitors general had all or most of the factors moving in a favorable direction, making their task easier. Others faced a recalcitrant Congress, an unsympathetic Court, or unfavorable issue evolution. Some faced all three. The constant presence of divided government has probably been a threat to the independence of the solicitor general.

Theoretically, the president, Congress, the agency, and the Court are part of the solicitor general's environment on every issue. In reality, their relative influence varies by the salience of the issue. Controversial issues develop and take shape in a charged atmosphere with a great deal of influence or interference from the political forces. Less salient issues are contested in what, by comparison, is a political vacuum and the solicitor general receives less interference. The history of the issue can also be a factor. If an issue has a long history—extensive precedents—the solicitor general's discretion is circumscribed. If an issue is new, the solicitor general could write on a blank slate and shape its contours. Of course, the OSG is less likely to get involved with new issues, even salient ones.

A significant measure of change comes from issue evolution. The Court creates dramatic precedents like *Brown*, which created opportunities for solicitors general, and *Roe,* which posed constraints. The landmarks establish a path for the development of doctrine. Issue evolution ensures that questions in the cases would become difficult enough to prompt the Court to retreat. This provided opportunities for administrations that wanted to rein in civil rights or reproductive rights and constraints for those who sought further expansion. External policy innovation alters the development of an issue and affects the solicitor general. Passage of the Civil Rights Act of 1964 and Voting Rights Act of 1965 changed the nature of activity for the solicitor general from a reliance on *amici* briefs to making the government a party, allowing the OSG to sequence litigation.

Policy unfolds in predictable ways. A breakthrough in policy tends to spread to related issues.[3] The Civil Rights Act and Voting Rights Act changed the nature of evolutionary development, advancing desegregation issues and ensuring that many new civil rights issues would develop. The NAACP and the CRD developed and transplanted doctrine and the solicitor general supported and carried those arguments forward. The solicitor general argued that disparate impact rather than intent should be the dominant standard in employment. After the Court accepted that position, the solicitor general helped transplant it to vote dilution and other areas.[4] Affirmative action was a natural consequence of disparate impact. When the Reagan administration came to power, its solicitors general targeted affirmative action, disparate impact in employment, and its doctrinal relative, vote dilution.[5]

Institutionally, the impact of different actors varied over time and across issues. All solicitors general have found it necessary to balance politics with law. In most issue areas, the legal component dominates their calculations. Civil rights and abortion issues required solicitors general to give great weight to the administration's priorities.

The Court has traditionally been the most dominant star in the solicitor general's constellation. The solicitor general may be the president's mouthpiece on certain issues, but the ultimate stage is the Court and the audience is the nine justices. The Court controls access to its docket and can limit the president's influence.[6] This means that solicitors general must calculate the judicial response to their briefs and arguments. Part of the calculus involves answering the question of whether the justices will decide cases in a legal manner, adhering to precedent, or in a more political manner, letting their sincere values dominate consideration of the issue. The need to react to the Court is both short term and long term. The solicitor general could not play a role in civil rights until the Court adopted judicial activism in individual liberties and group rights. The preferred position doctrine created the conditions for solicitors general who wanted to make extensive use of *amici* briefs.

Congress played a shifting role in the solicitor general's environment.

That role was limited in early civil rights and reproductive rights policy because of the constitutional nature of the cases. The extraordinary majorities necessary to overturn constitutional decisions were unlikely. Gender and race, after 1964, were dominated by statutory interpretation making Congress a major factor in the policy process. Since 1969, there has been almost constant divided government. This placed constraints on a solicitor general who might wish to follow the president's agenda. During the Reagan and Bush administrations, Congress played a significant role, overturning negative Court decisions. The Court seemed to react to the sitting Congress in its interpretation of statutory provisions. Indirectly, the OSG did as well, reacting to a Court that was reacting to Congress.[7]

Presidents, attorneys general, and their appointees to the CRD come to Washington with priorities, but it has often been difficult for them to direct solicitors general. A number of administrations tried to get solicitors general to do their bidding on civil rights before the Reagan administration allegedly politicized the office. Prior to that time, the OSG typically moderated political positions. The key has not been in putting pressure on the office in individual cases, but in choosing a solicitor general who reflects the administration's ideology.

The ability of the solicitor general to exert influence depends on the desire of the president and the attorney general to use the office to do their bidding. Advocate attorneys general will be more likely to utilize the solicitor general to pursue the administration's policy goals and opt for the political end of the politics-law spectrum. Neutral attorneys general would be more likely to insulate the office. Some attorneys general imposed themselves on the solicitor general, others imposed themselves between the political forces and the solicitor general.

According to Philip Heymann, "The independence of the Solicitor General's office depends on the relationship between the Attorney General and the Solicitor General. It depends on two conditions: an Attorney General who is powerful within the White House and an Attorney General who has respect for the Office of the Solicitor General and the individual Solicitor General."[8] Ultimately, it is reduced to the question of whether the attorney general will show deference to the solicitor general or attempt to treat the office as another weapon in the policy arsenal.

Kirsten Norman-Major maintains that "in the end, it is up to the President and the Court to decide how much of an activist the Solicitor General will be."[9] It reflects the tension between law and politics. There are payoffs to this strategy if a majority accepts the solicitor general's position, but there are risks in trying to move an agenda through a recalcitrant Court. An aggressive tack can have short and long-term consequences: it can thwart the president's goals, create harmful precedents, and damage the long-term relationship between the office and the Court.

Typically, the relationship between the CRD and the solicitor general is expected to be engine and brake, respectively. The normal expectation is that the legal forces and the careerists will have a moderating influence over the political forces. The most aggressive advances tended to occur when the political and legal forces were in concert.

During the Truman and Eisenhower administrations,[10] careerists in the office were more aggressive than the political operatives wanted. The reverse was true in the Kennedy administration. Cox held the line and moderated the scope and pace of the division's priorities. During the Johnson administration, the OSG was more willing to accept the position that the division adopted and even go beyond it. In the Nixon administration, solicitors general generally pushed the position that the legal forces adopted. This was due to the grudging willingness of the political operatives that their preferences had to give way. The division and the office convinced policy makers that a sudden and sharp retreat in civil rights would be self-defeating.

The Reagan administration represented a disjuncture, at least in degree. Solicitors general let some of the extreme positions reach the Court, but rejected and moderated others. The office had a number of battles with the EEOC. Issue expansion was often the result as the solicitor general ignored or discounted the position the EEOC favored. On the other side, the division had an aggressive agenda and there were a number of battles with the OSG, which tried to temper the tone of the briefs. These disputes had to be resolved by the attorney general. In reproductive rights, the intent was clear, to argue broadly and aggressively to undermine and then overturn *Roe*. Starr's tenure was marked by issue expansion in voting rights as the solicitor general tried to go beyond the position the division advocated. The Clinton administration had an unusual dynamic as the division and office wished to be more aggressive, but political operatives tried to rein them in.

There were similarities between the Truman and Reagan administrations. Their solicitors general pursued their agenda issues in the face of hostile precedents. There were differences between the Nixon and Reagan administrations in the work of their solicitors general. The retreat of the Nixon solicitors general was tied to issue evolution. Griswold and Bork tied their opposition to second-generation issues such as northern desegregation and remedies like busing. The work of Lee and Fried, however, was increasingly directed toward asking the justices to reconsider core precedents. Attacks on disparate impact, affirmative action, and reproductive rights did not focus on limiting civil rights solely because the cases were more difficult. Rather, they were frontal attacks.

While issue expansion and changing sides may be largely confined to the agenda issues and most prevalent in the voluntary *amici* cases, they are rare coin that the solicitor general typically spends frugally. Though civil rights and abortion were far from the norm for the solicitor general, they have implications for other issues. The solicitor general is in the unique position of arguing large numbers of cases on behalf of one client. The Court expects the solicitor general to carry the administration's flag for some agenda issues. But if the solicitor general abuses the privilege, there are potential consequences. In the short term, the Court can establish a harmful precedent in that area. More broadly, the solicitor general risks success in other areas if he antagonizes the Court in the agenda cases. In the long term, there are risks to the comity between the office and the Court.

The Changing Role of the Solicitor General?

The modern solicitor general is often constrained by the need to play a number of roles. In trying to assist the Court as tenth justice or fifth clerk, while fulfilling the president's agenda as "attorney general as policy maker" or pursuing the Justice Department's more neutral obligations as the "attorney general as law enforcement officer," the solicitor general has to balance a number of roles. In attempting to fulfill these roles, the solicitor general has several potentially competing constituencies to satisfy. When these factors move in the same direction, there are opportunities for the solicitor general, but that was rare in the last half-century, as divided government has been the rule.

The solicitor general previously faced constraints of a very different nature. At the outset, the office had little authority for entering cases. The solicitor general could be invited to play the role of an impartial fifth clerk. The lack of statutory authority limited the opportunities for the government to be a party to cases and did not allow the solicitor general to sequence litigation. Because there was little authority for the Justice Department and institutional mechanisms like the CRD and the EEOC did not exist, there was limited authority for the solicitor general acting as a law enforcement officer. The solicitor general had no history of using the *amicus* brief to assist private third parties. Thus there were few mechanisms to create an agenda issue and presidents and attorneys general were unwilling to invest their political capital in civil rights.

The changes that began in the Truman administration had important implications for the responsibilities of the solicitor general. The ability to become a party to litigation and file briefs when the government was not a party moved the solicitor general away from the Court to a degree. The addition of statutory authority and the ability to file an *amicus* brief pushed the solicitor general closer to the president and the attorney general.

The decline in support for civil rights and success is certainly a function of the ideological leanings of the president and the composition of the Supreme Court. Conservative presidents were less supportive of civil rights. Success was dictated, in part, by the Court. The Warren Court supported all manner of civil rights. The Burger Court opposed some extensions, but was generally supportive. On the other hand, as Paul Bender remarked about the Clinton solicitors general: "Our lower success rate in the Supreme Court was simply a matter of a conservative Court and our more liberal positions."[11]

Part of the reason for initial declines in civil rights support during the administrative phase was the increased difficulty of the cases. The solicitor general's participation was dominated by second-generation education cases (busing and northern cases), public/private cases, employment and affirmative action, and cases asking the Court to extend the Voting Rights Act.[12]

Affirmative action served as a bridge to the redefinition phase. The difficulty of the cases was partially responsible for the retreats. As Lawrence Wallace noted: "Civil rights work is very trying these days. There is a great complexity to the cases. Twenty-five years ago the cases were less technical. It was a lot more apparent who wore the white hats. There are much closer issues today with merits on both sides."[13] In the redefinition phase, solicitors general were not just content to ask the Court to freeze things where they were because the issues were difficult, rather they were willing to ask the Court to revisit and reverse existing precedents.

The dynamics are a bit more complicated, however. Skowronek argues that presidents shape the context that their successors inherent. During each phase of civil rights policy, the first president's solicitors general were instrumental in changing the nature of the office's activities and established a context for subsequent administrations.

In effect, there were three different regimes for civil rights issues. The Truman administration set the precedent for the litigation phase. Truman's solicitors general were the first to use *amici* briefs to extend the office's involvement and support the NAACP. The increased activism and more aggressive use of *amici* briefs enhanced Court dependence and reliance on the solicitor general, but enhanced the potential of presidential influence. This set a context for successors.

When the Civil Rights Act of 1964 was passed, the context changed. During the administrative phase, it was the Johnson solicitors general who established the path for their successors. Cox and Marshall not only defended the constitutionality of the Civil Rights Act and the Voting Rights Act, they argued for expansion of their provisions. Marshall tried to link moribund Reconstruction legislation to current civil rights acts. This created a broader range of tools for the Justice Department and increased the activity of the solicitor general.[14]

Reagan solicitors general set the context for the redefinition phase. It was marked by increased external pressure on the office. Changes in the institutional context of the office and the types of people chosen to be solicitor general were responsible. The administration tried to create a new definition of civil rights, reverse existing precedents, and limit new initiatives. If Lee and Fried did not achieve all the administration's goals, they established a momentum that would lead to important reversals and helped usher in a new dominant theory to guide judicial decision making. This served to create opportunities for Starr and constraints for Days, Dellinger, and Waxman.

In reproductive rights, solicitors general were not constrained by their predecessors because the OSG had stayed away from direct consideration of the issue. Solicitors general filled the roles of tenth justice and fifth clerk. Thus, they did not leave a paper trail for their successors. Since the Reagan administration attacked the issue directly, political forces dominated the legal forces. The solicitor general became the attorney general as policy maker.

In gender, solicitors general wrestled with the proper standard, opting to avoid the race paradigm. Because gender intersected with race and reproductive rights, the Court and the OSG had to consider the broader implications of potential decisions. In addition, gender issues raised a wide range of fact situations almost immediately. Further complicating the development of doctrine, some cases involved discrimination against men, while others involved discrimination against women. These factors posed more constraints than opportunities for the office as it tried to impose some consistency on a wide range of activity. The OSG often opted to move the issue toward the legal end of the law-politics dichotomy, acting initially as tenth justice to help the Court.

While one might be tempted to conclude that race and reproductive rights are the quintessential political issues, there were still legal components involved. On a number of occasions, solicitors general had to play the role of tenth justice or fifth clerk and argue positions that did not match the sincere goals of the presidents because they had to follow precedent or argue before a Court that was unsympathetic to their position.

Over the course of the development of civil rights, the role of the solicitor general changed dramatically. The sources of those changes were both exogenous and endogenous. Scholars typically attribute the strengths and weaknesses of the Supreme Court and presidents to historical,[15] institutional,[16] or individual factors.[17] Given that the solicitor general works at the intersections between the branches, it is not surprising that all three contributed to changes in the OSG. Historically, changes in the role and function of the Supreme Court led to institutional changes in the OSG. The Court carved a new role for itself through Footnote Four. The increased activism of the Court coupled with the willingness of the elected branches to abdicate their responsibility in some areas made the Court a more dynamic forum in those areas. As the Court's authority grew, the solicitor general became a more valuable vehicle for influencing the justices. Long periods of divided government have also enhanced the potential of the solicitor general.

Historical factors contributed to the institutional changes in the environment. Reproductive rights and, to a greater degree, civil rights have been responsible for redefining the role of the solicitor general. The creation and evolution of the CRD provided an increasingly powerful new actor in the office's environment. Because of civil rights, the OSG under Truman made more aggressive use of *amici* briefs and bequeathed that precedent to its successors. Passage of the Civil Rights Act and the Voting Rights Act strengthened the institutional hand of the office by permitting the government to intervene to as a party.

There were internal institutional changes as well. Civil rights issues carry important consequences and the political forces wanted to ensure that their views carried greater weight in making the calculations. The creation of the principal deputy was most symptomatic of the changes. While the principal deputy has not altered the OSG as many feared, it has demonstrated the vulnerability of the office's independence.

As a partial result of historical and institutional changes, there have been individual level changes. Has there been a sea change in the office and the type of people who are selected to be solicitor general? Once again, the question must be considered within the context of the law-politics tension. If the qualifications of the nominee are the central or sole criterion then legal considerations should dominate the solicitor general's tenure. If presidents have an ideological litmus test for nominees, then the potential for the infusion of politics is much greater.

Certainly, there is a widely shared perception that different factors matter in selecting a solicitor general. Carter's selection of Wade Mc-Cree brought a relative unknown to the office, following such noted legal scholars as Archibald Cox, Thurgood Marshall, Erwin Griswold, and Robert Bork. Some argue that the lack of an independent reputation was an impediment for a solicitor general trying to insulate the office from politics. The Reagan administration was charged with politicizing the OSG by making it more directly accountable to the attorney general. The confluence of these factors has contributed to the perception that politics is more prominent today in the solicitor general's calculations.

According to Andrew Frey, "There are two models of the solicitor general. The first is what I call the Harvard Law Professor Model:'I know what is best for the Court. My job is to help the Supreme Court reach the right result.' These solicitors general do not feel that they really have a client. The second see themselves as lawyers for a client, apart from their view of the general public interest. They see themselves as lawyers with the principal task of advancing the programmatic and litigation interests of the government."[18] Frey used Cox and Bork as examples of the Harvard Law Professor Model. More recent solicitors general seem to dominate the second group. Relatedly, Philip Heymann argued that traditionally the solicitor general could tell the president that the office could not take a certain position because it was contrary to the law. He argues that there has been a movement away from that today. Recent solicitors general are more likely to be advocates for a position and try to find grounds to argue that position.[19]

The evidence seems to support the impact of the changes. Solicitors general with formidable resumes and independent reputations could insulate themselves from the political winds. Cox did not move as fast as the attorney general wanted and Bork filed briefs that belied his ideological predilections. Griswold presents the best case study, serving presidents of different parties. Although Griswold tried to incorporate some of Nixon's views when the cases turned to busing, he was generally consistent in his filings across administrations.

While the solicitor general's position has traditionally been considered a stepping stone to the Supreme Court, it has been over a generation since it has occurred. Ironically, as ideology has become more important and solicitors general have appeared to be more willing to carry the administration's water to the Supreme Court, they have become more controversial, suggesting potential problems if the president nominated a solicitor general for a Court vacancy.

These changes have implications for the roles and goals of the solicitor general. As the solicitor general moves closer to the president, the goals appear to reflect that. There is also evidence that the changes have an impact on the roles that the solicitor general plays. In areas like civil rights, the solicitor general has increasingly assumed the role of the attorney general as policy maker. Part of this is a function of more aggressive use of the *amicus* curiae brief. But it has also reflected a conscious choice to assume a policy-making stance when the government was a party and in the less discretionary *amici* briefs. Whether coincidence or a reflection of these changes, the Court has been less likely to invite the government to participate.

NAMES CHANGE, BUT THE CONSTRAINTS REMAIN THE SAME

The competing constraints that are often brought to bear on the solicitor general influenced George W. Bush's administration as it prepared for its first Monday in October. Although the president and the attorney general had expressed antipathy for affirmative action, the administration asked the Court to uphold a disadvantaged business enterprise program. The case, *Adarand v. Mineta,* was a modified version of a 1995 decision *(Adarand v. Pena)* in which the Court struck down a minority business enterprise program that gave preference to minority contractors in government programs.[20] Thus, precedent favored the administration's sincere preferences. On the other hand, the Clinton administration had committed the government to support the program on its last day in office. When the Court voted to accept the case, the Bush administration had to determine whether to pay the price of reversing position.[21] Reversal of position is not common, but to the extent that it occurs, it happens in salient political issues, like civil rights. The Bush administration, constrained by the contested 2000 election that had to be settled by the Supreme Court, the defection of Senator James Jeffords that provided the Democrats a majority in the Senate, and the fact that this was Congressional policy, decided to stay the course the Clinton administration had established. Attorney General John Ashcroft and Solicitor General Theodore Olson decided not to reverse the Clinton administration's position. Ashcroft and Olson were controversial nominees who were considered very conservative and too political[22] and the constraints facing the new president may have forced them to moderate their position.

The reaction to the decision is a reflection of the intertwining of law and politics that the solicitor general faces. Conservatives, angry with Olson's decision not to oppose the program, criticized the position as political expedience. Liberals, surprised that the Justice Department stayed with the position staked out by the Clinton administration, applauded the attorney general and solicitor general for adopting a legal position even though their sincere preferences were very different.[23] But the salience of civil rights and reproductive rights issues ensures their re-emergence. Ashcroft and Olson are expected to oppose future affirmative action programs when the environmental conditions are more propitious to pursue the administration's sincere preferences.

CONCLUSION

In a sense, the solicitor general is arguably the most strategic actor in Washington. In addition to balancing the influence of the actors in their environment, solicitors general have to balance law and politics. Assuming that the office has been politicized, can the genie ever be put back in the bottle? Some of the historical, institutional, and individual level changes would need to be reversed. Generally, strengthening the political parties and limiting the incidence of divided government might reduce reliance on the solicitor general. More specifically, it would take one of three changes, which focus on the law–politics continuum. First, the president could change the criteria for selection, limiting political and ideological considerations and elevating traditional legal concerns. Second, the attorney general could take greater pains to insulate the solicitor general from the political forces. Finally, the Supreme Court could limit the efficacy of litigation. If the Court redefined its institutional role to reduce its policy-making proclivities, the administration would need to rely on other avenues.

There is little incentive for presidents to reduce the role of the solicitor general. The president and the office are on different clocks, one political and one legal. Presidents are trying to write their pages in history. Solicitors general have built up a reservoir of good will with the Court. A new administration may decide to borrow against that reserve. There is little reason for political operatives to be too concerned over the long-term relationship between the Supreme Court and the OSG.

Similarly, the likelihood that attorneys general who want to help presidents fulfill their perceived mandates will restrain themselves from the using the solicitor general is not great. To the extent that an attorney general is a member of the "Inner Cabinet," he or she is likely to be aggressive in using the solicitor general. An attorney general, particularly one categorized as a neutral, might be willing to establish a buffer for the solicitor general. Nancy Baker shows that presidents often appoint a neutral attorney general following a controversial advocate.[24] Considering that the advocate is likely to use the solicitor general aggressively, this would provide a mere respite for the office.

The final potential change might be the most likely. The Rehnquist Court has tried to change its institutional role, arguing that it will be less active in policy making. The Court seeks to be more restraintist and to fill interstices, rather than make law.[25] If the Court becomes a less inviting forum, the pressures on the solicitor general might be reduced. Part of the rationale for reducing the activism of the Court is that it will force the elected branches to become more active in policy making, particularly in controversial issues. In the past, the Court's willingness to consider those issues meant that Congress could safely resist involvement. Increased Congressional activity might mean more positive law and would constrain the solicitor general in adopting positions. If the Court was less willing to intervene in state matters, that would limit the opportunities to file voluntary *amici,* the primary vehicle for pursuing the president's goals. As the Court expands the legal or jurisprudential part of its role and contracts the policy component, it may lead to more invitations for the solicitor general's input. Invitations require less partisan responses from the OSG.

For the short term, though, the solicitor general will continue to make consequential decisions that involve the legal and political realms. As a strategic actor the solicitor general must balance law and politics in a dynamic political environment. The solicitor general will be trying to fulfill the administration's goals on the litmus test issues of the day, while trying to help the Court impose some consistency on the law in other issues. The solicitor general will continue to work beneath the public's radar. Perhaps the clearest evidence of the relative invisibility of the office is what is unsaid: virtually none of the biographies or autobiographies of recent presidents even mention a solicitor general. It seems to be an odd omission for an appointee whose successes and failures go a long way toward defining the most important issues of the day and determining the legacy a president will leave.

Appendix

INTERVIEWS

Donald Ayer (principal deputy: Fried), Jan. 30, 1998.
Paul Bender (principal deputy: Days), April 9, 1998.
Robert Bork (solicitor general: Nixon and Ford), Aug. 10, 1998.
Judge William Bryson (former deputy solicitor general), March 25, 1998.
Roger Clegg (former assistant to the solicitor general), April 16, 1998.
Archibald Cox (solicitor general: Kennedy and Johnson), Feb. 9, 1998.
Drew Days (solicitor general: Clinton), Nov. 24, 1997.
Walter Dellinger (acting solicitor general: Clinton), Dec. 12, 1999.
John Dunne (assistant attorney general for civil rights: Bush), April 16, 1998.
David Flynn (chief of appellate section), Jan. 27, 1998.
Andrew Frey (former deputy solicitor general), Jan. 29, 1998.
Judge Charles Fried (solicitor general: Reagan), March 3, 1998.
Kenneth Geller (former deputy solicitor general), Jan. 28, 1998.
Irving Gornstein (assistant to the solicitor general), Jan. 27, 1998.
Phillip Heymann (former assistant to solicitor general), March 6, 1998.
Nicholas Katzenbach (former attorney general), March 11, 1998.
Deputy Solicitor General Edwin Kneedler, Jan. 27, 1998.
Brian Landsberg (former chief of appellate section), April 7, 1998.
Jerris Leonard (assistant attorney general for civil rights: Nixon), April 27, 1998.
Mark Levy (former assistant to the solicitor general), Jan. 27, 1998.
Robert Long (former assistant to the solicitor general), April 20, 1998.

Burke Marshall (assistant attorney general for civil rights: Kennedy), March 4, 1998.

Deval Patrick (assistant attorney general for civil rights: Clinton), April 14, 1998.

Carter Phillips (former assistant to solicitor general), Jan. 29, 1998.

Stephen Pollak (assistant attorney general for civil rights: Johnson), June 25, 1998.

John Roberts (principal deputy: Starr), Jan. 28, 1998.

David Rose (former counsel for the EEOC), April 21, 1998.

W. Bradford Reynolds (assistant attorney general for civil rights: Reagan), Aug. 20, 1998.

Richard Seamon (former assistant to the solicitor general), April 28, 1998.

Kenneth Starr (solicitor general: Bush), Dec. 21, 1998.

James Turner (former acting assistant attorney general for civil rights), Jan. 27, 1998.

Deputy Solicitor General Lawrence Wallace, Jan. 29, 1998.

Seth Waxman (solicitor general: Clinton), Jan. 30, 1998.

Richard Wilkins (former assistant to the solicitor general), March 27, 1998.

Notes

PART I. THE SOLICITOR GENERAL AND AMERICAN POLITICS

1. Rebecca Salokar, *The Solicitor General: The Politics of Law*, p. 3.

2. Lincoln Caplan, *The Tenth Justice: The Solicitor General and the Rule of Law*, p. 3.

3. Charles Fahy, "The Office of the Solicitor General," *American Bar Association Journal* 28 (1942): 20–22.

4. Christopher Zorn, "U.S. Government Litigation Strategies in the Federal Appellate Courts" (Ph.D. diss., Ohio State University, Columbus, 1997), pp. 11–12. This does not suggest the attorney general is immune from pressures, Nancy Baker, *Conflicting Loyalties: Law and Politics in the Attorney General's Office, 1789–1990;* Cornell Clayton, *The Politics of Justice: The Attorney General and the Making of Legal Policy.*

5. An *amicus curiae,* or "friend of the court," brief is filed by a group that is not party to the case, but will be affected by the outcome. Such briefs provide the solicitor general with the opportunity to expand or contract issues in the case, provide expertise, and offer the Court an informal tally of public opinion (Richard Pacelle, *The Transformation of the Supreme Court's Agenda: From the New Deal to the Reagan Administration,* p. 31).

6. Karen O'Connor, "The *Amicus Curiae* Role of the U.S. Solicitor General in Supreme Court Litigation," *Judicature* 66 (1983): 256–64.

7. Salokar, *The Solicitor General,* chapter 2; Kevin McGuire, *The Supreme Court Bar: Legal Elites in the Washington Community,* pp. 165–66.

8. H. W. Perry, *Deciding to Decide: Agenda Setting in the U.S. Supreme Court;* Office of Legal Counsel, "Memorandum Opinion for the Attorney General: Role of the Solicitor General," *Loyola of Los Angeles Law Review* (1988): 1089–97.

9. Stephen Puro, "The United States as *Amicus Curiae*" in S. Sidney Ulmer, ed., *Courts, Law, and Judicial Processes;* John Jenkins, "The Solicitor General's Winning Ways," *ABA Law Journal* 69 (1983): 734–38.

10. Charles Epp, *The Rights Revolution: Lawyers, Activists, and Supreme Courts in Comparative Perspective,* pp. 60–63.

11. Jeffrey Segal, "*Amicus Curiae* Briefs by the Solicitor General During the Warren and Burger Courts: A Research Note," *Western Political Quarterly* 41 (1988): 135–44.

12. Kevin McGuire, "Repeat Players in the Supreme Court: The Role of Experienced Lawyers in Litigation Success," *Journal of Politics* 57 (1995), argues that expertise is the crucial determinant of the office's success.

13. Edward Carmines and James Stimson, *Issue Evolution: Race and the Transformation of American Politics.*

14. Stephen Wasby, "A Triangle Transformed: Court, Congress, and Presidency in Civil Rights," *Policy Studies Journal* 21 (1993): 565–74.

15. Louis Fisher and Neal Devins, *Political Dynamics of Constitutional Law.*

16. I include cases decided with a full opinion. The decision is the unit of analysis. Thus, *Roe v. Wade* and *Doe v. Bolton* count as one case because there was one opinion. Similarly, the trilogy of abortion funding cases count as one because the solicitor general filed one brief and the Court issued one decision.

17. Coding is based on the Supreme Court Data Base and Sheldon Goldman, "Voting Behavior on the United States Courts of Appeals Revisited," *American Political Science Review* 69 (1975): 493–95. Early gender cases involved laws that clearly discriminated against women. As the Court found these unconstitutional, attention turned to structural barriers to equality. Those issues often involved compensatory programs to remedy past discrimination. I distinguish between "invidious" and "helpful" programs (Judith Baer, *Equality Under the Constitution: Reclaiming the Fourteenth Amendment*). I coded support for compensatory programs, like benefits for widows that are denied widowers, as opposed to gender equality. Support for protective legislation that denied jobs to women was categorized as against equality, the perspective of groups litigating the cases. I coded support for affirmative action as pro-gender equality. I coded cases that do not recognize differences attendant to pregnancy as opposed to gender rights. Liberal feminist litigation, designed to eradicate male-created categories, was the dominant strategy (see Patricia Cain, "Feminism and the Limits of Equality" in *Feminist Legal Theory: Foundations,* ed. D. Kelly Weisberg, pp. 237–47).

18. William Eskridge, "Reneging on History? Playing the Court/Congress/President Civil Rights Game," *California Law Review* 79 (1991).

Chapter 1. Between Law and Politics

1. Ronald Chamberlain, "Mixing Politics and Justice: The Office of Solicitor General," *Journal of Law & Politics* 4 (1987): 379.

2. Paul Wahlbeck, "The Life of the Law: Judicial Politics and Legal Change," *Journal of Politics* 59 (1997): 779.

3. Salokar, *The Solicitor General.*

4. James Cooper, "The Solicitor General and Federal Litigation: Principal-Agent Relationships and the Separation of Powers" (Ph.D. diss., Indiana University, Bloomington, 1993).

5. Kenneth Starr, interview by author, Dec. 21, 1998.

6. Salokar, *The Solicitor General,* p. 12; William Brigham, "The Office of the Solicitor General of the United States" (Ph.D. diss., University of North Carolina, Chapel Hill, 1966), p. 1.

7. Robert Scigliano, *The Supreme Court and the Presidency,* p. 163.

8. Cooper, "The Solicitor General and Federal Litigation," p. 9.

9. Lawrence Wallace, interview by author, Jan. 29, 1998; Seth Waxman, interview by author, Jan. 30, 1998; Philip Heymann, interview by author, March 6, 1998; Walter Dellinger, interview by author, Dec. 12, 1999; Andrew Frey, interview by author, Jan. 29, 1998.

10. Drew Days, "The Solicitor General and the American Legal Ideal," *SMU Law Review* 49 (1995): 82.

11. Marc Galanter, "Why the 'Haves' Come Out Ahead: Speculations on the Limits of Legal Change," *Law & Society Review* 9 (1974).

12. Drew Days, "The Interests of the United States, the Solicitor General and Individual Rights," *Saint Louis Law Review* 41 (1996): 2–3.

13. John Aldrich, "Rational Choice Theory and the Study of American Politics" in *The Dy-*

namics of American Politics: Approaches and Interpretations, ed. Lawrence Dodd and Calvin Jillson, p. 227.

14. Lee Epstein and Jack Knight, *The Choices Justices Make.*

15. Mark Hurwitz, "The Nature of Agenda in the United States Supreme Court and Courts of Appeals" (Ph.D. diss., Michigan State University, East Lansing, 1998), pp. 41–51.

16. O'Connor, "The *Amicus Curiae* Role," p. 260.

17. David Mayhew, *Congress: The Electoral Connection.* Richard Fenno, *Congressmen in Committees,* argues that members of Congress choose committees based on individual goals.

18. R. Douglas Arnold, *Congress and the Bureaucracy: A Theory of Influence,* p. 24, maintains the hierarchy of goals is dominated by budget maximization.

19. Jeffrey Segal and Harold Spaeth, *The Supreme Court and the Attitudinal Model.*

20. Lawrence Baum, *The Puzzle of Judicial Behavior.*

21. *Chevron, USA, Inc. v. Natural Resources Defense Council, Inc.* 467 U.S. 837 (1984). John Osborn, "Legal Philosophy and Judicial Review of Agency Statutory Interpretation," *Harvard Journal of Legislation* 36 (1999): 115–16. For an argument that the Court has not been entirely faithful to *Chevron:* Richard Pierce, "The Supreme Court's New Hypertextualism: An Invitation to Cacophony and Incoherence in the Administrative State," *Columbia Law Review* 95 (1995): 749–53.

22. Eric Schnapper, "Becket at the Bar—the Conflicting Obligations of the Solicitor General," *Loyola of Los Angeles Law Review* 21 (1988): 1252.

23. Waxman, interview; Rex Lee, "Lawyering for the Government: Politics, Polemics & Principle," *Ohio State Law Journal* 47 (1986): 600–601.

24. Glendon Schubert, *The Judicial Mind Revisited;* Jeffrey Segal, "Predicting Supreme Court Cases Probabilistically: The Search and Seizure Cases, 1962–1981," *American Political Science Review* 78 (1984): 891–900; Tracey George and Lee Epstein, "On the Nature of Supreme Court Decision Making," *American Political Science Review* 86 (1992): 323–37.

25. Joseph Kobylka, "A Court-Related Context for Group Litigation: Libertarian Groups and Obscenity," *Journal of Politics* 49 (1987).

26. Stephen Wasby, "How Planned is 'Planned Litigation'?" *American Bar Foundation Research Journal* 32 (1984).

27. Richard Pacelle, "The Supreme Court's Agenda and the Dynamics of Policy Evolution" Paper presented at American Political Science Association meetings, 1990.

28. If the Court accepts an "easy" case, it often summarily reverses the lower court. Even if it contradicts their values, justices may support existing precedents. Donald Songer and Stefanie Lindquist, "Not the Whole Story: The Impact of Justices' Values on Supreme Court Decision Making," *American Journal of Political Science* 40 (1996).

29. In civil rights, gender, and reproductive rights, the solicitor general voluntarily entered fewer than one-third of the new cases. In later stages, the office entered well more than a half.

30. Robert Bork, interview by author, Aug. 10, 1998.

31. Pacelle, *The Transformation of the Supreme Court's Agenda;* Perry, *Deciding to Decide.*

32. At this stage, the solicitor general filed *amici* in more than three-quarters of the available civil rights cases.

33. Drew Days, interview by author, Nov. 24, 1997.

34. Edwin Kneedler, interview by author, Jan. 27, 1998.

35. Many studies of the solicitor general fail to divide *amici* briefs by the constraints and discretion. They often do not distinguish invited from voluntary briefs, for instance.

36. Salokar, *The Solicitor General,* pp. 77–85.

37. William Eskridge, *Dynamic Statutory Interpretation.*

38. Salokar, *The Solicitor General,* p. 79.

39. Jenkins, "The Solicitor General's Winning Ways," p. 737.

40. Salokar, *The Solicitor General,* p. 151.

41. Ibid., pp. 153–55.

42. Days, "The Solicitor General and the American Legal Ideal," p. 76.

43. Salokar, *The Solicitor General,* pp. 118–26, 154–56. The office may not oppose petitions because it feels optimistic about the prospects of success. The solicitor general may not oppose cert when there is a circuit conflict. The solicitor can also confess error or settle cases.

44. Lee, "Lawyering for the Government," pp. 599–600.

45. Mark Levy, interview by author, Jan. 27, 1998.

46. Lee, "Lawyering for the Government," pp. 599–600.

47. Salokar, *The Solicitor General,* pp. 158–63.

48. Levy, interview.

49. Samuel Krislov, "The *Amicus Curiae* Brief: From Friendship to Advocacy," *Yale Law Journal* 72 (1963).

50. In interviews, there was disagreement about the nonpartisan nature of invited briefs. Some argued the office files and justices expect nonpartisan views. Others claimed that the office does not file different briefs in invited cases.

51. Dellinger, interview.

52. Days, interview.

53. Starr, interview.

54. Wallace, interview.

55. Richard Seamon, interview by author, April 28, 1998.

56. William Bryson, interview by author, March 25, 1998.

57. Jeffrey Segal, "Supreme Court Support for the Solicitor General: The Effect of Presidential Appointments," *Western Political Quarterly* 43 (1990): 149, argues the success of the solicitor general is due to judicial deference to the executive branch.

Chapter 2. The Solicitor General as a Strategic Actor

1. *United States v. Carolene Products* 304 U.S. 144 (1938); Pacelle, *The Transformation of the Supreme Court's Agenda.*

2. Gary McDowell, *Equity and the Constitution,* p. 34.

3. Clement Vose, *Caucasians Only: The Supreme Court, the NAACP, and the Restrictive Covenant Cases.*

4. Drew Days, "In Search of the Solicitor General's Client: A Drama with Many Characters," *Kentucky Law Review* 83 (1994–95): 503; Frey, interview.

5. Scigliano, *The Supreme Court and the Presidency,* p. vii.

6. Salokar, *The Solicitor General.*

7. Days, interview. Days was only in the office in the Supreme Court before and just after oral arguments. He compared it to the green room that houses talk show guests.

8. Dellinger, interview.

9. Salokar, *The Solicitor General,* pp. 55–56.

10. Days, "In Search of the Solicitor General's Client," pp. 489, 493; Wallace, interview.

11. Days, "In Search of the Solicitor General's Client," p. 493.

12. Bork, interview.

13. Wallace, interview.

14. David Lewis and James Michael Strine, "What Time Is It? The Use of Power in Four Different Types of Presidential Time," *Journal of Politics* 58 (1996): 683–86.

15. Wallace, interview.

16. Chamberlain, "Mixing Politics and Justice," p. 409.

17. Victor Navasky, *Kennedy Justice,* pp. 283–87.

18. Dellinger, interview.

19. Caplan, *Tenth Justice,* p. 33; Salokar, *The Solicitor General,* p. 5; "Memorandum Opinion for the Attorney General."

20. Schnapper, "Becket at the Bar," pp. 1223–24.

21. N. Baker, *Conflicting Loyalties,* pp. 2–18.

22. Robert Dixon, "The Attorney General and Civil Rights 1870–1964" in *Roles of the Attorney General of the United States,* ed. Luther Huston, Arthur Selwyn Miller, Samuel Krislov, and Robert Dixon, pp. 145–48.

23. Brigham, "The Office of the Solicitor General," p. 24.

24. Donald Horowitz, *The Jurocracy.*

25. Days, "In Search of the Solicitor General's Client," p. 497; Frey, interview.

26. David Flynn, interview by author, Jan. 27, 1998; Kneedler, interview.

27. Flynn, interview; Wallace, interview; Kneedler, interview; Starr, interview.

28. Days, "In Search of the Solicitor General's Client," p. 497.

29. Kneedler, interview.

30. Levy, interview.

31. Wallace, interview; Levy, interview.

32. Chamberlain, "Mixing Politics and Justice," p. 388.

33. Schnapper, "Becket at the Bar," p. 1222.

34. Luther Huston, *The Department of Justice,* p. 77.

35. Brian Landsberg, *Enforcing Civil Rights: Race Discrimination and the Department of Justice.*

36. I refer to these attorneys as careerists to distinguish them from political appointees, although few spend their entire careers in the office. Some deputies rise through the ranks and spend more than a decade in the office. Most assistants spend a few years in the office before taking an academic or government position or joining a private firm.

37. Carter Phillips, interview by author, Jan. 29, 1998.

38. Some administrations allow solicitors general to choose their deputy, others take an active role in screening potential deputies.

39. Wallace, interview; Phillips, interview.

40. Waxman, interview.

41. Kenneth Geller, interview by author, Jan. 28, 1998; Days, "The Solicitor General and the American Legal Ideal," p. 77.

42. Donald Ayer, interview by author, Jan. 30, 1998; John Roberts, interview by author, Jan. 28, 1998.

43. James Turner, interview by author, Jan. 27, 1998.

44. Henry Reske, "A Flap Over Flip-Flops: Solicitor General Says Changing Court Stances Not Unusual or Wrong," *ABA Journal* 80 (1994): 12–13.

45. Geller, interview.

46. Dellinger, interview.

47. Heymann, interview.

48. Paul Bender, interview by author, April 9, 1998.

49. Heymann, interview.

50. Salokar, *The Solicitor General,* p. 55.

51. Geller, interview.

52. Bryson, interview.

53. Ayer, interview.

54. Bender, interview.

55. Seamon, interview; Dellinger, interview.

56. Kneedler, interview.

57. Richard Wilkins, "An Officer and an Advocate: The Role of the Solicitor General" *Loyola of Los Angeles Law Review* 21 (1988): 1179–80.

58. Starr, interview; Cooper, "The Solicitor General and Federal Litigation," p. 70; Caplan, *Tenth Justice,* p. 33.

59. Starr, interview.

60. Caplan, *Tenth Justice,* pp. 20–25; Waxman, interview.

61. Levy, interview.

62. Salokar, *The Solicitor General,* p. 5; Solicitor General Oversight, Hearing Before the Committee on the Judiciary, U.S. Senate, Nov. 14, 1995, p. 53.

63. Perry, *Deciding to Decide.*

64. Timothy Johnson, "Oral Advocacy and the Supreme Court" (Ph.D. diss., Washington University, St. Louis, 1998).

65. Schnapper, "Becket at the Bar," pp. 1203–205.

66. Cooper, "The Solicitor General and Federal Litigation," p. 71.

67. Perry, *Deciding to Decide,* pp. 132–33.

68. Schnapper, "Becket at the Bar," pp. 1197–202. Occasionally, mostly in criminal cases, the solicitor general will "confess error" in a case the government won in the lower court and ask the Supreme Court to reverse or vacate the judgment. In confessing error, the solicitor general is acting against the government's interest and as an agent of the Court.

69. Lee, "Lawyering for the Government," p. 597.

70. Starr, interview.

71. Kristen Norman-Major, "The Solicitor General: Executive Policy Agendas and the Court," *Albany Law Review* 57 (1994): 1087.

72. Wallace, interview.

73. Cooper, "The Solicitor General and Federal Litigation," p. 59.

74. Solicitor General Oversight, Hearing Before the Committee on the Judiciary.

75. Cooper, "The Solicitor General and Federal Litigation," p. 59. Cases concerning executive and legislative powers provide difficult problems for the Court and the solicitor general. In most of these cases, the solicitor general will defend executive power. To speak for its institutional power, Congress has the authority to get its own representation, see Salokar, *The Solicitor General,* pp. 86–94.

76. Robert Katzmann, *Courts and Congress,* p. 46.

77. Richard Fleisher and Jon Bond, "The President in a More Partisan Legislative Arena," *Political Research Quarterly* 49 (December, 1996): 729–48.

78. Charles Fried, interview by author, March 3, 1998.

79. Joshua Schwartz, "Two Perspectives on the Solicitor General's Independence," *Loyola of Los Angeles Law Review* 21 (1988): 1154–55.

80. Days, "In Search of the Solicitor General's Client," p. 502.

81. J. Schwartz, "Two Perspectives," p. 1153.

82. Bork, interview.

83. Fried, interview.

84. Lori Hausegger and Lawrence Baum, "Inviting Congressional Action: A Study of Supreme Court Motivations in Statutory Interpretation" 43 *Journal of Politics* (1999): 164–70.

85. J. Schwartz, "Two Perspectives," pp. 1158–60.

86. Eskridge, "Reneging on History?" Each solicitor general I interviewed denied reacting to the sitting Congress. Robert Bork dismissed Eskridge's theory out of hand. Charles Fried argued that there was concern, but having President Reagan's potential veto made Congress less of a threat. Similarly, Drew Days claimed that his office did not react to how the sitting Congress, a Republican majority, might interpret statutes. He had no incentive to do so. He could argue for a broad interpretation of statutes because President Clinton could veto attempts to tamper with the interpretation or the Court's decision. Walter Dellinger and Seth Waxman said virtually the same thing: that this was an interesting theory, but not applicable to their calculations. Still, Eskridge's evidence is persuasive.

87. Robert Long, interview by author, April 20, 1998; Roberts, interview.

88. D. Roderick Kiewiet and Matthew McCubbins, *The Logic of Delegation,* pp. 54–55.

89. Robert Spitzer, *President & Congress: Executive Hegemony at the Crossroads of American Government,* p. 249.

90. C. Lawrence Evans and Walter Oleszek, *Congress Under Fire: Reform Politics and the Republican Majority,* pp. 116–28.

91. Morris Fiorina, *Divided Government,* pp. 6–12.

92. Perry, *Deciding to Decide,* p. 132.

93. Days, "In Search of the Solicitor General's Client," p. 487.

94. Lee, "Lawyering for the Government," p. 597; Norman-Major, "The Solicitor General," p. 1090.

95. Lee, "Lawyering for the Government," pp. 599–601.

96. Lee Epstein and Joseph Kobylka, *The Supreme Court and Legal Change: Abortion and the Death Penalty.*

97. Starr, interview; Fried, interview.

98. Lee, "Lawyering for the Government," p. 600; Wallace, interview.

99. James Cooper, "The Solicitor General and the Evolution of Activism," *Indiana Law Journal* 65 (1990): 695–96; Norman-Major, "The Solicitor General," p. 1109.

100. Caplan, *Tenth Justice,* p. 12.

101. Lee, "Lawyering for the Government," p. 597.

102. Ibid., p. 601.

PART II. THE SOLICITOR GENERAL AND RACE LITIGATION

1. Sidney Milkis, *The President and the Parties: The Transformation of the American Party System Since the New Deal,* p. 176.

2. Hugh Davis Graham, *The Civil Rights Era: Origins and Development of National Policy 1960–1972,* pp. 9–11.

3. Lance LeLoup and Steven Shull, *The President and Congress: Collaboration and Combat in National Policy-Making 1960–1972,* p. 171.

4. Caplan, *Tenth Justice.*

5. I adapt this from Wasby, "A Triangle Transformed," and H. D. Graham, *The Civil Rights Era.*

CHAPTER 3. THE SOLICITOR GENERAL IN THE LITIGATION PHASE, 1945–63

1. Milkis, *The President and the Parties,* p. 161.

2. Jeffrey Hockett, *New Deal Justice: The Constitutional Jurisprudence of Hugo L. Black, Felix Frankfurter, and Robert H. Jackson,* pp. 151–52.

3. Robert Jackson, *The Struggle for Judicial Supremacy: A Study of a Crisis in American Power Politics;* Salokar, *The Solicitor General,* p. 141.

4. Donald Horowitz, *The Courts and Social Policy.*

5. Michael McCann, *Rights At Work: Pay Equity Reform and the Politics of Legal Mobilization.*

6. William Berman, *The Politics of Civil Rights in the Truman Administration,* p. x; Sean Savage, *Truman and the Democratic Party,* pp. 135–37.

7. David McCullough, *Truman,* pp. 638–40.

8. Richard Kluger, *Simple Justice,* pp. 249–52.

9. John Anderson, *Eisenhower, Brownell, and the Congress: The Tangled Origins of the Civil Rights Bill of 1956–1957,* pp. 8–12; John Elliff, "The United States Department of Justice and Individual Rights" (Ph.D. diss., Harvard University, 1967), pp. 211–12.

10. Sarah Binder and Steven Smith, *Politics or Principle? Filibustering in the United States Senate,* pp. 139–40.

11. Pacelle, *The Transformation of the Supreme Court's Agenda;* Thomas Walker, Lee Epstein, and William Dixon, "On the Mysterious Demise of Consensual Norms in the United States Supreme Court," *Journal of Politics* 50 (1988): 361–89.

12. Henry Abraham, *Justices and Presidents: A Political History of Appointments to the Supreme Court.*

13. C. Herman Pritchett, *Civil Liberties and the Vinson Court;* Frances Howell Rudko, *Truman's Court: A Study in Judicial Restraint.*

14. Lawrence Baum, "Measuring Policy Change in the U.S. Supreme Court," *American Political Science Review* 82 (1988): 905–12.

15. Richard Claude, *The Supreme Court and the Electoral Process,* pp. 47–54.

16. In addition, the solicitor general's office filed a brief in five cases consolidated under the banner *Brown v. Board of Education.* After oral arguments, the Court held the case over for the next term (Kluger, *Simple Justice,* p. 561).

17. Philip Elman, "The Solicitor General's Office, Justice Frankfurter, and Civil Rights Litigation" *Harvard Law Review* 100 (1987): 818.

18. Kluger, *Simple Justice,* pp. 249–51.

19. Vose, *Caucasians Only,* pp. 168–71.

20. Kluger, *Simple Justice,* pp. 252–53.

21. Vose, *Caucasians Only,* pp. 200–201.

22. Elman ("The Solicitor General's Office," pp. 819–21) notes that the *Shelley* brief transformed Perlman. The solicitor general was widely applauded for his efforts in the case and wanted to continue to press for civil rights.

23. Brief of Sam Hobbs as *Amicus Curiae,* no. 25, October Term, 1949, p. 35.

24. Kluger, *Simple Justice,* p. 277.

25. Stephen Wasby, Anthony D'Amato, and Rosemary Metrailer, *Desegregation from* Brown *to* Alexander: *An Exploration of Supreme Court Strategies,* pp. 49–50.

26. Elman, "The Solicitor General's Office," p. 822.

27. Kluger, *Simple Justice,* p. 558.

28. Caplan, *Tenth Justice,* p. 26.

29. Elman, "The Solicitor General's Office," pp. 813–15.

30. W. Berman, *Politics of Civil Rights,* p. 232.

31. Elman, "The Solicitor General's Office," p. 827.

32. James Sundquist, *Politics and Policy: The Eisenhower, Kennedy, and Johnson Years,* pp. 241–42; Charles Alexander, *Holding the Line: The Eisenhower Era, 1952–1961,* p. 197.

33. Gary Orfield, *Congressional Power: Congress and Social Change,* p. 64. Alexander (*Holding the Line,* p. 197) argued that Eisenhower worked hard behind the scenes for the Civil Rights Act, but his public pronouncements "suggested a lack of understanding, even interest."

34. Elmo Richardson (*The Presidency of Dwight D. Eisenhower,* p. 120) argues one of the primary motivations for Eisenhower sending troops into Little Rock was because disorder would abet Communist propaganda.

35. Milkis, *The President and the Parties,* p. 161; Mark Stern, "Presidential Strategies and Civil Rights: Eisenhower the Early Years, 1952–54," *Presidential Studies Quarterly* 19 (1989).

36. Anderson, *Eisenhower, Brownell, and the Congress,* p. 43; Herbert Brownell with John Burke, *Advising Ike: The Memoirs of Herbert Brownell,* chapter 12.

37. Roy Reed, *Faubus: The Life and Times of An American Prodigal,* pp. 212, 232.

38. Luther Huston, "History of the Office of the Attorney General" in *Roles of the Attorney General,* p. 22; Dixon, "Attorney General," p. 122.

39. Kluger, *Simple Justice,* p. 754; Robert Frederick Burk, *The Eisenhower Administration and Black Civil Rights,* pp. 191–98.

40. Orfield, *Congressional Power,* p. 61.

41. Carmines and Stimson, *Issue Evolution,* p. 59.

42. Walter Murphy, *Congress and the Court,* p. 152; Huston, "History" p. 23.

43. James Sundquist, *The Decline and Resurgence of Congress,* pp. 184–87.

44. Orfield, *Congressional Power,* p. 64. See Daniel Berman, *A Bill Becomes a Law: The Civil Rights Act of 1960.*

45. James Stimson, Michael MacKuen, and Robert Erickson, "Dynamic Representation," *American Political Science Review* 89 (1995): 561.

46. Brownell doubts Eisenhower actually uttered this quote. Warren initially accepted the position of solicitor general. The death of Chief Justice Vinson altered those plans (Brownell with Burke, *Advising Ike,* pp. 165–66, 173–75). Before settling on Warren, Eisenhower offered the position to Secretary of State John Foster Dulles, who refused and considered former Solicitor General John Davis, who had been retained to argue *Brown* on behalf of the southern schools (Stephen Ambrose, *Eisenhower: Soldier and President,* pp. 336–37).

47. Lawrence Baum, "Membership Change and Collective Voting Change in the United States Supreme Court," *Journal of Politics* 54 (1992).

48. Elman had clerked for Justice Frankfurter and remained close to him. Elman and Frankfurter discussed the *Brown* brief at length regarding the most appropriate strategy to use before the Court (Caplan, *Tenth Justice,* pp. 26–32; Kluger, *Simple Justice,* p. 650).

49. Dixon, "Attorney General," p. 115; Richardson, *Presidency of Dwight D. Eisenhower,* p. 125.

50. Sobeloff was a noted civil rights attorney (Brownell with Burke, *Advising Ike,* p. 144). Before Sobeloff was appointed, Rankin, an assistant attorney general, was *de facto* solicitor general for the *Brown* case. After Sobeloff was appointed to the federal court, Rankin was officially named solicitor general.

51. In *Colegrove v. Green,* the Court refused to get involved in the case claiming it was a political question and the province of the elected branches.

52. Elman ("The Solicitor General's Office," p. 832) claimed Frankfurter wanted the Eisenhower administration to be on record, as the Truman administration was, urging the Court to declare segregation unconstitutional. The original invitation came from the Vinson Court and Brownell (*Advising Ike,* p. 189) felt that Vinson was soliciting legal views "to tip the balance, either by encouraging the waverers on the Court to overturn *Plessy* if Eisenhower was on the side of that issue or to dodge the question until public and political support were greater and the Court would not have to risk its prestige in such a controversial area."

53. Kluger, *Simple Justice,* p. 650.

54. Eisenhower wanted the attorney general to decline the invitation. Brownell explained that the Justice Department had a special relationship with the Court and refusing the invitation would jeopardize that (see Dwight Eisenhower, *Waging Peace: The White House Years, 1956–1961,* p. 150; Brownell with Burke, *Advising Ike,* pp. 190–94).

55. Eisenhower invited Warren to the White House and discussed *Brown* with him and former Solicitor General Davis who was arguing on behalf of the southern school boards. Eisenhower praised Davis and opined that little white girls should not be required to go to school with big black boys (Burk, *Eisenhower Administration,* p. 142). Eisenhower asked to see the brief and marked it with comments.

56. Burk, *Eisenhower Administration,* pp. 136–40.

57. According to Elman, Frankfurter would predict how the justices would react to different arguments. The government's position evolved out of these discussions (Caplan, *Tenth Justice,* pp. 29–31).

58. Kluger, *Simple Justice,* pp. 650–53.

59. Caplan, *Tenth Justice,* p. 31.

60. Navasky, *Kennedy Justice,* p. 295; Kluger, *Simple Justice,* p. 726.

61. Burk, *Eisenhower Administration,* p. 141. Frankfurter and Elman referred to a number of miracles that led to *Brown.* These began with the scandal that forced McGrath to resign and led to the resignation of Perlman, who opposed an attack on segregation. The last "miracle" was the death of Chief Justice Vinson. Frankfurter was certain that the Court would not achieve unanimity with Vinson presiding. Indeed, he was uncertain whether they could even gain a majority. On hearing of the death of Vinson, Frankfurter supposedly remarked that this was "the first solid piece of evidence I've ever had that there really is a God" (Caplan, *Tenth Justice,* p. 29).

62. Wasby, D'Amato, and Metrailer, *Desegregation from* Brown *to* Alexander, p. 87. It is difficult to trace the causal chain. Did the brief influence the decision or did Frankfurter suggest language that the Court would eventually adopt?

63. Burk, *Eisenhower Administration,* p. 143.

64. Ken Gormley, *Archibald Cox: Conscience of a Nation,* pp. 143–50.

65. Mark Peterson, *Legislating Together: The White House and Capitol Hill from Eisenhower to Reagan,* pp. 241–42; Navasky, *Kennedy Justice,* p. 161.

66. Paul Light, *The President's Agenda: Domestic Policy Choice from Kennedy to Carter,* p. 104.

67. K. Gormley, *Archibald Cox,* p. 159.

68. Matthew Holden, "Race and Constitutional Change in the Twentieth Century: The Role of the Executive" in *African Americans and the Living Constitution,* ed. John Hope Franklin and Genna Rae McNeil, p. 126.

69. Gary Orfield, "Congress and Civil Rights: From Obstacle to Protector" in *African Americans,* p. 151.

70. Navasky, *Kennedy Justice,* p. 98.

71. Sundquist, *Politics and Policy,* pp. 256–58.

72. Wasby, "A Triangle Transformed," p. 567.

73. Richard Reeves, *President Kennedy: Portrait of Power,* pp. 518–24. Violence erupted in Birmingham in April, 1963, leading Kennedy to place civil rights on the agenda and creating national indignation. Taylor Branch, *Parting the Waters: America in the King Years 1954–1963.*

74. Burke Marshall, interview with author, March 4, 1998; Burke Marshall, *Federalism and Civil Rights.*

75. H. D. Graham, *The Civil Rights Era,* pp. 75–80, 94–99. This was controversial, but it allowed the bill to go to a sympathetic committee. The Judiciary Committee did not allow the Civil Rights Act of 1963 to go forward.

76. N. Baker, *Conflicting Loyalties,* p. 82.

77. Navasky, *Kennedy Justice,* pp. 97, 239; K. Gormley, *Archibald Cox,* pp. 155–56.

78. Heymann, interview.

79. K. Gormley, *Archibald Cox,* p. 158.

80. Marshall, interview.

81. Navasky, *Kennedy Justice,* pp. 291–92.

82. Orfield, *Congressional Power,* p. 65. It was opponents of the legislation who strengthened the Civil Rights Act on the premise that the stronger the bill, the more opposition.

83. Stimson, MacKuen, and Erickson, "Dynamic Representation."

84. Binder and Smith, *Politics or Principle?* p. 141.

85. Baum, "Measuring Policy Change."

86. Donald Jackson, *Even the Children of Strangers: Equality Under the U.S. Constitution,* pp. 92–93.

87. Marshall, interview.

88. Salokar, *The Solicitor General,* p. 141.

89. Marshall, interview.

90. K. Gormley, *Archibald Cox,* pp. 148–50. The night before oral argument, Cox went to the Eagle Coffee Shop. He observed that the flags of the United States and Delaware flew over

the coffee shop and parking garage. He tied this to state action and Justice Clark mentioned it in the opinion.

91. Navasky, *Kennedy Justice,* p. 290.

92. Caplan, *Tenth Justice,* pp. 200–201.

93. *Barr v. Columbia, Griffin v. Maryland, Robinson v. Florida, Bell v. Maryland,* and *Bouie v. Columbia.*

94. Wasby, D'Amato, and Metrailer, *Desegregation from* Brown *to* Alexander, p. 314.

95. Justice Brennan "surreptitiously helped enact" the Civil Rights Act of 1964 by convincing his brethren to avoid constitutional issues in sit-in cases, see Kim Isaac Eisler, *A Justice For All: William J. Brennan, Jr. and the Decisions That Transformed America,* p. 263.

96. Archibald Cox, interview by author, Feb. 9, 1998. Cox confirmed this was a consideration in seeking narrower grounds. Briefs of the United States as *Amicus Curiae,* nos. 6, 9, 10, 12, 60, October Term, 1962.

97. Wasby, D'Amato, and Metrailer, *Desegregation from* Brown *to* Alexander, pp. 314–15.

98. Cox, interview.

99. Wasby, D'Amato, and Metrailer, *Desegregation from* Brown *to* Alexander, p. 299.

100. Cox, interview.

101. K. Gormley, *Archibald Cox,* pp. 158–59.

102. Nicholas Katzenbach, interview by author, March 11, 1998.

103. Wasby, D'Amato, and Metrailer, *Desegregation from* Brown *to* Alexander, pp. 314–16.

104. While Kennedy was reluctant to challenge the solicitor general, the NAACP was not. Jack Greenberg (*Crusaders in the Court,* pp. 309–10) accused Cox of selling out to bigots. He argued that the policy of the administration was to oppose discrimination and the solicitor general was obligated to pursue that policy.

105. K. Gormley, *Archibald Cox,* pp. 158–59.

106. Royce Hanson, *The Political Thicket: Reapportionment and Constitutional Democracy,* pp. 53–54.

107. Marshall, interview.

108. Richard Cortner, *The Apportionment Cases,* p. 103; Gene Graham, *One Man, One Vote: Baker v. Carr and the American Levelers,* p. 209.

109. Robert Dixon, *Democratic Representation: Reapportionment in Law and Politics,* p. 177.

110. Cortner, *Apportionment,* p. 117.

111. Gordon Baker, *The Reapportionment Revolution: Representation, Political Power, and the Supreme Court,* pp. 126–27.

112. Bernard Schwartz, *Super Chief: Earl Warren and His Supreme Court—A Judicial Biography.*

113. Timothy O'Rourke, *The Impact of Reapportionment,* pp. 120–21.

114. Marshall, interview. Marshall felt that Ken Gormley (*Archibald Cox,* p. 169) exaggerated this point.

115. O'Rourke, *Impact of Reapportionment,* p. 2.

116. Cox, interview.

117. K. Gormley, *Archibald Cox,* pp. 172–74.

118. Ibid., pp. 159–60.

119. Chamberlain, "Mixing Politics and Justice," p. 425.

CHAPTER 4. THE SOLICITOR GENERAL IN THE ADMINISTRATIVE PHASE, 1964–80

1. James Pfiffner, *The Modern Presidency,* p. 148.

2. H. D. Graham, *The Civil Rights Era,* p. 152.

3. Lyndon Johnson, *The Vantage Point: Perspectives of the Presidency 1963–1969,* pp. 160–61; John Berg, *Unequal Struggle: Class, Gender, Race, and Power in the U.S. Congress,* p. 119.

4. H. D. Graham, *The Civil Rights Era*, pp. 163–70.

5. N. Baker, *Conflicting Loyalties.*

6. Clayton, *Politics of Justice*, pp. 135–36.

7. Hanes Walton, Jr., *When the Marching Stopped: The Politics of the Civil Rights Regulatory Agencies*, pp. 140–41.

8. Kenneth Thompson, *The Voting Rights Act and Black Electoral Participation*, pp. 2–3.

9. Donald Matthews and James Prothro, *Negroes and the New Southern Politics*, p. 475.

10. Robert Dallek, *Flawed Giant: Lyndon Johnson and His Times, 1961–1973*, p. 323.

11. Jeffrey Tulis, *The Rhetorical Presidency*, pp. 161–72.

12. Thomas Curtis and Donald Westerfield, *Congressional Intent*, p. 24.

13. Sally Kenney, *For Whose Protection? Reproductive Hazards and Exclusionary Policies in the United States and Britain*, p. 142.

14. Stimson, MacKuen, and Erickson, "Dynamic Representation."

15. Baum, "Membership Change."

16. Pacelle, *The Transformation of the Supreme Court's Agenda;* Jonathan Casper, *The Politics of Civil Liberties*, pp. 104–18.

17. Samuel Walker, *In Defense of American Liberties: A History of the ACLU*, p. 240. In several decisions, the Court limited the associational rights of alleged Communists. Justices Black and Douglas called attention to the difference between black (equal protection) and red (Communist) freedom of association cases (Peter Irons, *The Courage of Their Convictions*, p. 116).

18. Morton Horwitz, *The Warren Court and the Pursuit of Justice*, pp. 38–39.

19. Branch, *Parting the Waters*, pp. 291–93.

20. Greenberg, *Crusaders in the Court*, pp. 270–97.

21. Anthony Lewis, *Make No Law: The Sullivan Case and the First Amendment.*

22. Richard Cortner, *The Supreme Court and the Second Bill of Rights: The Fourteenth Amendment and the Nationalization of Civil Rights.*

23. Walker, *Defense*, p. 246.

24. Dallek, *Flawed Giant*, pp. 438–40. According to Juan Williams, (*Thurgood Marshall: American Revolutionary*, p. 315–17), LBJ had decided to put Marshall on the Supreme Court and wanted him to serve as solicitor general to prove to everyone, including himself, that Marshall could do the job. During his installation, Johnson referred to the new solicitor as Justice Marshall, but quickly corrected himself.

25. Wasby, D'Amato, and Metrailer, *Desegregation from* Brown *to* Alexander, p. 330.

26. Cox, interview.

27. Marshall, interview.

28. Katzenbach, interview.

29. Wasby, D'Amato, and Metrailer, *Desegregation from* Brown *to* Alexander, pp. 326–27.

30. *Katzenbach v. McClung,* Brief for the United States, no. 543, October Term, 1964.

31. *Katzenbach v. McClung* 379 US 294 (1964).

32. Randall Bland, *Private Pressure on Public Law: The Legal Career of Justice Thurgood Marshall, 1934–1991*, pp. 133–34.

33. Michal Belknap, *Federal Law and Southern Order: Racial Violence and Constitutional Conflict in the Post-*Brown *South*, p. 170.

34. J. Williams, *Thurgood Marshall.*

35. Belknap, *Federal Law and Southern Order*, pp. 173–76; Bland, *Private Pressure on Public Law*, pp. 133–34.

36. Belknap, *Federal Law and Southern Order*, pp. 176–79.

37. Stephen Pollak, interview by author, June 25, 1998.

38. Michael Davis and Hunter Clark, *Thurgood Marshall: Warrior at the Bar, Rebel on the Bench*, p. 259; Bland, *Private Pressure on Public Law*, p. 139.

39. Claude, *The Supreme Court and the Electoral Process*, p. 112.

40. Pollak, interview.

41. G. Edward White, *Earl Warren: A Public Life*, p. 305.

42. Pollak, interview.

43. Wasby, D'Amato, and Metrailer, *Desegregation from* Brown *to* Alexander, pp. 392–94.

44. Bernard Schwartz, Swann's *Way: The School Busing Case and the Supreme Court*, p. 65.

45. Pollak, interview.

46. Samuel Krislov, "The Role of the Attorney General as *Amicus Curiae*," in Huston et al., *Roles*, pp. 71–103. Ramsey Clark's father was the attorney general who approved the *Shelley* brief.

47. Pollak, interview.

48. H. D. Graham, *The Civil Rights Era*, p. 375; Derrick Bell, Jr., *Race, Racism, and American Law*, p. 498; C. Herman Pritchett, *Constitutional Civil Liberties*, p. 279; Pollak, interview.

49. Abigail Thernstrom, *Whose Votes Count? Affirmative Action and Minority Voting Rights*, pp. 22–27.

50. Richard Engstrom, "Racial Vote Dilution: The Concept and The Court" in *The Voting Rights Act: Consequences and Implications*, ed. Lorn Foster, pp. 22–32.

51. Raymond Wolters, *Right Turn: William Bradford Reynolds, the Reagan Administration, and Black Civil Rights*, p. 41.

52. Chandler Davidson, "The Evolution of Voting Rights Law Affecting Racial and Language Minorities" in *Quiet Revolution in the South: The Impact of the Voting Rights Act, 1965–1990*, ed. Chandler Davidson and Bernard Grofman, pp. 32–33.

53. Engstrom, "Racial Vote Dilution," pp. 14, 25.

54. B. Schwartz, *Super Chief*, p. 706.

55. Stephen Ambrose, *Nixon: Volume Two, 1962–1972*, pp. 364, 406–407.

56. James Reichley, *Conservatives In an Era of Change*, pp. 174–79.

57. John Aldrich (*Why Parties? The Origin and Transformation of Political Parties in America*, pp. 263–64) points out the genius of the southern strategy was that it did not focus on race but on an entire range of social issues.

58. Stephen Halpern, *On the Limits of the Law: The Ironic Legacy of Title VI of the 1964 Civil Rights Act*, pp. 105–108. The constitutionality of Nixon's proposed moratorium on busing was broadly challenged. Only Bork among the scholars Nixon consulted argued that the moratorium could be justified (Reichley, *Conservatives In an Era of Change*, pp. 198–99). This was instrumental in Bork's appointment (Caplan, *Tenth Justice*, p. 37).

59. Michael Genovese, *The Nixon Presidency: Power and Politics in Turbulent Times*, pp. 81–88.

60. N. Baker, *Conflicting Loyalties*, p. 121.

61. Turner, interview.

62. Clayton, *Politics of Justice*, pp. 138–39.

63. Solicitor General Bork was acting attorney general when he fired prosecutor Archibald Cox.

64. Reichley, *Conservatives In an Era of Change*, pp. 182–84.

65. Ambrose, *Nixon*, p. 364.

66. H. D. Graham, *The Civil Rights Era*, p. 319. Jerris Leonard, interview by author, April 27, 1998.

67. Erwin Griswold, *Ould Fields, New Corne: The Personal Memoirs of a Twentieth Century Lawyer*, pp. 270–71.

68. Leonard, interview.

69. John Robert Greene, *The Limits of Power: The Nixon and Ford Administrations*, p. 43.

70. Reichley, *Conservatives In an Era of Change*, p. 183.

71. Leonard, interview.

72. David Rose, interview by author, April 21, 1998.

73. Stimson, MacKuen, and Erickson, "Dynamic Representation."

74. Edward Keynes with Randall Miller, *The Court Versus Congress: Prayer, Busing, and Abortion,* pp. 219–27.

75. Orfield, *Congressional Power,* pp. 67–71.

76. Owen Fiss, *The Civil Rights Injunction,* p. 22.

77. Baum, "Measuring Policy Change."

78. D. Jackson, *Even the Children of Strangers,* pp. 102–11.

79. Bork, interview.

80. There was an additional case brought by an acting solicitor general.

81. Landsberg, *Enforcing Civil Rights,* pp. 144–45.

82. Richard Nixon, *RN: The Memoirs of Richard Nixon,* p. 440.

83. In *Keyes v. School District No. 1,* the office did not take a side.

84. H. D. Graham (*The Civil Rights Era,* p. 303) argues the southern strategy was really a "Rim" strategy directed at the border states. Leonard claimed: "There was a lot of talk by conservatives in the White House about the so-called Southern strategy. But it was smoke and mirrors. The truth was that it was promulgated by the people in the White House who thought that Nixon would not be re-elected if he was painted with the same brush as Kennedy and Johnson" (Leonard, interview).

85. Landsberg, *Enforcing Civil Rights,* p. 142.

86. B. Schwartz, *Swann's Way,* p. 67. Greene (*The Limits of Power,* p. 44) maintains that Senator John Stennis threatened to hold the anti-ballistic missile system hostage, unless Nixon slowed desegregation and the president "caved." Leonard said the reason for the slowdown was hurricane Camille, which damaged the schools (Leonard, interview).

87. Landsberg, *Enforcing Civil Rights,* p. 142.

88. Griswold, *Ould Fields, New Corne,* p. 274.

89. Wasby, D'Amato, and Metrailer, *Desegregation from* Brown *to* Alexander, pp. 400–401.

90. Leonard, interview.

91. Turner, interview; Leonard, interview; Nixon, *RN,* p. 440.

92. *Swann v. Charlotte-Mecklenberg Board of Education,* Memorandum for the United States as *Amicus Curiae,* 281, October Term, 1969.

93. Griswold, *Ould Fields, New Corne,* pp. 274–75.

94. Landsberg, *Enforcing Civil Rights,* p. 142.

95. *Swann v. Charlotte-Mecklenberg Board of Education,* Brief for the United States as *Amicus Curiae,* no. 281, 349, 436, October Term, 1969.

96. Landsberg, *Enforcing Civil Rights,* p. 143.

97. B. Schwartz, *Swann's Way,* p. 98.

98. Landsberg, *Enforcing Civil Rights,* p. 143. There was enough contradictory language in the opinion that Griswold (*Ould Fields, New Corne,* p. 275) could claim that his "was the view which was taken by the Court in an unanimous decision." The evidence and secondary sources do not support his conclusion, however.

99. Kluger, *Simple Justice,* p. 768; Bernard Schwartz, *The Ascent of Pragmatism: The Burger Court in Action,* p. 259.

100. Stephen Wasby, *Race Relations Litigation in an Age of Complexity,* p. 41.

101. *Keyes v. School District No. 1, Denver,* Memorandum for the United States as *Amicus Curiae,* no. 71-507, October Term, 1972.

102. Kluger, *Simple Justice,* pp. 768–69.

103. Salokar, *The Solicitor General,* p. 141.

104. Griswold, *Ould Fields, New Corne,* p. 317. The transition was unusual because Bork had agreed to teach at Yale Law School, so he did not take office immediately. In the interim, Griswold stayed in office, although Bork had input (Salokar, *The Solicitor General,* pp. 42–45).

105. Jeffrey Segal, Lee Epstein, Charles Cameron, and Harold Spaeth, "Ideological Values and the Votes of U.S. Supreme Court Justices Revisited," *Journal of Politics* 57 (1995): 812–23.

106. Wasby, *Race Relations*, p. 156.

107. Bork, interview.

108. *Milliken v. Bradley,* Memorandum for the United States as *Amicus Curiae,* no. 73-434, October Term, 1973. Together with *Allen Park Public Schools v. Bradley,* no. 73-435 and *Grosse Point Public Schools v. Bradley,* no. 73-436.

109. Landsberg, *Enforcing Civil Rights,* p. 145.

110. Girardeau Spann, *Race Against the Court: The Supreme Court and Minorities in Contemporary America,* p. 76.

111. Halpern, *On the Limits of the Law,* p. 93.

112. H. D. Graham, *The Civil Rights Era,* pp. 320–21.

113. This involved goals for hiring minority contractors. Assistant Attorney General William Rehnquist drafted a Justice Department opinion that the Philadelphia Plan was a lawful exercise, contradicting an opinion by the comptroller general that it violated Title VII. David Rose, "Twenty-Five Years Later: Where Do We Stand on Equal Employment Opportunity Law Enforcement?" *Vanderbilt Law Review* 42 (1989): 1141–42.

114. *Sullivan v. Little Hunting Park,* Brief for the United States as *Amicus Curiae,* no. 33, October Term, 1969.

115. *Tillman v. Wheaton-Haven,* Memorandum for the United States as *Amicus Curiae,* no. 71-1136, October Term, 1971; *Tillman v. Wheaton-Haven,* Brief for the United States as *Amicus Curiae,* no. 71-1136, October Term, 1972.

116. In *Sullivan,* the white petitioner conveyed property to a black man. One question was whether the white home owner had standing to challenge the racial exclusion policies.

117. *Palmer v. Thompson, Mayor of the City of Jackson* 403 U.S. 217 (1971).

118. Alfred Blumrosen, *Modern Law: The Law Transmission System and Equal Employment Opportunity,* pp. 98–99. Blumrosen was the EEOC's compliance chief and a force behind the broad redefinition of discrimination. His power was enhanced by frequent turnover at the top of the EEOC (Wolters, *Right Turn,* p. 152).

119. Eskridge, *Dynamic Statutory Interpretation,* p. 74. Perry (*Deciding to Decide,* pp. 125–28) finds dissensus on lower courts is a particularistic index, the votes of well-regarded judges are universal indices, and participation of the solicitor general is a universal signal for justices in deciding whether to grant a petition. In this instance, cues and indices moved in the same direction. Sobeloff was a respected judge and a former solicitor general and dissented in the case.

120. Landsberg, *Enforcing Civil Rights,* pp. 128–31. This position was known as "freezing relief" because neutral policies would freeze in place previous conditions, which were discriminatory. This position was developed in voting rights cases and a corollary was used in desegregation.

121. *Griggs v. Duke Power,* Brief for the United States as *Amicus Curiae,* no. 124, October Term, 1969 (on petition for certiorari to the U.S. Court of Appeals 4th Circuit); *Griggs v. Duke Power,* Brief for the United States as *Amicus Curiae,* no. 124, October Term, 1969 (on the merits).

122. *Griggs v. Duke Power,* quoted in Landsberg, *Enforcing Civil Rights,* p. 129.

123. According to Eskridge (*Dynamic Statutory Interpretation,* p. 74), the Court (and presumably, the solicitor general) can set policy at the point of the median member of the relevant committee, rather than the median member of the House. This appeared to occur in *Griggs.*

124. Wasby, *Race Relations,* p. 186.

125. Eskridge, *Dynamic Statutory Interpretation,* pp. 24–37, 79.

126. Ibid., pp. 17, 33–34.

127. *McDonnell-Douglas v. Green,* Memorandum for the United States as *Amicus Curiae,* no. 72-490, October Term, 1972.

128. Michael Levin-Epstein, *Primer of Equal Employment Opportunity,* pp. 123–24; Wasby, *Race Relations,* p. 41.

129. Reichley, *Conservatives In an Era of Change,* p. 276.

130. John Robert Greene, *The Presidency of Gerald R. Ford,* p. 90.

131. Norman Amaker, *Civil Rights and the Reagan Administration,* pp. 24–25.

132. N. Baker, *Conflicting Loyalties,* pp. 142–43; Gerald Ford, *A Time to Heal,* p. 235.

133. Amaker, *Civil Rights,* p. 25.

134. Brian Landsberg, interview by author, April 7, 1998; Bork, interview.

135. James Cannon, *Time and Chance: Gerald Ford's Appointment with History,* p. 527.

136. Stimson, MacKuen, and Erikson, "Dynamic Representation."

137. Reichley, *Conservatives In an Era of Change,* pp. 323–24.

138. Jeffrey Segal and Albert Cover, "Ideological Values and the Votes of U.S. Supreme Court Justices," *American Political Science Review* 83 (1989).

139. Baum, "Membership Change."

140. Ronald Kahn, *The Supreme Court & Constitutional Theory: 1953–1993,* p. 159.

141. D. Jackson, *Even the Children of Strangers,* pp. 102–107.

142. *Albemarle Paper Co. v. Moody,* Brief for the United States and Equal Employment Opportunity Commission, no. 74-389, October Term, 1974; *Halifax Local No. 425 Union of Papermakers and Paperworkers AFL-CIO v. Moody,* Brief for the United States and Equal Employment Opportunity Commission, no. 74-428, October Term, 1974.

143. *Albemarle Paper Co. v. Moody* 422 U.S. 405 (1975).

144. *Franks v. Bowman Transportation,* Brief for the United States and Equal Employment Opportunity Commission as *Amicus Curiae,* no. 74-728, October Term, 1974.

145. *Franks v. Bowman Transportation* 424 U.S. 747 (1976).

146. *Washington v. Davis,* Brief for the Federal Respondent, no. 74-1492, October Term, 1975.

147. Landsberg, *Enforcing Civil Rights,* p. 131.

148. *Washington v. Davis* 416 U.S. 229 (1976).

149. B. Schwartz, *Ascent of Pragmatism,* p. 267.

150. Landsberg, *Enforcing Civil Rights,* p. 132.

151. *Runyon v. McCrary,* Brief for the United States as *Amicus Curiae,* no. 75-62, October Term, 1975 (together with *Fairfax-Brewster School v. Gonzalez,* no. 75-66 and *South Independent School Association v. McCrary,* no. 75-278).

152. Salokar (*The Solicitor General,* p. 168) notes: Bork generally adopted the conservative side as *amici,* but in *Runyon,* he may have been constrained because the case was begun by Griswold.

153. *Runyon v. McCrary,* Brief for the United States as *Amicus Curiae,* no. 75-62; Robert Bork, *The Tempting of America: The Political Seduction of the Law,* p. 153.

154. *Runyon v. McCrary* 427 U.S. 160 (1976); Wasby, *Race Relations,* p. 16.

155. William Eskridge, "Overriding Supreme Court Statutory Interpretation Decisions," *Yale Law Journal* 101 (1991): 393–94. Stevens noted that it was extremely unlikely the enacting Congress in 1866 would have supported desegregation of private schools (Spann, *Race Against the Court,* pp. 45–46).

156. *Beer v. United States,* Motion to Affirm, no. 73-1869, October Term, 1974. *Beer v. United States,* Brief for the United States, no. 73-1869, October Term, 1974.

157. Thernstrom, *Whose Votes Count?* p. 151; Richard Engstrom, Stanley Halpin, Jean Hill, and Victoria Caridas-Butterworth, "Louisiana," in *Quiet Revolution,* pp. 114–15.

158. Richard Pacelle, "A President's Legacy: Gender and Appointment to the Federal Courts" in *The Other Elites: Women, Politics, and Power in the Executive Branch,* ed. MaryAnne Borrelli and Janet Martin.

159. Amaker, *Civil Rights,* p. 25.

160. Douglas Brinkley, *The Unfinished Presidency: Jimmy Carter's Journey Beyond the White House,* pp. 14–17.

161. N. Baker, *Conflicting Loyalties,* p. 155.

162. Clayton, *Politics of Justice,* p. 57.

163. Light, *President's Agenda,* pp. 46–47.

164. Charles Jones, *The Trusteeship Presidency: Jimmy Carter and the U.S. Congress,* pp. 57–60.

165. Peterson, *Legislating Together,* p. 262; Stimson, MacKuen, and Erickson, "Dynamic Representation."

166. Lawrence Baum, "Comparing the Policy Positions of Supreme Court Justices From Different Periods," *Western Political Quarterly* 42 (1989).

167. Halpern, *On the Limits of the Law,* pp. 149–60.

168. Landsberg, *Enforcing Civil Rights,* p. 149.

169. *Dayton v. Brinkman,* no. 78-267, and *Columbus v. Penick,* no. 78-610, Brief for the United States as *Amicus Curiae,* October Term, 1978, p. 13.

170. *City of Mobile v. Bolden,* Brief for the United States as *Amicus Curiae,* no. 77-1844, October Term, 1978.

171. According to Thompson (*Voting Rights Act,* p. 27), the Court misread congressional intent.

172. Don Edwards, "The Voting Rights Act of 1965, As Amended" in *Voting Rights Act,* p. 6.

173. Bernard Grofman, Lisa Handley, and Richard Niemi, *Minority Representation and the Quest for Voting Equality,* pp. 22–38.

174. Davidson, "The Evolution of Voting Rights Law," p. 34. Pollak, interview.

175. Grofman, Handley, and Niemi, *Minority Representation,* pp. 37–41.

176. Salokar, *The Solicitor General,* p. 75.

177. Robert McKeever, *Raw Judicial Power? The Supreme Court and American Society,* p. 136; Joseph Califano, *Governing America: An Insider's Report from the White House and the Cabinet,* p. 236. Caplan (*Tenth Justice,* p. 42) noted that Carter excluded the solicitor general from participation in writing the brief.

178. Landsberg, interview.

179. Fisher and Devins, *Political Dynamics,* p. 286.

180. Califano, *Governing America,* pp. 237–43. The two were Frank Easterbrook, later appointed to the Court of Appeals, and Lawrence Wallace, who would incur the wrath of the Reagan administration and survive attempts to fire him. Landsberg (*Enforcing Civil Rights,* p. 161) considers Wallace the classic example of the mistrust that political appointees hold for careerists: "This Johnson administration hire was considered a Nixon holdover under President Carter and a Carter holdover under President Reagan."

181. Peter Bourne, *Jimmy Carter: A Comprehensive Biography From Plains to Postpresidency,* p. 425.

182. Fisher and Devins, *Political Dynamics,* p. 286.

183. Caplan, *Tenth Justice,* pp. 41–47.

184. Griffin Bell with Ronald Ostrow, *Taking Care of the Law,* p. 30; Califano, *Governing America,* p. 242.

185. Cornell Clayton, *Government Lawyers: The Federal Legal Bureaucracy and Presidential Politics,* p. 19.

186. Bell with Ostrow, *Taking Care of the Law,* pp. 30–33; Landsberg (*Enforcing Civil Rights,* pp. 124–25) concurs: "It is alleged that officials in the White House attempted to influence the content of the brief. If that was so, those of us in the career staff who participated in that exercise were well insulated from White House pressure."

187. The intra-administration battles were often fought out in the press, prompting Chief Justice Burger to admonish McCree about the public dispute and news leaks (Howard Ball, *The Bakke Case: Race, Education & Affirmative Action,* pp. 74–75).

188. Califano (*Governing America,* p. 238) laments "the sea-change from Johnson's Justice

Department." But between the Johnson and Carter administrations, the Court had gotten more conservative, the string of success in the Court ended, negative precedents existed, issues were more difficult, and public opinion was less supportive. This was a different issue in a different context.

189. Bell with Ostrow, *Taking Care of the Law,* p. 32.

190. B. Schwartz, *Ascent of Pragmatism,* pp. 268–72.

191. *United States and the Equal Employment Opportunity Commission v. Weber,* Petition for Writ of Certiorari to the United States Court of Appeals for the Fifth Circuit, no. 78-436, October Term, 1978.

192. *United States and Equal Employment Opportunity Commission v. Weber,* Brief for the Federal Appellant, no. 78-436, October Term, 1978.

193. Ibid.

194. Eskridge, "Overriding," pp. 394–95.

195. Richard Epstein, *Forbidden Grounds: The Case Against Employment Discrimination Laws,* p. 429.

196. Because this was a federal program, the Fourteenth Amendment did not apply. In attempting to desegregate schools in Washington D.C., a result-oriented Court needed to find constitutional grounds and "created" an equal protection clause of the Fifth Amendment.

197. *Fullilove v. Kreps,* Brief for the Secretary of Commerce, no. 78-1007, October Term, 1979, p. 69.

198. *Fullilove v. Klutznick, Secretary of Commerce* 448 U.S. 448 (1980).

199. "Memorandum Opinion for the Attorney General."

CHAPTER 5. THE SOLICITOR GENERAL IN THE REDEFINITION PHASE, 1981–2000

1. Stephen Skowronek, *The Politics Presidents Make: Leadership from John Adams to Bill Clinton,* pp. 409–14.

2. Amaker, *Civil Rights,* pp. 157–59.

3. Halpern, *On the Limits of the Law,* p. 191.

4. William Gormley, *Taming the Bureaucracy: Muscles, Prayer, and Other Strategies,* pp. 173–74.

5. William French Smith, *Law & Justice in the Reagan Administration: Memoirs of an Attorney General,* pp. 90–93.

6. Eisler, *Justice For All,* p. 263.

7. W. Bradford Reynolds, interview by author, Aug. 20, 1998.

8. Lincoln Caplan, "The Reagan Challenge to the Rule of Law" in *The Reagan Legacy,* ed. Sidney Blumenthal and Thomas Byrne Edsall, pp. 216–17; Smith, *Law & Justice,* p. 59.

9. Joel Selig, "The Reagan Justice Department and Civil Rights: What Went Wrong?" *University of Illinois Law Review* (1985): 789.

10. Herman Schwartz, *Packing the Court: The Conservative Campaign to Rewrite the Constitution,* p. 182.

11. Wolters, *Right Turn,* pp. 24–33.

12. Salokar, *The Solicitor General,* p. 79; Charles Fried, *Order and Law: Arguing the Reagan Revolution,* pp. 40–44; Caplan, *Tenth Justice,* pp. 81–95.

13. Caplan, "Reagan Challenge," pp. 231–34; Sheldon Goldman, *Picking Federal Judges: Lower Court Selection from Roosevelt Through Reagan.*

14. Reynolds, interview.

15. Richard Watson, *Presidential Vetoes and Public Policy,* pp. 147–49.

16. Stimson, MacKuen, and Erickson, "Dynamic Representation."

17. H. Schwartz, *Packing the Court,* pp. 189–90.

18. Leroy Rieselbach, *Congressional Politics,* pp. 263–64.

19. Pacelle, "A President's Legacy."

20. Baum, "Membership Change."

21. Tinsley Yarbrough, *The Rehnquist Court and the Constitution.*

22. Robert Weiss, *"We Want Jobs": A History of Affirmative Action,* p. 222.

23. Richard Pacelle, "The Solicitor General and Gender: Litigating the President's Agenda and Serving the Supreme Court" in *The Other Elites.*

24. Rose, interview.

25. Caplan, *Tenth Justice,* pp. 218–28.

26. Reynolds, interview.

27. Salokar, *The Solicitor General,* p. 55.

28. Neal Devins, "Unitariness and Independence: Solicitor General Control over Independent Agency Litigation," *California Law Review* 82 (1994).

29. *Equal Employment Opportunity Commission v. Shell Oil* 466 U.S. 54; Brief for Petitioner, no. 82-825.

30. *W.R. Grace v. Local Union* 759 461 U.S. 757; Brief for the Equal Employment Opportunity Commission as *Amicus Curiae,* no. 81-1314, October Term, 1982. *Pullman-Standard v. Swint* 456 U.S. 273; Brief for the United States and the Equal Employment Opportunity Commission as *Amicus Curiae,* nos. 80-1190 and 80-1193, October Term, 1981. *Crown, Cork, & Seal v. Parker* 462 U.S. 345; Brief for the Equal Employment Opportunity Commission as *Amicus Curiae,* no. 82-118, October Term, 1982. *Cooper v. Federal Reserve Board* 467 U.S. 867; Brief for the United States and the Equal Employment Opportunity Commission as *Amicus Curiae,* no. 83-185, October Term, 1983.

31. Richard Wilkins, interview by author, March 27, 1998.

32. *City of Port Arthur v. United States* 459 U.S. 159; Motion to Affirm, no. 81-708, October Term, 1981; Brief for the United States, no. 81-708, October Term, 1981. *Lockhart v. United States* 460 U.S. 125; Brief for the United States, no. 81-802, October Term, 1981.

33. *McCain v. Lybrand* 415 U.S. 236; Brief for the United States as *Amicus Curiae. National Association for the Advancement of Colored People v. Hampton Election Commission* 470 U.S. 166; Brief for the United States as *Amicus Curiae.*

34. Salokar, *The Solicitor General;* Caplan, *Tenth Justice.*

35. Wolters, *Right Turn,* p. 232.

36. Reynolds, interview; Wilkins, interview.

37. Caplan, *Tenth Justice,* pp. 51–52.

38. *Goldsboro Christian Schools v. United States* and *Bob Jones University v. United States* Brief for the United States, nos. 81-1 and 81-3, October Term, 1980.

39. Selig, "The Reagan Justice Department," p. 817.

40. Salokar, *The Solicitor General,* p. 61.

41. *Goldsboro Christian Schools, Inc. v. United States* and *Bob Jones University v. United States,* Memorandum for the United States, nos. 81-1 and 81-3, October Term, 1981, p. 1.

42. *Goldsboro Christian Schools, Inc. v. United States* and *Bob Jones University v. United States,* Reply Brief for the United States, nos. 81-1 and 81-3, October Term, 1981, p. 1.

43. Devins, "Unitariness," p. 276.

44. *Goldsboro Christian Schools, Inc. v. United States* and *Bob Jones University v. United States,* Brief of *Amicus Curiae* in Support of the Judgment Below, nos. 81-1 and 81-3, October Term, 1982.

45. Reynolds, interview.

46. Selig, "The Reagan Justice Department," p. 820.

47. Caplan, *Tenth Justice,* pp. 61–62.

48. Selig, "The Reagan Justice Department," p. 821.

49. Landsberg, *Enforcing Civil Rights,* p. 168.

50. Amaker, *Civil Rights,* pp. 34–36.

51. Landsberg, interview.

52. Wilkins, interview.

53. Selig, "The Reagan Justice Department," pp. 807–10.

54. Ibid., p. 832.

55. *Washington v. Seattle School District No. 1* Memorandum for the United States, no. 81-9, October Term, 1980; Brief for the United States, no. 81-9, October Term, 1981.

56. *Crawford v. Board of Education, Los Angeles* Brief for the United States as *Amicus Curiae,* no. 81-38, October Term, 1981.

57. Wilkins, interview.

58. Amaker, *Civil Rights,* p. 124; Selig, "The Reagan Justice Department," p. 831.

59. H. D. Graham, *The Civil Rights Era,* pp. 109–13.

60. Wolters, *Right Turn,* pp. 211–18.

61. Fried, interview.

62. Robert Detlefsen, *Civil Rights Under Reagan,* p. 60.

63. Bryson, interview; Landsberg, *Enforcing Civil Rights,* p. 168; Selig, "The Reagan Justice Department," pp. 787–88.

64. Irving Gornstein, interview by author, Jan. 27, 1998.

65. Fried, *Order and Law,* p. 106.

66. *Firefighters Local Union 1784 v. Stotts,* Brief of *Amicus Curiae* for the United States, no. 82-206, October Term, 1982.

67. Wolters, *Right Turn,* pp. 236–37; Thomas Bagby, ed., *The Memphis Firefighters Case: The Impact of the Supreme Court's* Stotts *Decision on Affirmative Action, Equal Employment Litigation, Settlement, and Judicial Remedies,* pp. 12–14.

68. Wolters, *Right Turn,* p. 237.

69. Bagby, *Memphis Firefighters Case,* p. 31.

70. Douglas McDowell, *The 1986 Affirmative Action Trilogy: A Guide to Questions Left Open by the Supreme Court's Decisions in* Local 28, Wygant, *and* Cleveland Vanguards, p. 20; Landsberg, interview; Turner, interview.

71. Caplan, *Tenth Justice;* Reynolds, interview.

72. Caplan, *Tenth Justice,* pp. 87–95.

73. Geller, interview.

74. Caplan, *Tenth Justice,* pp. 102–107.

75. Phillips interview; Wilkins, interview.

76. Caplan, *Tenth Justice,* p. 107.

77. This was mentioned by a number of people in interviews.

78. Reynolds, interview.

79. Fried, *Order and Law,* pp. 41–42.

80. Rose, interview.

81. Reynolds, interview; Rose, interview.

82. Reynolds, interview.

83. D. McDowell, *1986 Affirmative Action,* p. 23.

84. Wolters, *Right Turn,* p. 253.

85. Fried, *Order and Law,* p. 117.

86. Douglas McDowell, *Affirmative Action After the* Johnson *Decision: Practical Guidance for Planning and Compliance,* pp. 31–35.

87. Weiss, *"We Want Jobs,"* p. 225.

88. Fried, *Order and Law,* p. 112.

89. D. McDowell, *Affirmative Action,* p. 64.

90. Blumrosen, *Modern Law,* p. 275.

91. Fried, *Order and Law,* p. 113.

92. Detlefsen, *Civil Rights Under Reagan,* p. 90.

93. Devins, "Unitariness," pp. 297–99.

94. Neal Devins, "Toward an Understanding of Legal Policy-Making at Independent Agencies," in *Government Lawyers,* p. 193.

95. Rose, interview.

96. Devins, "Toward an Understanding," p. 194.

97. Steven Shull, *A Kinder, Gentler Racism? The Reagan-Bush Civil Rights Legacy,* pp. 112–17.

98. Fried, *Order and Law,* pp. 226–27.

99. In a conversation, Stephen Shapiro did not remember the office being refused time to argue a case. Caplan (*Tenth Justice,* p. 260) has evidence that this has occurred only eighteen times in over three decades. James Cooper ("The Solicitor General and the Evolution of Activism," p. 693) isolates two periods and finds no refusals in 1954–57 and fourteen in 1984–87. Salokar *(The Solicitor General),* on the other hand, does not consider this unusual.

100. Fried, *Order and Law,* pp. 122–27.

101. Wolters, *Right Turn,* p. 283.

102. Fried, *Order and Law,* p. 129.

103. The Court had the last word when it refused to apply the acts retroactively. Lee Epstein and Thomas Walker, *Constitutional Law for A Changing America: Rights, Liberties, and Justice,* p. 680.

104. James Simon, *The Center Holds: The Power Struggle Inside the Rehnquist Court,* p. 81.

105. Blumrosen, *Modern Law,* p. 285.

106. Robert Smith, *Racism in the Post-Civil Rights Era: Now You See It, Now You Don't,* p. 60.

107. Wolters, *Right Turn,* p. 273.

108. *City of Richmond v. Croson,* Brief for the United States as *Amicus Curiae,* no. 87-998, October Term, 1987.

109. Wolters, *Right Turn,* p. 275.

110. Terry Eastland, *Ending Affirmative Action,* p. 125.

111. Detlefsen, *Civil Rights Under Reagan,* p. 194.

112. Nancy Maveety, *Justice Sandra Day O'Connor: Strategist on the Supreme Court,* p. 115.

113. Fried, *Order and Law,* pp. 122–24.

114. David Savage, *Turning Right: The Making of the Rehnquist Supreme Court,* p. 191. The Court discussed reconsidering *Jones v. Alfred Mayer,* which had been a basis for *Runyon,* see Bernard Schwartz, *Decision: How the Supreme Court Decides Cases,* pp. 238–39.

115. Simon, *Center Holds,* pp. 4–8.

116. Justice Scalia expressed dissatisfaction with the attorneys trying to overturn *Runyon.* In response to a point, Scalia said, "If that's all you have, I'm afraid it is nothing." David Savage *(Turning Right,* p. 223) claimed that "Scalia would need ammunition to fight for overturning *Runyon,* but the attorneys had not given him any."

117. Fried, interview.

118. Fried, *Order and Law,* pp. 125–26.

119. Simon, *Center Holds,* p. 42.

120. Fried, *Order and Law,* pp. 125–29.

121. Caplan, *Tenth Justice,* p. 240.

122. Fried, interview.

123. Caplan, *Tenth Justice,* p. 242.

124. Wolters, *Right Turn,* pp. 113–21.

125. Grofman, Handley, and Niemi, *Minority Representation,* p. 49.

126. Caplan, *Tenth Justice,* p. 243.

127. Reynolds, interview.

128. Fried, interview.

129. Wilkins, interview.

130. Bryson, interview; Selig, "The Reagan Justice Department," p. 796.

131. Wilkins, interview.
132. Kneedler, interview.
133. Landsberg, interview.
134. Wilkins, interview.
135. Reynolds, interview.
136. Simon, *Center Holds,* p. 81; Reynolds, interview.
137. Skowronek, *Politics Presidents Make,* pp. 429–39.
138. Shull, *Kinder, Gentler Racism?* p. 4.
139. Barbara Sinclair, "Governing Unheroically (and Sometimes Unappetizingly): Bush and the 101st Congress" in *The Bush Presidency,* ed. Colin Campbell and Bert Rockham, pp. 170–71.
140. Herbert Parmet, *George Bush: The Life of a Lone Star Yankee,* pp. 436–37.
141. Milkis, *The President and the Parties,* p. 297.
142. Clayton, *Politics of Justice,* pp. 227–29.
143. Turner, interview.
144. John Dunne, interview by author, April 16, 1998.
145. Roger Clegg, interview by author, April 16, 1998.
146. Spitzer, *President & Congress,* p. 74.
147. Stimson, MacKuen, and Erickson, "Dynamic Representation."
148. Richard Pacelle, "The Dynamics and Determinants of Agenda Change in the Rehnquist Court" in *Contemplating Courts,* ed. Lee Epstein; Mark Silverstein, *Judicious Choices: The New Politics of Supreme Court Confirmations,* pp. 126–27.
149. Paul Quirk, "Domestic Policy: Divided Government and Cooperative Presidential Leadership" in *Bush Presidency,* pp. 84–85.
150. Seamon, interview.
151. Clayton, *Politics of Justice,* p. 229.
152. Clegg, interview.
153. One case was *Georgia v. McCollum* involving the use of racial discrimination in preemptory challenges during the *voir dire.* This was a criminal procedure case assigned to Deputy William Bryson, who handled such matters.
154. Gornstein, interview.
155. Dunne, interview.
156. *United States v. Roemer,* Brief for the United States, no. 90-1032, October Term, 1990; *Houston Lawyers Association v. Mattox,* Brief of *Amicus Curiae,* no. 90-813, October Term, 1990.
157. *United States v. Roemer,* Brief for the United States, no. 90-1032, October Term, 1990.
158. *United States v. Roemer* 501 US 380 (1991).
159. Starr interview.
160. *Board of Education of Oklahoma City Public Schools v. Dowell,* Brief for the United States as *Amicus Curiae,* no. 89-1080, October Term, 1989.
161. Starr, interview.
162. *Board of Education of Oklahoma City Public Schools v. Dowell* 498 U.S. 237 (1991).
163. *Freeman v. Pitts,* Brief for the United States as *Amicus Curiae* Supporting Petitioners, no. 89-1290, October Term, 1990.
164. *Freeman v. Pitts* 503 U.S. 467 (1992).
165. Gary Orfield, "Turning Back to Segregation" in *Dismantling Desegregation: The Quiet Reversal of* Brown v. Board of Education, ed. Gary Orfield, Susan Eaton, and the Harvard Project on School Desegregation, pp. 10–11; Kenneth Meier, Joseph Stewart, and Robert England, *Race, Class, and Education: The Politics of Second-Generation Discrimination.*
166. Wolters, *Right Turn,* pp. 460–61.
167. Starr, interview.

168. Halpern, *On the Limits of the Law,* pp. 244–49.

169. Starr, interview.

170. *United States v. Mabus,* Brief for the United States, no. 90-1205, October Term, 1991; *United States v. Mabus,* Reply Brief for the United States, no. 90-1205, October Term, 1991.

171. John Domino, *Civil Rights & Liberties: Toward the 21st Century,* pp. 266, 281.

172. Halpern, *On the Limits of the Law,* p. 258; Kay Kindred, "Civil Rights and Higher Education," in *A Year in the Life of the Supreme Court,* ed. Rodney Smolla, p. 218.

173. Kahn, *The Supreme Court & Constitutional Theory,* p. 260.

174. *United States v. Fordice* 505 U.S. 717 (1992).

175. Devins, "Toward an Understanding," p. 199.

176. Devins, "Unitariness," pp. 294–97.

177. Roberts, interview.

178. *Metro Broadcasting v. Federal Communications Commission,* Brief of *Amicus Curiae* Supporting Respondent, no. 89-453, October Term, 1989; *Astroline Communications Co. v. Shurberg Broadcasting, Inc.,* Brief of *Amicus Curiae* Supporting Respondent, no. 89-700, October Term, 1989.

179. Joan Biskupic, *The Supreme Court Yearbook, 1989–1990,* pp. 17–19.

180. Eastland, *Ending Affirmative Action,* pp. 126–27.

181. David Brady and Craig Volden, *Revolving Gridlock: Politics and Policy from Carter to Clinton,* pp. 146–47.

182. Kenneth Collier, *Between the Branches: The White House Office of Legislative Affairs,* p. 260.

183. Brady and Volden, *Revolving Gridlock,* pp. 192–99.

184. Baird had no constituency to support her and had the baggage of allegations that she had hired illegal aliens and failed to pay income taxes. MaryAnne Borrelli, "Campaign Promises, Transition Dilemmas: Cabinet Building and Executive Representation" in *The Other Elites,* pp. 79–80.

185. See Lani Guinier, *The Tyranny of the Majority: Fundamental Fairness in Representative Democracy.*

186. For a view of the problems the administration had in filling positions in the Justice Department, Webb Hubbell, *Friends in High Places: Our Journey from Little Rock to Washington D.C.*

187. Bender, interview; Deval Patrick, interview by author, April 14, 1998.

188. Ibid.

189. Collier, *Between the Branches,* p. 260.

190. Paul Herrnson, *Congressional Elections: Campaigning at Home and in Washington,* p. 230.

191. Brady and Volden, *Revolving Gridlock,* pp. 146–47.

192. Patrick, interview.

193. Simon, *Center Holds,* p. 81; Leslie Friedman Goldstein and Diana Stech, "Explaining Transformations in Supreme Court Policy," *Judicature* 79 (1995).

194. Silverstein, *Judicious Choices,* pp. 170–75.

195. Dellinger had been nominated to the federal bench, but the nomination was blocked by Senators Jesse Helms and Lauch Faircloth. Orrin Hatch, head of the Judiciary Committee, was expected to block consideration of his nomination to be solicitor general, so Clinton made him the acting solicitor general.

196. Dellinger, interview.

197. Bender, interview.

198. Patrick, interview.

199. Jeffrey Toobin, "Clinton's Left Hand Man," *New Yorker,* July 21, 1997, pp. 30–31.

200. Landsberg, *Enforcing Civil Rights,* p. 152.

201. Seamon, interview.

202. Long, interview.

203. Landsberg, *Enforcing Civil Rights,* p. 153.

204. Days did not support civil rights claimants in just one case, the first time a Democratic solicitor general failed to do so, in a criminal case involving more severe penalties for crack cocaine than powder cocaine. The case turned on the question of whether this represented racial discrimination because whites were more likely to use powder, while crack cocaine was more prevalent among black drug users. Days argued that there was no intentional discrimination and the Court agreed.

205. L. Marvin Overby and Kenneth Cosgrove, "Unintended Consequences? Racial Redistricting and the Representation of Minority Interests," *Journal of Politics* 58 (1996): 540–41; Bernard Grofman, "*Shaw v. Reno* and the Future of Voting Rights," *PS* 28 (1995): 27.

206. Epstein and Walker, *Constitutional Law for A Changing America,* p. 790.

207. *Shaw v. Gerson,* Brief for the Federal Appellees, no. 92-357, October Term, 1992. Gerson was acting attorney general when the case was filed. Reno became the named party after her confirmation.

208. Maveety, *Justice Sandra Day O'Connor,* pp. 108–109.

209. Abigail Thernstrom, "More Notes from a Political Thicket" in *Affirmative Action and Representation:* Shaw v. Reno *and the Future of Voting Rights,* ed. Anthony Peacock, p. 101.

210. Days, interview; Patrick, interview. Quoted in Anthony Peacock, "Voting Rights, Representation, and the Problem of Equality" in *Affirmative Action,* p. 5.

211. Patrick, interview; Bender, interview.

212. Days, interview.

213. *United States v. Johnson,* Brief for the United States, no. 94-929, October Term, 1994. Together with *Miller v. Johnson,* no. 94-631 and *Abrams v. Johnson,* no. 94-797.

214. Thernstrom, "More Notes," p. 97.

215. Anthony Peacock, "*Shaw v. Reno* and the Voting Rights Conundrum: Equality, The Public Interest, and the Politics of Representation" in *Affirmative Action,* pp. 147–48; Peacock, "Voting Rights," pp. 7–8.

216. *Abrams v. Johnson; United States v. Johnson* 521 US 74 (1997).

217. *Adarand Constructors, Inc. v. Pena* 515 US 200 (1995).

218. Bender, interview.

219. Ibid.

220. Dellinger, interview.

221. Toobin, "Clinton's Left Hand Man," p. 31.

222. Dellinger, interview.

223. Toobin, "Clinton's Left Hand Man," p. 32; Bender, interview.

224. Dellinger, interview.

225. Symposium, "The Department of Justice and the Civil Rights Act of 1964," *Pacific Law Journal* 26 (1995): 765.

226. Days, interview; Dellinger, interview.

227. Patrick, interview; Dellinger, interview.

228. Patrick, interview.

229. Bender, interview.

PART III. THE SOLICITOR GENERAL AND GENDER DISCRIMINATION AND REPRODUCTIVE RIGHTS

1. J. Ralph Lindgren and Nadine Taub, *The Law of Sex Discrimination,* p. 1.

2. Fisher and Devins, *Political Dynamics,* p. 303.

3. Leslie Friedman Goldstein, *The Constitutional Rights of Women: Cases in Law and Social Change,* pp. 3–7.

4. The Supreme Court upheld laws that forbade women from practicing law *(Bradwell v. State)* and from working in bars unless they were related to the owner *(Goeseart v. Cleary)*.

5. Goldstein and Stech, "Explaining Transformations," pp. 80–85.

6. Pacelle, "The Solicitor General and Gender."

7. Justice Douglas found privacy at the intersection of freedom of association from the First Amendment, prohibitions against the quartering of troops in the Third Amendment, Fourth Amendment rights to be free from unwarranted searches, and due process guarantees of the Fifth Amendment, which cast shadows suggesting a right to privacy. Planned Parenthood argued for the inclusion of the Ninth Amendment, which states the enumeration of some rights does not foreclose exercise of others. Thomas Emerson, "Nine Justices in Search of a Doctrine," *Michigan Law Review* 64 (1965): 219–34.

8. Wendy Kaminer, *A Fearful Freedom: Women's Flight From Equality,* p. 169; Eva Rubin, *Abortion, Politics, and the Courts,* p. 4.

9. Many laws, such as the drinking age, make distinctions. The Court uses three levels of scrutiny to assess whether distinctions are legal. Under minimum scrutiny, the government needs to show only a rational purpose in passing the law. The Court ruled that the government must show a compelling reason for race-based distinctions. Few laws can survive this strict scrutiny. Moderate scrutiny was created for gender (Ruth Bader Ginsburg, "The Burger Court's Grappling with Sex Discrimination" in *The Burger Court: The Counter-Revolution That Wasn't,* ed. Vincent Blasi). Gender-based distinctions must further an important objective, which is easier for the government to demonstrate than the compelling standard.

10. McKeever, *Raw Judicial Power?* p. 178.

11. Kenney, *For Whose Protection?* p. 142.

CHAPTER 6. THE SOLICITOR GENERAL AND THE EMERGENCE AND DEFINITION OF GENDER AND REPRODUCTIVE RIGHTS POLICY

1. Eskridge, *Dynamic Statutory Interpretation*.

2. Keynes with Miller, *Court Versus Congress,* pp. 279–89.

3. Karen O'Connor and Lee Epstein, "Beyond Legislative Lobbying: Women's Rights Groups and the Supreme Court," *Judicature* 67 (1983): 134–43.

4. Baum, "Measuring Policy Change."

5. Lee Epstein, Jeffrey Segal, Harold Spaeth, and Thomas Walker, *The Supreme Court Compendium,* pp. 428–29.

6. Tracey George and Lee Epstein, "Women's Rights Litigation in the 1980s: More of the Same?" *Judicature* 74 (1991): 314–21.

7. Deborah Rhode, *Justice and Gender: Sex Discrimination and the Law,* p. 90.

8. Fisher and Devins, *Political Dynamics,* p. 303.

9. Stephanie Seymour, "Women as Constitutional Equals: The Burger Court's Overdue Evolution" in *The Burger Court: Counter-Revolution or Confirmation?* ed. Bernard Schwartz, p. 68.

10. Kahn, *The Supreme Court & Constitutional Theory,* p. 165.

11. Representative Howard Smith of Virginia added Title VII to increase the number of opponents to the bill. For that reason, some advocates of women's rights fought the addition (Rhode, *Justice and Gender,* p. 57). Because opponents of civil rights legislation formulated Title VII, there was no group to oversee implementation of sex discrimination provisions (Kenney, *For Whose Protection?* p. 142). If the intent of the framers of the Civil Rights Act was followed by the courts, the interpretation of its provisions would be narrower. But the Court tends to follow the intent of the sitting Congress (Eskridge, *Dynamic Statutory Interpretation*). Democratic control of Congress created an environment for aggressive interpretations of the Civil Rights Act and the amendments that strengthened the act. This constrained the solicitor general, often

requiring a broader interpretation than the president might have welcomed and led the conservative Court to relatively liberal interpretations of its provisions (Goldstein and Stech, "Explaining Transformations," pp. 80–85).

12. Levin-Epstein, *Primer of Equal Employment Opportunity,* pp. 26–29.

13. Baer, *Equality Under the Constitution,* pp. 162–63.

14. Timothy Cheney, *Who Makes the Law: The Supreme Court, Congress, the States, and Society,* pp. 4–5.

15. Jeffrey Segal and Cheryl Reedy, "The Supreme Court and Sex Discrimination: The Role of the Solicitor General," *Western Political Quarterly* 41 (1988): 553–68.

16. Baer, *Equality Under the Constitution,* p. 151.

17. Judith Baer, *The Chains of Protection: The Judicial Response to Women's Labor Legislation,* pp. 136–73.

18. Ginsburg, "Burger Court's Grappling with Sex Discrimination," p. 137.

19. Lindgren and Taub, *Law of Sex Discrimination,* p. 107; McKeever, *Raw Judicial Power?* p. 180.

20. Lindgren and Taub, *Law of Sex Discrimination,* p. 54.

21. Rhode, *Justice and Gender,* p. 113.

22. H. D. Graham, *The Civil Rights Era,* pp. 397–98.

23. Rhode, *Justice and Gender,* p. 301.

24. *Phillips v. Martin Marietta,* Brief for the United States as *Amicus Curiae,* no. 73, October Term, 1969.

25. Susan Gluck Mezey, *In Pursuit of Equality: Women, Public Policy, and the Federal Courts,* p. 47.

26. Rhode, *Justice and Gender,* p. 88.

27. *Frontiero v. Laird,* Motion to Affirm, no. 71-1694, October Term, 1972.

28. *Frontiero v. Laird,* Brief for Appellees, no. 71-1694, October Term, 1972, pp. 17–18.

29. Laura Otten, *Women's Rights and the Law,* p. 102.

30. Lindgren and Taub, *Law of Sex Discrimination,* p. 60.

31. Mary Frances Berry, *Why ERA Failed: Politics, Women's Rights, and the Amending Process of the Constitution,* p. 88.

32. David Kirp, Mark Yudolf, and Marlene Strong Franks, *Gender Justice,* p. 92.

33. Lindgren and Taub, *Law of Sex Discrimination,* pp. 63–64.

34. Bork, interview.

35. Joan Hoff, *Law, Gender, and Injustice: A Legal History of U.S. Women,* p. 273.

36. Rhode, *Justice and Gender,* p. 256.

37. *Schlesinger v. Ballard,* Jurisdictional Statement, no. 73-776, October Term, 1976; *Schlesinger v. Ballard,* Brief for the Appellants, no. 73-776, October Term, 1976.

38. Mezey, *In Pursuit of Equality,* p. 24.

39. D. Jackson, *Even the Children of Strangers,* p. 152.

40. *Weinberger v. Wiesenfeld,* Brief for the Appellant, no. 73-1892, October Term, 1973, p. 11.

41. Kirp, Yudolf, and Franks, *Gender Justice,* p. 101.

42. *Fiallo v. Levi,* Brief for the Appellees, no. 75-6297, October Term, 1976.

43. Mezey, *In Pursuit of Equality,* p. 28.

44. *Corning Glass Works v. Brennan,* Memorandum for the Respondent, no. 73-29, October Term, 1973, p. 5.

45. *Corning Glass Works v. Brennan,* Brief for the Secretary of Labor, no. 73-29, October Term, 1973.

46. Mezey, *In Pursuit of Equality,* p. 97.

47. Griswold's brief dealt with commercial speech. The creation of commercial speech doctrine was related to abortion rights. A Virginia newspaper had printed, in violation of state law,

an advertisement for a New York abortion clinic. The case, *Bigelow v. Virginia* (1975), recognized for the first time that commercial speech was deserving of First Amendment protection. It is doubtful that doctrine would have emerged at this time had it not been for *Roe,* which the Court was trying to protect and buttress with other favorable precedents. In his opinion for the Court, Justice Blackmun had to distinguish *Bigelow* from *Pittsburgh Press,* a potentially harmful precedent (Pritchett, *Constitutional Civil Liberties,* pp. 80–81). In both cases, the Court elevated the desire to protect women's rights and reproductive rights over the need for consistency in commercial law doctrine.

48. Eva Rubin, *The Supreme Court and the American Family,* p. 85.

49. Mezey, *In Pursuit of Equality,* pp. 113–15.

50. Rubin, *Supreme Court and the American Family,* pp. 87–88.

51. Bork, who was disqualified from the case, authorized filing the brief.

52. *Geduldig v. Aiello,* Brief of the U.S. Equal Employment Opportunity Commission, no. 73-640, October Term, 1973.

53. Rubin, *Supreme Court and the American Family,* pp. 88–90.

54. Otten, *Women's Rights and the Law,* p. 118.

55. Wendy Williams, "Equality's Riddle: Pregnancy and the Equal Treatment/Special Treatment Debate" in *Feminist Legal Theory,* p. 137.

56. Karen O'Connor, *Women's Organizations' Use of the Courts,* p. 131.

57. Landsberg, *Enforcing Civil Rights,* p. 207.

58. Hoff, *Law, Gender, and Injustice,* p. 295.

59. Lindgren and Taub, *Law of Sex Discrimination,* p. 114.

60. Kenney, *For Whose Protection?* pp. 152–54.

61. Hoff, *Law, Gender, and Injustice,* p. 324.

62. Karen Maschke, *Litigation, Courts, and Women Workers,* p. 30.

63. *Roskter v. Goldberg,* Brief for the Appellant, no. 80-251, October Term, 1980, pp. 16–21.

64. Kirp, Yudolf, and Franks, *Gender Justice,* p. 95.

65. Nancy Levit, *The Gender Line: Men, Women, and the Law,* p. 70.

66. D. Jackson, *Even the Children of Strangers,* pp. 159–60.

67. Rhode, *Justice and Gender,* p. 100.

68. Hoff, *Law, Gender, and Injustice,* p. 266; *Cannon v. University of Chicago,* Brief for the Federal Respondent, no. 77-926, October Term, 1978.

69. *General Telephone v. EEOC,* Brief for the Federal Respondent, no. 79-488, October Term, 1979.

70. Rhode, *Justice and Gender,* pp. 177–78.

71. *Personnel Administrator of Massachusetts v. Feeney,* Brief for the United States as *Amicus Curiae,* no. 78-233, October Term, 1978.

72. D. Jackson, *Even the Children of Strangers,* p. 157.

73. *Michael M v. Superior Court Sonoma County,* Brief for the United States as *Amicus Curiae,* no. 79-1344, October Term 1979, pp. 13–19.

74. Rhode, *Justice and Gender,* p. 102.

75. Levit, *Gender Line,* pp. 72–73.

76. Baer, *Equality Under the Constitution,* p. 125.

77. McCann, *Rights At Work.* Comparable worth is based on pay equity across different jobs. Traditionally, some jobs have gone to women, while others have been dominated by males. Comparable worth attempts to determine what occupations are worth and to seek comparable pay for comparable contributions. The impact would be to elevate remuneration for jobs that women have traditionally held.

78. Levin-Epstein, *Primer of Equal Employment Opportunity,* p. 36.

79. Hoff, *Law, Gender, and Injustice,* p. 254.

80. Lindgren and Taub, *Law of Sex Discrimination,* p. 153.

81. *City of Los Angeles Department of Water Power v. Manhart,* Brief for the United States and Equal Employment Opportunity Commission, no. 76-1810, October Term, 1977.

82. Kaminer, *Fearful Freedom,* p. 97.

83. Mezey, *In Pursuit of Equality,* p. 121.

84. *Great American Federal Savings & Loan v. Novotny,* Brief for the United States as *Amicus Curiae,* no. 78-753, October Term, 1978.

85. *Great American Federal Savings & Loan v. Novotny* 442 US 366 (1979).

86. Otten, *Women's Rights and the Law,* pp. 187–90.

87. Ibid., pp. 142–43.

88. Kristen Luker, *Abortion and the Politics of Motherhood,* pp. 1–2.

89. Bork, interview.

90. Epstein and Kobylka, *Supreme Court and Legal Change,* pp. 221–27, 292.

CHAPTER 7. THE SOLICITOR GENERAL AND GENDER AND REPRODUCTIVE RIGHTS POLICY

1. Berry, *Why ERA Failed,* p. 75.

2. *Newport News Shipbuilding and Dry Dock Co. v. Equal Employment Opportunity Commission,* Brief for the Equal Employment Opportunity Commission, no. 82-411, October Term, 1982.

3. Cheney, *Who Makes the Law,* p. 37.

4. Epstein and Knight, *Choices Justices Make,* pp. 15–16.

5. *North Haven Board of Education v. Bell,* Brief for the Federal Respondents, no. 80-986, October Term, 1980.

6. Mezey, *In Pursuit of Equality,* pp. 155–56.

7. Halpern, *On the Limits of the Law,* p. 196.

8. Reynolds, interview.

9. *Grove City College v. Bell,* Brief for the United States in Opposition, no. 82-792, October Term, 1982.

10. *Grove City College v. Bell,* Brief for the Respondents, no. 82-792, October Term, 1983, see footnote 18.

11. Halpern, *On the Limits of the Law,* pp. 197–98.

12. Hoff, *Law, Gender, and Injustice,* p. 242.

13. Lindgren and Taub, *Law of Sex Discrimination,* pp. 256, 279.

14. *Califano v. Webster* 430 US 313 at 317 (1977).

15. Otten, *Women's Rights and the Law.*

16. Goldstein and Stech, "Explaining Transformations," pp. 80–83.

17. Catherine MacKinnon, *The Sexual Harassment of Working Women,* pp. 32, 40.

18. Levin-Epstein, *Primer of Equal Employment Opportunity,* p. 33; John Semonche, *Keeping the Faith: A Cultural History of the U.S. Supreme Court,* p. 319.

19. Caplan, *Tenth Justice,* pp. 253–54.

20. Otten, *Women's Rights and the Law,* p. 221.

21. Cheney, *Who Makes the Law,* p. 52.

22. Martha Minow, "The Supreme Court 1986 Term, Foreword: Justice Engendered" in *Feminist Legal Theory,* p. 307.

23. Fried, *Order and Law,* p. 117; Fried, interview.

24. Melvin Urofsky, *Affirmative Action on Trial: Sex Discrimination in* Johnson v. Santa Clara, pp. 122–25.

25. *Johnson v. Transportation Agency, Santa Clara County,* Brief for the United States as *Amicus Curiae* Supporting Petitioner, no. 85-1129, October Term, 1986.

26. Urofsky, *Affirmative Action on Trial,* pp. 160–66.

27. Otten, *Women's Rights and the Law,* p. 221.

28. D. Jackson, *Even the Children of Strangers,* p. 163.

29. *Price Waterhouse v. Hopkins,* Brief for the United States as *Amicus Curiae,* no. 87-1167, October Term, 1987.

30. Hoff, *Law, Gender, and Injustice,* p. 270; Mezey, *In Pursuit of Equality,* pp. 56–57.

31. Lindgren and Taub, *Law of Sex Discrimination,* p. 163.

32. Rhode, *Justice and Gender,* pp. 119–20.

33. *California Federal Savings and Loan Association v. Guerra,* Brief for the United States as *Amicus Curiae* Supporting Petitioner, no. 85-494, October Term, 1985.

34. Lindgren and Taub, *Law of Sex Discrimination,* p. 107.

35. Simon, *Center Holds,* pp. 141, 156–58.

36. Suzanne Staggenborg, *The Pro-Choice Movement: Organization and Activism in the Abortion Conflict,* pp. 134–35.

37. *City of Akron v. Akron Center for Reproductive Health,* Brief for the United States as *Amicus Curiae* in Support of Petitioners, no. 81-746, October Term, 1982.

38. Caplan, *Tenth Justice,* pp. 105–106; Epstein and Kobylka, *Supreme Court and Legal Change,* pp. 239–44.

39. *Thornburgh v. American College of Obstetricians and Gynecologists,* Brief for the United States as *Amicus Curiae* in Support of Appellants, no. 84-495, October Term, 1985.

40. Epstein and Kobylka, *Supreme Court and Legal Change,* p. 254. Tanya Melich, *The Republican War Against Women,* pp. 184, 237.

41. Simon, *Center Holds,* p. 125.

42. Epstein and Kobylka, *Supreme Court and Legal Change,* p. 254; Fried, interview.

43. Fried, *Order and Law;* Salokar, *The Solicitor General.*

44. Caplan (*Tenth Justice,* p. 249) referred to this as the first major press conference held by a solicitor general.

45. Frey, interview.

46. Fried, interview.

47. Susan Moller Okin, *Justice, Gender, and the Family,* p. 41.

48. Susan Clayton and Faye Crosby, *Justice, Gender, and Affirmative Action,* p. 20.

49. Suzanne Uttaro Samuels, *Fetal Rights, Women's Rights,* p. 105.

50. Kaminer, *Fearful Freedom,* pp. 171, 174.

51. Samuels, *Fetal Rights,* p. 106; D. Savage, *Turning Right,* p. 373.

52. Robert Blank, *Fetal Protection in the Workplace: Women's Rights, Business Interests, and the Unborn,* p. 113.

53. Kenney, *For Whose Protection?* p. 142.

54. Lindgren and Taub, *Law of Sex Discrimination,* p. 186.

55. Samuels, *Fetal Rights,* p. 77.

56. Cheney, *Who Makes the Law,* p. 5.

57. Stephen Wermiel, "A Claim of Sexual Harassment" in *A Year,* pp. 249–51.

58. Marian Faux, *Crusaders: Voices from the Abortion Front,* p. 42.

59. Staggenborg, *Pro-Choice Movement,* pp. 137–38.

60. Faux, *Crusaders,* pp. 42–43.

61. Fried, interview.

62. *Webster v. Reproductive Health Services,* Brief for the United States as *Amicus Curiae,* no. 88-605, October Term, 1988.

63. Faux, *Crusaders,* p. 50.

64. Epstein and Kobylka, *Supreme Court and Legal Change,* p. 283.

65. *Hodgson v. Minnesota,* Brief for the United States as *Amicus Curiae* Supporting Respondents in no. 88-1125 and Supporting Cross-Petitioners in no. 88-1309, October Term, 1989.

66. Mark Graber, *Rethinking Abortion: Equal Choice, the Constitution, and Reproductive Rights,* p. 127.

67. Simon, *Center Holds,* pp. 151–52.

68. *Rust v. Sullivan,* Brief for the Respondent, no. 89-1391, October Term, 1990.

69. Graber, *Rethinking Abortion,* p. 127.

70. *Planned Parenthood of Southeastern Pennsylvania v. Casey,* Brief for the United States as *Amicus Curiae* Supporting Petitioner, no. 91-744, October Term, 1991.

71. Simon, *Center Holds,* pp. 155–56.

72. *Planned Parenthood of Southeastern Pennsylvania v. Casey* 505 U.S. 833 (1992).

73. Levit, *Gender Line,* p. 71.

74. *Bray v. Alexandria Women's Health Clinic,* Brief for the United States as *Amicus Curiae* Supporting Petitioners, no. 90-985, October Term, 1990.

75. Epstein and Walker, *Constitutional Law for a Changing America,* p. 271.

76. Lindgren and Taub, *Law of Sex Discrimination,* pp. 214–16.

77. *Harris v. Forklift Systems,* Brief for the United States and the Equal Employment Opportunity Commission as *Amicus Curiae,* no. 92-1168, October Term, 1993.

78. *Harris v. Forklift Systems* 510 US 17 (1993).

79. *Gebser v. Lago Vista Independent School District,* Brief for the United States as *Amicus Curiae* Supporting Petitioners, no. 96-1866, October Term, 1997.

80. *Gebser v. Lago Vista Independent School District* 524 US 274 (1998).

81. *Faragher v. City of Boca Raton,* Brief for the United States and the Equal Employment Opportunity Commission as *Amici Curiae* Supporting Petitioner, no. 97-282, October Term, 1997.

82. *Burlington Industries v. Ellerth* 524 US 742 (1998).

83. Bender, interview.

84. *United States v. Morrison,* Brief for the United States on Writ of Certiorari to the United States Court of Appeals for the Fourth Circuit, no. 99-5, October Term, 1999.

85. *United States v. Morrison* 529 US 598 (2000).

86. Semonche, *Keeping the Faith,* p. 391.

87. *National Organization for Women v. Scheidler,* Brief for the United States as *Amicus Curiae* Supporting Petitioners, no. 92-780, October Term, 1993.

88. *Madsen v. Women's Health Center,* Brief for the United States as *Amicus Curiae* Supporting Respondents, no. 93-880, October Term, 1993.

89. *Stenberg v. Carhart,* Brief for the United States as *Amicus Curiae* Supporting Respondent, no. 99-830, October Term, 1999.

90. *Stenberg v. Carhart* 530 US 914 (2000).

CHAPTER 8. THE SOLICITOR GENERAL

1. Of course, the OSG is also responsible for deciding which of the government's cases can be appealed to the Courts of Appeals. For the first systematic study of that stage see Christopher Zorn, *On Appeal: United States Government Litigation in the Federal Appellate Courts.*

2. S. Sidney Ulmer, "Issue Fluidity in the United States Supreme Court" in *Supreme Court Activism and Restraint,* ed. Stephen Halpern and Charles Lamb.

3. Matthew Crenson, *The Unpolitics of Air Pollution.*

4. Landsberg, *Enforcing Civil Rights.*

5. John Howard, *The Shifting Wind: The Supreme Court and Civil Rights from Reconstruction to Brown.*

6. Cooper, "The Solicitor General and the Evolution of Activism," pp. 695–96.

7. Divided government would seem to give the Court leeway to make decisions supported by the solicitor general. If the solicitor general has the backing of the president for a position

Congress opposes, the president could veto statutory retaliation. In effect, the two-thirds necessary to override a veto is equivalent to the majority needed to pass a constitutional amendment.

8. Heymann, interview.

9. Norman-Major, "The Solicitor General," p. 1109.

10. Also see Garth Pauley, *The Modern Presidency & Civil Rights: Rhetoric on Race from Roosevelt to Nixon*, pp. 204–207.

11. Bender, interview.

12. Thernstrom, *Whose Votes Count?*

13. Wallace, interview.

14. Griswold, *Ould Fields, New Corne.*

15. Skowronek, *Politics Presidents Make;* Robert McCloskey, *The American Supreme Court;* Bernard Schwartz, *A History of the Supreme Court.*

16. Richard Funston, *A Vital National Seminar: The Supreme Court in American Political Life;* William Lasser, *The Limits of Judicial Power: The Supreme Court in National Politics.*

17. Richard Neustadt, *Presidential Power: The Politics of Leadership with Reflections on Johnson and Nixon;* Segal and Spaeth, *Supreme Court and the Attitudinal Model;* Abraham, *Justices and Presidents.*

18. Frey, interview.

19. Heymann, interview.

20. The federal policy had been modified to give preference to subcontractors who fell beneath a certain economic threshold.

21. Neil Lewis, "Bush Administration Supports an Affirmative Action Position," *New York Times,* Aug. 11, 2001, p. A9.

22. Both Ashcroft and Olson faced significant opposition in the Senate. Even though Ashcroft had been a Senator, there were more than forty votes opposing his confirmation. The Judiciary Committee split 9-9 on Olson's nomination before the full Senate confirmed him. Olson also took the unprecedented step of doing the talk show circuit in the hours after the 2002 State of the Union address to defend the president.

23. Tony Mauro, "*Adarand* Vexes Administration: Solicitor General Draws Fire Over Affirmative Action Law," *Connecticut Law Tribune,* Aug. 20, 2001, p. 6.

24. N. Baker, *Conflicting Loyalties.*

25. Richard Pacelle, *The Role of the Supreme Court in American Politics: The Least Dangerous Branch?* pp. 46–47. Many argue that the professed move to restraint is nothing more than a new conservative activism couched in accepted normative terms (see, for instance, Yarbrough, *Rehnquist Court*).

References

Abraham, Henry. *Justices and Presidents: A Political History of Appointments to the Supreme Court*. New York: Oxford University Press, 1992.

Aldrich, John. "Rational Choice Theory and the Study of American Politics" in *The Dynamics of American Politics: Approaches and Interpretations,* edited by Lawrence Dodd and Calvin Jillson. Boulder: Westview, 1994.

———. *Why Parties? The Origin and Transformation of Political Parties in America*. Chicago: University of Chicago Press, 1995.

Alexander, Charles. *Holding the Line: The Eisenhower Era, 1952–1961*. Bloomington: Indiana University Press, 1975.

Amaker, Norman. *Civil Rights and the Reagan Administration*. Washington D.C.: Urban Institute, 1988.

Ambrose, Stephen. *Eisenhower: Soldier and President*. New York: Touchstone, 1991.

———. *Nixon: Volume Two, 1962–1972*. New York: Simon & Schuster, 1987.

Anderson, John. *Eisenhower, Brownell, and the Congress: The Tangled Origins of the Civil Rights Bill of 1956–1957*. Tuscaloosa: University of Alabama Press, 1964.

Arnold, R. Douglas. *Congress and the Bureaucracy: A Theory of Influence*. New Haven: Yale University Press, 1979.

Baer, Judith. *The Chains of Protection: The Judicial Response to Women's Labor Legislation*. Westport: Greenwood Press, 1978.

———. *Equality Under the Constitution: Reclaiming the Fourteenth Amendment*. Ithaca: Cornell University Press, 1983.

Bagby, Thomas, ed. *The Memphis Firefighters Case: The Impact of the Supreme Court's* Stotts *Decision on Affirmative Action, Equal Employment*

Litigation, Settlement, and Judicial Remedies. Washington, D.C.: National Foundation for the Study of Equal Employment Policy, 1985.

Baker, Gordon. *The Reapportionment Revolution: Representation, Political Power, and the Supreme Court.* New York: Random House, 1966.

Baker, Nancy. *Conflicting Loyalties: Law and Politics in the Attorney General's Office, 1789–1990.* Lawrence: University Press of Kansas, 1992.

Ball, Howard. *The* Bakke *Case: Race, Education, & Affirmative Action.* Lawrence: University Press of Kansas, 2000.

Baum, Lawrence. "Comparing the Policy Positions of Supreme Court Justices From Different Periods." *Western Political Quarterly* 42 (1989): 509–22.

———. "Measuring Policy Change in the U.S. Supreme Court." *American Political Science Review* 82 (1988): 905–12.

———. "Membership Change and Collective Voting Change in the United States Supreme Court." *Journal of Politics* 54 (1992): 3–24.

———. *The Puzzle of Judicial Behavior.* Ann Arbor: University of Michigan Press, 1997.

Belknap, Michal. *Federal Law and Southern Order: Racial Violence and Constitutional Conflict in the Post-*Brown *South.* Athens: University of Georgia Press, 1987.

Bell, Derrick, Jr. *Race, Racism, and American Law.* 2d ed. Boston: Little, Brown, 1980.

Bell, Griffin, with Ronald Ostrow. *Taking Care of the Law.* New York: William Morrow, 1982.

Berg, John. *Unequal Struggle: Class, Gender, Race, and Power in the U.S. Congress.* Boulder: Westview, 1994.

Berman, Daniel. *A Bill Becomes a Law: The Civil Rights Act of 1960.* New York: Macmillan, 1962.

Berman, William. *The Politics of Civil Rights in the Truman Administration.* Columbus: Ohio State University Press, 1970.

Berry, Mary Frances. *Why ERA Failed: Politics, Women's Rights, and the Amending Process of the Constitution.* Bloomington: Indiana University Press, 1986.

Binder, Sarah, and Steven Smith. *Politics or Principle? Filibustering in the United States Senate.* Washington D.C.: Brookings Institution, 1997.

Biskupic, Joan. *The Supreme Court Yearbook, 1989–1990.* Washington D.C.: Congressional Quarterly, 1991.

Bland, Randall. *Private Pressure on Public Law: The Legal Career of Justice Thurgood Marshall: 1934–1991.* Rev. ed. Lanham: University Press of America, 1993.

References

Blank, Robert. *Fetal Protection in the Workplace: Women's Rights, Business Interests, and the Unborn.* New York: Columbia University Press, 1993.

Blumrosen, Alfred. *Modern Law: The Law Transmission System and Equal Employment Opportunity.* Madison: University of Wisconsin Press, 1993.

Bork, Robert, *The Tempting of America: The Political Seduction of the Law.* New York: Free Press, 1990.

Borrelli, MaryAnne. "Campaign Promises, Transition Dilemmas: Cabinet Building and Executive Representation." In *The Other Elites: Women, Politics, and Power in the Executive Branch,* edited by MaryAnne Borrelli and Janet Martin. Boulder: Lynne Reiner, 1997.

Bourne, Peter. *Jimmy Carter: A Comprehensive Biography From Plains to Postpresidency.* New York: Scribners, 1997.

Brace, Paul, and Melinda Gann Hall. "Integrated Models of Judicial Dissent." *Journal of Politics* 55 (1993): 914–35.

Brady, David, and Craig Volden. *Revolving Gridlock: Politics and Policy from Carter to Clinton.* Boulder: Westview, 1998.

Branch, Taylor. *Parting the Waters: America in the King Years 1954–1963.* New York: Simon & Schuster, 1988.

Brigham, William. "The Office of the Solicitor General of the United States." Ph.D. diss., University of North Carolina, Chapel Hill, 1966.

Brinkley, Douglas. *The Unfinished Presidency: Jimmy Carter's Journey Beyond the White House.* New York: Viking, 1998.

Brownell, Herbert, with John Burke. *Advising Ike: The Memoirs of Herbert Brownell.* Lawrence: University Press of Kansas, 1993.

Burk, Robert Frederick. *The Eisenhower Administration and Black Civil Rights.* Knoxville: University of Tennessee Press, 1984.

Cain, Patricia. "Feminism and the Limits of Equality." In *Feminist Legal Theory: Foundations,* edited by D. Kelly Weisberg. Philadelphia: Temple University Press, 1993.

Califano, Joseph. *Governing America: An Insider's Report from the White House and the Cabinet.* New York: Simon & Schuster, 1981.

Cannon, James. *Time and Chance: Gerald Ford's Appointment with History.* Ann Arbor: University of Michigan Press, 1994.

Caplan, Lincoln. "The Reagan Challenge to the Rule of Law." In *The Reagan Legacy,* edited by Sidney Blumenthal and Thomas Byrne Edsall. New York: Pantheon Books, 1988.

———. *The Tenth Justice: The Solicitor General and the Rule of Law.* New York: Vintage Books, 1987.

Carmines, Edward, and James Stimson. *Issue Evolution: Race and the*

Transformation of American Politics. Princeton: Princeton University Press, 1989.

Casper, Jonathan. *The Politics of Civil Liberties.* New York: Harper & Row, 1972.

Chamberlain, Ronald. "Mixing Politics and Justice: The Office of Solicitor General." *Journal of Law & Politics* 4 (1987): 379–428.

Cheney, Timothy. *Who Makes the Law: The Supreme Court, Congress, the States, and Society.* Upper Saddle River: Prentice-Hall, 1998.

Claude, Richard. *The Supreme Court and the Electoral Process.* Baltimore: Johns Hopkins Press, 1970.

Clayton, Cornell. *Government Lawyers: The Federal Legal Bureaucracy and Presidential Politics.* Lawrence: University of Kansas Press, 1995.

————. *The Politics of Justice: The Attorney General and the Making of Legal Policy.* Armonk: M.E. Sharpe, 1992.

Clayton, Susan, and Faye Crosby. *Justice, Gender, and Affirmative Action.* Ann Arbor: University of Michigan Press, 1992.

Clegg, Roger. "Epilogue: Civil Rights in the Eighties and Nineties." *Louisiana Law Review* 54 (1994): 1605–17.

Collier, Kenneth. *Between the Branches: The White House Office of Legislative Affairs.* Pittsburgh: University of Pittsburgh Press, 1997.

Cooper, James. "The Solicitor General and Federal Litigation: Principal-Agent Relationships and the Separation of Powers." Ph.D. diss., Indiana University, Bloomington, 1993.

————. "The Solicitor General and the Evolution of Activism." *Indiana Law Journal* 65 (1990): 675–96.

Cortner, Richard. *The Apportionment Cases.* Knoxville: University of Tennessee Press, 1970.

————. *The Supreme Court and the Second Bill of Rights: The Fourteenth Amendment and the Nationalization of Civil Rights.* Madison: University of Wisconsin Press, 1981.

Crenson, Matthew. *The Unpolitics of Air Pollution.* Baltimore: Johns Hopkins University Press, 1971.

Curtis, Thomas, and Donald Westerfield. *Congressional Intent.* New York: Praeger, 1992.

Dallek, Robert. *Flawed Giant: Lyndon Johnson and His Times, 1961–1973.* New York: Oxford University Press, 1998.

Davidson, Chandler. "The Evolution of Voting Rights Law Affecting Racial and Language Minorities" in *Quiet Revolution in the South: The Impact of the Voting Rights Act, 1965–1990,* edited by Chandler Davidson and Bernard Grofman. Princeton: Princeton University Press, 1994.

Davis, Michael, and Hunter Clark. *Thurgood Marshall: Warrior at the Bar, Rebel on the Bench*. New York: Birch Lane Press, 1992.

Days, Drew. "In Search of the Solicitor General's Client: A Drama with Many Characters." *Kentucky Law Review* 83 (1994–95): 485–503.

———. "The Interests of the United States, the Solicitor General and Individual Rights." *Saint Louis Law Review* 41 (1996): 1–8.

———. "The Solicitor General and the American Legal Ideal." *SMU Law Review* 49 (1995): 73–82.

Detlefsen, Robert. *Civil Rights Under Reagan*. San Francisco: Institute for Contemporary Studies, 1991.

Devins, Neal. *Shaping Constitutional Values: Elected Government, the Supreme Court, and the Abortion Debate*. Baltimore: Johns Hopkins University Press, 1996.

———. "Toward an Understanding of Legal Policy-Making at Independent Agencies." In *Government Lawyers: The Federal Legal Bureaucracy and Presidential Politics,* edited by Cornell Clayton. Lawrence: University Press of Kansas, 1995.

———. "Unitariness and Independence: Solicitor General Control over Independent Agency Litigation." *California Law Review* 82 (1994): 255–327.

Dixon, Robert. "The Attorney General and Civil Rights 1870–1964." In *Roles of the Attorney General of the United States,* edited by Luther Huston, Arthur Selwyn Miller, Samuel Krislov, and Robert Dixon, 105–52. Washington, D.C.: American Enterprise Institute, 1968.

———. *Democratic Representation: Reapportionment in Law and Politics*. New York: Oxford University Press, 1968.

Domino, John. *Civil Rights & Liberties: Toward the 21st Century*. New York: Harper-Collins, 1994.

Eastland, Terry. *Ending Affirmative Action*. New York: Harper-Collins, 1996.

Edwards, Don. "The Voting Rights Act of 1965, As Amended." In *The Voting Rights Act: Consequences and Implications,* ed. Lorn Foster. New York: Praeger, 1985.

Eisenhower, Dwight. *Waging Peace: The White House Years, 1956–1961*. Garden City: Doubleday, 1965.

Eisler, Kim Isaac. *A Justice For All: William J. Brennan, Jr. and the Decisions That Transformed America*. New York: Simon & Schuster, 1993.

Elliff, John. "The United States Department of Justice and Individual Rights." Ph.D. diss., Harvard University, 1967.

Elman, Philip. "The Solicitor General's Office, Justice Frankfurter, and Civil Rights Litigation." *Harvard Law Review* 100 (1987): 817–52.

Emerson, Thomas. "Nine Justices in Search of a Doctrine." *Michigan Law Review* 64 (1965): 219–34.

Engstrom, Richard. "Racial Vote Dilution: The Concept and The Court." In *The Voting Rights Act: Consequences and Implications,* ed. Lorn Foster. New York: Praeger, 1985.

Engstrom, Richard, Stanley Halpin, Jean Hill, and Victoria Caridas-Butterworth. "Louisiana." In *Quiet Revolution in the South: The Impact of the Voting Rights Act, 1965–1990,* edited by Chandler Davidson and Bernard Grofman. Princeton: Princeton University Press, *1994.*

Epp, Charles. *The Rights Revolution: Lawyers, Activists, and Supreme Court in Comparative Perspective.* Chicago: University of Chicago Press, 1998.

Epstein, Lee, and Jack Knight. *The Choices Justices Make.* Washington D.C.: CQ Press, 1998.

Epstein, Lee, and Joseph Kobylka. *The Supreme Court and Legal Change: Abortion and the Death Penalty.* Chapel Hill: University of North Carolina Press, 1992.

Epstein, Lee, Jeffrey Segal, Harold Spaeth, and Thomas Walker. *The Supreme Court Compendium.* 2d ed. Washington D.C.: Congressional Quarterly, 1997.

Epstein, Lee, and Thomas Walker. *Constitutional Law for a Changing America: Rights, Liberties, and Justice.* 3d ed. Washington, D.C.: Congressional Quarterly, 1998.

Epstein, Richard. *Forbidden Grounds: The Case Against Employment Discrimination Laws.* Cambridge: Harvard University Press, 1992.

Eskridge, William. *Dynamic Statutory Interpretation.* Cambridge: Harvard University Press, 1994.

———. "Overriding Supreme Court Statutory Interpretation Decisions." *Yale Law Journal* 101 (1991): 331–417.

———. "Reneging on History? Playing the Court/Congress/President Civil Rights Game" *California Law Review* 79 (1991): 613–84.

Evans, C. Lawrence, and Walter Oleszek. *Congress Under Fire: Reform Politics and the Republican Majority.* Boston: Houghton Mifflin, 1997.

Fahy, Charles. "The Office of the Solicitor General." *American Bar Association Journal* 28 (1942): 20–22.

Faux, Marian. *Crusaders: Voices from the Abortion Front.* New York: Birch Lane Press, 1990.

———. *Roe v. Wade.* New York: Macmillan, 1988.

Fenno, Richard. *Congressmen in Committees.* Boston: Little Brown, 1973.

Fiorina, Morris. *Divided Government.* 2d ed. New York: Macmillan, 1996.

Fisher, Louis, and Neal Devins. *Political Dynamics of Constitutional Law.* St. Paul: West, 1992.

Fiss, Owen. *The Civil Rights Injunction.* Bloomington: Indiana University Press, 1978.

Fleisher, Richard, and Jon Bond. "The President in a More Partisan Legislative Arena." *Political Research Quarterly* 49 (December, 1996): 729–48.

Ford, Gerald. *A Time to Heal.* New York: Harper & Row, 1979.

Fried, Charles. *Order and Law: Arguing the Reagan Revolution.* New York: Simon & Schuster, 1991.

Funston, Richard. *A Vital National Seminar: The Supreme Court in American Political Life.* Palo Alto: Mayfield, 1978.

Galanter, Marc. "Why the 'Haves' Come Out Ahead: Speculations on the Limits of Legal Change." *Law & Society Review* 9 (1974): 95–160.

Genovese, Michael. *The Nixon Presidency: Power and Politics in Turbulent Times.* New York: Greenwood, 1990.

George, Tracey, and Lee Epstein. "On the Nature of Supreme Court Decision Making." *American Political Science Review* 86 (1992): 323–37.

———. "Women's Rights Litigation in the 1980s: More of the Same?" *Judicature* 74 (1991): 314–21.

Ginsburg, Ruth Bader. "The Burger Court's Grappling with Sex Discrimination." In *The Burger Court: The Counter-Revolution that Wasn't,* edited by Vincent Blasi. New Haven: Yale University Press, 1983.

Goldman, Sheldon. *Picking Federal Judges: Lower Court Selection from Roosevelt Through Reagan.* New Haven: Yale University Press, 1997.

———. "Voting Behavior on the United States Courts of Appeals Revisited." *American Political Science Review* 69 (1975): 491–506.

Goldstein, Leslie Friedman. *The Constitutional Rights of Women: Cases in Law and Social Change.* Madison: University of Wisconsin Press, 1988.

Goldstein, Leslie Friedman, and Diana Stech. "Explaining Transformations in Supreme Court Policy." *Judicature* 79 (1995): 80–85.

Gormley, Ken. *Archibald Cox: Conscience of a Nation.* Reading: Addison-Wesley, 1997.

Gormley, William. *Taming the Bureaucracy: Muscles, Prayer, and Other Strategies.* Princeton: Princeton University Press, 1989.

Graber, Mark. *Rethinking Abortion: Equal Choice, the Constitution, and Reproductive Rights.* Princeton: Princeton University Press, 1996.

Graham, Gene. *One Man, One Vote:* Baker v. Carr *and the American Levelers.* New York: Little, Brown, 1972.

Graham, Hugh Davis. *The Civil Rights Era: Origins and Development of National Policy 1960–1972.* New York: Oxford University Press, 1990.

Greenberg, Jack. *Crusaders in the Court.* New York: Basic Books, 1994.

Greene, John Robert. *The Limits of Power: The Nixon and Ford Administrations.* Bloomington: Indiana University Press, 1992.

———. *The Presidency of Gerald R. Ford.* Lawrence: University Press of Kansas, 1992.

Griswold, Erwin. *Ould Fields, New Corne: The Personal Memoirs of a Twentieth Century Lawyer.* St. Paul: West, 1992.

Grofman, Bernard. "*Shaw v. Reno* and the Future of Voting Rights." *PS* 28 (1995): 27–36.

Grofman, Bernard, Lisa Handley, and Richard Niemi. *Minority Representation and the Quest for Voting Equality.* New York: Cambridge University Press, 1992.

Guinier, Lani. *The Tyranny of the Majority: Fundamental Fairness in Representative Democracy.* New York: Free Press, 1994.

Halpern, Stephen. *On the Limits of the Law: The Ironic Legacy of Title VI of the 1964 Civil Rights Act.* Baltimore: Johns Hopkins University Press, 1995.

Hanson, Royce. *The Political Thicket: Reapportionment and Constitutional Democracy.* Englewood Cliffs: Prentice-Hall, 1996.

Hausegger, Lori, and Lawrence Baum. "Inviting Congressional Action: A Study of Supreme Court Motivations in Statutory Interpretation." *American Journal of Political Science* 43 (1999): 162–83.

Herrnson, Paul. *Congressional Elections: Campaigning at Home and in Washington.* 2d ed. Washington, D.C.: CQ Press, 1998.

Hockett, Jeffrey. *New Deal Justice: The Constitutional Jurisprudence of Hugo L. Black, Felix Frankfurter, and Robert H. Jackson.* Latham: Rowman & Littlefield, 1996.

Hoff, Joan. *Law, Gender, and Injustice: A Legal History of U.S. Women.* New York: New York University Press, 1991.

Holden, Matthew. "Race and Constitutional Change in the Twentieth Century: The Role of the Executive." In *African Americans and the Living Constitution,* edited by John Hope Franklin and Genna Rae McNeil. Washington, D.C.: Smithsonian Institution Press, 1995.

Horowitz, Donald. *The Courts and Social Policy.* Washington, D.C.: Brookings Institution, 1977.

————. *The Jurocracy.* Lexington: Lexington Books, 1977.

Horwitz, Morton. *The Warren Court and the Pursuit of Justice.* New York: Hill and Wang, 1998.

Howard, John. *The Shifting Wind: The Supreme Court and Civil Rights from Reconstruction to Brown.* New York: State University of New York Press, 1999.

Hubbell, Webb. *Friends in High Places: Our Journey from Little Rock to Washington, D.C.* New York: Morrow, 1998.

Hurwitz, Mark. "The Nature of Agenda in the United States Supreme Court and Courts of Appeals." Ph.D. diss., Michigan State University, East Lansing, 1998.

Huston, Luther. *The Department of Justice.* New York: Praeger, 1967.

————. "History of the Office of the Attorney General." In *Roles of the Attorney General of the United States,* edited by Luther Huston, Arthur Selwyn Miller, Samuel Krislov, and Robert Dixon, 1–39. Washington, D.C.: American Enterprise Institute, 1968.

Irons, Peter. *The Courage of Their Convictions.* New York: Macmillan, 1988.

Jackson, Donald. *Even the Children of Strangers: Equality Under the U.S. Constitution.* Lawrence: University Press of Kansas, 1992.

Jackson, Robert. *The Struggle for Judicial Supremacy: A Study of a Crisis in American Power Politics.* New York: Knopf, 1941.

Jenkins, John. "The Solicitor General's Winning Ways." *ABA Law Journal* 69 (1983): 734–38.

Johnson, Lyndon. *The Vantage Point: Perspectives of the Presidency 1963–1969.* New York: Holt, Rinehart, and Winston, 1971.

Johnson, Timothy. "Oral Advocacy and the Supreme Court." Ph.D. diss., Washington University, St. Louis, 1998.

Jones, Charles. *The Trusteeship Presidency: Jimmy Carter and the U.S. Congress.* Baton Rouge: LSU Press, 1988.

Kahn, Ronald. *The Supreme Court & Constitutional Theory: 1953–1993.* Lawrence: University Press of Kansas, 1994.

Kaminer, Wendy. *A Fearful Freedom: Women's Flight From Equality.* Reading: Addison-Wesley, 1990.

Katzmann, Robert. *Courts and Congress.* Washington, D.C.: Brookings Institution Press, 1997.

Kenney, Sally. *For Whose Protection? Reproductive Hazards and Exclusionary Policies in the United States and Britain.* Ann Arbor: University of Michigan Press, 1992.

Keynes, Edward, with Randall Miller. *The Court Versus Congress: Prayer, Busing, and Abortion.* Durham: Duke University Press, 1989.

Kiewiet, D. Roderick, and Matthew McCubbins. *The Logic of Delegation.* Chicago: University of Chicago Press, 1991.

Kindred, Kay. "Civil Rights and Higher Education." In *A Year in the Life of the Supreme Court,* edited by Rodney Smolla. Durham: Duke University Press, 1995.

Kirp, David, Mark Yuldorf, and Marlene Strong Franks. *Gender Justice.* Chicago: University of Chicago Press, 1986.

Kleven, Thomas. "The Constitutional Philosophy of Justice William H. Rehnquist." *Vermont Law Review* 8 (1983): 1–54.

Kluger, Richard. *Simple Justice.* New York: Knopf, 1975.

Knight, Jack. *Institutions and Social Conflict.* New York: Oxford University Press, 1992.

Kobylka, Joseph. "A Court-Related Context for Group Litigation: Libertarian Groups and Obscenity." *Journal of Politics* 49 (1987): 1061–79.

Krislov, Samuel. "The *Amicus Curiae* Brief: From Friendship to Advocacy." *Yale Law Journal* 72 (1963): 694–721.

———. "The Role of the Attorney General as *Amicus Curiae.*" In *Roles of the Attorney General of the United States,* edited by Luther Huston, Arthur Selwyn Miller, Samuel Krislov, and Robert Dixon. Washington, D.C.: American Enterprise Institute, 1968.

Landsberg, Brian. *Enforcing Civil Rights: Race Discrimination and the Department of Justice.* Lawrence: University Press of Kansas, 1997.

Lasser, William. *The Limits of Judicial Power: The Supreme Court in National Politics.* Chapel Hill: University of North Carolina Press, 1988.

Lee, Rex. "Lawyering for the Government: Politics, Polemics & Principle." *Ohio State Law Journal* 47 (1986): 595–601.

LeLoup, Lance, and Steven Shull, *The President and Congress: Collaboration and Combat in National Policy-Making 1960–1972.* Needham Heights: Allyn & Bacon, 1997.

Levin-Epstein, Michael. *Primer of Equal Employment Opportunity.* 4th ed. Washington, D.C.: Bureau of National Affairs, 1987.

Levit, Nancy. *The Gender Line: Men, Women, and the Law.* New York: New York University Press, 1998.

Lewis, Anthony. *Make No Law: The Sullivan Case and the First Amendment.* New York: Vintage Books, 1991.

Lewis, David, and James Michael Strine. "What Time Is It? The Use of Power in Four Different Types of Presidential Time." *Journal of Politics* 58 (1996): 682–706.

References

Lewis, Neil. "Bush Administration Supports an Affirmative Action Position," *New York Times,* Aug. 11, 2001, p. A9.

Light, Paul. *The President's Agenda: Domestic Policy Choice from Kennedy to Carter.* Baltimore: Johns Hopkins University Press, 1982.

Lindgren, J. Ralph, and Nadine Taub. *The Law of Sex Discrimination.* 2d ed. Minneapolis: West, 1993.

Luker, Kristen. *Abortion and the Politics of Motherhood.* Berkeley: University of California Press, 1984.

MacKinnon, Catherine. *The Sexual Harassment of Working Women.* New Haven: Yale University Press, 1979.

Marshall, Burke. *Federalism and Civil Rights.* New York: Columbia University Press, 1964.

Maschke, Karen. *Litigation, Courts, and Women Workers.* New York: Praeger, 1989.

Matthews, Donald, and James Prothro. *Negroes and the New Southern Politics.* New York: Harcourt, Brace & World, 1966.

Mauro, Tony. "*Adarand* Vexes Administration: Solicitor General Draws Fire Over Affirmative Action Law." *Connecticut Law Tribune,* Aug. 20, 2001, p. 6.

Maveety, Nancy. *Justice Sandra Day O'Connor: Strategist on the Supreme Court.* Latham: Rowman & Littlefield, 1996.

Mayhew, David. *Congress: The Electoral Connection.* New Haven: Yale University Press, 1974.

McCann, Michael. *Rights At Work: Pay Equity Reform and the Politics of Legal Mobilization.* Chicago: University of Chicago Press, 1994.

McCloskey, Robert. *The American Supreme Court.* Chicago: University of Chicago Press, 1960.

McCullough, David. *Truman.* New York: Simon & Schuster, 1992.

McDowell, Douglas. *Affirmative Action After the* Johnson *Decision: Practical Guidance for Planning and Compliance.* Washington, D.C.: National Foundation for the Study of Equal Employment Policy, 1987.

———. *The 1986 Affirmative Action Trilogy: A Guide to Questions Left Open by the Supreme Court's Decisions in* Local 28, Wygant, *and* Cleveland Vanguards. Washington, D.C.: National Foundation for the Study of Equal Employment Policy, 1987.

McDowell, Gary. *Equity and the Constitution.* Chicago: University of Chicago Press, 1982.

McGuire, Kevin. "Repeat Players in the Supreme Court: The Role of Experienced Lawyers in Litigation Success." *Journal of Politics* 57 (1995): 187–96.

————. *The Supreme Court Bar: Legal Elites in the Washington Community.* Charlottesville: University of Virginia Press, 1993.

McKeever, Robert. *Raw Judicial Power? The Supreme Court and American Society.* 2d ed. Manchester: Manchester University Press, 1995.

Meier, Kenneth, Joseph Stewart, and Robert England. *Race, Class, and Education: The Politics of Second-Generation Discrimination.* Madison: University of Wisconsin Press, 1989.

Melich, Tanya. *The Republican War Against Women.* New York: Bantam, 1996.

Mezey, Susan Gluck. *In Pursuit of Equality: Women, Public Policy, and the Federal Courts.* New York: St. Martin's, 1992.

Milkis, Sidney. *The President and the Parties: The Transformation of the American Party System Since the New Deal.* New York: Oxford University Press, 1993.

Minow, Martha. "The Supreme Court 1986 Term, Foreword: Justice Engendered." In *Feminist Legal Theory: Foundations,* edited by D. Kelly Weisberg. Philadelphia: Temple University Press, 1993.

Murphy, Walter. *Congress and the Court.* University of Chicago Press, 1962.

Navasky, Victor. *Kennedy Justice.* New York: Atheneum, 1971.

Neustadt, Richard. *Presidential Power: The Politics of Leadership with Reflections on Johnson and Nixon.* New York: John Wiley, 1976.

Nixon, Richard. *RN: The Memoirs of Richard Nixon.* New York: Simon & Schuster, 1978.

Norman-Major, Kristen. "The Solicitor General: Executive Policy Agendas and the Court." *Albany Law Review* 57 (1994): 1081–109.

O'Connor, Karen. "The *Amicus Curiae* Role of the U.S. Solicitor General in Supreme Court Litigation." *Judicature* 66 (1983): 256–64.

————. *No Neutral Ground?: Abortion Politics in an Age of Absolutes.* Boulder: Westview, 1996.

————. *Women's Organizations' Use of the Courts.* Lexington: Lexington Books, 1980.

O'Connor, Karen, and Lee Epstein. "Beyond Legislative Lobbying: Women's Rights Groups and the Supreme Court." *Judicature* 67 (1983): 134–43.

Office of Legal Counsel, "Memorandum Opinion for the Attorney General: Role of the Solicitor General." *Loyola of Los Angeles Law Review* (1988): 1089–97.

Okin, Susan Moller. *Justice, Gender, and the Family.* New York: Basic Books, 1989.

Orfield, Gary. "Congress and Civil Rights: From Obstacle to Protector." In *African Americans and the Living Constitution,* edited by John Hope Franklin and Genna Rae McNeil. Washington: Smithsonian Institution Press, 1995.

———. *Congressional Power: Congress and Social Change.* New York: Harcourt Brace Jovanovich, 1975.

———. "Turning Back to Segregation." In *Dismantling Desegregation: The Quiet Reversal of* Brown v. Board of Education, edited by Gary Orfield, Susan Eaton, and the Harvard Project on School Desegregation. New York: New Press, 1996.

O'Rourke, Timothy. *The Impact of Reapportionment.* New Brunswick: Transaction Books, 1980.

Osborn, John. "Legal Philosophy and Judicial Review of Agency Statutory Interpretation." *Harvard Journal of Legislation* 36 (1999): 115–59.

Otten, Laura. *Women's Rights and the Law.* Westport: Praeger, 1993.

Overby, L. Marvin, and Kenneth Cosgrove. "Unintended Consequences? Racial Redistricting and the Representation of Minority Interests." *Journal of Politics* 58 (1996): 540–58.

Pacelle, Richard. "The Dynamics and Determinants of Agenda Change in the Rehnquist Court." In *Contemplating Courts,* edited by Lee Epstein. Washington, D.C.: Congressional Quarterly, 1995.

———. "A President's Legacy: Gender and Appointment to the Federal Courts." In *The Other Elites: Women, Politics, and Power in the Executive Branch,* edited by MaryAnne Borrelli and Janet Martin. Boulder: Lynne Reiner, 1997.

———. *The Role of the Supreme Court in American Politics: The Least Dangerous Branch?* Boulder: Westview, 2002.

———. "The Solicitor General and Gender: Litigating the President's Agenda and Serving the Supreme Court." In *The Other Elites: Women, Politics, and Power in the Executive Branch,* edited by MaryAnne Borrelli and Janet Martin. Boulder: Lynne Reiner, 1997.

———. "The Supreme Court's Agenda and the Dynamics of Policy Evolution." Paper presented at American Political Science Association meetings, 1990.

———. *The Transformation of the Supreme Court's Agenda: From the New Deal to the Reagan Administration.* Boulder: Westview, 1991.

Parmet. Herbert. *George Bush: The Life of a Lone Star Yankee.* New York: Scribner, 1997.

Patterson, James. Brown v. Board of Education: *A Civil Rights Milestone and its Troubled Legacy.* New York: Oxford University Press, 2001.

Pauley, Garth. *The Modern Presidency & Civil Rights: Rhetoric on Race from Roosevelt to Nixon*. College Station: Texas A&M University Press, 2001.

Peacock, Anthony. "*Shaw v. Reno* and the Voting Rights Conundrum: Equality, The Public Interest, and the Politics of Representation." In *Affirmative Action and Representation:* Shaw v. Reno *and the Future of Voting Rights,* edited by Anthony Peacock. Durham: Carolina Academic Press, 1997.

————. "Voting Rights, Representation, and the Problem of Equality." In *Affirmative Action and Representation:* Shaw v. Reno *and the Future of Voting Rights,* edited by Anthony Peacock. Durham: Carolina Academic Press, 1997.

Perry, H. W. *Deciding to Decide: Agenda Setting in the U.S. Supreme Court*. Cambridge: Harvard University Press, 1991.

Peterson, Mark. *Legislating Together: The White House and Capitol Hill from Eisenhower to Reagan*. Cambridge: Harvard University Press, 1990.

Pfiffner James. *The Modern Presidency*. 2d ed. New York: St. Martin's, 1998.

Pierce, Richard. "The Supreme Court's New Hypertextualism: An Invitation to Cacophony and Incoherence in the Administrative State." *Columbia Law Review* 95 (1995): 749–81.

Pritchett, C. Herman. *Civil Liberties and the Vinson Court*. Chicago: University of Chicago Press, 1954.

————. *Constitutional Civil Liberties*. Englewood Cliffs: Prentice-Hall, 1984.

Puro, Stephen. "The Role of the *Amicus Curiae* in the United States Supreme Court." Ph.D. diss., State University of New York, Buffalo, 1971.

————. "The United States as *Amicus Curiae*." In *Courts, Law, and Judicial Processes,* edited by S. Sidney Ulmer. New York: Free Press, 1981.

Quirk, Paul. "Domestic Policy: Divided Government and Cooperative Presidential Leadership." In *The Bush Presidency,* edited by Colin Campbell and Bert Rockham. Chatham: Chatham House, 1991.

Reed, Roy. *Faubus: The Life and Times of an American Prodigal*. Fayettesville: University of Arkansas Press, 1997.

Reeves, Richard. *President Kennedy: Portrait of Power*. New York: Touchstone, 1993.

Reichley, A. James. *Conservatives In an Era of Change*. Washington, D.C.: Brookings Institution, 1981.

Reske, Henry. "A Flap Over Flip-Flops: Solicitor General Says Changing Court Stances Not Unusual or Wrong." *ABA Journal* 80 (1994): 12–15.

Rhode, Deborah. *Justice and Gender: Sex Discrimination and the Law.* Cambridge: Harvard University Press, 1989.

Richardson, Elmo. *The Presidency of Dwight D. Eisenhower.* Lawrence: Regents Press of Kansas, 1979.

Rieselbach, Leroy. *Congressional Politics.* Boulder: Westview, 1995.

Rose, David. "Twenty-Five Years Later: Where Do We Stand on Equal Employment Opportunity Law Enforcement?" *Vanderbilt Law Review* 42 (1989): 1121–82.

Rubin, Eva. *Abortion, Politics, and the Courts.* Westport: Greenwood, 1987.

———. *The Supreme Court and the American Family.* Westport: Greenwood, 1986.

Rudko, Frances Howell. *Truman's Court: A Study in Judicial Restraint.* New York: Greenwood, 1988.

Salokar, Rebecca. *The Solicitor General: The Politics of Law.* Philadelphia: Temple University Press, 1992.

Samuels, Suzanne Uttaro. *Fetal Rights, Women's Rights.* Madison: University of Wisconsin Press, 1995.

Savage, David. *Turning Right: The Making of the Rehnquist Supreme Court.* New York: Wiley, 1992.

Savage, Sean. *Truman and the Democratic Party.* Lexington: University of Kentucky Press, 1997.

Schnapper, Eric. "Becket at the Bar—the Conflicting Obligations of the Solicitor General." *Loyola of Los Angeles Law Review* 21 (1988): 1187–271.

Schubert, Glendon. *The Judicial Mind Revisited.* New York: Oxford University Press, 1974.

Schwartz, Bernard. *The Ascent of Pragmatism: The Burger Court in Action.* Reading: Addison-Wesley, 1990.

———. *Decision: How the Supreme Court Decides Cases.* New York: Oxford University Press, 1996.

———. *A History of the Supreme Court.* New York: Oxford University Press, 1993.

———. *Super Chief: Earl Warren and His Supreme Court—A Judicial Biography.* New York: New York University Press, 1983.

———. *Swann's Way: The School Busing Case and the Supreme Court.* New York: Oxford University Press, 1986.

Schwartz, Herman. *Packing the Court: The Conservative Campaign to Rewrite the Constitution.* New York: Scribners, 1988.

Schwartz, Joshua. "Two Perspectives on the Solicitor General's Independence." *Loyola of Los Angeles Law Review* 21 (1988): 1119–66.

Scigliano, Robert. *The Supreme Court and the Presidency.* New York: Free Press, 1971.

Segal, Jeffrey. "*Amicus Curiae* Briefs by the Solicitor General During the Warren and Burger Courts: A Research Note." *Western Political Quarterly* 41 (1988): 135–44.

———. "Predicting Supreme Court Cases Probabilistically: The Search and Seizure Cases, 1962–1981." *American Political Science Review* 78 (1984): 891–900.

———. "Supreme Court Support for the Solicitor General: The Effect of Presidential Appointments." *Western Political Quarterly* 43 (1990): 137–52.

Segal, Jeffrey, and Albert Cover. "Ideological Values and the Votes of U.S. Supreme Court Justices." *American Political Science Review* 83 (1989): 557–65.

Segal, Jeffrey, Lee Epstein, Charles Cameron, and Harold Spaeth. "Ideological Values and the Votes of U.S. Supreme Court Justices Revisited." *Journal of Politics* 57 (1995): 812–23.

Segal, Jeffrey and Cheryl Reedy. "The Supreme Court and Sex Discrimination: The Role of the Solicitor General." *Western Political Quarterly* 41 (1988): 553–68.

Segal, Jeffrey and Harold Spaeth. *The Supreme Court and the Attitudinal Model.* New York: Cambridge University Press, 1993.

Selig, Joel. "The Reagan Justice Department and Civil Rights: What Went Wrong?" *University of Illinois Law Review* (1985): 785–835.

Semonche, John. *Keeping the Faith: A Cultural History of the U.S. Supreme Court.* Lanham: Rowman & Littlefield, 1998.

Seymour, Stephanie. "Women as Constitutional Equals: The Burger Court's Overdue Evolution." In *The Burger Court: Counter-Revolution or Confirmation?* edited by Bernard Schwartz. New York: Oxford University Press, 1998.

Shull, Steven. *A Kinder, Gentler Racism? The Reagan-Bush Civil Rights Legacy.* Armonk: M.E. Sharpe, 1993.

Silverstein, Mark. *Judicious Choices: The New Politics of Supreme Court Confirmations.* New York: Norton, 1994.

Simon, James. *The Center Holds: The Power Struggle Inside the Rehnquist Court.* New York: Simon & Schuster, 1995.

Sinclair, Barbara. "Governing Unheroically (and Sometimes Unappetizingly): Bush and the 101st Congress." In *The Bush Presidency,* edited by Colin Campbell and Bert Rockham. Chatham: Chatham House, 1991.

Skowronek, Stephen. *The Politics Presidents Make: Leadership from John Adams to Bill Clinton.* Cambridge: Belknap Press, 1997.

Smith, Martin. *Pressure Power & Policy: State Autonomy and Policy Networks in Britain and the United States.* Pittsburgh: University of Pittsburgh Press, 1993.

Smith, Robert. *Racism in the Post–Civil Rights Era: Now You See It, Now You Don't.* Albany: State University Press of New York, 1995.

Smith, William French. *Law & Justice in the Reagan Administration: Memoirs of an Attorney General.* Stanford: Hoover Institution Press, 1991.

Songer, Donald, and Stefanie Lindquist. "Not the Whole Story: The Impact of Justices' Values on Supreme Court Decision Making." *American Journal of Political Science* 40 (1996): 1049–63.

Spann, Girardeau. *Race Against the Court: The Supreme Court and Minorities in Contemporary America.* New York: New York University Press, 1993.

Spitzer, Robert. *President & Congress: Executive Hegemony at the Crossroads of American Government.* New York: McGraw-Hill, 1993.

Staggenborg, Suzanne. *The Pro-Choice Movement: Organization and Activism in the Abortion Conflict.* New York: Oxford University Press, 1991.

Stern, Mark. "Presidential Strategies and Civil Rights: Eisenhower the Early Years, 1952–54." *Presidential Studies Quarterly* 19 (1989): 769–95.

Stimson, James, Michael MacKuen, and Robert Erickson. "Dynamic Representation." *American Political Science Review* 89 (1995): 543–65.

Sundquist, James. *The Decline and Resurgence of Congress.* Washington, D.C.: Brookings Institution, 1981.

———. *Politics and Policy: The Eisenhower, Kennedy, and Johnson Years.* Washington, D.C.: Brookings Institution, 1968.

Symposium. "The Department of Justice and the Civil Rights Act of 1964." *Pacific Law Journal* 26 (1995): 765–811.

Thernstrom, Abigail. "More Notes from a Political Thicket." In *Affirmative Action and Representation:* Shaw v. Reno *and the Future of Voting Rights,* edited by Anthony Peacock. Durham: Carolina Academic Press, 1997.

———. *Whose Votes Count? Affirmative Action and Minority Voting Rights.* Cambridge: Harvard University Press, 1987.

References

Thompson, Kenneth. *The Voting Rights Act and Black Electoral Participation.* Washington, D.C.: Joint Center for Political Studies, 1984.

Toobin, Jeffrey. "Clinton's Left Hand Man," *New Yorker,* July 21, 1997, pp. 28–32.

Tribe, Laurence. *Abortion: The Clash of Absolutes.* New York: Norton, 1990.

Tulis, Jeffrey. *The Rhetorical Presidency.* Princeton: Princeton University Press, 1987.

Ulmer, S. Sidney. "Issue Fluidity in the United States Supreme Court." In *Supreme Court Activism and Restraint,* edited by Stephen Halpern and Charles Lamb. Lexington: Heath, 1982.

Urofsky, Melvin. *Affirmative Action on Trial: Sex Discrimination in Johnson v. Santa Clara.* Lawrence: University Press of Kansas, 1997.

Vose, Clement. *Caucasians Only: The Supreme Court, the NAACP, and the Restrictive Covenant Cases.* Berkeley: University of California Press, 1959.

Wahlbeck, Paul. "The Life of the Law: Judicial Politics and Legal Change." *Journal of Politics* 59 (1997): 778–802.

Walker, Samuel. *In Defense of American Liberties: A History of the ACLU.* New York: Oxford University Press, 1990.

Walker, Thomas, Lee Epstein, and William Dixon. "On the Mysterious Demise of Consensual Norms in the United States Supreme Court." *Journal of Politics* 50 (1988): 361–89.

Walton, Hanes, Jr. *When the Marching Stopped: The Politics of Civil Rights Regulatory Agencies.* Albany: State University of New York Press, 1988.

Wasby, Stephen. "How Planned is 'Planned Litigation'?" *American Bar Foundation Research Journal* 32 (1984): 83–138.

———. *Race Relations Litigation in an Age of Complexity.* Charlottesville: University of Virginia Press, 1995.

———. "A Triangle Transformed: Court, Congress, and Presidency in Civil Rights." *Policy Studies Journal* 21 (1993): 565–74.

Wasby, Stephen, Anthony D'Amato, and Rosemary Metrailer. *Desegregation from* Brown *to* Alexander: *An Exploration of Supreme Court Strategies.* Carbondale: Southern Illinois University Press, 1977.

Watson, Richard. *Presidential Vetoes and Public Policy.* Lawrence: University Press of Kansas, 1993.

Weiss, Robert. *"We Want Jobs": A History of Affirmative Action.* New York: Garland, 1997.

Wermiel, Stephen. "A Claim of Sexual Harassment." In *A Year in the*

References

Life of the Supreme Court, edited by Rodney Smolla. Durham: Duke University Press, 1995.

White, G. Edward. *Earl Warren: A Public Life.* New York: Oxford University Press, 1982.

Wilkins, Richard. "An Officer and an Advocate: The Role of the Solicitor General." *Loyola of Los Angeles Law Review* 21 (1988): 1167–86.

Williams, Juan. *Thurgood Marshall: American Revolutionary.* New York: Times Books, 1998.

Williams, Wendy. "Equality's Riddle: Pregnancy and the Equal Treatment/Special Treatment Debate." In *Feminist Legal Theory: Foundations,* edited by D. Kelly Weisberg. Philadelphia: Temple University Press, 1993.

Wolters, Raymond. *Right Turn: William Bradford Reynolds, the Reagan Administration, and Black Civil Rights.* New Brunswick: Transaction, 1996.

Yarbrough, Tinsley. *The Rehnquist Court and the Constitution.* New York: Oxford University Press, 2000.

Zorn, Christopher. *On Appeal: United States Government Litigation in the Federal Appellate Courts.* Ann Arbor: University of Michigan Press, forthcoming.

———. "U.S. Government Litigation Strategies in the Federal Appellate Courts." Ph.D. diss., Ohio State University, Columbus, 1997.

Index of Cases

Index of Cases

Index

Index

Index

Republican Party, 95, 109, 123, 220, 255; civil rights and, 50, 59, 132, 138; gender and, 202

Reske, Henry, 279n

Restrictive covenant cases, 70, 73, 91

Reynolds, W. Bradford, 168, 169, 179, 244; affirmative action and, 154–56, 158; and Civil Rights Division, 145, 146, 170, 235; desegregation and, 153, 174, 175; relation with OSG under Lee, 148, 150–52; relation with OSG under Fried, 156–58, 166; voting rights and, 163, 164

Rhode, Deborah, 221, 299–301n, 303n

Richardson, Elmo, 282n

RICO statutes, 256

Rieselbach, Leroy, 293n

Roberts, John, 39, 49, 177, 178

Rogers, William, 75

Roosevelt, Franklin, 29, 57, 67, 68, 143; battle with Supreme Court, 29, 52; New Deal, 143; presidential power and, 32

Roosevelt Court, 68, 69

Rose, David, 111, 148, 160, 289n

Rubin, Eva, 217, 299n, 301n

Rudko, Frances Howell, 282n

Sacks, Albert, 41

Salokar, Rebecca, 31, 33, 275n–78n, 280n, 284n, 288n–93n, 295n

Samuels, Suzanne Uttaro, 303n

Savage, David, 295n

Savage, Sean, 281n

Scalia, Antonin, 232, 238, 256, 295n

Schnapper, Eric, 15, 37, 279n, 280n

Schubert, Glendon, 277n

Schwartz, Bernard, 285n, 292n, 287n, 288n, 290n, 295n, 305n

Schwartz, Herman, 292n, 293n

Schwartz, Joshua, 280n

Scigliano, Robert, 30, 276n

Scrutiny standard, 6, 201, 208; in gender cases, 205, 210, 212–15, 217–19, 223–25, 228, 267; in affirmative action, 134, 135, 137, 154, 159, 162, 171, 178, 186–88, 193, 238, 253–55

Seamon, Richard, 26, 43, 171, 184, 185

Segal, Jeffrey, 275n, 277n, 278n, 289n, 290n, 299n, 300n, 305n

Segregation, 57, 68, 73; *de facto,* 112, 115, 117, 123, 126, 128; *de jure,* 112, 115–17, 126, 128, 133

Selig, Joel, 146, 152, 153, 167, 293n, 294n

Semonche, John E., 304n

Sexual harassment, 162, 163, 233; Bush (G.H.W.) administration, 246, 247; Clinton administration and, 251–53, 255, 258; hostile environment, 236, 237, 253; *quid pro quo,* 236, 237, 253; Reagan administration and, 236, 237

Seymour, Stephanie, 208

Shapiro, Stephen, 295n

Shull, Stephen, 281n, 295n, 296n

Silverstein, Mark, 297n

Simon, James F., 161, 169, 295n, 297n, 303n, 304n

Sinclair, Barbara, 296n

Skowronek, Stephen, 170, 266, 292n, 296n, 305n

Smith, Howard, 75, 299n

Smith, Robert, 161, 295n

Smith, Steven, 282n, 284n

Smith, William French, 146, 292n

Sobeloff, Simon, 77, 79, 119, 120

Solicitor General, 5, 9, 10; in administrative phase, 60, 62, 93–41, 193, 194, 266, 267; as "Attorney General" as law enforcement officer, 20, 23, 29, 34, 91, 265, 267, 268; as "Attorney General" as policy maker, 20, 23, 24, 29, 34, 91, 265, 267, 268, 270; balance of law and politics, 9–17, 20–27, 29–53, 58, 60, 62, 259–72; changes in types of, 41–43; as Fifth Clerk, 20, 24–26, 29, 66, 91, 206, 265, 268; goals of, 13–15, 27; Harvard Law Professor Model, 269; in litigation phase, 60, 62, 65–91, 140, 193, 194, 266, 267; president and 67, 69, 72–76, 78, 80, 82, 84, 89–91, 95, 99, 107–109, 112–16, 118, 122, 123, 130, 134, 135, 138–40, 143, 148–54, 158, 163, 165–68, 170, 172, 175–79, 181, 183, 188–95, 218, 220, 226, 229, 231, 236–38, 241–46, 248–51, 253–59, 264, 267, 269–71; in redefinition phase, 60, 62, 143–95, 266, 267; roles of, 20–25; as Tenth Justice, 20–24, 26, 29, 265, 268. *See also* individual administrations, individual solicitors general, and Office of the Solicitor General

Songer, Donald, 277n

Souter, David, 171, 179, 245, 251, 255

Spaeth, Harold, 277n, 289n, 299n, 305n

Spann, Girardeau, 289n, 290n